QUALITATIVE RESEARCH

A Personal Skills Approach

SECOND EDITION

Gary D. Shank
Duquesne University

PEARSON

Merrill
Prentice Hall

Upper Saddle River, New Jersey
Columbus, Ohio

Library of Congress Cataloging-in-Publication Data

Shank, Gary D.
   Qualitative research : a personal skills approach / Gary D. Shank.—2nd ed.
      p. cm.
   Includes bibliographical references and index.
   ISBN 0-13-171949-1
1. Social sciences—Methodology. 2. Qualitative research. I. Title.

H61.S5138 2006
001.4'2—dc22

                                         2005040825

Vice President and Executive Publisher: Jeffery W. Johnston
Publisher: Kevin M. Davis
Editorial Assistant: Sarah N. Kenoyer
Production Editor: Mary Harlan
Production Coordinator: Norine Strang, Carlisle Publishers Services
Design Coordinator: Diane C. Lorenzo
Cover Design: Jason Moore
Cover Image: SuperStock
Text Design: Carlisle Publishers Services
Production Manager: Laura Messerly
Director of Marketing: Ann Castel Davis
Marketing Manager: Autumn Purdy
Marketing Coordinator: Brian Mounto

This book was set in Berkeley by Carlisle Communications, Ltd. It was printed and bound by R. R. Donnelley & Sons Company. The cover was printed by R. R. Donnelley & Sons Company.

Pearson Prentice Hall™ is a trademark of Pearson Education, Inc.
Pearson® is a registered trademark of Pearson plc
Prentice Hall® is a registered trademark of Pearson Education, Inc.
Merrill® is a registered trademark of Pearson Education, Inc.

Pearson Education Ltd.   Pearson Education Australia Pty. Limited
Pearson Education Singapore Pte. Ltd.   Pearson Education North Asia Ltd.
Pearson Education Canada, Ltd.   Pearson Educación de Mexico, S.A. de C.V.
Pearson Education–Japan   Pearson Education Malaysia Pte. Ltd.

10 9 8 7 6 5 4 3 2 1
ISBN: 0-13-171949-1

To the memory of Michael Crotty—
a true friend I never got the chance to meet in person.

Preface

Conceptual Framework and Organization of the Text

When I set out to write an introductory textbook in qualitative research, I had several goals in mind. First and foremost was my desire to create a hands-on learning environment that gives instructors and students freedom to tailor and modify the text for their own needs. To that end, I created 10 exercises that are built into the text itself. Personally, I feel that the exercises associated with the basic skills are the most important, but instructors should feel free to augment, modify, omit, and substitute based upon their particular needs and goals. The important part is that this text offers a vehicle for incorporating hands-on learning into the overall process.

Second, I have long felt that qualitative research is in need of a basic vision, and that such a vision ought to be an integral part of any introductory text. To that effort, I have attempted to articulate an inclusive yet clarifying vision in the very first chapter of this text. This vision does not attempt to supplant or replace anyone's understanding of qualitative research. Instead, I have tried to look at as many points of view and approaches within qualitative research as possible, and then distill out a set of common principles. Those common principles all seem to center on the notion of looking at meaning in empirical settings, and thus the vision used here was born.

Finally, I attempted to integrate the first two points into a cohesive approach that takes advantage of what I feel is the big secret of all qualitative research: Qualitative research is based on skills that we already possess. Learning qualitative research is not like learning statistics. When we look at all we do, we see that we are really refining such basic activities as talking, observing, pitching in, and the like. Furthermore, we all have our own areas of strengths and weaknesses. We can use the exercises and the materials dealing with personal skills to tailor our own development programs as qualitative researchers, even as we move beyond the boundaries of the course materials themselves. This should allow us to work from our strengths and to chart out systematic areas of growth at the same time.

Features of the Text

This text is essentially divided into four parts. The first part contains Chapter 1, which lays out what I feel are the crucial assumptions and principles that we need in order to learn and then perform qualitative research.

The second part consists of the basic skills necessary to participate in any and all forms of qualitative research. Chapter 2 outlines and discusses the skill of observing using the framework of an observation exercise. Chapter 3 focuses on the skill of conversing, and this skill is related via exercises pertaining to and examples of the art of interviewing. Chapter 4 tackles the broad area of participating using a case study project, and Chapter 5 rounds out the basic skills by taking a careful and hands-on look at the complex and often implicitly addressed skill of interpreting. Music is used as the foundation for the exercise for this chapter. One reason that music is used is to highlight the realization that, unlike other forms of research that are primarily visual, qualitative research has a large auditory component to its basic makeup.

The third part moves us past the basic skills toward the more advanced skills. These advanced skills often play key roles in qualitative research, but they are less obvious and more intuitive. Chapter 6 starts readers out by considering the task of questioning. How we think through the process of eventually asking a qualitative research question is examined. Chapter 7 takes us into the realm of data gathering. Here we examine some of the major processes and techniques we use to collect our actual data, and see how those processes relate to our questions. Chapter 8 looks at the task of analyzing. Here, great efforts have been made to present as broad a spectrum of analytic tools, perspectives, and styles as possible. Chapter 8 is designed not so much to teach various analytic strategies but to situate as many strategies as possible in relation to each other. Guidance is then given to direct students to more explicit prescriptions and procedures for particular analytic methods. In this way, students have some valuable perspective on the range of analytic possibilities that they might choose from.

Chapter 9 deals with the skill of narrating, and Chapter 10 deals with the skill of writing. Many books combine these skills, but I feel that it is important to look at them separately. In Chapter 9 we concentrate on the art of identifying and understanding narratives, whereas in Chapter 10 we tackle practical and theoretical issues dealing with the difficult but highly important task of writing up qualitative research findings.

In the fourth and final part, crucial evaluative and historical issues are addressed. We start with a look at the thorny task of evaluating qualitative research. The metaphor of the seven deadly sins is used in Chapter 11 as a guide to help us see areas for self-improvement. Finally, Chapter 12 ends the book at the point where many other texts begin—with a look at the history of the field. Why do we look at history so late in the game? The answer is simple: Once students have experienced qualitative research from the perspective of their own skills and insights, they are then in the position to be more critical consumers of methods based on various historical positions. That is, we do not strive for privileged methods strictly because they have historical pedigrees. Instead, students should understand why these methods have been adopted so often and so extensively by past researchers in the field.

Changes in This Edition

The second edition of a textbook gives its author two key benefits. First of all, it provides a validation of the original vision. I wanted to write a book that was comprehensive yet helpful and engaging at the same time. I am so grateful to all the readers and adopters who have told me how much they and their students have enjoyed working with the first edition of this book. As I prepared the second edition, I worked hard to make sure I kept those things that people valued in the book, and I thank them for their kindness and loyalty from the bottom of my heart.

At the same time, a second edition is a second chance. There were some things that, frankly, I did not get quite right the first time around. I hope that I have found and corrected all of these issues. If I missed some, or made new mistakes, please let me know.

It is also a chance to make some changes to better address the needs of my readers and adopters. To that end, I have made a number of revisions. I have updated references and examples. In the four short years since the first edition, much has changed in the field. To reflect these changes, I have added nearly 200 new references. Many of those references, in addition, are from valid and respected online sources, as these sorts of sources are becoming more and more important in the qualitative research field.

In addition to updating, I have also reorganized. Several of the original chapters have been replaced with topics that, upon reflection and feedback, appear to be more central to the vision and skills of the field. I did not eliminate such skills as conceptualizing and reasoning, but moved them to more subordinate roles. With such skills in their place, I was then able to elevate and examine in more detail such topics as questioning and data gathering. I streamlined and reorganized the chapters on participating and interpreting, moving most of the practical details of data gathering to the appropriate later chapter, making the chapter on analyzing both more practical and more user-friendly.

Finally, I sought to rethink several key areas. In the first edition, I did not capture the sense of tension and diversity that epitomizes the qualitative research field. Although much of our rhetoric calls for unity among ourselves and other types of researchers, it seems that there are at least two broad camps within qualitative research—qualitative science and qualitative inquiry, as I have come to label them. I bring out this distinction not to sow seeds of discord in the field but to help us situate ourselves along this broad and diverse continuum. By acknowledging that there are fundamental differences between, say, grounded theory and critical theory, we can help ourselves stay focused and clear on what we are trying to do without attacking or condemning the work of others. This is the spirit of the distinctions that I have sought to raise here.

The other areas of rethinking were more practical in nature. I examined each and every one of the 10 exercises to see if they were working as intended. As a result, I replaced a few of the exercises with new exercises that are intended to be both easier to do and clearer in their focus and intent. At the same time, I added a whole new series of exercises to the end of the first 10 chapters. These exercises were designed as practical guides to help graduate students through the process of preparing a qualitative research proposal. Because every institution, and in fact every professor, approaches this task in a different way, I tried to offer a set of steps that would complement, and not interfere with, particular tasks and processes that actual graduate students might be called to do. At the same time, to acknowledge that the different ends of the continuum call for different approaches, I had Carol and Albert work toward the ends of that continuum as more- or less-extreme cases. Actual proposals, I am sure, will be more tempered and moderate in their use of qualitative science and qualitative inquiry techniques and insights.

Acknowledgments

I would first like to thank my editor, Kevin Davis, and his helpful and friendly staff. Kevin continued to believe in this project at every stage of its rather labyrinthine path of development. I would also like to thank my former graduate students at Northern Illinois University who helped me develop much of the content and many of the exercises used in this work. In these students I found many willing and trusted colleagues. I thank my doctoral advisees at Duquesne University for their help in reading and refining these materials and procedures. Of course, I am grateful to the School of Education at Duquesne University for its support, financial and otherwise, toward this effort.

In addition, I would like to acknowledge the efforts of the many reviewers of this book in its various stages. Those who were instrumental in getting the original edition off the ground are Carole B. Shmurak, Central Connecticut State University; Dia Sekayi, Cleveland State University; Armando Trujillo, University of Texas, San Antonio; Shelley Roberts, University of Illinois; Michelle D. Young, The University of Iowa; Peter A. Hessling, North Carolina State University; James H. Banning, Colorado State University; and Janice Williams, Oklahoma State University.

Reviewers for this edition gave me generous help and advice and feedback in finding ways to make sure the second edition was more truthful, clearer, better organized, and better prepared to address the theoretical and practical needs of the readers: Janina Brutt-Griffler, The University of Alabama; Elizabeth Meador, California State University, Monterey Bay; Bette Speziale, The Ohio State University; and Benjamin H. Welsh, Ball State University. Without their extensive comments and suggestions, this would have been a far different work. All mistakes and blunders, of course, are still my own fault.

Finally, I would like to thank the Admirals, who were the best friends a person could possibly have and who helped me navigate many a stormy sea. I hope you are both having a great time in that vast Beyond, and I miss you both.

Educator Learning Center: An Invaluable Online Resource

Merrill Education and the Association for Supervision and Curriculum Development (ASCD) invite you to take advantage of a new online resource, one that provides access to the top research and proven strategies associated with ASCD and Merrill—the Educator

Learning Center. At **www.educatorlearningcenter.com**, you will find resources that will enhance your students' understanding of course topics and of current educational issues, in addition to being invaluable for further research.

HOW THE EDUCATOR LEARNING CENTER WILL HELP YOUR STUDENTS BECOME BETTER TEACHERS

With the combined resources of Merrill Education and ASCD, you and your students will find a wealth of tools and materials to better prepare them for the classroom.

Research

- More than 600 articles from the ASCD journal *Educational Leadership* discuss everyday issues faced by practicing teachers.
- A direct link on the site to Research Navigator™ gives students access to many of the leading education journals, as well as extensive content detailing the research process.
- Excerpts from Merrill Education texts give your students insights on important topics of instructional methods, diverse populations, assessment, classroom management, technology, and refining classroom practice.

Classroom Practice

- Hundreds of lesson plans and teaching strategies are categorized by content area and age range.
- Case studies and classroom video footage provide virtual field experience for student reflection.
- Computer simulations and other electronic tools keep your students abreast of today's classrooms and current technologies.

LOOK INTO THE VALUE OF EDUCATOR LEARNING CENTER YOURSELF

A four-month subscription to Educator Learning Center is $25 but is **FREE** when packaged with any Merrill Education text. In order for your students to have access to this site, you must use this special value-pack ISBN number **WHEN** placing your textbook order with the bookstore: 0-13-225927-3. Your students will then receive a copy of the text packaged with a free ASCD pincode. To preview the value of this website to you and your students, please go to **www.educatorlearningcenter.com** and click on "Demo."

Brief Contents

Contents

CHAPTER 7

Data Gathering   124

CHAPTER 8

Analyzing   145

CHAPTER 1

Becoming a Skilled Qualitative Researcher

The purpose of this book is fairly simple—to help all of us who strive to do qualitative research to be more skilled. This simple purpose, however, leads to many complex questions: How can I get to be more skilled in what I do? Does skill simply depend on mastering certain techniques, or is it a broader notion? Is there more than one way to be a skilled qualitative researcher? Where exactly do I start? How will I finally know if I am really skilled, and I that am doing a good job?

Let us start with a very basic question. What does it mean to be skilled in the first place? In short, to be skilled means to be *aware*. Skilled qualitative researchers are aware of, and confident of, their strengths. They are alert in their assessments of situations, competent in their abilities to choose and apply appropriate techniques, and willing to set aside all they know and to set off in different directions if need be. Skilled qualitative researchers are also well-versed in theory and are particularly sensitive to both overt and hidden assumptions associated with their chosen research processes. Skilled qualitative researchers are well aware that they have much to learn about doing research, but they never lose sight of the fact that research is done by persons who bring both commitment and enjoyment to the process. They bring a positive, relaxed, and seeking presence to their endeavors.

TECHNIQUE SKILLS AND PERSONAL SKILLS

As we can see from the previous discussion, being a skilled qualitative researcher is a rich and comprehensive process. So where do we start? One very useful starting place involves the sorting and ordering of skills. When we look at the overall picture, we can see that there are two fundamental types of skills in qualitative research. We need to look at each of these fundamental areas in turn.

The most obvious, and often most prized, set of skills we will call *technique skills*. These are the sorts of skills that prescribe how to do certain types of qualitative procedures and analyses. You can always identify a technique skill by the presence of some explicit or implicit list of prescriptions, or some set of rules, for its use. Technique skills dominate many qualitative research texts, and we will talk about certain important technique skills here as well. For example, when we get to such areas as grounded theory, the use of proper techniques is critical.

Though technique skills are important, they are only part of the picture. We have been consistently taught to respect technique skills in research. Often, this is because many of us first learned social science research methods from a statistically guided perspective. In order to compute a mean or perform an Analysis of Variance (ANOVA), for instance, it is important to use the right techniques and follow the proper computational rules. But even so, the best statistically guided researchers go beyond technique to combine proper procedure, clear thought, and insight. That is what makes their work special.

For qualitative research, the reliance on technique is much more muted. Specific techniques are most often less definitive. There are few analogues in qualitative research, for example, to getting an ANOVA right. Furthermore, mastery of technique alone will make you at best a qualitative artisan. You may be able to apply specific ideas and techniques developed by other researchers with great skill. So long as you stay within the "straight and narrow," you will do okay. But if you ever need to reach out, to push the boundaries of your techniques and the field itself to look at truly significant questions, you cannot depend on technique alone. You must be able to dig down to a more basic level, to look at what you have in front of you with new and fresh eyes, to ask the sort of questions the situation requires, and to craft research methods and approaches to fit your questions. In essence, you must rely on your skills as a curious and seeking human being. These are the skills that we call *personal skills,* and these are the skills that will be the main focus of this text.

Why should we concentrate here on these personal skills? Because a primary truth of qualitative research is this: We already possess the personal skills we need to be good qualitative researchers. We now need only learn how to channel those skills in particular directions to address certain types of goals. And once we meet these research goals, we often find (as an added bonus!) that we also have achieved a richer, more mature, and more balanced perspective on life in general.

In short, personal skill mastery is less obvious, more implicit, but far more important in the long run. It shows up in the intersection between our lives as qualitative researchers and our lives in general. As we get to be better researchers, we often find that we are also becoming better human beings. For that reason alone, a personal skills approach is worth pursuing.

THE BASIC PLAN FOR THIS TEXT

How can we reach such lofty heights? Toward that aim, this book is built on three main assumptions:

1. There are certain basic personal skills that are found in nearly all forms of qualitative research.
2. These basic personal skills are linked to certain fundamental aspects of qualitative research that go beyond theory and practice to shape a coherent *vision* of the field itself.
3. The combination of fundamental vision and basic personal skills leads toward more advanced personal skills that are not as universal but are nonetheless critically important.

The flow of this text will be simple. First we will describe the basic personal skills. Then we will move toward a new vision of qualitative research as a unique form of empirical inquiry. After that, we will address each basic skill in turn. Once we have laid out these basic personal skills through exercises, examples, and theories, we will work our way through the more advanced skills in the same fashion. We will next look at some pitfalls that we might find along the qualitative path, and we will finally end with an overview of the past, present, and future of qualitative research.

IDENTIFYING AND UNDERSTANDING THE BASIC PERSONAL SKILLS

There is nothing magical or surprising about the set of basic personal skills needed to do qualitative research. Remember, the art of learning qualitative research starts with refining the basic skills that you already have.

Each of these basic skills will have its own chapter, but let us start with a very quick look at each in turn. There are four basic personal skills in all: observing, conversing, participating, and interpreting.

Observing

All forms of qualitative research make use of observational skills. Like all creatures, human beings are highly skilled and sophisticated observers. Otherwise, we would have a hard time surviving. We observe when we pay careful attention to something in the world of experience.

When we talk about observing, we mean far more than just looking. We might look at something, but we might also hear it, feel it, taste it, or smell it. Or we might use some combination of any or all of these actions. Observing as a qualitative research skill is grounded in our ordinary understanding of observation, but it is more focused, refined, and directed.

Conversing

Humans are unique in that they engage in conversation. Conversation is more than talking. It is the interplay of talking and listening that allows for genuine vocal communication. There is no form of qualitative research that, at some level, does not make use of the skill of conversing. Most of us begin conversing at an early age, and most of us are fairly good at it. But qualitative research is not just about talking and listening. Certain highly developed techniques, like interviewing, are used by qualitative researchers to heighten and focus basic conversational skills.

Participating

It is impossible to do qualitative research without getting involved at some level. But human beings are quite good at getting involved. We are social creatures at heart. None of us, for example, could have survived the first year or so of our lives without some social order, such as the family or even an orphanage, to make sure that we were fed and protected. Seeking participation seems to be built into our very fiber.

Qualitative research extends our efforts toward participation through a set of varied research strategies. In general, we can organize these participatory actions under several broad categories, including fieldwork and action research. Each of these areas (which sometimes overlap as well) use refined and focused techniques to help us get involved within generally complex social settings.

Interpreting

The difference between qualitative research and any other form of empirical inquiry is the fact that qualitative research is first and foremost about meaning. This point will become clearer when we talk about the unique vision that all forms of qualitative research share. But here we acknowledge the basic skill of discerning meaning in any given setting.

Just as nature abhors a vacuum, human beings abhor any setting that is not meaningful. We have to settle issues of meaning, and we are good at doing this quickly and efficiently. In fact, the qualitative skill of interpretation is not about doing meaning resolution more quickly or more effectively, but in learning not to jump to an interpretative conclusion too soon.

This is an important point. With the first three basic skills, we learn how to mold those things we do already into a more refined and focused set of tools. When we learn qualitative research interpretive skills, we often have to go against our own instincts. Whether or not you can master this final basic skill will have much bearing on how good of a qualitative researcher you will eventually become.

LOOKING AT THE WORLD IN A DIFFERENT WAY

The first part of learning qualitative research is the task of identifying and working with the four basic skills just listed. But we cannot just mechanically apply a set of skills and call the result "research." Research flows from a larger context. In our case, that larger context is based upon a fundamental vision of what qualitative research really and truly is. The first step toward such a context or vision is a definition.

A Matter of Definition

There are quite a few definitions of qualitative research. Without going into specifics, we can say that these definitions fall into a number of different categories.

Some definitions emphasize the history and development of the field (e.g., Jacob, 1987). They talk about how qualitative research, as a field, began with fieldwork, urban sociology, symbolic interactionism, grounded theory, and other forms of research in natural settings. These definitions focus on the evolution of qualitative methods and theories in such fields as anthropology, sociology, education, and nursing and health sciences, to name a few.

Other definitions focus on the conditions of data gathering and interpretation. They emphasize the use of verbal and observational data, the importance of conducting qualitative research in ecologically valid and holistic settings, and the power of critical modes of thought to understand people in their day-to-day settings (e.g., Lancy, 1993).

Finally, still other definitions concatenate the differing sorts of methodologies that most researchers consider qualitative in nature. They point out that qualitative research most often is built around such research tools as interviews, focus groups, participant observation, ethnography, case studies, narratives and oral history, and the like (e.g., Cresswell, 1998).

Although these definitions have a certain practical and clarifying value, we need a definition of qualitative research that is more basic and abstract. To address that need, I would like to offer one of my own definitions of *qualitative research*. In its most basic terms, qualitative research is a form of *systematic empirical inquiry into meaning* (Shank, 1994).

"Unpacking" the Definition

Why do we need such a complex set of terms to define qualitative research? Because we need to be very careful and precise at the outset about what we mean when we say certain things about qualitative research. To see this last point in action, we will "unpack" the basic definition very carefully. "Unpacking" means that we will look at each word and phrase very carefully to see what is really and actually being said.

Let us start with *systematic empirical* inquiry. Both of these words have been chosen carefully. First of all, qualitative research is *systematic*. That is, it not haphazard, nor idiosyncratic, nor even subjective (in the popular sense of that term). It is planned, ordered, and public.

At the same time, it is not mechanical or reductionistic. Just because something is not mechanical or reductionistic, however, does not mean that it is anything anyone wants it to be. By being public and rooted in social understandings and activities, this sort of inquiry can be just as systematic as inquiry mapped out by, say, a mathematical model. It will be systematic in a different way, however, much as steak and carrots are much different forms of the same thing—namely, food.

Second of all, it is *empirical* inquiry. *Empirical* inquiry means any form of inquiry that depends upon the world of experience in some fundamental way. Here we have to be very careful not to fall into old patterns of thinking right away. We normally think that the only time an inquirer turns to the world of experience in a systematic way is when that inquirer wants to determine whether or not some claim is true. That is, we look toward the world of experience to verify our predictions or claims. But, if we think about it, this is only one of many ways we might use the world of experience in a systematic way as an inquirer. We will talk about this in more detail in a bit, when we look at the two broad domains within qualitative research.

When you take on the task of doing an *inquiry into meaning,* the rules are different. Meaning, for a qualitative researcher, is always an incomplete picture. It is not so much the case that we do not have the right meaning; it is far more often the case that we do not have enough meaning. Our picture of anything is always too simple. And, rather than applying simplifying moves, we are the sort of empirical inquirers who want instead to develop a more complex picture of the phenomenon or situation. Only we prefer not to call it complex. We prefer terms like *rich, deep, thick, textured, insightful*, and, best of all, *illuminative*.

There is yet another task in our unpacking exercise. We need to see how this definition operates in the real world to frame research conducted in the qualitative tradition. The first thing we see is the fact that our definition of qualitative research allows for a great variety of different approaches.

The Big Deal about Meaning

Because it is a systematic inquiry into meaning, it is obvious that meaning is a big deal for qualitative research. At the same time, meaning is paradoxically the most overrated and the most underrated concept in contemporary Western thought. We simply do not understand the role and use of meaning all that well. So it is no surprise that a systematic empirical inquiry into meaning ends up being a complex task to navigate.

We have addressed some of these issues theoretically, but for now we need to be a bit more practical. What are some key aspects about meaning that all qualitative researchers need to keep in mind at all times? Here is a short list:

- *The path to truth always goes through meaning.* Qualitative research is not an excuse to discard the concept of truth. Deep in our hearts, no matter how often we might see others rail against and denigrate the notion of truth, ultimately we cannot deny its existence. The problem is that we have not properly understood the role of meaning in the search for truth. We cannot really understand and perform qualitative research until we have a clear sense of the role of meaning in our inquiry.

- *The world is full of meaning.* One of the worst mistakes we can make as qualitative researchers is to assume that there is no meaning in the world at large (or in that little part of the world that we are studying) unless we put it there. The world is perfused with meaning. The world is intelligible, but always on its own terms. Why would we assume that the world was put together in such a way as to make it easy to be understood by humans? We are just not that important in the cosmic scheme of things. So we need to be willing to look for meaning on the world's terms, not our terms.
- *We only know something to the degree that we first understand it.* This is a paraphrase of the first point. It does, however, point us toward the necessity of taking the act of understanding, of discerning and reconciling meaning, seriously and on its own terms. Changes in knowledge are incremental and accumulative; we know more and more about something. Changes in understanding are powerful and revolutionary. How often are we awash in facts and true claims, only to lack the understanding to see what all these facts and claims really mean?
- *Sometimes, things are only meaningful.* Even in the empirical world, there are things that matter only as sources of meaning. Because we are continually oriented toward the approach of taking care of meaning as quickly as possible, we often overlook the significance of these things in the empirical world.

Here is a simple example of what I mean. When my kids were little, I told them the story of *The Three Little Pigs.* In case you have forgotten or never heard the story, each of the pigs builds his own house. The first pig builds a straw house, the second pig builds a house of sticks, and the third pig builds a brick house. The big bad wolf manages to blow down the straw house and the house of sticks, but he cannot blow down the brick house. When all three pigs finally end up in the brick house, built by the wisest pig, then they are all safe from the big bad wolf.

My kids loved this story, and they asked many questions about the pigs and the wolf. Why weren't the first two pigs smart enough to build brick houses? Were they too lazy? Why did the smart and hard-working pig let them in? These are questions about meaning.

Here are some of the questions they did not ask: Did the three little pigs really talk? Did they really live? Do we really know anything factual about their lives? These are silly questions, because the "truths" embodied in parables, like *The Three Little Pigs,* are truths that are rooted only in meaning. How many other parables are waiting to be discovered in the empirical world, serving in their own ways as guides to insight into practice and understanding?

QUALITATIVE RESEARCH AS A "BIG TENT"

When we consider our working definition of qualitative research as a "systematic empirical inquiry into meaning," we see that this is a very big tent, indeed. Atkinson, Coffey, and Delamont (2001) point out that "in terms of methodologies, perspectives, and strategies, qualitative research is an umbrella term which encompasses many approaches" (p. 7).

In other words, there is room for many different types of views about qualitative research that can easily and comfortably fit into this definition. This is a good thing, as there is a wide variety of views in the field. The history and nature of some of these views will be addressed in the last chapter. In the final chapter we will also look at some of the major trends of qualitative research. For now, though, we will settle for looking at one of the most important of these trends—exploring the role of science in qualitative research. This crucial trend is based on the fact that qualitative research tends to operate within two broad domains. We need to look at each of these domains in some detail.

The Two Domains of Qualitative Research

There are two broad domains within qualitative research as a whole. Taken together, these two domains define the field as currently understood and practiced. That is, the dazzling variety of qualitative methods, theories, and approaches can be roughly sorted into these two "camps."

First of all, there is *qualitative science*. Qualitative science is that branch of qualitative research that sees itself as working within the broader framework of science as a whole.

The second domain we might call *qualitative inquiry*. Qualitative inquiry does not see itself as part of the scientific enterprise, but as a systematic and empirical alternative to science.

We will examine each domain briefly in turn, starting with qualitative science.

Qualitative Science

How is qualitative science like other forms of science? Briefly, qualitative science is grounded in the scientific method; it often advocates the use, testing, and development of theory; and it sees science as the guide to practice in all forms of empirical inquiry.

Some researchers feel that all empirical inquiry needs to be grounded in the *scientific method*. This is not an unreasonable position to take. Science has had much success in allowing us to predict, control, and understand the empirical world. The key to that success has been the fact that the scientific method has allowed researchers to test theories and hypotheses in a public and objective way, and to replicate the findings of others. The scientific method has allowed researchers to focus on research questions and to address those questions directly. Science has also allowed us to look for simple processes that underlie and determine many of the complex processes and phenomena that we find in the empirical world. For these and other reasons, it is quite easy to understand why some qualitative researchers respect, and even treasure, the nature of science and the role of the scientific method in empirical inquiry.

Qualitative science also often advocates the use of *theory* (Harre, 2004). At the most basic level, what do we mean when we call something a theory? In short, theories are tools that allow us all to be on the same page, meaning-wise. Theories are patterns of meaning, and in science, they are only as good as the data that substantiate them. They are also sensitive to the facts at hand, such that even just one contrary fact can send even the most respected theory tumbling to the ground. The history of science is filled with theories that were once highly respected and followed (like the phlogiston theory in chemistry or the ether theory in physics) that are now discarded and forgotten. Finally, theories are also ways of making complex situations simpler to predict and understand.

When we do qualitative research, however, the question of theory is not so simple. In one sense, we respect the notion of theory as an overarching perspective that helps us coordinate a wide range of findings and understandings. But the scientific role of theory, where theory is used to settle questions of meaning, often impedes genuine qualitative inquiry. This is because the primary focus of qualitative research is, front and center, an examination and inquiry into meaning.

If theory can help us coordinate and orchestrate our growing sense of richness of meaning as we do our qualitative inquiry, then it is a useful tool for qualitative researchers. If we find that theory forces us to take a premature stand on certain issues of meaning that need further exploration, then we are best advised to defer its presence, or even set it aside. Qualitative science also feels that the *rules of practice of science* are important guidelines for all forms of empirical inquiry.

There are a number of key models that embrace both qualitative research and the scientific method. For now, we will simply describe these models. Details and critiques of these approaches will be covered in later chapters.

Most obviously, there is the notion of *mixed methods* designs. In a mixed methods design, or a *mixed research* design, the researchers are deliberately combining both qualitative and quantitative methods in an attempt to get a more comprehensive picture of the area of study. The key characteristic of mixed methods studies is the fact that these studies are based on research questions that can be tackled both qualitatively and quantitatively. Traditional concerns of scientific research in the social sciences, like reliability, validity, generalizability, bias, and error, are also addressed in these designs.

There are a number of *inductive, data-driven* approaches to qualitative research that fall within the realm of qualitative science. The most famous and best-developed example is *Grounded Theory* (GT). Like many other branches of empirical inquiry, GT seeks to create theory. Unlike many other top-down approaches, which seek to create new theory from old theory, GT strives to generate theory bottom-up from the data itself. It uses a systematic process, most notably the constant comparative method.

Some examples of qualitative science are less programmatic, and more *practice specific*. One good example is in the use of interviews in a qualitative study. Researchers might choose to use semistructured interviews, instead of unstructured interviews, because the researchers want to make sure each participant was asked the same set of questions on the same topic. This sort of standardization of design is used to reduce the likelihood of error in a scientific design. By seeking to reduce this sort of error, the researchers are working within a qualitative scientific framework.

Qualitative science also shows up, less systematically, in the choices researchers often make in *analyzing their data*. Even if the research design is not overtly scientific, the treatment of the data often is. This is seen most often when the rules of practice of science are enforced in the data analysis. For example, a qualitative research team might use a case study design, which is fairly neutral. When they look at the data, however, the team might choose to pay careful attention to scientific principles. For instance, issues of validity and generalizability are often addressed here.

What makes qualitative science different from ordinary science? There are many cases where qualitative science can operate in a much different way than traditional science operates. We can see this in a number of assumptions that researchers who do qualitative science often hold.

First of all, there is the notion that it is perfectly appropriate to turn to the world of experience in an *exploratory* way. Furthermore, this act of exploration of meaning can be viewed as not just preliminary, but as the whole point of the empirical inquiry. This happens when we do not know enough to make any serious predictions, and we have to look around first and get the lay of the land, so to speak. Many researchers feel that this situation describes those cases where qualitative research is most useful as a method of empirical inquiry. A number of mixed methods studies operate along this design, where a qualitative investigation leads to questions that are addressed more stringently using a quantitative design.

Second, there are those who hold that qualitative science allows us to extend scientific thinking and methods into areas where *the phenomena to be studied are not easily measured.* Labuschagne (2003) illustrates this point clearly. Quantitative research, says Labuschagne, deals with phenomena that "possess certain properties, states and characters, and the similarities, differences, and causal relations that exist within and between these" (p. 100).

Qualitative science deals with different sorts of phenomena. This form of research, Labuschagne (2003) continues, "is mainly concerned with the properties, the state, and the character (i.e., the nature) of phenomena. The word qualitative implies an emphasis on processes that are rigorously examined, but not measured in terms of quantity, amount or frequency" (p. 100).

Finally, there are those who practice qualitative science who feel that these methods allow researchers to *study processes in more naturalistic and less artificial settings.* In the traditional sciences, experimentation has always been held up as an important standard. In qualitative research, however, the notion of experimentation is problematic (Howe, 2004). Ever since the early days of ethnography, when researchers went on site to study people and cultures in their native settings, qualitative research has favored working within natural settings to understand complex processes as they unfold in their own ways. Even those who favor developing theory in qualitative research emphasize that we ultimately need to turn to these sorts of holistic settings in order to validate and confirm our understandings.

As we have seen, the qualitative science perspective is best viewed as operating along its own continuum. What all of these examples and issues share in common is this: in some fashion, they address the concerns and goals of science. We should hasten to add, however, that qualitative scientists still see themselves as doing different types of research than their more purely scientific colleagues. Because all qualitative research, including qualitative science, is grounded in the systematic empirical pursuit of meaning, qualitative science can never be completely assimilated into what we usually call "science." At best, it can be linked to more traditional scientific efforts via a mixed methods approach, but at some level it still stands as an example of that unique process we call qualitative research.

Qualitative Inquiry

When we believe that our current levels of meaning are not rich enough, this position leads us inevitably to study things on their own terms, at their own levels, as wholes. We resist the urge to factor, to decompose, to compartmentalize, in order to explain. We do not resist this urge for dogmatic reasons, but because when we look toward enriching our meaningful understanding of something, we cannot ever afford to lose sight of the whole. Therefore, a major skill in qualitative research is this ongoing conceptualization and reconceptualization of some holistic focus of attention.

At least some qualitative researchers believe that we are not required to turn to science in order to do systematic empirical inquiry. From their view, science is a well-understood, well-respected, and extremely useful form of empirical inquiry, but it is not the only form of empirical inquiry.

What is to be gained, you might ask, by looking away from science? For one thing, science is committed to the notion that complex phenomena are best understood as composites of simpler phenomena. If we can study and understand and predict these simpler phenomena, then we can get a handle on what really make these complex phenomena "tick." This drive to reduction and simplification is at the very heart of science.

The basic tenets of qualitative inquiry are less familiar to us than are the basic tenets of scientific inquiry. In addition, qualitative inquiry approaches often cover a wide terrain of perspectives, beliefs, and methods. Therefore, it is hard to come up with any set of basic tenets that can characterize the field as a whole. By necessity, our basic tenets in qualitative inquiry will be broader and less specific than the basic tenets of qualitative science, because the field itself is so diverse by nature. For now, we will look at these tenets in very brief form. As we progress through the book, these tenets will be explained and illustrated in greater detail as they become relevant.

There are three basic tenets in the qualitative inquiry approach. The first tenet holds that *the researcher matters*. By this, I mean that researchers are not merely gatherers of information; they are an active part of the research process itself. Their actions, their interpretations, and their decisions are often an integral part of the research procedures and the research findings as well. Qualitative inquiry is often grounded and shaped by issues of culture, society, history, gender, and the like. This grounding invariably starts with the researchers themselves—who they are, what they do, why they are there, and how they see what they find. Qualitative inquirers often put these issues right out front for all of us to see and evaluate.

The second basic tenet of qualitative inquiry is that *the inquiry into meaning is in service of understanding*. By this, I mean that qualitative inquirers seek understanding not just to build theories and other generalizations about knowledge; often, they have critical agendas as well. These researchers sometimes go beyond trying to understand what they see. They also seek to change things for the better. At the same time, they reject naive notions about what "better" might actually be. Most often, these sorts of critical efforts are in service of marginalized people, or persons who need to be empowered in various ways for various reasons.

The final basic tenet is this: *qualitative inquiry embraces new ways of looking at the world*. Some of those ways include phenomenology, hermeneutics, structuralism, poststructuralism, postmodernism, critical theory, and so on. Some of these methods are complex and difficult to understand. We will look at some of these approaches in later chapters, both in terms of theory and practice.

When it is at its best, qualitative inquiry is not about attacking or opposing qualitative science. It is simply about doing a different sort of inquiry. But, having said this, we need to return to the notion of qualitative research proper—how can we bring together all these disparate threads and agendas? Our basic definition is helpful, but it is not enough. We need to go on, and talk about an overarching vision of qualitative research that incorporates and situates these domains in a reasonable and meaningful fashion.

VISION AND RESEARCH

So far we have been unpacking our definition of qualitative research and seeing how our efforts as researchers tend to fall within two major domains. In order to further our basic understanding of qualitative research per se, however, we now have to move away from definitions and "big tents" and start looking more closely at the notion of vision.

Anything that is special and unique has its own vision. This is certainly true of qualitative research. Before we can begin the task of developing basic and advanced qualitative research skills, we should first examine what makes the process of qualitative research truly unique.

I do not think we can underestimate the importance of having a unique vision when we set out to conduct our own research activities. Is there only one type of "seeing" in research, or are there multiple ways to "see"? If there is more than one way to "look," do these multiple ways of seeing stand apart or can they be reconciled? And finally, how is each of these ways of seeing unique?

It is with the consideration of these apparently simple and humble issues that we can start to make some real headway on the thorny issue of discovering a unique and powerful vision for grounding qualitative research.

First we need to see what sorts of "visions" have dominated and shaped empirical inquiry as a whole. Then, we can discern the aspects of qualitative research that give it its own unique vision. Once we do that, we can then compare that unique vision with the other visions that we find in the history of doing empirical inquiry.

We will approach the question of vision by looking at the three fundamental technological innovations that have allowed human beings to see things that they ordinarily would not be able to see: the mirror, the window, and the lantern. As we will discover, each of the three broad areas of empirical inquiry in Western thought brings one of those technologies to the forefront as its organizing idea. We now will look at these efforts chronologically.

The Mirror

The discovery of the mirror has to be one of the greatest technological advancements in human inquiry. It allows the inquirer to correct for the fact that, ordinarily, he or she cannot see himself or herself seeing. But the mirror has a much richer connotation as well.

We have a mirror when we look into any reflective surface and see ourselves. The first mirror was probably a clear pool of water on a cloudy day. Our prehistoric ancestors perhaps bent down to drink and were surprised to see themselves in the act of drinking.

All reflections, however, need not be so direct or so simply visual. Is it possible for more complex phenomena or occurrences to be "reflective" in a less direct, more metaphorical way? Suppose, for example, we see an albatross gliding gracefully and effortlessly above the ocean, only to hit the water in a gangling and comical fashion when it tries to land. We might be tempted to laugh, but might we not also be tempted to see a parallel in our lives, or in the lives of others? Are there times when we, too, must abandon our natural grace and crash into the only kind of "landing" we are equipped to make? Does the flight and landing of the albatross metaphorically reflect our strengths and shortcomings in being a teacher, a parent, a theorist, a human being?

Reflective-based inquiry into the world was called *speculative* (after the Latin word *speculum,* meaning "mirror"), and was the earliest form of empirical inquiry in Western civilization. Speculative inquiry had its heyday in the Hellenistic period and especially during the Middle Ages. It is important for us to remember that speculative inquirers were doing their version of empirical inquiry. For instance, when they asked about the moral meanings of the acts of animals, they turned to the world of experience to discover those animals and to chronicle their acts. Speculative inquiry was neither science nor qualitative research, but its own form of empirical inquiry grounded in the vision of the mirror.

Though we do not perform much explicit speculative empirical inquiry anymore, stop and think about how much informal or implicit speculation we use in our everyday lives, and how much of a covert role it plays in theoretical thinking. In short, the speculative vision is somewhere in the background of contemporary empirical inquiry, but it is far from absent. It was pushed into the background because of a conflict with the next great technology of "seeing" in Western thought, the window.

The Window

The window is the prototypical scientific visual device. Its job is to give us as clear and undistorted a look as possible at something, where such a look was not possible at all before the advent of said window. A typical window is a piece of wall that, unlike the rest of the wall, is clear enough to look through. A microscope is a window that gives us a relatively undistorted look at something quite small, and a telescope is a window that gives us a relatively undistorted look at something quite far way. All of these windows allow our eyes to be somewhere and looking at something as if it were the most natural thing in the world to be doing so. This is an incredibly powerful enhancement of our ability to "see."

Coupled hand in hand with this new way of looking is a new way of thinking about those things that we see. Our first priority is no longer discerning the significance of what we see. Now we are far more concerned with making sure that what we see has not been distorted by any substance or event that might occlude our window.

The vision of the window plays a major role in the way that science is done on a day-to-day basis. First of all, there is the matter of the transparency of the window. When the window is smudged, we are not seeing the true view but only that part of the view that the window will allow us to see. The more that the window controls the view, the more *biased* we say that view is. Bias, in the scientific world, is anything that keeps our window from being purely transparent. Bias can range from errors in using measuring systems to the prejudices and opinions of the scientists involved.

Sometimes, our window is not just smudged, but is actually flawed. The window is distorted in some fashion, so that we are not getting a truly transparent look at the world through it. When we turn these same flaws to our outward vision, then we get *error*. Errors are similar to biases, in that they distort the genuine record. But they are more serious, harder sometimes to find, and usually need to be controlled because they cannot be totally eliminated.

Error is the admission that even the most unbiased and well-crafted window is imperfect, and that we need to acknowledge and work with and around the inevitable presence of errors. For this reason, probability plays a key role in all scientific claims. Because of uncertainty at all levels, we can only be relatively sure of our claims. Issues like *generalizability* and *validity* are based on our admission that error, and to a lesser degree bias, cannot be eliminated from scientific work. So we make probability-based reliability and validity determinations to tell us how confident we can be of the results of our work.

Transparency plays one more key role in science. The ultimate recording devices in science are the scientists themselves. Therefore, there is a need for their recording and reporting to be as transparent as possible, so that they can create a clear channel between the phenomena and the readers of the work. As a consequence, we find a standard of transparency in science writing. Anything "subjective" is seen to be a source of either error or bias, or both. Therefore, scientists need to "objectify" their outlooks and their reporting. Any observation that can be taken as a personal interpretation must be excluded. "Two men were fighting" is okay (objective), but how do you know for sure that "they were fighting over a woman's love" (subjective)?

Finally, all writing must be transparent as well. We see that the first-person writing style is shunned as subjective and biased, and third-person writing is used exclusively. "I" never did anything; only "the researcher" is present in these reports. Furthermore, "I" never "observed these effects" but rather "these effects were observed." Third-person and passive voice are two of the main rhetorical tools used to signal objectivity and transparency in scientific reports.

Scientifically based empirical inquiry sought to relegate speculative empirical inquiry into oblivion. Speculation was sometimes allowed, but only within the carefully defined and controlled confines of scientific theory. Other forms of speculation were deemed too subjective to be useful; they could only fuel eventual bias and error. To oversimplify, speculation per se became welcome only in the humanistic areas of endeavor, such as creative writing and the arts. Genuine empirical work was the purview of the masters of the window.

The lure of the window is also quite compelling for many qualitative researchers for several reasons. First of all, we have been socialized as inquirers to accept the window as the basic vision for *all* empirical inquiry. This is such a basic notion for so many of us that it is very hard to step back and question it. Second, many of the mirror issues appear to have direct relevance to our qualitative efforts. This is particularly true of such statistically grounded notions as reliability, validity, and especially generalizability. These issues will be addressed in some detail in Chapter 6, but for now we can say that we need to realize that perspective, which is critical in qualitative research, looks like mere bias within traditional window models. Finally, we need to realize that, like the mirror before it, there are always overtones of the window in any form of empirical research. This point will show up time and again when we look at both basic and advanced qualitative skills.

Qualitative research is not a child of the mirror or the window. It is linked with a third fundamental vision based on a completely different technology of seeing. We will argue that the basic vision that guides qualitative research is centrally grounded in a third fundamental innovation in the art of seeing, the lantern.

The Lantern

What can be as basic as the mirror or the window? Arguably, the third great technological advance for the skill of looking came with the introduction of the lantern. The first lantern was most likely a smoldering branch, picked up and used as a torch by some prehistoric ancestor. With this smoldering branch, our ancestor was able to shed light in dark corners, where no light had been shed before. Whereas the great advance of the mirror was reflection, and the great advance of the window was transparent access, the lantern's great contribution is illumination.

When we look at qualitative researchers over the decades as they have struggled to craft conceptual tools for their trade, we find an implicit reaching for illuminative concepts. We see them use such words as *illumination, insight,* and *understanding.* We see researchers going to faraway places and to ordinary settings, seeking to make the strange familiar and the familiar strange. We find researchers struggling to see the world through the eyes of others, to understand acts in terms of strange motives and to fathom cultures in terms of strange presuppositions. We find other qualitative researchers using interpretative tools and techniques to decipher cultural codes and social mores ranging from marriage rituals to dealing with uncommunicative students.

Therefore, the goals of qualitative research are insight, enlightenment, and illumination. We are neither contemplative mirror researchers nor unbiased window researchers. We are searchers and discoverers and reconcilers of meaning where no meaning has been clearly understood before, and we do not feel that our understanding of meaning is complete until we discover and understand its role in practice and experience.

TYPES OF VISION AND THE TWO DOMAINS

It is tempting to argue that quantitative research is window research and qualitative research is lantern research, but this is too simplistic. All forms of empirical inquiry have all three aspects of vision embedded in them. What is important is the degree to which these views dominate basic thinking, and the degree to which these various visions are either foregrounded or relegated to the background.

We will leave it up to quantitative thinkers to apply these aspects of vision to their field. In the meantime, we will look at the "blend" of the three modes of vision in each of the two main domains of qualitative research.

Vision and Qualitative Science

First of all, it is important to state that in all forms of qualitative research, the notion of the lantern will be a dominant concept. All major forms of qualitative research seek illumination and insight. The question is this: Which other modes of vision come into play, and how do they relate to our basic lantern stance?

In qualitative science, the window is critically important. Though qualitative scientists are not seeking to be transparent, they do embrace many of the concerns that predominate window thinking. In particular, qualitative scientists seek to be *systematic* by being *objective.* As we will see throughout this book, there are a number of ways to be systematic. Qualitative science, like science in general, turns to objectivity as a primary tool for establishing and maintaining systematicity. Along with objectivity, related concepts like reliability, validity, and generalizability come into play as well.

Do not think, however, that the mirror plays no role in qualitative science. On the contrary, the mirror has played an important role in sciences of all forms and natures. Science, qualitative or otherwise, is also done by persons who have stances to take and lessons to learn from their efforts. All good inquiry is, to some degree, reflective inquiry. In some ways, qualitative scientists are freer than other scientists to allow the mirror to hold forth in their work.

This is because qualitative science, in the final analysis, is about meaning. And meaning at some level always has a reflective and speculative dimension to it.

Vision and Qualitative Inquiry

Qualitative inquiry, like qualitative science, embraces the concept of the lantern. At the same time, qualitative inquiry also foregrounds the notion of the mirror. The stance, perspectives, and reflections of the individual qualitative inquirer have always been an important dimension to this domain. Starting with the sole ethnographer alighting into a strange and new culture, and proceeding through the most intimate personal analysis of a racialized or gendered experience, the subjective experiences and characteristics of the qualitative inquirer have been important. Just because these experiences are grounded in specifics does not make them unsystematic, however. Systematicity in qualitative inquiry comes not from an objective stance, but from an honest, open, and revealed stance.

As with qualitative science, all three modes of vision are important in qualitative inquiry as well. The window, though less important, still has a role to play. Qualitative inquirers need to do work that stands up to scrutiny on its own terms. It cannot hide behind the defense that it is what the researcher believes or wants it to be. It has to take its place in the community of inquiry, and so it must have values that can be transparently seen and appreciated.

ADVANCED SKILLS AND THEIR ROLES

Earlier in this chapter, we summarized the four basic skills that allow us to approach the world in a qualitative fashion. Looking at the world in this different way also requires us to develop a more specialized set of different sorts of research tools and skills. We will consider these to be advanced skills. Not all forms of qualitative research employ all these skills, or employ them in the same ways, but they are certainly necessary skills for developing skilled qualitative researchers. As with the basic skills, each will have its own chapter later on, but for now we will take a quick look at each skill in turn. The more advanced qualitative research skills are questioning, data gathering, analyzing, narrating, and writing.

Questioning

The problem of stating a proper research question is a thorny issue for qualitative research. Qualitative researchers are always looking for meaning, whether they pursue hypotheses, explore unexplored issues, dig deeper into the meanings we find in everyday life, or make a call for action and change. To get at meaning, qualitative researchers ask questions. In some cases, these questions lead to formal *research questions,* much as we find in scientific research. In other cases, these types of general questions lead qualitative research to *research target areas.* We will compare and contrast these approaches in our chapter on questioning (Chapter 6).

Part of the skill of asking good research questions, or identifying good research targets, is at the theoretical level. In particular, three theoretical issues surface over and over, and need to be addressed in nearly every qualitative study: (1) How do we address issues like reliability, validity, and generalizability? (2) What is our view of reality, especially regarding the notion of multiple realities? and (3) What are our particular ethical responsibilities? All of these issues can and often do play key roles in how we approach a topic or area of study.

It is quite possible to argue that research is nothing more than applied logic. Though we will not go that far, we will also realize that different modes of research, and different types of research questions, employ different forms of reasoning. Asking research questions and finding research targets often require careful logical reasoning as well. Some of these modes of reasoning are quite distinct to the qualitative research process, and so will be examined. In particular, we will talk about reasoning to meaning, and the role it can play in qualitative research.

The most practical application of reasoning in qualitative research involves its use in creating and shaping the literature review. A literature review is nothing more than a logical argument that uses current research to support its claims. How does the nature of reasoning change the nature of the literature review in qualitative research?

The nature of the literature review is a tricky issue for most qualitative researchers. Some qualitative researchers hold that a qualitative study should not start with a literature review, but that the researcher should enter the setting with a blank slate. But can researchers really set aside their preconceptions? If it does make sense to review the literature for a qualitative study, what sort of literature review should it be? How should it resemble a standard literature review? How should it be different? These questions will also be addressed in Chapter 6.

Data Gathering

You cannot do empirical research without data. And you will not have data unless you gather it. While this simple truth seems so obvious, the task of data gathering is anything but simple and obvious.

Different modes of qualitative research employ different data-gathering strategies. We will examine some of the most common data-gathering strategies in qualitative research in Chapter 7. These strategies run the gamut from careful case studies with a single individual to large programmatic participatory projects.

Analyzing

Analysis is probably the most common concept in empirical research. Research findings are no good unless we analyze them. Is there a sharp break between qualitative and quantitative methods of analyses, or do they lie along some kind of continuum? These are some of the issues we will examine in Chapter 8.

The goal of analysis in quantitative research is twofold: to describe things according to preestablished measurement criteria, and to test predictions based on theory. Statistics is most often used as the final analysis tool, and so the two types of analyses just described are often grounded, respectively, in descriptive and inferential statistics. The term *analysis* comes from a Greek word meaning "to break apart." This breaking apart is an integral part of quantitative research. Complex wholes are broken into descriptive measurement criteria. Complex causal settings are broken into independent and dependent variables. And comprehensive theoretical claims are broken into testable hypotheses.

Does analysis in qualitative research have to follow the same trends? Are complex wholes broken down into units and then studied, or do we try to keep things whole? What role does synthesis play? How do synthesis and interpretation allow us to find illumination and insight, and go beyond current models and levels of understanding? Are some forms of qualitative research closer to traditional analysis models than others, and why is this so? These issues will also be addressed.

Narrating

Stories seem to play an integral role in many forms of qualitative research. Why is this so? Is it true, as some have charged, that qualitative research is nothing more than a form of story-telling? Chapter 9, on narrating, will address these concerns.

The closest thing to story in quantitative research is the concept of theory. A theory is a formal account of meaning used to make sense of complex phenomena and to allow researchers to derive testable hypotheses. For quantitative research, there is a necessary link between meaning and explanation, and prediction. A theory that only explains something, but that cannot be used to make predictive hypotheses that can be verified or falsified, is no good. At best, such a theory is only a story.

Qualitative research does not treat story as a poor cousin to theory, but takes the form seriously on its own terms. First of all, there are many different types of story, from fable to myth to narrative. Each has its own character and plays its own role in helping us to understand complex phenomena. Second, stories follow overt rules. Therefore, they can be studied as carefully and as objectively as any other natural phenomenon. Finally, story is the enemy of chance. If we find that certain accounts and findings and observations and happenings all fit neatly together into a lawful and coherent story, then we have uncovered a powerful source of order in the world.

Do stories play the same role in qualitative research that theories play in quantitative research? Or should we look at them as separate sorts of entities, and not try too hard to compare them? This issue will also be examined in Chapter 9.

Writing

Writing (Chapter 10) plays a crucial role in qualitative research. It goes beyond the task of merely creating the record. In quantitative research writing, we find the tacit adoption of what we called earlier a rhetoric of transparency. The rhetoric for qualitative research is much more complex.

We tend to think of rhetoric as being mainly about persuasion, and so the notion that rhetoric is crucial for qualitative research makes us suspicious. But we need to expand our definition of rhetoric. Rhetoric is not just about persuading. On a larger level, rhetoric is about being able to convey a complex or subtle notion or description of experience from one person to another. It involves more than being good with words. It involves the ability get inside another person's frame of reference, as best as possible, and to see and describe the world from that other frame.

Is it possible to say that the analysis of a qualitative study is over prior to the writing? Or is the writing the critical last piece of the puzzle? Is qualitative research writing an act of chronicling, or is it the last stage of the research process? Are there preferred forms of writing for qualitative research? What practical writing skills do qualitative researchers need to develop and hone? What is the role of tale and genre in qualitative research writing? These issues will be addressed in Chapter 10.

MOVING FROM EXPERIENCE TO REFLECTION TO CREATE A SKILL

Let me conclude this chapter by describing the basic strategy of personal skill building that will be used.

We will start out each skill with an exercise grounded in the world of experience. Exercises have long been noted as a useful way to learn qualitative skills. Janesick (1998) is one of the best current examples of the use of such exercises in this fashion.

It is best if you go ahead and do the exercise before you read the rest of the chapter. I know that most of us want to do well, and one of the best ways to do well is to read ahead, and try to do what is expected of us. In this case, however, reading ahead will work against the purposes of the exercises. The exercises are meant to provide us with the "raw materials" of experience that all of us can use in common to pursue mastery of the skills in question.

As we reflect on our own experiences in light of the basic principles of each skill, we gain important insight into our own strengths. Good researchers know their own strengths, and build upon them. This is a far more useful strategy than trying to identify and correct our weaknesses. Once we know and understand our strengths, we can use them to compensate and correct for our weaknesses. This is the fundamental and natural path for growth of any kind.

Once we have reflected on our emerging skill development, we need to ground those skills in traditional and current understandings in the field. As neophyte qualitative researchers, we need to look upon those broad domains of understanding in the field that bear upon each of our skill areas.

We must be careful to realize that any understanding is a work in progress, not only for ourselves but also for the field as a whole. That is one reason we do not emphasize any particular manifestation of a skill strictly in terms of technical practices alone. Those technical practices are prone to change, but the skill area will almost certainly persist. For instance, interview strategies and techniques may change and evolve, but researchers will certainly continue to talk and listen to people.

Then, we will concentrate on putting our skills to work on a broader level. Now that we are working within the framework of an overarching vision, with a set of our own experiences, and with a sense of where the field is situated in terms of these skills, we can confidently put our emerging skills to work. Learning qualitative research is a lifelong process, and the only way to do it is to become a qualitative researcher. But a basic mastery of fundamental skills is probably the best way to start.

Finally, we will conclude each of our first 10 chapters with an ongoing practical exercise. Specifically, we will follow two graduate students through the process of preparing their first qualitative research proposals. As they ask themselves the questions they need to ask, we will look over their shoulders and ask ourselves the same questions.

PLANNING YOUR RESEARCH PROPOSAL: INTRODUCTION

It is time to meet Albert and Carol. First of all, these are not real students, and the projects that they are doing are not real projects. At best, they are composites of students I have taught over the years. Many of their issues, and their actual topics, are complete inventions.

Carol

Carol is pursuing her doctorate in Sociology at a private university. Carol has been a social worker for many years, and so she has come to know the plight of poor, single women trying to receive the education they need for career advancement while trying to find a life partner at the same time. She is not comfortable with the surveys and questionnaires she has seen on this topic; too often, these instruments seem to lead the women in the directions the researchers have already decided were important. At the same time, she is dissatisfied with many of the open-ended interview studies she has read. In these studies, it seems as if the researchers were not concerned with building a bigger picture and allowing some sort of general and theoretical understandings to emerge. Fortunately for Carol, her department specializes in qualitative science research. Carol feels that this sort of rigor and appeal to the concerns of science is a perfect match for her own research concerns.

For these reasons, Carol will be our example of a student developing a research proposal based on the qualitative science approach.

Albert

Albert is a doctoral student in an education department at a large state university. Before he came back to school, he was a secondary-level classroom teacher for a number of years. His teaching area was mathematics. He was most happy in his geometry classes, where his students generally displayed a great deal of math anxiety. Helping these students relieve their anxiety was his greatest source of pleasure and satisfaction as a teacher. When he decided to pursue his doctorate in Mathematics Education, he also decided that he was going to conduct research that would help make things better for math-anxious students.

Early in his graduate studies, Albert took a course on qualitative inquiry methods. Prior to that course, he had assumed that he would rely upon his considerable mathematical skills and insights, and pursue qualitative approaches in his research. After his exposure to qualitative inquiry, however, he realized that this approach seemed to be most relevant to the kinds of issues and basic questions about math anxiety that he might wish to pursue.

For these reasons, Albert will be our example of a student developing a research proposal based on the qualitative inquiry approach.

Ourselves

Now that Albert and Carol have introduced themselves, it is time for us to introduce our own research thinking. Take a few moments to reflect on the following points:

- Write a brief career autobiography. If you are a full-time student, what did you do before you went back to school? If you have never held a full-time job, what sort of job would you like to have when you graduate? If you are a part-time student, what are you doing now? How will your degree affect the sort of career you would like to have? What three goals would you most like to pursue, career-wise, after you complete this degree? Why?
- Look at your three career goals. Are they practical or theoretical? If they are theoretical, what sorts of research efforts would allow you to start moving toward those goals? If they are practical, what sorts of research efforts might get you moving in the right direction?

- Write the phrase *qualitative science* on a piece of paper. List three things about this approach that appeal to you personally. List another three areas where you might have personal concerns. Does this approach seem viable to you? Does it relate well to your goals?
- Write the phrase *qualitative inquiry* on a piece of paper. List three things about this approach that appeal to you personally. List another three areas where you might have personal concerns. Does this approach seem viable to you? Does it relate well to your goals?
- Finally, we will look at our areas of basic interest. Take two more sheets of paper. On one sheet, write the words *Areas of personal curiosity* on the top. Then proceed to list those broad areas where you are curious, and where you would like to do research. On the other sheet, write the words *Areas of practical concern* on the top. Then proceed to list those broad areas where you have serious personal or professional concerns, and where you would like to do research. Which list is longer? If you have more areas of curiosity, try to think of some additional areas of concern. If you have more practical concerns, try to let your curiosity run free a bit. The idea is to generate a broad pattern of potential research areas, based on both curiosity and concerns.
- Feel free to repeat any of these exercises as you wish. The idea is to open up your thinking to who you are, what you wish to achieve, and some of the broad areas and approaches to research that might appeal to you.

CHAPTER 2

Observing

Exercise One—*The Quiet Place*

There are certain enduring traditions that seem to be a part of many cultures. For instance, when some seekers have needed to think in peace, to sort out what is central and what is peripheral in their lives, they have turned to the desert. Native American youths of the Southwest headed into the desert on Vision Quests, in search of true identity. Eastern Rite monks of the early Christian Era turned away from cities and from the merging of religion and culture to lead solitary and ascetic lives in the deserts of the Middle East. Australian native people set off on "walkabouts" in the Outback to discover themselves and their place in the world. There is something about the emptiness of the desert that allows the seeker to discover substance in apparent emptiness.

Our first exercise is designed to tap into the enormous power that resides in the "desert." However, this exercise is not meant to be either spiritually or philosophically profound. We are seekers of a different sort, and we need to take advantage of emptiness for different reasons.

It is hoped that this exercise will allow you to discover some of your own basic observational preferences and orientations. In order to do any form of qualitative research, you need to find your own observational strengths and hone your own basic observational skills. But you need to do this first under simplified conditions.

Therefore, you need to find a "desert." It need not be a real desert. It can be a metaphorical desert; that is, any place that is relatively empty. Perhaps it is a spot on campus that is off the beaten trail. Perhaps it is a restaurant on a slow day. Feel free to use your imagination to find a simple and bare place where you can settle in and observe, without being overwhelmed or being observed yourself.

The procedures for doing this first exercise are quite simple:

- Find a place that is very quiet and isolated. The less human activity associated with this place, the better. Even a very isolated and empty place is much busier and harder to observe than you might suppose.
- Take paper and pencil with you to this place. Record the date and time that you begin your observations. For this particular exercise, it is better to use paper and pencil than to use a tape recorder. Tape recorders allow us to babble unless we are very skilled at dictation. It is also better to use paper and pencil than, say, a notebook computer. Computers have a nasty tendency to run out of battery power, or to manifest other glitches. Besides, for most of us, it takes more attention to type on a keyboard than to jot down notes on a pad. With a paper and pencil, you can spend more time with your eyes on the site, and not on your computer screen.
- Begin observing. Note the day and time that you begin. Observe for at least 30 minutes, but for no more than 60 minutes. When you are done, record the finishing time.

- For now, don't worry about whether or not you are observing properly. There is no magic to observation—it is something we have done all our lives. Good research observational skills are built through practice. Be alert and reflective about what you perceive, about what these things mean to you, and also try to develop a sense of what you are not observing.
- To finish this exercise, pull your observational findings into an observational report. Again, do not worry about proper format at this time. Simply decide what to include and what to exclude, and make a report. You may wish to share your report with fellow students or with your instructor.

The goal of this exercise is to help you discover what sort of observer you are under natural and ordinary conditions. Do not worry about trying to follow some preconceived observational protocol. These protocols will only interfere with your own inherent observational tendencies. What do you consider important? How do you proceed with this sort of task? What are some of your basic strategies? Your basic tactics? Do not worry about these matters until after you have done your observational exercise. Just relax and do what seems most natural to you.

REFLECTING ON OBSERVING

Observation is both the most basic and the single trickiest skill for qualitative researchers to master. That is why we start with it.

As human beings, we are programmed to observe. We cannot ignore our surroundings or the activities that go on in those surroundings unless we actually make a sustained effort to ignore these things. Even in the midst of shutting off our normal observational processes, a truly unusual or unexplained event will snap us back to full awareness and back into the regular observational process, whether we want to or not. We can no more stop observing than we can stop breathing. Sure, we can hold our breaths and we can hold our observations, but sooner or later we are forced to both breathe and observe.

WHY IS QUALITATIVE RESEARCH OBSERVATION SO DIFFICULT?

Given the constant presence and prevalent role of observation in our ordinary lives, why should it be a tricky skill for a qualitative researcher? Very simply, it is hard to turn away from our ordinary uses of observation per se and move toward a research orientation. There are at least three primary reasons for this basic difficulty.

First of all, most of our ordinary observational efforts are geared toward what we might call "maintenance." This can be a subtle point to grasp. Think of it this way—suppose you are driving down a familiar street. Perhaps you are listening to the radio and daydreaming about an upcoming vacation. What are you actually observing under these circumstances? More often than not, you are checking out the familiar terrain just to make sure there are no serious changes or surprises lurking there. That way, we do not have to invest a lot of time or attention to the observational process. Though this helps us lead our everyday lives, it works against us as qualitative researchers.

We can step outside this ordinary casual "maintenance" process to some degree when we observe as researchers, but we usually sustain more of this ordinary maintenance functioning than we might realize. It is as if we have to work against our instincts in order not to see the ordinary and the everyday. That is, we see what we expect to see. Something out of the ordinary has to happen, or we have to pay very careful attention, to do otherwise.

The second source of difficulty is the fact that genuine qualitative research observation is intense and is usually very taxing. This is because such acts of observation have to both take note of and then go beyond the ordinary and everyday. You are spending more energy than usual, and this is both more demanding and more tiring.

To emphasize this last point, let us go back to our driving example. Suppose we run into a sudden traffic problem. It turns out that, say, a raspberry jam truck has overturned up ahead. Fortunately, no one has been injured, but the road is a real mess. Smashed jars of raspberry jam are strewn all over the place. You might say that this is a real traffic jam!

Under these circumstances, you are observing the road in a careful and intense way. You have put aside your ordinary "maintenance" observation. Your concentration is totally given over to looking out for glass shards and slippery patches of jam. You are also watching your fellow drivers to see what they are doing.

When you finally navigate through this sudden and treacherous obstacle course, you are surprised to find that the radio is in the midst of playing one of your favorite songs. Normally, as soon as that particular song would come on, you would start to sing along with your usual gusto. On this occasion, you missed singing along with this song because you literally did not heart it. You were so busy observing the road that you shut off your awareness of everything else. You also notice that you have been perspiring, your eyes are achy and tired, and you feel somewhat fatigued.

Now, imagine a situation where you have to make sure that you are paying attention, not only to the road and to the other drivers, but where you also have to note the presence of your favorite song as it comes on the radio! In other words, you have to be able to observe the extraordinary and the ordinary at the same time, without one type of observation getting in the way of the other. A perfect qualitative observer could do this, but this level of observational skill tends to be beyond us mere mortals. However, we should continue to work on our abilities to observe in more than one direction at a time.

There is a third complicating factor that we have already addressed implicitly in our traffic example: ordinary observation tends to adopt what we might call a *convergent observational focus*. We saw this point illustrated quite nicely in the previous example. When a crisis arose, we focused entirely on the road and lost track of the song that was playing on the radio. We also failed to notice, say, that a familiar billboard had changed its message, and that a car that had been following us had turned off before we got to the end of the jam mess. Convergence observational focus, in these sorts of settings, is nothing less than a tool we use instinctively to increase our chances of survival. No wonder it is so prevalent in all of our observational activities.

In everyday life, convergence observational focus can be quite powerful, but qualitative research observation requires us to be divergent as well. We have to be able to turn our eyes and ears away from a central focus and pay attention to what is happening on the edges and at the limits of the observational setting. This is perhaps the single most difficult skill for the qualitative research observer to learn, but the one that potentially can yield the most benefits.

Given these difficulties and complications and circumstances, what can you do to improve your observational skills? The most important first step is to understand yourself as an observer. We can begin this process of understanding by looking at different sorts of observer types.

OBSERVER TYPES

As a result of your observational exercise, you now have a more explicit sense of the sort of observer that you are. Did you pay a great deal of attention to sounds? Sights? Human interactions? One way to understand widely differing approaches to observation is to categorize observers themselves by creating idealized observer types.

The following sections lay out a series of such idealized observer types. There is nothing particularly scientific or theoretical about this list. It is actually a list that I have compiled and modified over the years by looking at observation reports done by my students as they performed an observational exercise similar to the one that began this chapter. These idealized observer types are presented as a guide to help you identify your own observational preferences and tendencies.

This list is not exhaustive or exclusive; it is far from definitive. If you feel that you, or others, fit into some undefined type, feel free to create a new category.

Also remember that each category is an extreme type. No one real person is an example of a "pure" category. All of us embrace aspects of at least several of these categories. But we can usually turn to one of these types and say that it reflects our basic orientation toward observation.

Having stated the disclaimers, let us examine eight of the most common types of observers that I have been able to document.

The Embracer

The Embracer seeks to take in as much as humanly possible. No detail is too unimportant, no incident too trivial. The Embracer does not seek to sample, but to capture the whole. In this fashion, the Embracer is dedicated to bringing a richness to the act of observation that respects the richness and complexity of life itself.

The positive side to the Embracer stance is that it can be used to create an observational experience and subsequent report that is dazzling in its richness and texture. A skilled Embracer experiences and documents so much so effectively that you do not just consume the observational account, you nearly reexperience it.

The negative side lies in the term *nearly reexperience*. The Embracer, regardless of effort and skill, always falls short of being able to re-create or totally document a complete experience, no matter how apparently empty or sparse the original setting. The world of experience, at every turn, is just too rich to be completely contained in human reports. Therefore, the Embracer is forced to make choices, and more importantly, omissions. But the Embracer is not temperamentally suited to making these choices and omissions. Such choices often seem to the Embracer to be merely examples of failing to perform the observational task to its fullest extent.

The Photographer

The Photographer is an observer who is overwhelmingly visual. For the Photographer, observation is looking. Findings from other sensory modalities may be duly noted, but most of them are intimately linked or even grounded in the visual record. For example, suppose we are observing and a dog wanders onto the scene. Because we *saw* the dog, we note its bark and its smell. If the dog had been out of our visual range, and we had only heard its bark, then more likely than not the bark would not have been recorded in our observational protocols.

The positive side to the Photographer stance is the fact that visual information is incredibly useful and important to all of us, and a careful visual record is more often than not a highly useful record. It is also the record that is usually most familiar and most compelling. For many of us, seeing is the beginning and the end of observation. By staying within the visual frame, the Photographer is actually addressing observational issues that are traditionally most important for research.

On the negative side, however, is the realization that sometimes focusing on the visual array causes us to miss crucial information unfolding via other sensory modalities. Because we depend so much on our sense of sight, we often shortchange our other sensory modalities. These other modalities are crucial for complete observing.

There is a great deal of difference between turning first to the visual record and staying exclusively within the visual record. Unless there are compelling reasons to do otherwise, there is nothing wrong with the first position. It is the overdependence or exclusive dependence on the visual record that can get us into trouble as qualitative observers.

The Tape Recorder

The Tape Recorder is an observer who is drawn toward sounds and sound patterns. Usually, the Tape Recorder is drawn most deeply to human speech and conversation. All of us know the importance of language, but no one is more aware of this than the Tape Recorder. For the Tape Recorder, instances of speech take precedence over any and all other events on the scene.

The positive side to the Tape Recorder stance is the fact that speech is critical for most human interactions, and the Tape Recorder is well situated and well disposed to taking full advantage of the richness of such speech. In qualitative research, transcripts of verbal records usually play an important role. Observers who are keenly aware of the nuances of verbal communication often uncover subtle cues and bits of information that would elude a less careful listener.

On the negative side, too often speech per se is overrated as a source of information. Anyone who has wrestled with the problem of interpreting transcripts knows this. How was something said? What were the facial expressions of the speaker? The mannerisms? How did the listener react nonverbally to what was said? If the observational record is strictly verbal, then it is difficult or impossible to answer such important questions.

Are there Tape Recorders who are attuned to sounds other than speech? Perhaps, but I have not come across any in my classes. Those students who concentrated on documenting sounds when there were no other people in the setting were quick to shift to documenting speech records when other people came upon the scene. If they were observing in settings where there were no other people, I usually found that an initial focus on sound eventually faded into an awareness of other sensory inputs, usually visual. That is why I feel that the Tape Recorder is really primed for the appearance of a verbal encounter.

The Categorizer

The Categorizer is an observer who creates sorting categories and assigns observations to them as a basic and ongoing part of the observational process. Each major datum point is assigned a place within the developing category process.

One of the most popular forms of qualitative research, namely grounded theory, is in many ways a formalized and refined version of the Categorizer stance. Grounded theory reflects the positive side to the Categorizer stance. When we categorize, we organize. The process of observing becomes an active and evolving process of understanding. If we are particularly skilled Categorizers, then we also enrich and expand our observational processes to take advantage of the richer picture we are building of the scene.

As with any other observational strategies, there is of course a negative side to the Categorizer stance. First of all, it is difficult to split our attention on observing and organizing simultaneously. If we are not careful, we tend to allow our organizational structure to sway our observing, instead of vice versa. Once we start to build a categorical scheme, it is harder than we might suppose to modify or even abandon it.

Before we leave the Categorizer type, however, we need to be aware of the dangers of being an ideological Categorizer. There is a crucial difference between a natural Categorizer and an ideological Categorizer.

Natural Categorizers gravitate immediately to the formation and elaboration of observational categories. For such people, finding and building categories is not particularly strenuous, and so it is not that hard to move back and forth between categorizing and observing without missing anything important.

Ideological Categorizers, however, are committed always and everywhere to being "scientific." They want to make sure that their observations fit into their preconceived ideas of what good research should be about. So they set out to force fit their observations into the sorts of categories they feel that good researchers would use.

The formation of categories is not a natural act for ideological Categorizers, but instead it is a major and taxing chore. In their response to the fear of being taken as "unscientific," ideological Categorizers tend to produce thin, stilted, and barren categories whose only virtue is that they are usually so pedestrian that they are totally uncontroversial.

There is no need to be reckless or bohemian as an observer. However, a misplaced zeal for scientific precision and accuracy more often than not produces an observational record of dubious worth. In short, if the categories flow naturally, do not worry about being a Categorizer. If, however, you find yourself laboriously editing your language and thoughts and limiting your observations to conform to some standard of objectivity, then abandon the use of categories as an observational tool. They are only serving to keep you from doing really interesting observational work.

The Baseliner

The Baseliner organizes experiences along some sort of temporal, or time, dimension. That temporal dimension can be as arbitrary as the act of recording an observation at predetermined time intervals, or as episodic as observing and noting critical events as they arise within the observational process.

The positive side of the Baseliner stance is that it is sensitive to the role of time in the observational process. Too often, we take time for granted. But the skilled Baseliner is aware of the role and place of time in the observational setting and the observational process. Some crucial aspects of a situation cannot be understood unless and until their temporal characteristics are taken into account. This is particularly true of things that happen in cycles. Do certain things seem to occur at the same time of day? At the same time of year? These dimensions can be both subtle and crucial.

On the negative side, sometimes things just happen to be unfolding in time. Placing a temporal dimension on their presence can suggest a level of process that is just not there. One event may have just happened to have occurred at the beginning of the observation period, and another event may have just happened to have occurred at the end of the same period. Baseliners have to be careful not to draw too much of a process link between such events without making sure that there is other evidence that they are related.

The Abstracter

The Abstracter tries to be as objective as possible. In this way, the Abstracter resembles a Categorizer. There are important differences, however. Categorizers tend to focus on categories that allow for descriptive organization. Therefore, observations that fall into the evolving categories can still be rich in sensory data. With Abstracters, however, there is a move up to a more abstract level of description. Specific sensory information is less important for these observers, while overall conceptual links become more important. In other words, Abstracters tend to look upon the observation process as an intellectual task, first and foremost.

On the positive side, Abstracter reports are the easiest to coordinate directly with other, scientifically oriented, research efforts. The intellectual character of such findings also allows for easy integration into other forms of theoretical thinking. The skilled Abstracter is also more likely to see more complex, higher-order patterns in the observational data.

On the negative side, the Abstracter can sometimes strive so completely to be objective that he or she actually discards crucial information that is not easily translated into objective accounts. There is nothing wrong with Abstract forms of observation, of course. The problem lies in their exclusive use. For one thing, highly intellectualized and abstract observations tend to be less specific and less richly invested with concrete sensory information. In their rush to move to the abstract level, Abstracters have to be careful to leave behind enough of a sensory record to allow others to interpret and evaluate their observations at more basic levels.

The Interacter

The Interacter sees observation as the study of people, and so pays attention to persons in settings and their interactions. The Interacter obviously chooses settings that will guarantee the presence of people.

On the positive side, there are few things more interesting to people than other people. By observing others in a skillful way, Interacters can help us see important aspects about our culture and ourselves as played out in natural and unforced settings. Such information is potentially of the highest use to any social scientist.

On the negative side, Interacters can run the risk of missing important cues from the setting that do not involve people in any explicit way. Does it matter, for instance, that the bench upon which a couple is sitting is made of concrete instead of wood? What about the fact that they are sitting under a maple tree? The concrete sidewalk is broken and in general poor repair—does this matter? Interacters have to remember that human interactions, as fascinating as they are, take place within physical settings that confine, and sometimes define, the nature of those interactions.

A skilled Interacter is not a voyeur. It is unethical and probably unhealthy to observe complex and extended human interactions without all parties knowing that such an observation is taking place.

The Reflecter

The Reflecter tends to see observation as at least in part an exercise in self-discovery, and so constantly monitors the impact of these observational experiences on himself on herself.

On the positive side, the Reflecter stance is one of the most humane of all observational processes. When we read the work of a skilled and careful Reflecter, we can almost look through that person's eyes. Skilled Reflectors focus on and reflect upon those things that are universal and significant to other human beings. The process of self-discovery can then serve as a guide for other persons as well.

On the negative side, the Reflecter stance can be prone to narcissism. In this case, the process is not one of self-discovery and growth, but of self-absorption. The Reflecter does not learn anything new about himself or herself, and the poor reader is treated to a self-indulgent and tiresome account as a result.

The Reflecter is closest in nature to the speculative inquirers of the mirror tradition, and so Reflecters can learn much by studying that tradition. The best speculative researchers in the past were careful enough to hold the mirror of nature far enough at arm's length so that they could see more than their own faces, metaphorically speaking. Skilled Reflecters follow that same process when they function as qualitative research observers.

Working with Observational Types

First of all, try your best to identify your own observational style. Feel free to use the categories just described to help you decide, but do not feel limited by them. Also, don't worry about being a pure anything, observation-wise. Sometimes, the particular setting has a lot to say about the way we go about employing our observational skills. But you can identify some of your comfort zones as an observer and understand them as personal areas of strength. As with anything else, it is better to work from your strengths in order to improve and refine your observational skills.

Second, you can work on integrating other observational types into your own natural style. Here, you are going beyond merely practicing other observational stances. Reflect instead on the positives and strengths that are manifested by each particular observational style. Then, try to put some of those strengths to work in your own observations. At first, this will be very difficult. Also, your observational results will suffer while you are practicing these unfamiliar skills. But if you are patient with yourself, you can reap some real benefits as a more balanced observer.

Finally, all of us can work on our ability to be more divergent observers. Remember that the twin forces of "maintenance" and "convergence" usually lead us to latch onto what is most active and most obvious in our given observational settings. But, as often as not, the really interesting things in a particular observational setting are happening at the edges and boundaries of awareness. Don't be afraid to spend some time looking into corners and under rocks, observationally speaking. After all, if we are taking a lantern approach toward searching for meaning, we need to move around and look in unfamiliar places.

GROUNDING OBSERVATIONAL SKILLS

So far, we have been discussing observational issues from an informal perspective. We also need to ground these skills within classic and current qualitative research thinking. Adler and Adler (1994) summarize many of the key points that currently impact the practice of observation in qualitative research. Some of the key issues they raise are: (1) subordination, (2) selection issues, (3) focus issues, and (4) saturation.

Subordination

Observation is often viewed as subordinate to other aspects of research. This means that we rarely just observe, and in addition, observation is rarely the primary strategy we adopt when collecting data. At best, observation is most often seen as part of the process, or as a means to a larger and more complex methodological end.

Gold (1958) lays out one of the earliest examples of this overall perspective. Gold locates observation along a four-stage continuum that also addresses participation. The *complete observer,* who is rare, simply watches. More often we find either *the observer-as-participant,* or the *participant-as-observer.* The difference between these last two strategies is a matter of involvement. The observer-as-participant is joining in, but mostly to observe. The participant-as-observer is more involved, but has still made it clear to the others involved that they are under observation. Finally, we occassionaly may find the use of the *complete participant,* where the researcher is simply a member of the group under study. Complete observation and complete participation can both be morally suspect, if the groups involved have no notion of the research aims and purposes of the researcher.

As you strive to find the role that observation plays in your approach to qualitative research, you will need to be clear on the subordination question. Does observation usually play a central role in your work? Or does it take a backseat to other modes of collecting data? Why do you work the way you do? Is it a function of the questions you ask, the way you like to collect data, or both?

Selection Issues

Selection issues deal with how a researcher goes about choosing where and whom to observe. Obviously, these selection issues are driven by the goals and purposes of the given research project. Let us look at each issue in turn.

The first issue in the selection process addresses where to do your observing. Choosing a setting is a crucial part of the observation process. Some site-selection issues are obvious. If you are looking for a particular type of behavior or a particular type of person, is there a high probability of finding each in the site you have selected? Is your site manageable? That is, have you chosen a site that you can observe without being overwhelmed? Think back to the exercise at the beginning of this chapter. Even though you deliberately selected an "empty" place, recall how busy, involved, and complex it really was. Make sure you do not bite off more than you can chew, site-wise, or you will end up missing most of the important things you want to observe.

Finally, there are several key logistical issues related to site selection. Is the site safe? Can you be sure that observing on this site will not compromise your personal safety, or do you need a guide or protector? Or do you need to leave this observation task to someone else? Do you need permission, either formal or informal, to observe on this site? If you need permission, from whom do you need it? Will your presence change the sorts of behaviors or interactions that you are there to observe? If so, how do you minimize the impact of your own presence? These and other logistical matters are often not apparent until you are actually on site doing observation. So you need to be aware of their potential presence, and monitor your own presence as an observer.

The second major selection issue deals with whom you are observing. Kuzel (1999) reviews the complex issue of how we go about getting a sample of persons for qualitative research in general. There are three basic sampling strategies we can use to decide whom to observe. Each strategy encompasses a "family" of selection processes.

The first strategy is the personal characteristic strategy. Here we focus in on some characteristic or set of characteristics of the persons we choose. We can choose to look along a dimension from maximum variation to homogeneity. At one end of the spectrum we find extreme cases, critical cases, or deviant cases. At the other end we find typical cases. Our choice is obviously governed by our purposes for doing observations. If I want to observe the typical office worker at lunch, for instance, then I would employ a different selection strategy from the one I would use, say, to find the best office worker in New York City.

The second strategy is the theoretical sampling strategy. Here you are sampling with a purpose. The purpose can be demographic, as in stratified and modified random samples. The purpose can also be more directly based on testing theory, such as theoretical or criterion sampling strategies. Finally, you can select participants who are either politically or informationally rich sources of data.

The third and final strategy is the pure logistical strategy. Here, often because of the trickiness of the problem or the setting, you are willing to take what you can get. Convenience samples, opportunistic samples, and snowball samples are examples of this strategy. Convenience sampling is the least systematic. With an opportunistic sample, you are acting a bit like a detective, tracking down leads. With the snowball sample, you are depending on previous participants to refer you to new participants.

Site selection and person selection are critically important decisions. As long as you understand up front why you are observing where you are observing, and why you are observing whom you are observing, then you are probably on the right track.

Focus Issues

What sorts of things do we choose to concentrate upon as observers? One of the first and most important models of observation (Spradley, 1980) is based on starting with description and then shifting to more focused matters. We will use this model as the basis for bringing up key focus issues for observation.

Spradley's (1980) model begins the process of observational research with an activity he calls the *grand tour* observation. A grand tour observation strategy is a comprehensive observation plan that addresses the following issues (p. 78):

1. *Space*. What does the physical place (or places) look like? Is this a common or unique type of setting? How might the setting restrict certain possible activities and interactions? How might it encourage others?

2. *Actor.* Who are the people involved? Why are they present? Is their presence usual or unusual? Are they related in any fashion to other people present?

3. *Activity.* What are people doing? How are these activities related to each other? Are they expected or unexpected? Are they easy or skilled activities?

4. *Object.* What are the physical "props" in this particular setting? What roles do they play? How would the setting change if these objects were not here? How would the activities of the participants change if these objects were missing?

5. *Act.* An act is a single event performed by a participant. How common is it? Is it related to others acts? Are other people doing the same or similar acts?

6. *Event.* An event is a set of related activities that people carry out. How do we know when acts come together to make events? Which events are most common? Which events seem to be most important? Do people coordinate events?

7. *Time.* What kinds of sequencings can be observed? Are these sequences cyclical or unique? Are they apparent or subtle? How are they linked to the physical nature of the setting? To the motives of the participants?

8. *Goal.* What sorts of things are the participants trying to accomplish? How are these goals present in the setting and the actions? Are they steady or do they change?

9. *Feelings.* What sorts of emotions are being expressed by the participants? How can you be sure? What sorts of feelings does this setting bring out in you?

Spradley (1980) held that as we shift from description to focus, we also shift from descriptive matters to structural matters. That is, as we get observational answers to what we see, when we see it, who does it, and the like, then we are in the position to start thinking about some initial answers to "why" questions. But observation by itself is not enough to build these structures of understanding. We need more direct participation with the persons involved, if at all possible.

While society and research methods have changed a great deal since Spradley's day, his advice still rings true for many circumstances. But the world has become more complex, more global, more fragmented, more politically aware, and more gendered. Angrosino and de Perez (2000) provide a good starting place for looking at how current thinking has brought about a shift in our understanding of both the context and the methods we use for making research observations.

Saturation

One of the more common guidelines used in current qualitative research is the strategy of saturation. First laid out by Glaser and Strauss (1967), saturation simply means that you have studied in a particular setting long enough so that you are now only finding things that you have already found. This principle is often found in observation activities, but it obviously extends to interviewing, document collection, and most other forms of qualitative data gathering.

Saturation most often makes its presence known in observation via the process of anticipation. Suppose you are watching a group of people engage in some complex task. When you find that you can anticipate and predict what they will do, and predict the consequences of their actions, then you are probably pretty close to the saturation point. Ease of categorization is another giveaway. If you can effortlessly assign each and every act or occurrence to preexisting category, then you have probably exhausted the uniqueness of this particular observational setting.

In a way, the concept of saturation is simply a restatement of the law of diminishing returns. There is no way that you can be sure that you have observed everything that you are likely to find in a given setting. But the patterns of repetition you are experiencing make it less likely that investing any more observational time and effort will pay off with any really new or unique observational experiences. We will return to the matter of saturation when we look at grounded theory in some detail in Chapter 7.

CURRENT FRONTIERS OF OBSERVATION IN QUALITATIVE RESEARCH

In all of the cases we have looked at so far, observation has more or less been involved with an observer being on scene and recording what he or she hears, sees, or feels. In recent years, qualitative researchers have extended these boundaries of observations in interesting ways. We will look at three of those ways here: (1) extending our concepts of the parameters and settings of observing; (2) extending our capabilities by incorporating new technical tools; and (3) treating observation as an artistic endeavor.

Parameters and Settings of Observation

In one of his last articles, Peshkin (2001) invited us to reconsider the role of perception in observation. He reminds us that anthropologists are paying more and more attention to the roles of such "peripheral" senses as smell, touch, and taste, and how they help shape our observations and actions in field settings. He suggests that we actively sample our perceptions in field settings, using a series of "lenses" that can help us gather richer and more complex observational data. His set of lenses consist of: (1) searching for patterns as we are observing; (2) being sensitive to both the passage of time and the role of history and how both of these factors affect our perceptions; (3) seeking to perceive and observe in an *emic* way, or a way that is grounded to the lives and experiences of those whom we are observing; (4) shifting our observational perspective across such positional dimensions as age, race, religion, social class, and the like, to see if we observe new and different things; (5) reflecting on the possible impact of ideology, both others' and our own, and its possible impact on our observations; (6) actively searching for themes and metaphors as part of our observational work; (7) being sensitive to irony, especially when observing artistic acts or products; and (8) paying attention to all forms of silence, or the lack of what we might have expected, in our observational settings (pp. 243–250). By using these sorts of lenses, Peshkin is inviting us to become more active and more constructive observers, working with and within our settings to create rich and subtle observational "texts."

Agee (2002) explores a similar theme. She suggests the use of six observational lenses to allow us to understand the symbolic and dynamic nature of settings. These lenses focus on the following properties of observational settings: (1) Observational settings are bounded, but those boundaries are often permeable to some degree, allowing observers to pay particular attention to these sorts of edges, and the people who are allowed into these settings; (2) People often move across settings, and these sorts of movements are fertile ground for observers; (3) There is often a great degree of variability within settings, and this variability is important to observe and track; (4) Settings come with their own histories, and tapping into those historical dimensions can be a rich and important observational task; (5) The physical nature of many settings are determined by cultural dynamics, and need to be included as part of the observational task; and (6) Few settings are simple, and so observers need to be aware at all times of the complex cultural ecologies that often underlie even the most simple of settings (pp. 572–582). In short, Agee, like Peshkin earlier, reminds us that observation is often not a simple act. Observers are often plunged into rich and complex social, cultural, and historical domains, and tapping into those complexities is often a necessary part of any observational task.

Observation and Technology

Technology has had a profound impact on qualitative research as a whole. Therefore, it is no surprise that technology is altering the ways that we can do observations. Any discussion of technology in research runs the risk of becoming instantly obsolete, so we will only look at broad and general trends.

The most obvious technology to impact observation is video recording. Penn-Edwards (2004) outlines a series of practical recommendations for using video recording in qualitative research, both at the point of recording and at the point of viewing the final product. Such technical dimensions as lighting, angle, camera placement, and editing can have a major impact on the target of the observation and the viewer as well. In spite of the need to be careful in the use of video recording, Penn-Edwards points out that this technology can expand our current understanding and practice of observation to include such new areas as subject self-reflections captured on video and observing the reactions of others observing the original video product. Paterson, Bottorff, and Hewatt (2003) recommend the "blending" of live observation and video observation to enhance both observational techniques.

When it comes to technology, we can depend on the fact that new advances in representations and breakthroughs in making once-expensive forms of technology cheap and available will alter the observational face of qualitative research. On the other hand, very little in the way of innovation really moves us radically away from the basic core of observational practice itself. So while technology continues to change, one of our best strategies is to practice and refine our basic observational skills. In that fashion, we will be well prepared to put them to the new uses that new technologies will inevitably offer to us.

Observation and the Arts

We do not often think of the arts as an observational technique, but researchers who do arts-based research are often taking their highly refined observational techniques, combined with their artistic skill, to render important acts of qualitative research. Barone (2003) argues for the use of visually critical observational skills in order to understand film-based research. Finley (2003), in reviewing a large body of arts-based qualitative research, raises a number of questions to guide our observations of arts-based qualitative research, including: (1) Is the research useful or harmful for its target community? (2) Can you hear both the voices of the researchers and the participants, and are the researchers being careful in their treatment of participants? (3) Are the researchers experimenting with form and representations, and are those experimentations opening up dialogue and interaction among researchers and participants? (4) Is the research practice and representation passionate and visceral, and is there a blurring between researchers and participants? and, (5) Does the research, through its form and content, connect to a larger audience (p. 294)?

In short, observing artistic works and arts-based research is a special sort of observation, and as such requires its own set of specialized artistic observational skills and procedures.

OBSERVATION IN QUALITATIVE SCIENCE AND QUALITATIVE INQUIRY

In Chapter 1, we saw that the field of qualitative research can be divided into the broad domains of qualitative science and qualitative inquiry. Are there different observation strategies for research in qualitative science and qualitative inquiry?

The answer is yes and no. In one sense, observation is observation. The things that we see and perceive with our other senses do not change based on our theoretical or methodological outlook.

In another sense, our outlook can make a big difference in whether or not we pay attention to something in the first place. If our theories and practices predispose us to expect certain things, then it is not surprising when those things surface. A qualitative science researcher might miss something that a qualitative inquiry researcher would spot right away, and vice versa. In qualitative research, like all forms of empirical inquiry, it is important to make sure the data come first.

There are also differences in some observational methods in the practices of qualitative science and qualitative inquiry. A qualitative science study might sample persons and settings with more of an eye toward generalization. This same study might also use observational techniques that depend upon time or event sampling—say, making an observation every 2 minutes, or recording every fifth example of a particular target action or behavior. On the other hand, a qualitative inquiry might sample in a completely different way, looking purposely for particular people or settings that might contribute unique or important information. The inquiry study might be much more interested in recording critical or unusual events, rather than worrying about a standardized rubric of sampling.

MASTERING OBSERVATIONAL SKILLS

We have looked at many different types of observers, ways of observing, and sites and sources of observation. In the final analysis, however, there are really only four main things you need to keep in mind as you set forth to grow and develop as an observer:

1. *Build on your observational strengths.* There is no magic time when you become an expert qualitative observer. Remember, you are already a skilled and competent observer of life. As you continue to do qualitative research, pay attention to what comes easily to you. Are you good at detail? At getting the confidence of others, so that they behave naturally around you? Are you good at seeing small, subtle changes and shifts? Try to extend the range and scope of these skills outward.

2. *Reflect on key issues.* When we were grounding qualitative observational skills, we did so by focusing on such key issues as site selection, sampling, saturation, and ethical concerns. With practice, these issues will become part of your natural framework. Have I selected the right settings and people for my observations? Have I done enough observation to get a clear picture? How valid are my conclusions about my observations? How ethical are my actions? These and other key issues are an important part of the qualitative landscape.

3. *Focus on the big picture.* Qualitative research specializes in taking a holistic perspective. Don't focus too much on individual, discrete observational techniques. Concentrate instead on the big picture. You can end up with a very rich record, full of details, that is still holistic in its orientation.

4. *Keep a record.* One of the key areas of practice for all observers is the task of note-taking. We will not talk about formal models or techniques of note-taking, as these tend to be a matter of personal style for most qualitative researchers. If you are looking for a checklist, Spradley's (1980) set of focus areas is one of the most comprehensive set of factors in the literature, and looking for these factors can help you develop detailed notes. But note-taking is more than just making sure you have gotten all the details. Have you gotten them correctly? Don't be afraid to record your opinions and impressions if you want to refer to them later on. But remember, you cannot look into other peoples' heads and observe what they are thinking. Try to keep those notes that describe the actions of others as free of motives as you can. That child, for instance, may be crying, but are you sure he is crying from shame? Record context and circumstances instead, and see if you can infer what is going on from the experiential record instead. If you really want to keep a record of your on-the-spot interpretations, make sure you label them as interpretative notes, not fieldnotes.

OBSERVATION AND THE MIRROR, WINDOW, AND LANTERN

If we return to our three technologies of looking from Chapter 1, we can use them to help us sort out some of the key observational issues that we experience as practicing qualitative researchers.

Observation and the Mirror. Several of our observational types are mirror inquirers at heart. In particular, the Reflecter and the Interacter seek out circumstances and other people as sources of personal introspection and growth. So long as we are not self-absorbed or self-deluded, this is not a bad path. We have to be aware, however, that there are times when we need to step out of the way and let the record speak for itself.

Observation and the Window. Most of us try to follow the implicit rules of the current culture of inquiry and be good windows. The Camera, the Tape Recorder, and especially the Embracer all start out with sensory data as the bedrock for observation. The Baseliner and the Categorizer impose a temporal and conceptual structure, respectively, as the "basic frame" of the window, and the Abstracter is busy creating scientific findings as an integral part of the observation process. So long as we do not try to hide our own thoughts and feelings behind an artificial veil of "objectivity" we can be very effective as observers from any of these stances. We have to be aware, however, that there are times when we need to step forward and make our voices heard over and above the record.

Observation and the Lantern. Most of the observation types we have found so far are rooted in the older and more familiar mirror and window traditions. We have not identified specific observer types for the lantern metaphor, so let us do so now. Here are three to start with, for your consideration and rumination.

Our first lantern observer is the Spelunker. A Spelunker is a person who goes underground into caverns, carrying a lantern into these dark recesses. Traditional ethnographers, or people who venture into strange and alien cultures with the intent to survive and learn, are good examples of Spelunkers.

The second lantern observer is the Detective. A Detective is a person who is committed to looking carefully and systematically to see what others have not seen, to uncover order that is there to be found. Interpretative researchers of all types tend to have a strong Detective streak in them.

Our last lantern observer is the Diogenist. This observer is named after Diogenes (d. about 320 B.C.), a Greek philosopher who wandered the earth, bearing a lantern, searching for an honest man. Diogenists are qualitative researchers who refuse to acknowledge that qualitative research must abandon the concept of truth. For them truth is often grounded in humane conduct, so that the honest man is also the moral man. Action researchers, particularly those who follow a path toward liberation, are good examples of Diogenists.

FINAL THOUGHTS ON OBSERVATION

As we turn from observing to our other skills, we cannot forget the fundamental importance that observation plays in qualitative research. We seek to see those things that others have overlooked, to hear those things that others failed to notice, and in general to find things that make our understanding richer and deeper. Good qualitative researchers do not take their observational skills for granted, nor do they allow themselves to settle into comfortable observational patterns. Keeping observational skills fresh and sharp is a hard task, but a rewarding and necessary one.

PLANNING YOUR RESEARCH PROPOSAL: LOOKING FOR POTENTIAL RESEARCH TOPICS

One of the best things about practicing your observational skills is the fact that you start seeing new and exciting things everywhere. Nowhere is this more advantageous than in your efforts to identify new and exciting potential research topics.

In traditional quantitative research, new topics are often derived from a closer look at previous findings and theory. It is often the case that a new piece of research must first be grounded in existing theory in order to be pursued in the first place. This is because much quantitative research depends upon the notion of hypothesis testing, and most hypotheses are derived from existing theory.

Qualitative research, be it qualitative science or qualitative inquiry, puts much less weight on existing theory and more weight on taking the world as you find it. We can see this process at work as we watch Albert and Carol think about various potential research topics.

Carol

Carol has decided on a very broad topic. She is interested in how poor, single women balance the search for education and career advancement with the search for a life partner. She knows that much of the current literature is anecdotal. Jane has no problem with that, but she also believes that there are systematic aspects of this topic that have not been explored. Though she thinks that questionnaires and surveys are excellent sources of data, she fears that we do not know enough about these balancing efforts to write good instruments yet. She wants the women in the field to have a "say" in setting up her research agenda.

Albert

Albert is our "math anxiety" scholar. He realizes that math anxiety is an important phenomenon, but he also knows that it has been studied extensively. He wants to be able to use his extensive experience in math classrooms to identify some aspect of math anxiety that has not been looked at yet, but he is also concerned that he might fall into patterns of thought that researchers in math anxiety are already using. He wants to find something important, but he also wants his research to be fresh and new.

Ourselves

At this stage, potential research topics are still fairly general and global. Too often, novice qualitative researchers make the mistake of trying to pin down their research too early. Qualitative research is creative in nature, and all creative efforts require some percolation time. If you wish, you can illustrate this percolation process with yourself by doing the following exercise:

- Write down a list of potential research topics that might interest you.
- Underneath each topic, write a few thoughts about how you might approach that topic if you were going to start doing the research today.
- Put these notes in an envelope, and mail them to yourself.
- With any luck, you should have the list back in a few days. If by some chance it comes back the next day, put it aside and wait another day or two. Now read your list and your thoughts.
- Have your topics changed? Have your thoughts changed? Any changes are most likely due to percolation. Whether you realize it or not, you have been thinking about these issues and topics, at some level, all along.

It is important to give yourself enough time to allow your basic ideas to percolate. At the same time, it is important not to procrastinate unnecessarily. Over time, you should get to the point where you will know one from the other. If you are in doubt, then you are probably procrastinating. Go ahead and take a stab at writing down your latest thoughts and ideas. At the worst, all you are wasting is a little effort instead of time.

CHAPTER 3

Conversing

Exercise Two—*Table Talk*

It is almost impossible to do good qualitative research without learning how to interview someone. There are any number of sources for excellent advice on conducting the qualitative interview (e.g., Fontana & Frey, 2000; McCracken, 1988; Miller & Crabtree, 1999; Rubin & Rubin, 1995; Seidman, 1991). My personal favorite is Steiner Kvale's *InterViews* (1996). But most of these (more or less) technical guides to the art of interviewing tend to lose sight of one very simple point—an interview is a form of conversation. A very specialized and skilled type of conversation to be sure, but a conversation nonetheless. And no one can develop into a better interviewer than his or her current conversational skills will allow. So it makes sense to work on conversational skills, with an eye toward enhancing more specialized interview skills down the road.

The purpose of this exercise is to help you get relaxed and comfortable with the notion of talking to someone and getting insights from him or her in the process.

As we focus on our conversational skills, we find ourselves operating in a different fashion than we have learned to expect as researchers. Most quantitative research in the social sciences tends to gather information by using the following path: We start at Point A. We decide we need to get to Point B. What is the best way to get from A to B?

In other words, when gathering information for most quantitative studies, if you don't have a strategy you are lost. Most of the time in qualitative research, however, too much strategy only gets in the way of gathering information. We have to learn how to strip down these strategic needs, so that we can take advantage of the information the circumstances give us. Mostly, this is nothing more than being relaxed and alert in the moment of contact. Our eyes and ears are open, but we feel at ease with our ability to follow the situation and not lead it.

Where can we practice these basic skills? How can we put ourselves in a situation where we can get information and insights from another person, but not feel compelled to structure the interaction so strategically? How do we allow the circumstances unfolding before us to guide our efforts tactically? How do we fight off the compulsion to make sure we nail down the information that we decided beforehand we absolutely had to have, while perhaps ignoring much more important information in the process? These are the issues that this exercise will help you address.

The exercise itself is quite simple:

- Pick a friend or family member or colleague with whom you feel comfortable, and with whom you would enjoy sharing a meal.

- Inform your instructor of some insight that you want to get from this person. Be fair; pick an insight that you want to acquire, not one you already have. At the same time, try to pick an area of insight that will not be uncomfortable or controversial for the person you have selected. This is not in-depth analysis; it is an act of uncovering some fairly innocent but unrevealed aspect of this person's life.
- Now, invite this person to dinner. Sit across from him or her, and converse with him or her as naturally as possible. Try to make your research agenda and your natural desire to converse with your friend blend with each other. If it makes you more comfortable, tell your dinner companion what you are trying to achieve, and ask for his or her help.
- See if you can steer the discussion in the direction of the insight you wish to reach, without doing damage to the normal flow of conversation. But be prepared to shift gears if the conversation takes you away from your original area toward some other, perhaps more important, destination.
- Don't tape record the conversation or take notes. Rely on your memory.
- Pay attention to all the subtle nuances that make up any ordinary conversation. Note the shifts of attention, and the rise and fall of energy between you and your friend.
- Gear your conversation to the available time. You have a very natural time span to work with. Most of us have a clear, if not always articulated, sense of the cultural time boundaries that define dinner and after-dinner conversations.
- If you have not already done so by the end of the conversation, explain to your friend the nature of your exercise. Ask his or her permission to transfer your insights to paper and write them up for your instructor. Discuss the insights you reached as you understand them, and see what your friend thinks of your conclusions.
- Ask his or her honest opinion of your conversational skills in this regard. Did you try too hard to steer the conversation toward the insights you wanted to explore? Were you unnatural at any time in the process? Did your motives interfere with what was, at another level, a casual discussion among friends?
- If you feel that the person you have selected for this project would feel awkward or uncomfortable doing any of these tasks, then you have chosen the wrong person. Pick someone else, someone you know well enough to be able to accept and understand all the activities just described without feeling threatened, angry, or guarded.
- When you have finished your dinner meeting, go home and write up your findings and impressions as soon as possible. Then, let them sit for a day or so before you revisit your notes.
- By now, you should be ready to write a summary report for your instructor. Usually it is best to turn in both your notes and your summary report. Remember to protect the anonymity of your friend, in both your notes and your report.
- You might also want to share a copy of your report with your dinner partner. If all goes well, you should both enjoy reading it.

Conducting a conversation exercise, like this one, serves as an important intermediate step in the development of more formal interviewing skills. Keep in mind how this exercise differs from casual conversation at one extreme and a full-blown interview at the other extreme. When you conduct a more ambitious and formal interview, you still need to be able to move up and down all of these conversational dimensions as the moment dictates.

You will take up an interview task proper for your next exercise, so for now be patient and learn and enjoy this exercise on its own terms.

REFLECTING ON CONVERSING

For the most part, unless we are physically incapable, we already know how to talk and listen. We do it every single day of our lives. What is the longest period of time you have gone without talking to another person? For most of us, the answer can be measured in days, at the most. How long have you gone without hearing another person talk? Again, for most of us, the answer is usually measured in days or perhaps even hours.

THE FINE ART OF RESEARCH CONVERSING

Given that we talk and listen so often in our lives, why is it that we are often so apprehensive about using our talking and listening abilities as research skills? There are three reasons that come immediately to mind.

First of all, we tend to think of our daily routines of talking and listening as life skills, and not research skills. To some degree, this is correct. As we will see later, some of the skills we use in ordinary conversation can actually interfere with our ability to interview people.

Second, we see that some people are much better at talking and listening than others are, and we assume that we have to be at the top of the pyramid, so to speak, to be effective research interviewers. This, of course, is not true. In fact, the opposite is often the case. A good conversationalist tends to have a personal style. A good interviewer cannot afford to have a personal interview style. An interviewer must be able to move flexibly across different modes of conversation, depending on the conversational strengths and areas of comfort of the interviewee. Therefore, a well-established conversational style can actually interfere with the ability to conduct a good interview.

Finally, we realize, at least intuitively, that everyday conversations are different from the type of interviews we need to conduct when we perform research. Of the three reasons, this one is the most compelling. But in order to explore the differences between interviews and personal conversations, we need to step back and look at communication per se. Once we have examined the basics of all forms of human verbal communication, then we can trace their effects on more specialized forms such as conversing and interviewing.

CONVERSATION AND HOLISTIC COMMUNICATION

Why is conversation so important to us? The simple answer is that conversation is one of the primary ways that we gain information. But the dynamics of conversation are much richer than just the sending and receiving of information. Good interviewers have always been aware of the previous point, if only implicitly.

How can we gain a richer, more explicit understanding of the dynamics of conversation? The quickest way is to look at theories of communication, and especially at models derived from these theories. One of the best of these models is an important model of verbal communication first articulated by Roman Jakobson (1976).

THE SIX FUNCTIONS OF VERBAL COMMUNICATION

Jakobson's complete model covers many aspects of the linguistics of conversation, and as such is beyond our needs here. We will focus instead on only one part—but a crucial part—of the whole model. That is, we will concentrate on the six functions of any act of verbal communication: the referential function, the emotive function, the conative function, the metalingual function, the poetic function, and the phatic function.

To understand these six functions, we need to look first at the basic structure of Jakobson's model. The two primary agents in any verbal communication model are the *sender* of the message and the *receiver* of the message. In addition, there is the *content* of the message. This content is encoded into some linguistic *code* by the sender, and then decoded by the receiver. The message passes along some *channel* of communication, which also exists within some *context* of communicating. Finally, the content of the message usually makes some true or false reference or *claim* about the world.

By looking at the operation of this system as a holistic activity, Jakobson was able to identify six primary functions contained in every communicative act. It is important for us to realize that each and every one of these functions is operating during each and every act of conversing, including research interviewing. We will look at each function in turn, with some suggestions about how the function in question plays a role during the interview experience.

Before we go on, though, let me warn you: If you try to focus on these functions during an actual interview, you will most likely impede the natural flow of the interview process. These functions are best used as a debriefing tool. They can give you a way to see what you have done well or poorly in a given interview setting, with the goal of learning from your experience so as to improve future interviews.

The Referential Function

Perhaps the most basic function of any act of verbal communication is the passing of information from the sender to the receiver. We then analyze that information in terms of what we already know about the world.

Another way of looking at the referential function is to say that it is related to the truth content of the message. Is the message saying something about the world? Is what it says true or not?

The role of the referential function in the interview process centers on the flow of information. In many cases, it is important to know whether the information being conveyed is true or not. Lincoln and Guba (1985), for instance, talk about trustworthiness. Their complete view of trustworthiness has many facets, but one of the most important forms of trustworthiness deals with being able to tell whether or not your interviewee is telling the truth or not.

There are two ways that an interviewee can lie to you: by telling a deliberate lie, and by telling a lie that the interviewee thinks is true. Deliberate lies are usually easier to spot. Very few of us are really good at lying, especially when our lies must hold up over an extended conversation.

More often than not, we have to deal with interviewees who "lie" because they are either confused or misinformed. These falsehoods are harder to spot and to correct because the interviewee believes them to be true. If you know from your own knowledge, or it is clear in context, that the interviewee is telling you something that is simply not true, then take note of the fact mentally and document it as soon as possible.

Falsehoods that are reported in good faith as truths are also often a source of interesting data. Ask yourself why your interviewee believes these things to be true. Are these beliefs anchored to a particular culture or a particular worldview? Do these falsehoods represent a gap between your world and that of your interviewee? Are you sure you are communicating clearly, or that you are not misunderstanding what you are being told?

Very rarely, however, is it a good idea to challenge the interviewee on the matter of falsehoods. Is the interviewee being hurt by holding these false beliefs, or are they relatively benign? If there is no real harm in holding these beliefs, it is best for you to leave the matter alone. More often than not, you will not change the interviewee's mind. You are much more likely to do damage to your rapport instead.

The Emotive Function

We are not computers or tape recorders. Verbal messages have an impact on us over and beyond the information they possess. The message is often more than just a vehicle to deliver information from the sender to the receiver. The sender often has real feelings about the content of the message, and about the way that the message needs to be perceived by the receiver. This is known as the emotive function of the message.

The role of the emotive function in the interview process often centers on our ability to process all the nonverbal information that the interviewee sends along with his or her message.

One source of nonverbal information is the way in which a message is delivered verbally. What is the tone of the interviewee's voice? Is he or she confident about what he or she is saying? Is there some uncertainty? Is this a casual topic for the interviewee, or one that he or she feels very passionately about? One of the drawbacks of transcribing is the fact that transcripts preserve the words, but not these important clues about the meaning of the message to the interviewee. You need to revisit your original tapes to touch base on these sorts of cues. There are also techniques of conversational analysis, which we will look at later on when we talk about studying narratives, that can document some of these other sources of information.

Your interview tapes may preserve the tone in which things were said, but there is no way an auditory record can capture paratactic sources of information. *Paratactic* information usually involves such things as posture, distance between you and the interviewee, and body language. These are just as much a part of the communicative process as the actual words. If you are a skilled reader of body language, note your findings as soon as possible after the interview. If you are less sure of your body reading, then only document those episodes that you feel you can understand. It is better to lose information than to document incorrect interpretations.

Videotaping interviews can help preserve much of this paratactic information, but it is not as reliable as you might think. The interviewer and the interviewee often move in subtle ways in relation to each other to preserve a certain flow of information and to convey dynamic aspects of the conversational process. A fixed video camera cannot accurately cue on these sorts of movements, and so tends to constrain the visual frame of reference for communication. A video record, however, can be very useful in documenting important body language messages and posture shifts. For instance, we have already looked at the impact of video recording on observation in Chapter 2.

If you are not skilled in the use of video, or if there is no easy way to transcribe the auditory information from the videotape, you might consider carefully whether videotaping is the way you want to proceed as a way to record interviews. Of course, we must be sensitive to changes in technology. For instance, Givens (2004) suggests that mind-disc recorders may render tape recording obsolete. Who knows what other technological advances will be on the market by the time this book gets into print or in the years to come!

The Conative Function

People rarely tell us things just for the sake of passing along information. More often than not, messages have a persuasive function. From the point of view of verbal communication, persuasion is most clearly seen in those cases in which words by the sender lead to actions on the part of the receiver. This impact of the message on the receiver is called the conative function.

The role of the conative function in the interview process centers around the impact of the interview process on you, the interviewer. The easiest and most seemingly natural type of conative impact occurs when you are able to maintain a smooth and easy flow of understanding. Everything the interviewee says makes sense, and it all fits together effortlessly. The only problem with such a scenario is that you are not learning anything new, nor are you getting any new or fresh insights into the situation.

More often than not, the interviewee wants the interview process to be easy for you. He or she might strive to tell you what you want to hear, in terms that are acceptable. Though this is a considerate thing to do, it can be the death of research. You must steer the interviewee away from trying to please you, toward informing you. One way to do this is by signaling your pleasure in hearing things that take you by surprise. Jump upon these surprise openings and press the matter further. If the interviewee is comfortable with your responses, then he or she is free to respond in as natural a way as possible.

The Metalingual Function

Language is a code, but it is only one of many codes that permeate most acts of communication. For instance, Barthes (1957) showed that such things as advertisements, clothing fashions, and even professional wrestling matches can be deciphered in terms of their own codes. The metalingual process centers around building a joint awareness of all codes involved, what they mean, and how they are used.

The role of the metalingual function in the interview process centers around the evolution of understanding that takes place in an interview process. In a real sense, it is often a matter of speaking the same language. Does the interviewee live in a world where special terms are used to describe important features? Are there rules of dress? Rules of conduct? A skilled interviewer looks for codes at every turn, and seeks the explicit help of the interviewee in reading and interpreting these codes. As the communicative possibilities grow richer by the introduction and clarification of relevant codes, the likelihood of genuine discovery and insight also increases.

The Poetic Function

A good interview usually is more than getting good information. In addition, it is often good information told well. When we turn toward the message itself, to see how it is crafted and what choices were made to create it in its present exact form, then we are dealing with the poetic function of language.

Jakobson (1976) is using the term *poetic* in a technical sense. He is not talking about how the interviewee creates artistic speech, or how we render our interview findings into art. Poetry is just too hard for us to attempt for any reason other than its own merits. By poetics, all we mean here is close and careful attention to the form of the communication act itself.

The role of the poetic function in the interview process centers around the way the interviewee tells his or her story. When people speak of things they know and understand quite well, there is often a natural eloquence present. That eloquence might sound quite different from what we would normally think of as polished speech, but if we listen to it carefully and seek to understand it on its own terms, then it can open up subtle and fresh avenues of understanding for us. Capturing that "voice" is often an essential part of the research process.

The Phatic Function

This function is simultaneously the least important and the most important function in operation during an act of communication. The phatic function consists of those things that we do to signal to the receiver, and then back to the sender, that there is an open channel between us. Have you noticed that, if you walk down a hall three times in one hour and pass the same person, you make a slight act of acknowledgment each time? That is a phatic signal conveying that if more needs to be said, then the channel is open and ready. To ignore such signals is to say that there is no channel between us, and in our culture at least, it is a very rude thing to do to someone you know.

The role of the phatic function in the interview process centers around making sure the channel is as open as possible, within the grounds of propriety. Although interviewing can take on intimate characteristics, it is at heart a formal process. For instance, female interviewers who have interviewed males have reported to me that at times their interest in maintaining open communications had sometimes been misunderstood. It goes without saying that the rules of civility and decorum need to be diplomatically but firmly insisted upon in such situations. Most males will acknowledge their mistaken understanding and move on. If the person does not, or will not, understand, then you are better off not interviewing him at all.

On a less charged note, part of the role of the phatic process is to signal when an interview is winding down. Once you have done enough interviews, you will learn that there is a real and tangible connection between the interviewer and the interviewee. In my own case, I feel it as a flow of energy back and forth between me and the person I am interviewing. When all is going well, that back and forth energy flow is strong and focused. When I begin to feel it fade or wane, then I know that it is time to start moving this particular interview toward a smooth conclusion.

FROM CONVERSING TO INTERVIEWING

Now that we have a firm grounding on the nuances of communication, and how they can affect the interview process, we need to take a more formal look at the interview process. Our first step in that direction is to clarify how interviewing is different from conversing.

We need to start by remembering that all acts of conversing involve the transfer of information. In normal conversation, there is a pattern of reciprocation. One party reveals a bit of personal information, and the second party reciprocates with a similar bit of personal information. There is a symmetry of disclosure. But, by design, disclosure is asymmetric in an interview setting. One party is seeking information and the other party is providing that information. It is not an equal process. But how does a skilled interviewer deal with the inevitable tug toward disclosure?

One trick of the trade is to seek out alternative signals of intimacy. During a typical conversational setting, ongoing disclosure grows more and more intimate. One party starts by revealing a fairly prosaic piece of personal information. The listener, to indicate trust, tends to reciprocate with a slightly more intimate piece of information. The cycle continues until the conversational pair reaches a level of mutual intimacy that they are comfortable with.

As a qualitative researcher, you want your interview to go beyond superficial levels. In your attempt to seek depth, you instinctively drive the conversation toward a more intimate level. For most of us, the only way we know how to do this is to use disclosure. However, standard disclosure by the interviewer is almost always a bad idea. It moves the discussion away from an exploration of the interviewee toward the establishment of some shared understanding. It puts the interviewee in an uncomfortable situation because the interviewee probably is not really seeking to gain a more intimate relationship with you. Finally, it wastes valuable interview time.

Skilled interviewers use informal signals to sustain a growing sense of intimacy, thus inviting the interviewee to control the flow and nature of disclosure in a fairly comfortable situation. Nodding your head, or shifting your body forward, signals to the interviewee that you are listening and that you are sharing an intimate relation. Opening gestures with your body also indicate that you are taking in the information, even if you are not reciprocating verbally. One word of warning, however. Nonverbal signals are very powerful and can often be misunderstood. Make sure you do not overdo your openness signals, or else you may be sending out a stronger invitation for intimacy than you might intend.

The time-honored strategy for all interviewers, however, is to be quiet. Don't feel you have to say something when your interviewee pauses. He or she may be just collecting his or her thoughts, and you need to allow time to do so. Inserting a comment for the sake of conversational flow is intrusive in interview situations. It is better to make some phatic signal, such as "go on" or "what do you mean?". Let the interviewee know that you are listening, but that he or she controls the topic. Finally, don't be afraid of silence. It may be uncomfortable at first, but as the interview progresses, it will become more and more natural and you and the interviewee understand the nature of the interaction between you.

GROUNDING INTERVIEW SKILLS

There has been a long and detailed history of interview process refinement in qualitative research. We will look at an established model of field interview techniques, a current vision of the nature of qualitative interviewing, and an area of interviewing that has become more prominent in recent years—the notion of group interviewing and, in particular, focus group models.

The Classic Field Interview

Once again, we turn to the classic work of James Spradley to ground our understanding of the field interview. Many of the advances in this field have been built directly from these basic ideas. Spradley (1979) emphasized the combination of descriptive (pp. 78–91) and structural (pp. 120–131) approaches when conducting field interviews. Each approach involves its own unique flow.

When asking descriptive questions, the researcher begins with a sense of uncertainty and apprehension. Without some degree of uncertainty, it is difficult to move on to the next phase, or the asking of exploratory questions. Here, don't be afraid to repeat questions if you do not understand the answers you are getting. Through exploration, you also build rapport with your interviewees. As rapport increases, you move from exploration to cooperation, and perhaps even participation.

Once full rapport has been reached, then descriptive questions can be properly raised. Spradley talks about five general types of descriptive questions.

The first and often most important type is the grand tour question. A grand tour question invites the interviewee to lead you on a grand tour of the topic or setting. Grand tour questions are very broad and unfocused. You can ask about a typical day, or what is going on. My personal favorite is "What does it mean to be who you are, or to live and work where you work?".

During the grand tour process, it is sometimes useful to stop the tour for a bit and focus in on some specific aspect in more detail before moving on. Spradley calls such questions mini tour questions. They involve short side stops from the ongoing grand tour. Once a mini tour question is answered, then the grand tour continues.

Spradley concludes the descriptive process with example questions, experience questions, and native language questions. These are all calls for greater specification. "Can you give me an example of what you are talking about?" "Can you tell me about some personal experience you have had that relates to what you are saying?" "How would you describe some important aspect in the language that you and others use everyday?"

Structural questions go beyond description to elicit understanding or verification. In pursuing structural matters, Spradley suggests that you pay attention to both the context and cultural framework of the answers you get. Do not be satisfied with one person's take on the matter. You are looking for evidence of structural principles, so this evidence needs to be found in the accounts of many informants on the scene. Finally, it is best to ask structural questions, whenever possible, concurrently with descriptive questions. That way, you are building a picture of structure as you are getting a sense of the nature of the culture and setting you are studying.

Conducting the Qualitative Research Interview

From the classic field interview approach of Spradley (1979), we can move directly to the more contemporary notion of the qualitative research interview. The qualitative research interview is different from any other sort of interview. Kvale (1996) stresses 12 crucial aspects of qualitative interviewing (pp. 30–31):

- A qualitative interview seeks to discover the everyday lived world of the interviewee.
- Once the interviewee's everyday lived world is discerned, the interview goes on to search for key meaningful themes that are part of that lived world.
- The interview seeks to explore those themes in ordinary, qualitative language.
- Different aspects of the interviewee's life are sought, and are expressed in carefully nuanced descriptions.
- Abstractions are set aside in favor of a search for specific concrete actions and settings.
- The interviewer cultivates a deliberate openness and, if possible, naiveté instead of trying to pull everything together too soon.
- The interviewer walks a tightrope between a tight structure and a totally nondirective line of questions.

- Ambiguities and contradictions are accepted and duly noted, not brushed away or ignored.
- If the interview itself creates new insights and forms of awareness for the interviewee, those new insights are welcomed as part of the process and are properly documented as such.
- The interviewer must always be aware of the fact that the interview process is sensitive to the interviewer's awareness and sensitivity to the issues that arise during the interview.
- An interview is an interpersonal event, and any knowledge generated by the interview is inexorably shaped by these interpersonal dynamics, whether that shaping is apparent or not.
- A good interview can do much good and be the source of much knowledge and insight, not only for the research project, but often for the interviewee, and in some cases, for the interviewer's personal life as well.

One final logistical point needs to be addressed. By and large, interviews work best when they are face to face. At times, however, it might be necessary or even desirable to conduct an interview via the telephone. For example, it might be physically dangerous to conduct an interview on site, or the topic might be so sensitive that the interviewee feels more comfortable talking over the phone. In spite of the loss of face-to-face dynamics, Sturges and Hanrahan (2004) found that there were no real differences when face-to-face and telephone interviews were conducted with the same populations. So, if it is not possible to physically meet with your participants, all is not lost. Telephone interviews can fill in quite well, although it just makes sense to talk face to face whenever it is feasible.

Interactions in Interviews

One of the key dynamics of interviewing is the ongoing interaction between the interviewer and the interviewee. Rapley (2001) reminds us that our actions as interviewers are critical in getting our subjects to open up and work with us to create solid interview data.

Interactions between interviewers and interviewees are particularly important when dealing with sensitive topics. Given the potential risks of such topics on those we interview, Corbin and Morse (2003) recommend that we be sensitive and reciprocate in appropriate ways to make sure we are not doing harm as we gather our data.

At a theoretical level, these interactions can be described using positioning theory (Ritchie & Rigano, 2001). Positioning theory holds that we are not just interacting in interview settings, but that we are jointly producing storylines. This theory starts with the idea that everyday life is an interplay between discourses that resonate between our biographies and our take on the social world: "The skills that people have to talk are not only based on capacities to produce words and sentences but equally on capacities to follow rules that shape the episodes of social life" (p. 744). In other words, interviewing is as much a social skill as it is a communicative skill.

Like any other set of skills, good interviewing skills are learned. In evaluating their intensive course on interviewing, Roulston, deMarrais, and Lewis (2003) took a look at some of the challenges and struggles their students faced. Some of the key challenges that these novice interviewers faced included: (1) learning how to phrase and negotiate questions, avoiding closed questions, and asking the sorts of questions that opened further dialogue and reflection; (2) dealing with unexpected answers and/or behaviors from their interviewees; (3) dealing with the consequences of their own actions, including their own unexamined beliefs and assumptions; (4) dealing with sensitive issues; and (5) dealing with the arduous and time-consuming process of transcription (pp. 648–657). These novices did benefit greatly from the training, however, and were able to reflect upon their challenges and successes with each other.

Focus Groups

Another major development and expansion of the interview in qualitative research has been the use of the focus group. Morgan (Morgan, 1988, 1998) has pioneered much of our current thinking on the use of focus groups in qualitative research. Other useful guides to focus group research include works by Greenbaum (1997, 2000) and Barbour and Kitzinger (1999). Morgan and Krueger (1997) have also developed an extensive focus group research kit.

A focus group is a group of people whom you interview at the same time. The first focus groups arose from the awareness that, in group therapy, people were often more likely to discuss complex and intimate issues when they were participating in a group discussion.

Focus groups are most useful for getting at complex underlying notions in a setting where the sharing of experiences can help guide the other participants to greater awareness and participation. There are a few practical rules that help make sure a focus group will be fruitful.

First of all, keep your lists of questions short. You need to make sure there is enough time to answer each question in depth, so you need to limit the actual number of questions you will use. Therefore, it is important to select your questions carefully.

Second, make sure you can identify participants later on. If you are audiotaping, have each participant state his or her first name. That way, you can keep track of who said what when you are transcribing. If you are videotaping, there is obviously no need to do this. It is a good idea, whether you are audiotaping or videotaping, to use a PZM (sometimes called a flat or paddle) microphone. These microphones are omnidirectional. Place the microphone in the center of the table, and the results should be quite good.

Finally, make sure each participant answers each question. If the participant answers the question as part of the flow of the focus group, then all is well and good. If not, explicitly invite that person to address the issue before moving on. As the moderator of the focus group, you have to be a bit more directive than you would be during an ordinary interview. It is often a good strategy to ask a question and then immediately invite a participant by name to address the question. When you follow this procedure, you can then vary the order that participants answer. This way, you do not settle into the rut of having the same person always answer first, or last.

Online Focus Groups

In recent years, there has been an expansion of focus groups into the realm of the Internet. There are a number of reasons for considering online focus groups. First of all, conducting a focus group online greatly expands the pool of possible participants. Using online formats makes data collection and data organization much easier because the responses are more or less already transcribed by participants. The online format also can make it easier for some people to respond to sensitive questions and areas. Online communication tends to be more egalitarian, and so there are fewer instances of certain people trying to dominate the interaction (Franklin & Lowry, 2001; Oringderff, 2004).

At the same time, the dynamics of online conversation in general can work against the effective use of online focus groups. For one thing, the lack of physical and verbal cues can lead to misunderstandings and even conflicts. If the group is conducted in an asynchronous fashion, there can be long gaps in conversations. If the conversations are synchronous, it can be sometimes hard to determine who is saying what, and in response to whom. Finally, there is the potential problem that different participants have different levels of skills with the computer hardware and software. Like many other Internet initiatives, online focus groups offer a great deal of promise, but there are ongoing issues of concern that need to be addressed carefully (Franklin & Lowry, 2001; Oringderff, 2004).

SPECIALIZED TYPES OF INTERVIEWS

By and large, the basic interview model presented by Spradley (1979, 1980) and modified and enhanced by others has served us well. Over the years, though, researchers have felt the need to develop a number of different specialized types of interviews. We will look at a few of these types that have emerged within qualitative research as a whole.

Witzel (2000) developed the *problem-centered interview* (PCI) as a method to enhance theory generation in qualitative research. As such, it is seen as an offshoot of Grounded Theory. True to its name, the problem-centered interview is focused on a specific area where the researchers wish to gather interview data. The PCI process starts with a short questionnaire to gather social characteristics data. The interviewer then uses a set of predetermined guidelines to make sure comparable questions are asked in each interview: Communication strategies, including preformulated introductory questions, general exploration questions, and specific exploration questions, are part of these guidelines. Interviews are recorded, and researchers add postscripts to capture their impressions and observations of the interview process per se. We can think of a PCI process as a highly regulated form of semistructured interview. It is also a solid example of qualitative science thinking translated into methodology.

Our other specialized examples come from the qualitative inquiry tradition. Torronen (2002) advocates the use of *stimulus texts,* such as pictures, films, news accounts, and the like, in the interview process. In his work, interviewees react to these texts, and Torronen employs *semiotic* techniques to analyze these responses. In this way, interview data is treated as a complex set of clues based on responses to these stimulus texts.

Denzin has long been a champion of *reflexive methods* and procedures in qualitative research. He has expanded this perspective into the realm of *interviewing and performance* (Denzin, 2001). Denzin sees the interview not as a data-gathering device, but an interpretive performance. Interviews are not linear; interviewees tell their stories using such techniques as montage, where they jump ahead and back in time to weave their accounts. For Denzin, the boundaries between interview and performance are often blurred, and we need to apply performative thinking in our reflexive understanding of interviews and the interview process.

Boufoy-Bastick (2004) combines the notion of interviewing and autoethnography to create the idea of autointerviewing. Autointerviewing allows us to explore our own worldviews by asking ourselves a series of critical and reflexive questions. By focusing on oral history, personal biography, and critical incidents, we can use the interview process to come to know ourselves and our worldviews.

MASTERING INTERVIEW SKILLS

Anyone who has little or no experience as an interviewer enters the process with a number of questions. More often than not, those questions are very similar from interviewer to interviewer. Also more often than not, those same questions are not nearly as important as the novice interviewer thinks they are. But it would be remiss of us if we did not address the three most common questions that novices tend to raise.

Should I Conduct a Structured or an Unstructured Interview?

Novices realize that there are two broad types of interviews—structured and unstructured. How can we decide which type of interview to use in a given situation?

Many qualitative researchers avoid the traditional structured interview. They ask—If I want to ask the same questions, the same way, at the same place in the process, then why wouldn't I use a survey instrument instead? Surveys have the advantage of being easily distributed to lots of people at the same time, and the people can take their time and think about their answers before they write them in. So long as researchers provide room for narrative comments in their surveys, there does not seem to be any reason to do a strictly structured interview. In fact, a strictly structured interview is most useful as a pilot tool for writing an effective survey instrument.

Semistructured interviews are often favored by people doing qualitative science. In particular, the semistructured interview is most often used in these circumstances. A semistructured interview allows the interviewer some latitude in how questions are asked, and in what order, but it is still the case that all interviewees are asked the same basic questions. By standardizing the interviews to some degree, the researcher preserves a degree of comparability across interviews.

There are many models of semistructured interviews. Here is one that I find generally useful and easy to conduct. Generate a list of, say, six critical questions. Decide which question is most important, and start with that one for each interview you conduct. Then, use the rest of the list as a checklist. If the interviewee touches on the area as part of the conversation, simply cross it off. Before the interview is over, make sure all the questions are either ticked off naturally or raised by you.

As your interview becomes more and more structured, you also run the risk of asking leading questions. A leading question is a question that guides the interviewee toward giving you an answer that you are looking for. Though it is not impossible to ask leading questions with unstructured interviews, they are more common in semistructured and structured interviews. Look over the list of questions you intend to ask and think about how you yourself would answer them. Are you pushing your interviewee, either explicitly or implicitly, in that direction? If the question cannot be answered except in the manner you want it answered, then eliminate or change it. For instance, do not ask "Do you feel that being a beauty pageant contestant is demeaning?" Instead, ask something like "What would be hard for a person on the outside, like me, to understand about being a beauty pageant contestant?" That way, you will get the answer they want to give, not necessarily the one you want to hear.

The unstructured interview has the virtue of being guided by the interviewee. The reason that I am conducting an interview with the person in the first place is because I suspect that he or she knows more about the topic than I do. Why not let that person guide the process, then?

Conducting an unstructured interview requires a great deal of skill. The interviewer has to know when the interview is just drifting, and how to nudge it back along a more productive track without forcing the tone or the nature of the interview. Novice interviewers often are more successful using semistructured interviews. Unstructured interviews, however, are usually more relevant and useful for qualitative inquiry studies. This is because the free form of the unstructured interview allows researchers to explore issues of meaning with a great degree of methodological freedom.

How Many Questions Should I Ask?

This is the simplest question to answer. Most novices plan to ask too many questions; as a result, one of two counterproductive things usually happens. Sometimes, they set out to ask a lot of questions and only get to a few, thereby feeling guilty and frustrated. Other times, they force themselves to ask all the questions they want, but at the expense of cutting off valuable information and forcing the interview along a predetermined path.

You are better off asking too few questions, or getting through too few of your questions, than forcing answers to too many questions. If you ask too few questions, one of two things will happen. Either your interviewee will take up the slack and lead the interview process himself or herself (which is usually a good thing when it happens) or else the interview will end early. If it ends early, you can always go back later and set up another interview with more questions derived from answers to the original question. That is usually not such a bad thing, either.

On the other hand, when you force the issue by plowing through a list of questions that is too long, then several bad things can happen. Your interviewee picks up your sense of rushing through the material, and cooperates by giving quick, superficial answers. Or else the interviewee senses that you are more interested in your questions than his or her answers, and withdraws psychologically. These problems can be avoided by taking your time and letting the interviewee pace the interview. If you really need to ask all of the questions, you can always schedule another interview.

How Long Should Any Given Interview Be?

This question is based on a desire to use time properly. Is it best to have one long interview, a few medium-length interviews, or a lot of short interviews?

The answer to this question depends on you and your interviewee. Each interview setting seems to have its natural length. When you are conducting an interview, you will feel a tangible energy connection between you and the person you are interviewing. As that energy begins to dip, the interview moves toward conclusion. Let this unfold on its own accord. If you need to go back and get more information, do it. Don't try to force an interview beyond its natural zone of energy.

Sometimes, you will find that your energy is waning and the interviewee is still going strong. This is not at all unusual. In many cases, it is actually easier and less demanding to be interviewed than it is to conduct an interview. If you can muster up the extra energy, by all means keep going while your interviewee is going strong. You may never get the chance to get this information so easily again. If you just cannot go on, exit as gracefully as possible and set up another interview at the earliest possible date.

How Should I Conduct My Interviews?

Earlier, we looked at the emerging trend of online focus groups. Other forms of online interviewing have become more common as online environments become more familiar. Some of these forms include the use of email, listservs, and online course software.

More and more, researchers are having to decide whether or not to interview face to face or online. There are no hard and fast rules for making these sorts of decisions.

If there are compelling logistical reasons to conduct interviews online, then it makes sense to do them that way. Some of these reasons might include logistical issues such as distance and availability. Other potential factors include considerations of safety for the researchers or the interviewees, and the possibility that the interviewees might feel more comfortable dealing with sensitive subjects by typing in their thoughts, particularly in an asynchronous setting where the interviewees can take time to think out their answers.

In the final analysis, however, it makes sense to conduct interviews face to face whenever feasible. In this way, the researchers and interviewees get to react to each other as human beings in real-time and real-place settings. Researchers also benefit by gaining information and impressions that go beyond the actual words used.

CONVERSING AND THE MIRROR, WINDOW, AND LANTERN

If we go back to our three technologies of looking from Chapter 1, we can sort out the kinds of conversing issues that will guide us as qualitative researchers.

Conversing and the Mirror.   There is a great deal of mirror thinking in most interviews. How can we help but reflect on what we hear from others?

Some of the most important work during the speculative era in the Middle Ages consisted of mock interviews and mock conversations. The conversation was taken as a natural vehicle to allow people with opposing points of view to air those views, to examine their differences, and to see what common beliefs they held. An element of this sort of mock conversation for the sake of elucidating views is a good thing to cultivate in most interviews.

Although talking about views is important, it is a good idea to steer clear of debate. When debates break out during interviews, more often than not they are informal arguments over points of view. Formal debates are a highly stylized form of such interactions, with the difference that formal debates are used to evaluate debating skills more than as devices to get at the truth. It is usually a good idea not to get into any sort of debate during an interview. If your interviewee is putting forth beliefs that you cannot accept, perhaps the best thing to do is to simply note them and move on. Intellectual debates too often lead to genuine conflict, which shuts down all rapport on the spot.

Conversing and the Window.   The chief virtue of the window perspective is a dogged determination to get at the unvarnished truth. In qualitative interviewing, that pursuit of truth is most often related to the truthfulness and knowledgability of the interviewee. Misinformed interviewees are not deliberate liars, but in a sense they are telling lies. Here is where you, as an interviewer, have to keep clear on the difference between beliefs and truths. People hold beliefs, and they are allowed to report those beliefs as if they were true. They are not allowed, though, to insist upon things that are errors of fact. Sorting out fact from belief from error is best done, most of the time, by yourself and after the interview. You have to make sure your own commitment to the truth, however, is not compromised by how you report your interviewee's thoughts and opinions. For instance, if your interviewee holds strong racist views, and puts them forth as truth, you are not required to put them forth as facts in your research. They were your interviewee's beliefs and they are important for the record as beliefs. You do not have to elevate them to truth claims to hold that they are important information.

Conversing and the Lantern.   When you are shining light into dark corners, more often than not you will be surprised by what you find. Are you prepared to deal with surprise in an interview setting? Are you comfortable when the interview takes off in a productive direction that is far different from the one you intended? Can you resist the urge to bring it back to where you wanted it to go originally?

Over and over again, we will find that surprise is one of the greatest gifts that a qualitative research setting can give us. If nothing else, it tells us that we are not dealing with our own presuppositions anymore. Therefore, we have to embrace surprise, and not explain it away. Moving forth in the face of surprise is the single best tool you can use in a qualitative interview to get really new and fresh insights.

FINAL THOUGHTS ON CONVERSING

Conversing is one of the most important human skills we possess. When we are interviewing, we are bending those skills somewhat, while trying to make the process look as unforced and as natural as possible. We must be careful not to allow this bending process to slip into a form of manipulation. We must respect the privacy and the rights of the interviewee, and if we uncover material that the interviewee might not wish to be part of a more public record, we must give the interviewee a chance to make these wishes known.

Does this mean that the interviewee has the right to edit the results of an interview? This is a complex matter. First of all, you should always use a consent form with any person you seek to interview. The interviewee's rights and privileges should be spelled out explicitly in that consent form. The form should also lay out your expectations for using the material. Make sure the interviewee understands each of the tenets of the consent form before he or she signs it.

If you wish to use potentially sensitive material, and you feel that its use is protected under the consent form, check with the interviewee anyway. Just because something might be legal does not mean that it is the right thing to do. Allowing the interviewee the right to edit the record can seriously compromise the integrity of the research; you are not writing an authorized biography but are trying to get at the truth as you best understand it. If the material is seen by the interviewee to be unacceptably damaging, consider this and make the decision to edit or modify the record yourself. If you feel you cannot edit the material, and the interviewee cannot tolerate its use, the court of last resort is to abandon all of the interview material. This is a preferable alternative to allowing the interviewee the right to edit.

In the final analysis, however, most interview situations are pleasant for both parties, so do not be anxious about conducting interviews. Wade in and let the process unfold. You may be surprised at how much you enjoy it.

PLANNING YOUR RESEARCH PROPOSAL:
IDENTIFYING POSSIBLE SETTINGS AND PARTICIPANTS

Both Albert and Carol will be doing their research in field settings. For Albert, the setting will be a series of middle school math classrooms. For Carol, the setting will be a series of corporate offices, a series of informal gathering places for young urban singles, and personal dwelling places. Carol will be looking at multiple settings for each of her participants, while Albert will restrict his access to school settings only.

Carol

Carol knows that she will be keeping her research into her participants to a minimum, in order to not compromise her grounded theory approach to studying them. Therefore, she will have to describe them demographically instead. In this fashion, she will be able to demonstrate that she understands these participants before she is allowed to study them.

Carol compiled the following demographic characteristics to use in her search for participants:

- Each participant would be a single female without children
- Each participant would live in a nearby urban setting
- Each participant would be working either a part-time job or a job whose salary level was in the lower quartile of salaries in the region
- Each participant would be working on a GED or attending college full- or part-time
- Each participant would be actively looking for a husband or a permanent male companion or significant other

Carol then began her preliminary search for potential participants. She started by exploring three sources: (1) word of mouth among friends and acquaintances, (2) advertising on local computer bulletin boards, and (3) advertising on free urban newspapers targeted to single people. At this stage, she would like to be able to contact 10 to 20 young women in order to tap into a good mix of potential participants for her actual study.

Albert

Albert wants to move beyond his personal base of knowledge to decide on whom to select as the participants for his study. He is well aware that he has many math anxious students in his own classrooms. But these students seem to match the profiles of typical math anxious students he finds in his review of the literature. He wants to look at something different, but he just cannot seem to put his finger on what it is.

His big breakthrough came one day in the teacher's lounge. He was talking to another math teacher about math anxiety. The other teacher, who has been teaching math for two decades, was reflecting on one of his algebra students. This student, whom we will call Troy, was an outstanding math student the previous year. As it turns out, Troy has always been good at math, and has enjoyed math. This year, however, Troy had finally run into trouble with math. The strange thing is that Troy is acting just like any other math anxious student. The previous years of success seem to play no role in Troy's approach to math or his own math anxiety.

Albert was immediately struck by this example. Nowhere in the literature has he read about students who are math anxious for the first time after years of prior success. What are these students like? Are they like other math anxious students? Are they different in some way? The questions seemed to fly in to his head, one after another.

Albert had found his pool of participants, at least in theory. Now he has to be able to find them in real life. He begins by contacting all local middle school math teachers to see if they might help him compile a list of likely participants. He has no idea how many potential participants he will find. So far, he knows of at least one.

Ourselves

As you think about designing your own research, think about the following issues:

- How important is the potential setting for your research?
- Do you need a special setting, or can you conduct your research nearly anywhere?
- Do you need a special group of participants, or can you more or less sample from the general population? If you need certain people to participate, can you explain why? Can you identify possible alternatives, in case you cannot find any or all of the target people you are seeking?
- Roughly, how many participants do you think you will need? Why do you think you need this many? Would you be able to settle for less? Do you think you might need more than you anticipate?

CHAPTER 4

Participating

Exercise Three—*The Expert Case Study*

At this time, we are going to start working on a major project. Over the years, I have used this project in my own Qualitative Research Methods classes, and it has yielded exceptional results. I call this project the "Expert Case Study." Of course, you or your instructor may choose to modify this exercise to fit your own needs and goals.

Here are the rules that I have used for this exercise:

- Select a person who is an expert in some area, and do a case study on that person. The focus of this study should be on the person's experiences, practices, history, and thoughts about being an expert. The actual content and nature of the case study itself will be highly dependent on the nature of the area of expertise and the personality of the expert.
- You need to gather and present some evidence to explain why you consider your case study person to be an expert. The nature of the evidence will depend on the person and the area of expertise. You do not want to belabor this effort, though. You are just making a basic case to your reader, and not putting together an airtight defense of your choice.
- You and your expert must both sign an informed consent form. A generic consent form model can be found at the end of this chapter.
- Your case study research must fall in the category of "expedited research." That is, your expert must be at least 18 years old, your expert cannot be a member of any special or protected population (e.g., incarcerated or institutionalized for any reason), and you are restricted to collecting interview, observational, and archival data only.
- Most important, your expert's area of expertise must fall outside any area where you personally have any real knowledge or experience. In other words, your expert must be an expert in an area that is completely foreign to you. For many of us, this means that your expert cannot be an expert in any area having to do with education or academia. If you have other areas of knowledge or special experience, those areas are ruled out as well.
- A good rule of thumb is to pick an expert in an area of which you have no knowledge, but that is potentially interesting to you. It is also a good idea to interview your expert at least once and to tape any and all interviews.
- We will leave the task of creating an actual written report for later.

Over the years, I have managed to accumulate a dazzling list of "experts" from my students. My students have conducted expert case study research with Nobel Laureates, manicurists, Tony Award actors, criminal profilers, journalists, musicians, insurance agents, veterinary acupuncturists, sanitary landfill operators, arboretum managers, plane crash site investigators, ministers, blacksmiths, Negro League ballplayers, dentists, long haul truckers, concrete fabrication engineers, leather crafters (this person also made special costumes for movies), cake decorators, funeral directors, skyscraper ventilation consultants, and many, many more.

The following simple procedures usually work well:

- Identify and contact an expert. If you are adventurous, you can contact someone you do not know. For many, a casual acquaintance works out quite well. Even close friends or family members can work out, if you make sure that they are taking the project seriously. You will be surprised at how little you really know about their expertise.

- Set up a time for at least one interview. Bring taping or other recording equipment to the interview. Analog cassette recording is the most common and reliable recording system to date, although you can use digital recorders, CD recording technology, or computer recording if you are comfortable and familiar with the technology.

- If you are recording on analog cassette, I recommend using a full-size recorder rather than a micro recorder. Make sure you have fresh batteries, spare batteries, and an extension cord. If you can run the tape recorder using AC current, do so.

- Use archive-quality tape. Maxell XLIIS 90 tapes are famous for their dependability and durability, and so that is all that I personally use. If you cannot find Maxell XLIIS tapes, or do not wish to use them, then Maxell XLII 90 tapes are a reasonable substitute. Some field recorders prefer TDK SAX 90 or TDK SA 90 tapes, although they have a very small track record of jamming or stretching. I do not personally recommend any other analog cassette tapes for use. Maxell XLIIS 90 tapes are rarely more than $4.00 each, and you will rarely use more than two or three tapes, so don't try to save money at the expense of the security of your data.

- Usually, a list of four or five questions is sufficient. Some questions could include: Are you an expert? How did you get to be an expert? What is it like to be an expert? Then, sit back and let your person talk. Try not to interrupt or cut off your expert. Let your person lead you; he or she knows the material far better than you do.

- Pay careful attention to answers that surprise you. No matter what their fields are, we all have some preconceptions about our experts and their worlds. A surprising answer takes us away from our preconceptions. When you get a surprising answer, follow up with probing questions. You are now lucky enough to be out of your own preconceptions and on totally new ground—make sure you take advantage of this opportunity.

- Whether or not you transcribe your tapes is up to you or your instructor. Make sure you at least listen to them several times, and take good notes. Pay attention not only to the words, but also to inflections, pauses, and the like. Try to reconstruct a visual memory of the interview as you listen to the tapes.

- It is not a good idea to videotape unless both you and your expert are very comfortable with the use of videotaping equipment. If you are fussing with the camera and paying too much attention to it, you are hurting the flow of information. Also, people tend to feel much less at ease when they are being videotaped than when they are being audiotaped. They tend to forget about the tape recorder fairly soon, but the presence of a video camera is much harder for people to ignore.

- If you feel, upon review of your tapes, that there are "holes" in your understanding of your expert, schedule another interview. Minimally, contact your expert by phone and share concerns or ask for clarification. Tape record those comments if possible. In some states and countries, however, it is illegal to tape record telephone conversations even with a person's permission. Make sure you follow all applicable laws if you wish to tape record these follow up conversations.

This should be enough to get you started. As you gather your data, and as you think about what your report might look like, feel free to use the advanced skills you will be mastering later on as this project starts to take form. There will be no official links between this project and most of the advanced skills, however. That is because there is no guarantee that your particular project will require all of these advanced skills. We will officially revisit the expert case study project in Exercise 9, when it is time to write your final draft.

REFLECTING ON PARTICIPATION

Most types of qualitative research depend on some form of fieldwork. Therefore, it is necessary for you to learn and practice fieldwork skills. In its most fundamental form, fieldwork is about participation on the part of the researcher. The researcher is involved in some fashion, if only by being present and on site. In other words, all fieldwork skills are built on basic participation skills.

In this chapter, we will endeavor to learn the basic skills of participation. This usually means that we will identify those skills that are most often emphasized in most types of experiential training. The key to participation in qualitative research is the concept of *participant observation*. We will start by examining the basics of this mode of operation. Once we understand the basic dynamics of participant observation, we can examine some of the main forms of participative activities in qualitative research.

There is a temptation, as we learn about fieldwork, to want to find out the rules that we need to learn to be properly trained in these methods. Instead, we find that traditionally participants often receive very little formal training. This is particularly true of that branch of fieldwork known as *ethnography*, where the researcher is immersed in some other culture. Most ethnographers learn ethnography by diving into settings and learning as they go along. This same tradition, to a lesser degree, is found in other sorts of fieldwork settings, such as *action research*.

Why are fieldwork skills most often taught on site? The answer is based on the fact that field research is much different from laboratory and other forms of experimental research. In short, when we learn to do experimental research, we learn how to strategize and implement a study. When we do field research, we learn how to participate tactically in real-world settings, and to learn from those settings and our maneuvering.

We will explore the notions of strategic and tactical investigation styles in Chapter 7. In the meantime, we need to take a close look at the three basic forms of fieldwork that are most commonly used in qualitative research: participant observation, ethnography, and action research. They have many similarities, but each form has its own unique characteristics.

Most of us will find ourselves gravitating toward one form of fieldwork, or perhaps even away from one or more of these basic methods. But we must be ready to use any of these forms if our particular research interests lead us in their direction. Therefore, an awareness of the major forms of fieldwork is the best place for us to start on the path of developing our own basic participation skills.

PARTICIPANT OBSERVATION

Perhaps the most fundamental form of fieldwork is the notion of participant observation. Participant observation is exactly what it says it is. Participant observation occurs when we enter a setting and become involved in two ways. First of all, we are acting as observers. Second, we are attempting to "work our way" into these settings as active participants. By starting at the periphery, we can eventually move closer and closer to the center of the action, so to speak (Lee & Roth, 2003).

More often than not, participant observation is a set of skills used in field research studies. Some of the most important of these skills are described in the following paragraphs.

Entry

One issue that seems to be present in all field studies is the topic of entry. How are we to go about gaining access, or entry, into a particular field setting? Entry strategies can be as simple as just showing up in some public space and starting to observe, to some form of participation or even initiation to be able to gain access to more restricted locales. Fieldwork has more often than not been characterized as an art (e.g., Wolcott, 1995a, among others) and nowhere is this "art" more subtle than in the process of entry. Bogdevic (1999) reminds us that you must ask permission to gain access to any field setting. Sometimes, that permission must be formal. Do not hesitate to seek permission in writing if need be. Also, make sure that you have permission, formal or informal, from all necessary parties. Quite often, a setting is a complex place, and there are many "players" on the scene. Make sure you have permission from every side or every faction within a setting. This will help you maintain the neutrality you will need if you are doing fieldwork in a setting where there is potential for conflict or for struggle between different perspectives.

Rapport

Formal or informal entry is all about permission. Getting people to accept you, once you are on scene, is all about rapport. Rapport is governed by one main factor—who you are. You can only develop genuine rapport by being yourself. If your natural bent is toward caution and care, then you must plan your excursions into field settings to match your careful nature. Can you find someone who can help you get the access you need? On the other hand, if you are adventurous and outgoing, then you are best served by allowing your basic nature to help guide you into the setting. But you cannot establish rapport by pretending to be someone you are not. Bogdevic (1999) goes on to suggest that when seeking to build rapport, be prepared to spend some time and effort. Be unobtrusive, especially at first. Be honest and open. Play down your own skills and knowledge, and engage instead in as much reflective listening as possible. But do not be secretive—be willing to reveal your own thoughts, feelings, and background if asked. If you balance these pointers with patience and take your own personality and inclinations into account, then you should be able to build good on-site rapport.

Finding and Cultivating Informants

Informants have been a time-honored part of the fieldwork process. How can you find and develop the informants you need to give you the information you need? Gilchrist and Williams

(1999) emphasize developing key informants. A key informant is a person who can give you an inside look into the culture you are studying. Here is a set of simple questions to keep in mind as you attempt to judge the validity of a key informant: Is this person trustworthy? Is this person a member in good standing of the culture? Does this person have access to the information you need? Could this person have an ulterior motive for being an informant? Can this person lead you to other informants? If you pay attention to the flow of information from your informants, and use your own knowledge and experiences as a checkpoint, then you should be able to gather valuable information on an ongoing basis.

Fieldnotes

In order to record their experiences, field researchers often turn to the task of writing fieldnotes. Fieldnotes are important for all forms of field research, but they are particularly central for ethnography (Wolfinger, 2002). In the early days, most fieldnotes were composed late at night from bits and scraps of written memos and from memory. With the advent of new technology, however, fieldnotes can be recorded on audio or videotape, on compact disc, or directly onto computer hard drives.

Two points need to be emphasized, however. First of all, fieldnotes are just as much about your impressions and your observations as they are records of who said what. Mechanical recording devices, such as tape recorders, can capture words but not your thoughts (unless you use these devices as dictation tools). Thus tapes and transcripts cannot replace fieldnotes—they can only support them with a more accurate record.

Second, when you move away from paper-and-pencil notes, however, take care to make sure that your notes are in permanent form. If you lose your fieldnotes, your research will suffer. Also, remember that your fieldnotes are for your use. Do not force yourself to adopt any one note-taking style just because you think it might be the right way. Just as there are different ways to observe, there are different ways to take notes. You are free to be as detailed or as global as you wish. Do take care to document important events by time and place, though. You will need these time and space "anchors" for later reporting.

As participant observation becomes more formalized, it takes on different forms. Three of the most important of these forms are ethnography, applied field research, and action research. Each of these forms will be discussed in some detail.

ETHNOGRAPHY

The oldest formal type of participatory fieldwork is the field of ethnography (see Hammersley, 1990; Hammersley & Atkinson, 1983; LeCompte, 2002; and LeCompte & Preissle, 1993 for useful summaries and descriptions of the history of, and an overview of traditional and emerging issues in, ethnography). In ethnographic research, you participate, over an extended period of time, in the lives of the people you are studying. You do this to try to see the world from their cultural perspectives and to understand the meanings in their rituals and cultural artifacts and activities.

Basic Ethnographic Skills

Ethnography has developed a simple ethic of training. In most traditional ethnographic training programs, the future ethnographer is literally dropped into the culture in question, and is expected to learn ethnography techniques on site. Very little emphasis is placed on developing and practicing field techniques beforehand, as such practice was seen to be more likely to set up preconceived strategies on the part of the fieldworker, interfering with the fieldworker's ability to craft ethnographic tools "as needed" in the actual setting.

The ethnographer as participant observer.

First of all, it is important to remember that the basic skills of participant observation apply directly to most forms of ethnography. This is not surprising because most of those skills were first delineated by researchers conducting traditional ethnographic work. Entry, rapport, finding and using informants, and recording observations and impressions are at the heart of the ethnographic process. In addition, there are a number of more specific approaches that ethnographers often adopt.

The ethnographer as "recording device."

The requirement to master ethnographic technique on-site ultimately depends upon a view of research that puts the ethnographer to work on the task of discovering and discerning aspects of culture as they exist "in the wild." Here, the ethnographer is not concerned about how the culture in front of him or her is like or unlike his or her own home culture. The culture under study must be experienced on its own terms.

Under such a worldview, it makes sense for the ethnographer to act as a recording instrument. And like any good recording instrument, preset conditions should be avoided. If the ethnographer is a blank slate, then it will be easier for him or her to see what the people in the cultural setting really think. The clutter of the ethnographer's own opinions and prior assumptions must be set aside, as much as possible.

The ethnographer as narrator.

Everyday settings usually require not only a change in what ethnographers might see, but also a change in what they might do. What should a budding ethnographer do when going into a cultural setting that may already be somewhat, or even very, familiar? Often, the role of the ethnographer shifts from that of being a simple chronicler of events and structures to being a chronicler and teller of tales.

We cannot tell the tales of a culture unless we have some basic prior understanding of that culture. Otherwise, all we are doing is transcribing their accounts, and leaving it to others to understand what these accounts mean. When we feel that we understand the basic dynamics of a culture going in, however, we have a different task at hand (see Pratt, 1986, for an extended discussion of this situation). On the positive side, we can use these research accounts to transform our initial understandings into more comprehensive structures of meaning. On the negative side, our preconceptions can be so powerful that we cannot break free from them, even in the face of new data.

One thing seems to be true, though. There is a growing sense that ethnographies, especially when they are conducted on familiar cultures, are "made" as much as "found." This leads us to the matter of ethnography as "telling" and the ethnographer as "narrator."

Clifford (1986) and Marcus (1986), in particular, have emphasized the ethnographer as narrator. This strategy works, regardless of whether the ethnographer is studying a strange or a familiar culture. If we are discovering a culture, are we not discovering it through our eyes, and are we not really telling the story of that culture as it impacts upon us? If we are not really discovering a culture, but are taking a closer look at a familiar culture, then are we not telling our story as a member of that culture? (See Peshkin's 1982 work for a further discussion of subjective dynamics in ethnographic settings.)

One interesting approach to the telling of the story of a culture takes this "telling" as an ethnohistorical task. Precourt (1982) is a good example of such an effort; he examines the role of the history of an alternative Appalachian school as a key part of understanding its current functioning.

The emphasis of the role of narrative skills in ethnography is also particularly important for those ethnographers who hold a postmodern perspective (e.g., Denzin, 1989, 1997; Wolcott, 1995b). We will talk about postmodernism in some depth in Chapter 5.

The personal cost of ethnography.

One last point needs to be made about doing major ethnographic fieldwork. Most classic ethnographers actually did very few field studies in their careers. Many did only one long extended study, often with visits and revisits as part of the process. Why was this the case? Apart from the time and expense involved, and the need to devote as much time to writing up the findings as was actually spent in the field (an unwritten rule of thumb in ethnography), there was another subtle but powerful reason.

An extended ethnographic stay in an unfamiliar culture was, more often than not, an exercise in controlled "split personality." What do I mean by this? Simply enough, the ethnographer usually had to think, act, respond, live, and interact like a "native" by day, and then retire to his or her tent or hut or igloo or whatever and think, act, and write like a social scientist by night. To do this well, you cannot just shift perspective. You have to be able to actually, as much as possible, switch back and forth between identities.

Engaging in such extensive identity switching over a long period of time is the sort of change that inevitably takes its toll on the researcher. I am not saying that ethnographers go mad. They are more like marathon runners. Marathon running is a controlled activity, but it takes a cumulative physical toll on the body. It is common wisdom that a marathon runner only has so many peak "runs" in his or her body before the body loses its ability to sustain the exertion and energy transfer needed to perform a marathon run at competitive times. In similar fashion, perhaps the human psyche has only so many extended dual-identity performances in it before it loses the focus needed to perform in peak fashion.

In other words, it is a demanding and telling task to master the process of becoming an ethnographer. This process can have a profound personal impact on the individual (see Van Maanen, 1995). Coe (1991) demonstrates this quite clearly as he leads us through the process by which he changed from being a naive beginner to becoming an adept practitioner. Coe's message is simple: Ethnography changes ethnographers.

You should not be afraid to do field research, but you need to be aware of what you are getting into. An extended ethnographic performance is very demanding, however, so you need to choose your extended field projects wisely.

Advances and Evolutions in Ethnography

Nowadays, traditional ethnographies are getting rarer. This is due in part to globalization, as there are no longer any remote and untouched cultures in the world. These changes are also due to changes in the way that researchers understand and conduct the ethnographic process, and changes in sites for ethnographic research. Some of these changes and trends are detailed in the following subsections.

Ethnography in everyday settings.
Ethnographic research has changed, and there are few traditional training programs left in existence. One reason is the fact that traditional methods were best suited for those cases in which the culture under study was fundamentally different from prevailing Western culture. In this global age, such cultures simply do not exist anymore. We would be hard pressed to find a place on earth where globalization has not left its mark. Therefore, we cannot expect to be able to walk into a "pristine" culture and have the differences between that culture and ours leap out at us (Tedlock, 2000).

More and more, ethnography has become concerned with examining subcultures or other pockets of cultural organization (Whyte, 1955 is an early and famous example). The differences between these subcultures and prevailing Western culture are more subtle (see Chambers, 2000 for a look at ethnographic approaches to the study of the workplace, for example). We have to be more deliberate in our search for differences, and so a simple immersion strategy is often inadequate (see Schatzman & Strauss, 1973 for their description of field techniques for what they call "natural sociology").

Microethnography.
Also, there has been a growing use in everyday settings of a technique known as microethnography. Microethnography occupies an interesting middle ground between a limited case study on one hand and a full-blown ethnography on the other hand. The researcher does go into a setting, but not for very long. There is also a tendency to focus on only a few predetermined characteristics of the setting. Such areas often include the search for specialized knowledge, the study of specialized settings, or an emphasis on communication patterns. Erickson and Mohatt (1982) provide a good example of a microethnography conducted in an educational setting.

Autoethnography.
One trend that has also emerged in the use of narrative in current ethnographic practice is an approach known as autoethnography. Ellis (Ellis, 1995; Ellis & Bochner, 2000) is one of the key advocates of this approach. By bringing her personal and reflective perspective into her work, she attempts to show us how the setting and the events affect real lives. We cannot know those real impacts, autoethnographic practitioners argue, unless we know them from the view of those who are involved, in their own words. Other recent work in autoethnography has also attempted to expand the approach beyond an autobiographical narrative frame. For instance, Spry (2001) combines autoethnography with performative methodologies to allow for the combining of self-reflective and embodied approaches.

Critical ethnography.
Traditional ethnography saw itself as scientific. As ethnography has evolved and changed, ideas from qualitative inquiry have come to play more prominent roles. This is nowhere more clear than in the development of critical ethnography.

Critical ethnography can be thought of as a blend between critical theory and ethnography. We will talk about critical theory in Chapter 5, but for now we can think of critical theory as a process where we engage reflexively with the world of experience in order to heighten our consciousness and awareness. When we do critical ethnography, we acknowledge that we are not going innocently into some setting, but that we arrive with a worldview and a set of ideas and expectations about culture and the human condition.

Foley (2002) argues that critical ethnography did not rise up overnight, but grew out of decades of concern and examination of the basic processes and goals of ethnography. As ethnographers became more aware of their roles as agents of culture and purveyors of certain viewpoints, it became necessary to become aware of those factors. Segall (2001) argues for the combination and weaving of various voices, including those of the researchers, into the act of gathering and forming the ethnography proper. Alexander (2003) illustrates these sorts of dynamics in his study looking at the powerful impact of gender roles and expectations within his particular ethnographic setting.

Online ethnography.
One final area that has been rapidly developing in recent years is the notion of doing ethnographic research online. Over the years, it has become clear that communities are arising and thriving in online settings, and these sorts of communities are appropriate targets for ethnographic study. For instance, Eichorn (2001) looked at a community based on specialized texts and treatises known as *zines*. Zines are becoming more and more an online phenomenon, as online publishing becomes a viable alternative to traditional print publishing. As she traces her community both in print and online, the hybrid dynamics point toward a changing community. Gatson and Zweerink (2002), on the other hand, looked at a community that primarily existed in online space. This group, which was spawned from the office website for the television series *Buffy the Vampire Slayer,* also spilled out into the "real world" in exciting and interesting ways. As more and more of these sorts of communities arise, the need to research and understand their natures and dynamics will increase.

APPLIED FIELD RESEARCH

Field researchers often do their work in applied settings. More often than not, the researchers are not just participant observers, but members of these applied communities. As an example, we will look briefly at a few recent applied field studies in the area of education. The following paragraphs describe recent examples of such applied field research.

Learning in Groups

Collaborative learning in schools has become a dominant pedagogical methodology in recent years. But how do students engage in collaborative discussions in schools, and what are those discussions typically like? Furthermore, how can teachers make sure that students are being as effective and efficient as possible in these sorts of collaborative groups?

Corden (2001) set out do to fieldwork to address these sorts of questions. Specifically, in this article he chose to explore "how pupils' culturally based definitions and the attitudinal baggage they bring to lessons shape their use of language during group discussions" (p. 348).

Corden (2001) adopted a mixed methods approach to his field research. First of all, he videotaped various small-group student interactions in four high schools in England over a year. He analyzed those tapes in an inductive fashion, looking for patterns and themes. From these interactions, he was able to discern four main categories of utterances: (1) exploring ideas; (2) reasoned evaluations of topics; (3) desultory, or off-task, comments; and (4) disputational talk, where students disagreed in a nonconstructive way. Corden went on to illustrate examples of these categories within actual patterns of comments, and to tabulate general percentages of occurrences of each category within different types of learning contexts.

By working with these illustrative and tabulated data, Corden (2001) was able to conclude that students made many more productive comments, and fewer desultory and disputational comments, when they knew what was expected of them. Otherwise, the students would revert to their tendencies to work independently. Corden found that teachers need to develop specific strategies if they wish their students to pursue lively exchanges of ideas in a collaborative and critical fashion. As he concludes: "Paradoxically, it may be that teachers need to structure tasks carefully and provide unambiguous ground rules for learning if they wish to encourage exploratory discourse during group activities" (p. 364).

School Countercultures

Kipnis (2001) was interested in the phenomenon of countercultures within schools. Rather than conducting his own fieldwork on the topic, he instead sought to assimilate fieldwork results from studies across a variety of national and cultural boundaries. Because the very nature of a counterculture implies resistance, Kipnis first set out to try to distinguish the concept of a school counterculture from other forms of resistance. Then, he sought to describe the social forces that both foster and inhibit the formation of ideal, well-articulated school countercultures.

Toward the first goal, Kipnis (2001) was able to identify four forms of student resistance that did not involve the actions of a counterculture. These results, drawn mainly from research in China, included such acts of resistance as: (1) disrespecting teachers, (2) criticizing examinations systems, (3) ostracizing more academically oriented peers, and (4) cheating on exams (pp. 485–487).

Kipnis also found a number of dynamics that worked to help create well-articulated and stable countercultures in schools across cultural and national boundaries. In general, these countercultures serve to sustain existing class, ethnic, linguistic, and gender differences. Forces such as immigration, the decoupling of education from social mobility in many cultures, and need for individual expression often fuel such persistent countercultures.

In the final analysis, Kipnis (2001) was not interested so much in creating a theory of school countercultures. Instead, he sought to bring together a variety of findings to create a practical guide for the nature and types of such countercultures, regardless of where we might find them. In that sense, he was not so much doing either science or interpretation as he was providing applied guidance.

Scientific Literacy

Hogan and Corey (2001) were interested in how well at-risk elementary children understood the mores and norms of science. In their study, they looked at the efforts of 16 children in one poverty-level fifth-grade class. The researchers were participant observers and guest lecturers in this class. Over the course of the spring semester, they gathered video and audio data on an experimental project to test the effects of different sorts of compost materials on growing plants. Data analysis was conducted at the micro level on the various interactions, and thematic analyses were also conducted. The researchers gathered data that addressed four main areas:

1. The teacher and the researchers sought to guide the students into collaboratively designing a controlled experiment. Instead, the students wanted to work alone. The students designed tests and controls that put their own ideas at an unfair advantage. Finally, the students saw no need for replications or back ups to support their work.
2. The teacher and the researchers sought to guide the students into evaluating their designs using peer reviews. Instead, they found that students resisted offering constructive criticism and feedback, and often reacted negatively when their own ideas were criticized.
3. The teacher and the researchers sought to guide the students in the creation of fair and valid tests for their hypotheses. Instead, students were suspicious of each other, and did not trust each other to carry out testing procedures in a competent fashion.
4. The teacher and the researchers sought to guide the students in pooling their data to help strengthen their analyses. Instead, students focused almost exclusively on their own data. They felt that confirming their own ideas was the most important task, and that their data were more convincing than overall class trends. They also felt that there was no need to draw conclusions from overall data because a single demonstration seemed more convincing to them.

Hogan and Corey (2001) concluded that these students needed explicit teaching on the goals, norms, and values of science. Note that the researchers did not attempt to foster this instruction as part of their study. The goal of the study was to discern current levels of understanding of these norms, not to try to make things better.

Education Beyond Schools

Fine, Weis, Centrie, and Roberts (2000) studied two examples of educational "spaces" that existed in the community and beyond the walls of a classroom. In particular, these spaces existed as special places for young men and women living in ravaged urban settings "within their geographic locations, their public institutions, and their spiritual lives to sculpt real and imaginary corners for peace, solace, communion, and personal and collective identity work. These are spaces of deep, sustained community-based educative work, outside the borders of formal schooling" (p. 132).

Two representative spaces were examined in this study. The first, MollyOlga, was a neighborhood art center on the East Side of Buffalo, New York. It served not only as an art center but also as a safe haven from drugs and violence. The second space was Orisha, a heterogeneous spiritual community in New York City.

Although much of the article was concerned with exploring theoretical aspects of these communities, two practical dimensions also surfaced. The first dimension was that of "free space." The notion of free space indicates openness to any and all segments of society. At the same time, there is a respect for individual differences of all sorts, from personal to race, gender, ethnicity, and sexuality. This combination of free space and difference grounded many of the day-to-day efforts of both places.

Basic Researchers and Teacher-Researchers

Hammond and Spindler (2001) offer a variety of insights on the conduct of research in educational settings. In their work, we find a basic anthropological researcher (Spindler) and a teacher as a practitioner-researcher (Hammond) comparing and contrasting their approaches to doing research. In their reflections, we can derive the following basic points that can help us get a clear handle on the fundamental differences between basic and applied field research:

1. *Type of research questions.* Basic researchers are mainly concerned with questions dealing with identifying and studying fundamental processes. Applied researchers are also interested in fundamental processes, but in terms of how they can be programmatically incorporated into new and existing projects and programs.
2. *Data-collection strategies.* Basic researchers draw upon the wide range of tools available for participant observation research. Applied researchers go about doing their jobs in a more reflexive and documented fashion.
3. *Communication of findings.* Basic researchers are looking to publish books and articles for the academic community. Applied researchers seek to share the information directly with communities of practice.
4. *Research purposes.* Basic researchers are looking for new understandings. Applied researchers value understanding, but they also value improvements in practice.

Reflections on Classroom-Based Fieldwork

As a form of summary of our discussions on applied field research in education, we turn to the advice of a long-standing practitioner in the field. Wax (2002) reflects on some of the dynamics of classroom-based fieldwork that have evolved over his own long career. In particular, he advises that "novice researchers orient themselves toward doing fieldwork rather than constructing a science of anthropology" (p. 129).

He goes on to assert that when studying human social life, "the ideal of science leads to impersonality, lifeless objectivity, and bureaucratic inflexibility. Terms like culture become reified. Those who seek a science of culture lose the ability to observe and interpret the dramas of living" (Wax, 2002, p. 129).

Wax (2002) also reminds us that it is possible to go too far in the other direction as well. "It is not an error to be a critic and crusader, but ideologies—including ideologies of a scientific anthropology or an anthropology of 'liberation'—can blind, and one thereby loses the capacity to learn from one's hosts" (p. 129).

As the consummate applied field researcher, Wax (2002) reminds us that we are not so much pursuing qualitative science or qualitative inquiry, as we are doing applied fieldwork. When we are studying schools, "one needs to learn from the children, and appreciate how collectively they work toward dealing with the problems posed for them by an institution dominated by alien adults" (p. 129).

ACTION RESEARCH

The far end of the participation spectrum finds the researcher not only studying a set of circumstances, but also trying to help make those circumstances better for the people involved. Ideally, the researcher takes a backseat whenever possible, and the people involved take control themselves of the process of improving their lives and circumstances in partnership with the researcher. Whenever we have a commitment to leave a research scene, having helped facilitate a positive and fundamental change for the participants in that setting, then we have engaged in action research.

Practical Participation

One style of action research focuses on the notion of practical participation. In this case, we have a setting that needs improvement. We also have individuals who have access to that setting, and can work within that setting to help bring about positive change.

Stringer (1996) lays out the basic steps for this sort of practical participation. First of all, the researcher makes a careful observational record of the setting. Then, the researcher comes up with a plan to make the necessary positive changes. Next, working with the people in the setting, the researcher implements the plan. Finally, the researcher evaluates the effectiveness of the plan in operation and makes necessary modifications and corrections.

One of the largest and most lively areas of practical participation has been in the field of education and the "teacher as researcher" movement. Bullough and Gitlin (1995) advocate this initiative as a basic part of learning how to be an effective teacher. Kincheloe (1991) sees the teacher-as-researcher movement as empowering, and Wells (1999) sees it as a necessary part of sustaining an authentic dialogic learning community among teachers.

All of these views share the insight that teachers and other practitioners need to move away from being consumers of research to become more active and more involved in the research that will impact their lives and their careers.

Participatory Action Research

Sometimes, action research needs to go beyond the idea of "fixing" something that is wrong within a given social or cultural setting. There are situations in which the changes that are needed go far beyond simple corrective actions. Mind-sets need to be changed, and awareness needs to be raised. When we are dealing with these more serious situations, action research often requires a degree of participation that is quite extraordinary. This form of action research is often called *participatory action research*.

An early and important example of a participatory action research can be seen in the work of Heath (1982, 1983). Heath started her inquiry with an apparently intractable problem. Minority children in a school district were refusing to communicate and cooperate with their White teachers. This refusal was interpreted by the White community as evidence that the minority children were not interested in improving themselves via access to educational opportunities. Exasperated, they asked Heath to see if she could come in and "fix the problem."

Heath quickly saw that the main problem was a crisis of meaning. When she observed in the classrooms, she noted that the minority students appeared to be uncomfortable with the questions their White teachers raised. Could it be that each side was misunderstanding what the other side was doing?

To test her "misunderstanding" hunch, Heath did an in-depth analysis of questioning behavior in minority households. She found that the sorts of questions asked in class were fundamentally different from the sorts of questions that were raised at home. In short, most of the classroom questions were rhetorical. It was clear to everyone that the teacher knew the answer. For a child raised in a White household, such rhetorical questions were often used as part of the learning process. But rhetorical questions were not part of the minority culture. In that situation, a rhetorical question was an insult. It was as if the questioner was saying "Could you at least give me the right answer to this obvious question?".

There was the further dimension that not everyone in a minority culture had the right to ask questions. This was especially true when an outsider came into a minority setting and started asking questions. More often than not, this was seen as a precursor to trouble. There-fore, if a White person came around asking questions, most minority children were instructed to ignore those questions.

As a result of her fieldwork, Heath was able to show that two completely different per-ceptions were operating against each other in the classroom setting. The teachers felt that they were asking innocent, traditional, and time-honored types of questions, and that the minority children were either too stupid or too belligerent to answer. The children felt that the teach-ers were insulting their intelligence, and that, anyway, when White people started asking ques-tions, especially questions they already knew the answers to, then there was likely to be trouble for the children if they answered.

Heath (1982, 1983) made the move from ordinary researcher to action researcher when she took the next step. She endeavored to help bring this welter of misunderstandings to an end. She worked with both White and minority groups to raise each group's awareness of the perceptions of the others, and cooperated with them in the task of reaching common solutions.

Action Research as a Revolutionary Act

Finally, the most extreme and the most overtly political form of action research is dedicated not to making changes in settings and subcultures but to turning around the culture as a whole. In these instances, action research becomes part of an overall strategy seeking libera-tion of oppressed peoples, or the liberation of oppressed minorities within larger cultures.

The architect of action research as liberation of the oppressed was Paulo Freire (1968/1983). Freire began his career in the late 1950s, when he was sent by the Brazilian gov-ernment into the impoverished northwest part of the country to teach literacy skills to the peasants there. Freire took the radical stance that illiteracy was a form of oppression, and tied the teaching of literacy to the task of helping the peasants see themselves as oppressed and in need of liberating themselves. Freire was so successful, on both counts, that he was sent into exile by the Brazilian government. Eventually, Freire was allowed to return to Brazil, where he continued to pursue his agenda to help the poor seek liberation through self-examination, ed-ucation, and political action.

Many contemporary critical theorists have embraced and extended the Freirean agenda. McLaren (1986) has combined Marxism and a Freirean perspective toward postcolonial lib-eration in his work. Giroux has stressed the role of power (1983), marginality (1992), and multiculturalism (1993) in his theoretical writings. And Kincheloe (1991, 1993) has com-bined empowerment and postmodern consciousness in his efforts to shed new light on areas of overt and covert oppression of teachers and students.

These and other contemporary thinkers and activists are extending the traditional do-mains of research, even action research, into the boundaries of revolution. Should we follow suit? That is for each and every one of us to decide on our own.

PARTICIPATION IN QUALITATIVE SCIENCE
AND QUALITATIVE INQUIRY

As we look at the participation strategies and methods of ethnography, applied field re-search, and action research, we find evidence of both qualitative science and qualitative in-quiry perspectives.

Perspectives Within Ethnography

Traditional ethnography has always had an uneasy relationship with traditional science. Though traditional ethnography emphasized careful, value-free, and objective observation, it was clear that this sort of field research did not fit with more familiar modes of doing scientific inquiry. Traditional ethnography respects the perspectives of the scientific method more than it employs clearly identifiable scientific methods per se.

Many of the revolutionary activities within ethnography have been done within the qualitative inquiry perspective. For instance, the recent emphasis on narration, the emergence of ethnographies and microethnographies within common, everyday settings, and the growth and development of such new directions as critical ethnography and autoethnography are all in line with qualitative inquiry thinking.

Perspectives Within Applied Field Research

Applied field research is concerned with addressing and answering practical questions. Therefore, questions of which methods to use are driven by the programmatic needs of the researchers. Some of our illustrative studies, such as Corden (2001), made extensive use of the techniques and assumptions of qualitative science. Other studies, such as Fine et al. (2000) were much more oriented to the qualitative inquiry side of the spectrum. Applied researchers are most often looking for results, and will adopt those methods they feel they need to get the job done.

Perspectives Within Action Research

Like our other forms of participation, we can find both qualitative science and qualitative inquiry approaches within the broader spectrum of action research. As a general guideline, those forms of action research that are looking for specific types of improvements or results are much more likely to incorporate qualitative science considerations and techniques. For instance, the model laid out by Stringer (1996) is very much in line with most forms of qualitative science thinking.

On the other hand, most forms of participatory action research, and especially those forms that favor such notions as emancipation and empowerment, are more likely to adopt qualitative inquiry aspects. For most action researchers of this ilk, Freire (1968/1983) is the guide and model of their efforts.

A Quick Aside on *Emic* Versus *Etic*

Sometimes, an insider perspective is described as an *emic* perspective. In contrast, the view from the outside is called an *etic* perspective. I prefer the terms *insider* and *outsider* because they are more self-evident. *Emic* and *etic* are best reserved for those aspects of cultural study that seek to identify units of culture in practice. It was for this task that Kenneth Pike (one of the world's greatest phonologists) first drew the distinction between emic and etic. He meant for them to be the cultural equivalent of phonemic and phonetic units in language (personal conversion, Pike, 1995). Etic units were meant to be more abstract, and emic units were meant to be more production oriented. Briefly, an outsider approach deals with the ethnographer looking at, and describing field circumstances from the ethnographer's own native cultural perspective. The insider approach requires the ethnographer to try, as best as possible, to capture these circumstances from the perspectives of members of the actual culture under study. Most often, a field study benefits by trying to incorporate and coordinate both perspectives if possible.

MASTERING FIELDWORK SKILLS

Doing fieldwork is a matter of actually going into the field and gaining experience. This is a tactical process. There is no shortcut for getting this sort of experience and there is no real guide for doing it the "right" way. There are, however, a series of questions you can continually ask yourself to monitor your experiences:

- Have I seen or learned anything yet that I did not know coming into this experience? If not, why not?
- What am I trying to find? Am I prepared to abandon my preconceptions if need be? Or am I trying to "stay on task" and discover what I meant to discover all along?
- Am I keeping good and accurate records of my experiences? Do I need to document certain things for my future use?
- Have I left things the way I found them? Or are things better? If they are better, by whose definition of better?
- Do I need to go back? If so, for how long? And why?
- Is it time to start writing yet?

PARTICIPATION AND THE MIRROR, WINDOW, AND LANTERN

As we seek to get a clearer picture of the complex array of possibilities that we find when we look at fieldwork, once again we can benefit by going back to our three technologies of looking from Chapter 1.

Participation and the Mirror.   When we participate in the lives of others, we are inevitably holding those lives before ourselves as a mirror of our own lives. But it can create problems for each type of fieldwork.

When we do case study research, we explore another person's world. It is hard for us not to compare that world to ours, but we must be careful not to pursue this line of thought too far. If we are not careful, we run the risk of slipping away from the case study as an exploration, into the case study as an act of personal affirmation on the part of the researcher. We must allow the case study person's world to be different from our own.

In ethnography, the concept of the mirror is deliberately avoided. The culture must be described on its own terms. Ethnographers tried to minimize this mirroring effect by getting the field researcher lost at the very start in the day-to-day intricacies of the strange new culture.

Compassion plays an unstated but important role in action research. When we see others suffer, we do not fail to understand that we could have been in their circumstances. But we must be thoughtful, alert, and reflective about our compassion in these circumstances. It is not our job to get the folks to "be somebody, like me." We must have the wisdom to let the solutions be *their* answers, not *ours*.

Participation and the Window.   As usual, when we are talking about the window, we are talking about the scientific perspective. Just how scientific is fieldwork? How transparent is the field researcher? How generalizable are the findings from a single case? How is actively changing the circumstances of a setting the test of the validity of a theory? Why is it not contamination instead?

As you can see from these questions, there is a certain tension between fieldwork and science. A scientist often sees fieldwork as a means to an end. If there are real effects there, then we can find them in the field and then refine and test those effects in the laboratory. But field participation is a fundamentally different sort of activity. A field researcher becomes a part of the process in a way that any traditional scientist would avoid. Therefore, we must be extremely careful when we apply scientific thinking, and particularly scientific ideologies, to our field research endeavors.

Participation and the Lantern.   The ideology of the lantern is all about shining light into dark places. Fieldwork is all about getting to those dark places instead of waiting for them to come to you.

When you get to dark places in case study research, you do so by asking questions to which you do not already know the answer, and letting the person lead you someplace where you have never been before. Is it uncomfortable to give up this much control? Of course. Are you running the risk of setting out in a direction that will eventually lead to some dead end? Of course. But you need to take these sorts of chances if you really want to find out anything new.

Ethnography is about nothing if not about going to the strange and dark place. This was relatively easy to accomplish when strange places were the highlands of New Guinea, the frozen Arctic plains, or the depths of the Brazilian rainforest. But strangeness also dwells in the suburb, the shopping mall, the elementary classroom, and at the sign of the double arches—it is just more subtle and harder for us to find.

Action research, if done well, is also about self-discovery. In one way, that is a bit like the mirror approach. But in another way, it is just as much an adventure as, say, a wilderness trek. Helping others move themselves away from false consciousness to awareness is one of the fundamental tasks of action research. Genuine self-awareness and realization is just as elusive as any wild prey, and requires just as much patience and skill and care to stalk.

FINAL THOUGHTS ON PARTICIPATION

As we turn from participation to our last basic skill, it makes sense for us to revisit the roles of observing and conversing in participation.

First of all, good participation depends on good observation and good conversation skills. That is why we addressed those skills first. But though these skills are necessary to do fieldwork, they are not sufficient. There is an element to participation that goes beyond our cumulative abilities to observe and to converse.

In short, participation also depends on placement skills. How do you make yourself and others comfortable with your presence? How do you get them to talk to you in the first place? These are skills of practice. You must allow yourself to develop these skills over time. You will make mistakes. You will endure awkward and uncomfortable moments. You must take heart from the fact that you are learning from your mistakes and that you are constantly improving.

Some people start off being better natural field researchers than others, in that they expend less energy learning, make fewer mistakes, and feel more comfortable with the process. But all of us can learn to be competent field researchers if we give ourselves the time and the chance.

PLANNING YOUR RESEARCH PROPOSAL: FIRST INFORMAL OUTLINE

Carol and Albert have been busy. Carol has found 16 young women who have agreed to consider participating in her study. She has shown them a copy of the consent form that she will use, and they have no problems with any aspects of the study. Furthermore, they are spread across a number of different career areas. All of the young women are working on a college degree; 5 are going full time and 11 are going part time. Their ages range from 19 to 27. Half of them still live at home, and half live with one or more female roommates.

Albert has identified five first-time math anxious students in the middle school grades. Because these students are minors, he has taken special care to contact their parents and teachers. Like Carol, he has shown them preliminary consent forms, and all parties are interested in participating. All five students are above-average students. Three of them are female and two of them are male.

Now the time has come for both of our students to clarify their overall thoughts. To do this, they use the following informal outline. In this outline, they are confined to making one-sentence responses in each area. This is to allow them to develop an initial global picture of their overall thoughts.

Carol

I. *What do I want to do:* Look at the interaction of career and love pressures on the lives of young, single working women

II. *Who are my participants:* Sixteen young, single, poor working women who are going to college and who are looking for a life partner at the same time

III. *What do I already know:* All of the pressures and commitments are difficult to juggle and can lead to stress and feelings of discouragement

IV. *What will I surely find:* I hope to find systematic patterns of interaction among school and love pressures

V. *What is my theoretical perspective:* I want to come up with a sound theory that is derived from my data

VI. *What methods will I most likely be using:* Grounded theory

Albert

I. *What do I want to do:* Look at math anxiety among middle school students who have traditionally been happy and successful math students

II. *Who are my participants:* Five middle school children, three females and two males, who have been successful in math until now

III. *What do I already know:* Math anxiety is stressful and often leads to feelings of despair and helplessness

IV. *What will I surely find:* These students will be struggling with their unaccustomed failures in math

V. *What is my theoretical perspective:* I am not sure yet

VI. *What methods will I most likely be using:* I am not sure yet

SAMPLE INFORMED CONSENT FORM

Researcher Name:
Address:
Phone:

Thank you for agreeing to participate in this study, which will take place from (date) to (date). This form outlines the purposes of the study and provides a description of your involvement and rights as a participant. The purposes of this project are:

(insert purpose here)

The methods to be used to collect information for this study are explained below.

(describe your methods briefly here)

You are encouraged to ask any questions at any time about the nature of the study and the methods that I am using. Your suggestions and concerns are important to me; please contact me at any time at the address/phone number listed above.

I will use the information from this study to write a case report about you (the respondent). This report will be read by you, the course instructor, and optionally, by one other person if you give permission, in order to check on the accuracy of the report. The case report will not be available for any other person to read without your permission.

I guarantee that the following conditions will be met:

1) Your real name will not be used at any point of information collection, nor in the written case report; instead, you and any other person and place names involved in your case will be given pseudonyms that will be used in all verbal and written records and reports.
2) If you grant permission for audiotaping, no audiotapes will be used for any purpose other than to do this study, and will not be played for any reason other than to do this study. At your discretion, these tapes will either be destroyed or returned to you.
3) Your participation in this research is voluntary; you have the right to withdraw at any point of the study, for any reason, and without any prejudice, and the information collected and records and reports written will be turned over to you.
4) You will receive a copy of the report before it is submitted, so that you have the opportunity to suggest changes to the researcher, if necessary.
5) You will receive a copy of the final report that is submitted to the instructor.

Do you grant permission to be quoted directly?   Yes _____   No _____

Do you grant permission to be audiotaped?   Yes _____   No _____

I agree to the terms:

Respondent _____   Date _____

I agree to the terms:

Researcher _____   Date _____

Ourselves

Take a few moments to lay out your own informal outline. Try to keep your responses no longer than one sentence each. Do not be afraid to say that you do not know something yet, like Albert, or that you are still undecided. It is still early in the game, and you are better off thinking in global terms.

CHAPTER 5

Interpreting

Exercise Four—*Just Listen to the Music Play . . .*

This exercise is extremely simple to conduct. The instructor selects music, plays it for the class, and the students listen and comment afterwards. But, as with nearly everything, there is more than meets the eye (or in this case, the ear). We need to talk a bit.

Let me start by talking to the instructors first—

One of the key skills in qualitative research is to learn to be comfortable in a state of ambiguity. There is no better way to create an atmosphere of ambiguous meaning than to bombard students with music they do not currently understand, and then ask them to take a crack at interpreting what they have heard. This is an optional exercise, as it involves a lot of class time. When I do this myself, I devote at least 2 hours to the activity. You can use less time, but I find that spending too little time diminishes the impact of the exercise. It takes time to build up a collective sense of being inundated in unfamiliar meaning. There is also another purpose to this exercise. Auditory information is important for any sort of qualitative research. Any exercise that requires your students to sit and listen carefully for an extended period of time can only be good for them.

Picking the music is a major challenge. There are a number of ways to do this. One is to ask the help of a knowledgeable colleague. Another is to create a task force of students who can help you find and select choices for the entire class. I prefer to select the music myself. Over the years, I have honed my musical selections fairly carefully, so that I have a set of pieces that I know will most likely evoke certain responses from my students. Here are some of the guidelines I have evolved:

- Don't shy away from long pieces. There is a temptation to play only short pieces, or snippets from longer pieces. The trick is not to cover as many types of music as possible; it is instead to present selections with real depth. And most often, musical depth takes some time to unfold. I recommend playing fewer, but longer, pieces.
- Choose pieces which will be unfamiliar to your students. One reason is that you want your students to hear these pieces with fresh ears. The other reason relates to the basic rationale of this exercise. Music offers a wonderful opportunity for those of us teaching an inquiry based on meaning. This is because music is always meaningful, and we all are already aware of this fact. Therefore, if we hear music that we do not understand, we cannot simply dismiss it as meaningless. We have to acknowledge that the music has meaning, but that we do not know what the meaning is. Furthermore, we are not free to simply make the music mean what we want it to mean. We have to respect the fact that the music was written and performed by people who wanted it to mean something, whether or not we ever find out what that meaning is. At best, we can develop our own interpretations . . . and attempt to meet the composer and/or performers' intentions halfway.

- Arrange your choices carefully. Generally, you will have a primary rationale for each piece you select. How do these rationales relate to each other? What is the best order to address each one? Also, how demanding is each piece? I typically find that the more demanding the piece, the more subtle points about meaning I want to make by using it. Therefore, it usually is best to start with the less demanding pieces and work up to the most demanding pieces at the end.

- What should you tell your students to listen for? Any number of things. We tend to think that music is just about feelings—and it can be. But it is always better when we dig deeper. When Tori Amos, in the song "Winter," relates to us an anecdote of a father saying to his young daughter, "When you gonna love you as much as I do?", we are moved by the poignancy of paternal love and awkward adolescence. But what does this say about the larger human condition? If we catch the joke, then Phish's wry command to "wash your feets and drive me to Firenze" in "You Enjoy Myself" makes us smile. Sometimes we can use our prior knowledge of lyrics when we hear certain remarkable excursions into music, like Miles Davis or Chet Baker taking us to the edge in "My Funny Valentine" or John Coltrane taking us beyond in "My Favorite Things." John Adam's "Christian Zeal and Activity" peacefully drifts along seeking a cadence, and then is ruptured by the strange insistence of the sound poem "Sermonette." Students often struggle with the oddness of Schoenberg's "Violin Concerto," and yet they hear order and passion and beauty seemingly move in and out of the piece as they try to resolve their ears to 12-tone structure. The key is to get your students to face the meaning of the music head on, whether they get it or not, wait for the music to unfold, and respect the meaning that is already there and driving the art.

- So you don't know anything about music? Neither do I, really. But I have managed to learn a thing or two from album notes. I am not afraid to turn to music colleagues for answers to my questions. Also, I have found that most students love to listen to music they already know, but they are intimidated by the idea of listening to unfamiliar music. I think this is because they understand that you cannot just bluff an understanding of a musical piece. So don't be afraid to turn to them and tell them that you don't completely understand some of the pieces either. At some point in time they need to learn that every interpretation is provisional and incomplete. Why not help model that realization for them?

- Help students before you move on to another piece. Start off by asking for their interpretations. More often than not, they will be hesitant to offer any. This is because they do not want to be wrong. You need to emphasize that the point of this exercise is not to get the right answer, but to use interpretation strategies in a public way, and then modify those interpretations based on further input. So do not be shy about giving them further input after they have struggled for awhile. Let me clarify this point with an example. One piece I like to use with students was performed by the Kronos Quartet and written by Ishvan Marta, a contemporary Hungarian composer. It is called "Doom: A Sigh" and consists of a string-quartet piece performed over tape recordings of old women singing in archaic Hungarian in a remote Rumanian village. Because It is highly unlikely that anyone in your class will be able to understand archaic Hungarian, there is a good chance that the meaning of the words of the songs will not be understood. So, when they have finished talking and interpreting based solely on what they have heard and what they already know in their lives, I read aloud from the liner notes on the CD, where Marta talks about his project. This always makes the exercise more meaningful. Students will venture to guess what those songs might be about, and will offer evidence for their interpretations, but it is always good to nail down any actual facts before the collective interpretative process moves along to the next musical piece.

Now it is time to talk directly to students—

What if your instructor does not want to do this exercise in class, but you find it intriguing and you would like to pursue it? There are a number of ways that you can proceed:

- Find out if there are other interested students, and set up a time and place to do this on your own. Invite each person to bring one or two really obscure pieces, and then select them at random.
- If you are alone in your interest, or it is logistically impossible to get together with other students, be resourceful. Talk to friends and family about their tastes in music. Can they recommend unusual choices? Will they play them for you? What about the local library? Many libraries have music collections, and they often contain selections that are unusual or outside the comfortable mainstream of musical tastes.

In summary, it is hard to think of a better example of the interdependent interplay of consciousness and sensation than the experience of listening to and appreciating music. In short, listening to music is a perfect example of finding meaning "in the wild."

REFLECTING ON INTERPRETATION

Of all the exercises I do with my students, the music exercise is the one that makes them the most uncomfortable. After each selection, I ask them to tell me about the piece. Inevitably, I meet with an uneasy silence. People are literally afraid to speak. It takes us forever to finally relax and allow ourselves to say what we think about the pieces we have heard.

Why do people fear interpretation? Are they concerned that they will look foolish if they do not come up with the perfect interpretation? Are they afraid that they will miss something important? Do they feel that the task of interpretation is a highly specialized skill that is beyond their abilities?

It is hard to blame people for having these feelings about interpretation. We have painted a picture of interpretation in research that resonates with all of the stereotypes, just listed, and then some. We need to stop and take a simpler view of the matter, so that we do not get overwhelmed or burdened by these kinds of stereotypes.

Remember our earlier definition of qualitative research as the systematic empirical inquiry into meaning. Interpretation is that part of the process where we continue examining the meanings that we feel we already have, while we think about other meanings that we might seek. Interpretation is not the whole of qualitative research, but there can be no qualitative research without it.

The key to interpretation, simple as it may be, is the art of description. So let us start there.

MASTERING DESCRIPTION AND THICK DESCRIPTION

The most basic form of interpretation is description. At first, this sounds like a contradiction. Isn't description the act of rendering an account of something without interpreting it? That is, when we describe, aren't we just describing? Isn't interpreting something else, something beyond mere description?

First of all, there is no such thing as "mere description." Every descriptive act involves choice, and that choice is a form of interpretation. You might mention, for example, that the first five people to enter a room were females. Why did you choose this framework for description? Why is gender an important aspect of this descriptive setting? And, for that matter, how can you really be sure that the people you have identified as female are really and truly female? Aren't you making some sort of interpretation when you assign labels?

It is very easy to be defensive in light of these, and other, concerns. But that is not the issue at hand. Interpretation always involves taking some form of chance, and taking the risk that your interpretation might not be accurate or even correct. You do not guard against these circumstances by making timid descriptions. Instead, you make sure your interpretations are as "up front" as possible. If your interpretation ends up being incorrect, it is best for it to be incorrect in a public and correctable way. In many ways, it is better to be clear and wrong than muddled and correct.

The most powerful, and most easily misunderstood, form of description in qualitative research is the category that Geertz (1973) first labeled as *thick description.* Good interpretation in qualitative research more often than not is grounded in, and flows from, thick description. Therefore, it is important that we understand this concept thoroughly.

Geertz acknowledged that he borrowed the notion of thick description from the British philosopher Gilbert Ryle. Ryle was interested in being able to describe any complex phenomenon on its own terms. Upon inspection and reflection, Ryle discovered, among other things, that seemingly simple and innocent terms often served as "code" or "shorthand" for complex social and cultural settings and activities.

The Wink

Ryle's famous example of thick description was that of the "wink." Ryle pointed out that a wink could be described at many levels, and that each description detailed some level of interpretation. At the most basic physical level, a wink involved the opening and closing of the eye for a certain length of time, using a certain series of muscles. This basic process could be studied in great detail, with split-second timing of the opening and closing and pinpoint precision in terms of the number and sequence of muscles used to perform the act.

However, said Ryle, none of this precise description actually describes a wink. Though you cannot have a wink without eyelids and muscles and timed sequences, these pieces do not describe the wink proper. A wink, properly understood, is a cultural signal. As a cultural signal, it is remarkably subtle and precise. The turn of the head, the angle of the head, and the length of the wink all play key roles in determining precisely what this act was intended to mean.

Also at play is the interpretative skill of the receiver of the wink. A wink does not truly end until it has an interpretative impact on the person who is the target of the wink. For Ryle, then, a thick description is an interpretative process that seeks to understand a phenomenon in its fullest meaningful context.

Geertz was quick to understand that all description in social science research is thick description, to some degree. Since Geertz's declaration, it has become increasingly popular to think about and practice thick description in qualitative research. However, there are a number of pitfalls to avoid. Perhaps these are best understood by saying what thick description is *not.*

What Thick Description Is Not

First of all, thick description is not voluminous description. This is the most common misunderstanding that beginners hold. They feel that if they pile descriptive detail upon descriptive detail, then they have captured the essence of the thing described. What is missing is the reason behind each and every detail. Some details are crucial, and others just happen to be there.

Think back to the wink example. The precise length of time that a person holds the "squeeze" of the shut eye before finishing the wink conveys important information. A quick squeeze most likely signals a wink that was meant to be subtle and not perceived by anyone other than the intended target. A long squeeze is an indicator of an exaggerated wink, perhaps one that is not to be taken seriously. So, it is important to record this precise and specific piece of information.

However, suppose that we report that the person winking has blue eyes. Or that the person has thick eyelashes. Or that the person is wearing bifocals. These details are not just useless; they get in the way of genuinely important details. We have to wade through observations like these to get to the observations that really matter. Also, they create a sense of anxiety on the part of the reader and perhaps even the researcher. If the researcher has bothered to note and describe these factors, doesn't that mere fact make them important? The answer is, of course, no. But the presence of such carefully detailed information is hard to ignore. We assume that it must mean something.

Second of all, thick description is not idiosyncratic description. That is, a thick description is not some personal or private look at the world that is being shared with the rest of us. There must be some anchor to the rest of humanity as a whole in order for the description to make sense. Otherwise, it is nothing more than propaganda.

Let us look at an extreme and unpleasant example. Suppose that I am a racial bigot, and that I am observing a cultural ritual performed by members of the race that I despise. My description will most likely be "thick" with overt and covert racial slurs. I am using the process of description to attempt to sway others to come over to my way of thinking and looking at the world. The more I am skilled at bigotry, the more covert and subtle my cues, and the harder they are to ferret out to refute.

This sort of programmatic observation is easy to see in examples dealing with issues we disagree with, but often much harder to see when the observer is making programmatic descriptions from more popular stances. In this latter case, both the observer and the reader must be aware of these programmatic agendas. We are not claiming that an observer should not and cannot take a moral stance, only that the moral stance be clearly identified such that observers and describers at least strive to find some degree of universality in their observations and descriptions. If something cannot be seen at all outside the programmatic frame of reference, how can we be sure that it is not an artifact of that frame of reference?

One final point on the idiosyncratic problem is needed. Some describers are just more subtle and more skilled than others are. Are their descriptions more "thick," or are they merely programmatic? The answer is simple. The farther we can wander from their original frame of reference, and still garner insight, the more skilled and effective they were.

Again, let us turn to a sublime and ridiculous example. First, the sublime side. I do not have to be a Buddhist to appreciate at least some of the wisdom of Buddha. The same can be said about Mohammed, Jesus, and Moses, just to name a few.

Now, let's get a bit ridiculous. Suppose I am a member of the Church of Jerry Garcia (the late and much lamented lead guitarist and vocalist for the defunct 1960s rock band The Grateful Dead). I point to his guitar solo on "Sugar Magnolia" on 14 October 1983 (on *Dick's Picks Vol. (6)*, or his vocal rendition of "Friend of the Devil" on 26 December 1979 (on *Dick's Picks Vol. 5*), and claim that these are messages of enlightenment and redemption for those few fortunate souls who can hear what is "really" going on there.

In this case, I am much more likely to be in the grip of a delusion. I am making the world fit to Jerry Garcia, rather than the other way around. In this particular case, there were actual tragic overtones. Because of this misguided fanaticism on the part of some of his fans, who hung on his every word, poor Garcia was not able to say anything in public without it being examined microscopically for cosmic meaning by these fans. And so, for the last 10 or so years of his life, he was virtually silenced by this sort of adulation and praise. How can this be anything but "thick description" gone totally haywire?

Finally, thick description is not artistic description. Thick description is not about creating art. It is about describing what is present, on its own terms and at its own level. Very often, artistic description seeks to create tension between levels of description. An artistic description of the wink might move between the wink as a physiological muscle response and the wink as a cultural signal, creating dissonance in understanding.

A genuine thick description always strives to be clear. This is not to say that artistic description can never be clear. Artistic description is in fact as clear as it can be, given the goals of the artist. But the artist is prepared to use ambiguity as a necessary tool for artistic insight. Thick description seeks to avoid ambiguity for its own sake. If there is ambiguity inherent in the situation, it is described and clearly marked as such. Although the richness of thick description might mimic certain types of artistic descriptions, the intent is quite different. In all cases, thick description strives to make meaning clear.

One last point—is thick description more common in qualitative science or in qualitative inquiry? The flippant answer is "yes." Description in general, and thick description in particular, is an interpretive process found in all forms of qualitative research. That is why we started with a careful look at its meaning and how it is done. Careful and attentive use of thick description is important for all qualitative researchers. It is the first step in the process of making meaning clear.

SUBJECTIVITY AND OBJECTIVITY

Description, particularly thick description, is a necessary part of the interpretive process in qualitative research. But there is another key issue regarding interpretation that needs to be addressed before we can talk about approaches and techniques for interpretation: To what extent do we feel that interpretation is a subjective process, and to what extent is it objective (Ratner, 2002)?

Our stance as qualitative researchers on the nature of subjectivity and objectivity in interpretation affects not only how we go about doing interpretations, but also our decisions of what kinds of interpretations we might accept or reject. Because these concepts are not well understood by many qualitative researchers, we need to examine some basic definitional and historical issues.

A Brief Summary of Subjectivity and Objectivity

Originally, subjectivity and objectivity were fairly technical and limited concepts. The best way to understand their original use is to think of an ordinary simple sentence. For example, consider the following basic sentence: *Lassie barked.* We will assume that the "Lassie" in this sentence is the legendary collie from television and the movies.

As we all learned back in elementary school, this little sentence consists of a *subject* and a *predicate*. The subject, in this case, is Lassie. The predicate is the word *barked*. As you may remember, the predicate describes some action and condition that can be applied to the subject. In this case, we predicate the fact that our subject, the famed collie, engaged in the act of barking.

Whenever we have a subject, we can predicate certain things to that subject. In this case, we say that Lassie is capable of barking. But Lassie is not the only thing that can bark. Most other dogs bark. Wild dogs, jackals, hyenas, and even grouchy bosses can bark. This is a key point for many predicates—not only can predicates apply to the given subject at hand, but also to many other subjects as well. They are not linked to any single given thing, but can be applied to many other things as well.

There is another key aspect to this sort of predication. We can predicate the fact that Lassie barks based on our prior knowledge that Lassie is a dog. This is because we know that dogs bark. This sort of predicate, then, is an example of what we might call an *objective* predicate. We expect Lassie to bark not because she is Lassie, but because she is a dog, and dogs bark.

This aspect of objective predication is the basis of our current understanding and use of the concept of objectivity. That is, when we are being "objective" we are looking for those properties that go with the bigger category and not the individual.

Now, let us modify our original sentence to: *Brave Lassie barked.* We have added another predicate—the term *brave*. Like the objective predicate, this predicate can also be applied to a variety of phenomena. We can have brave dogs, brave women, brave soldiers, and so on. But these predicates cannot be applied across an entire class. That is, not all dogs are brave. It is not a general property of dogs, women, soldiers, or the like. We must decide on a case-by-case basis whether or not a given dog, woman, soldier, or whatever is brave. Therefore, this sort of property is predicated at the subject level, and so becomes a *subjective* predication.

When we want to look at a subject as a member of a larger class, then we pay attention to objective predications. When we want to understand a given subject on its own terms and get to its essence, then we pay attention to subjective predications. Objective predications tend to be more categorical, and subjective predications tend to be more biographical.

Historical Changes in Subjectivity and Objectivity

If we had stayed within this fairly technical domain, all would have been well and good. However, the notions of objectivity and subjectivity began to expand with the growth and development of empirical inquiry. First of all, Descartes (1596–1650) split apart the objective and subjective realms. For Descartes, the objective realm became anything that could be physically observed or else inferred from such physical observation. The subjective realm became the mental, private, and idiosyncratic domain of the individual thinker.

It was not long, then, before science began to champion the objective cause. After all, it is only the observable and the inferable that can serve as the "raw data" of science. The subjective, as the mental and the idiosyncratic, were beyond the reach and frankly the interest of science. In fact, subjective phenomena became one of the prime candidates as a source of potential error in the conduct of science. By the time we reach Comte and positivism in the late

19th century, we see that subjectivity is nearly banished from all forms of empirical research in Western thought.

Rethinking Subjectivity in Qualitative Research

Issues associated with subjectivity have also been associated with the search for meaning. Therefore, subjectivity plays a key role in qualitative research (Morgan & Drury, 2003). However, if we continue to think of subjectivity in the ways described earlier, then qualitative research will be at a permanent disadvantage. So we need to reclaim important aspects of subjectivity as part of the pursuit of meaning.

The first step is to free our notion of meaning itself. As discussed in Chapter 1, meaning is not the personal and private plaything of individual meaning makers. It is not idiosyncratic and unsystematic. Like any other part of the empirical world, meaning plays a systematic and public role. More often than not, we discern meaning rather than just make it up.

Traditional science freed meaning from the grip of subjectivity (as science understood that concept) by making sure that meaning was always linked and derived from things that are true. The motto of meaning in traditional science might be this: "First I find out what is true, and now I know what to believe."

Charles Peirce, the brilliant 19th-century logician and philosopher of science, turned that idea on its ear. He said, "I cannot know anything that I do not first believe." For Peirce, the act of believing is our fundamental way of operating in the empirical world. We get our beliefs from a variety of sources—our personal experiences, our friends and family, our teachers, and the like. These beliefs are subjective not only because we hold them personally but also because they help shape who we are. We operate confidently in the world as if those beliefs were perfectly true. However, if our beliefs are not true, then sooner or later they will betray us in the world of experience. At that point, we must examine and test our beliefs. Once we reconcile our beliefs, we will have a richer and truer picture of the world.

Peirce would grant that our beliefs might be subjective, but our operations in the world certainly are not. Therefore, our subjective beliefs play a crucial role in how we conduct ourselves, and this conduct is living proof that our subjective beliefs are not totally private or idiosyncratic. Instead, our subjective beliefs are the very source of our personal and individual actions as researchers. If we return to the notion of subjective that emphasizes those things that are predicted to us as active subjects or agents in the world, who engage in correctable activities based on those beliefs, then we can acknowledge that subjectivity can be both personal and systematic. This allows us the room we need to conduct systematic empirical inquiry into meaning by acting as believing persons.

Self and Other

One way that subjectivity plays a role in qualitative research is by allowing for a focus on the nature of the *Self* (Gonzalez, 2001). As we will see when we look at critical models of interpretation, issues of the Self also involve issues of the *Other*. That is, our identities are often intertwined with notions of race, ethnicity, gender, social class, and other dimensions used to sort humans within the complex fabric of culture.

Addressing the differences and tensions between Self and Other can be tackled with straightforward ethnographic investigation. As we will see, it is also often the focus of various critical approaches, from feminism to critical race theory to postcolonial research. This tension can also be addressed artistically (Rolling, 2004) and performatively (Pedelty, 2001). Performative and scientific dimensions can also be brought together in an exploration of these dynamics by the use of ethnodrama (Barone, 2002).

Intersubjectivity

Qualitative research has traditionally made another move in relation to subjectivity and method. Remember that many of our beliefs are not totally personal and private. They are beliefs that we have gained from others, or that we share with others. Therefore, it is important to note that our culture, from the level of our families to such large international modes of communication and interchange as popular culture, television, and the Internet, help shape our views of our world. Furthermore, this shaping is grounded in constant interaction and communication.

This sense of a shared and interactive process of beliefs and meanings about our world is called *intersubjectivity*. Many phenomenological and hermeneutic theories emphasize intersubjective dynamics. Intersubjectivity is a key concept in a number of other approaches and methods related to qualitative research, including symbolic interactionism (Crotty, 1998) and social constructivism. We will examine many of these theoretical and methodological systems later in this chapter, and in other chapters as well.

The Nagging Issue of Multiple Realities

Finally, we end this excursion into subjectivity and objectivity by taking a look at one of the most controversial areas in qualitative research. The quarrel between looking at things objectively or subjectively impacts contemporary research theories and practices in many deep ways. Nowhere is this truer than in the task of trying to get a handle on the concept of reality as it applies to qualitative research.

First of all, there is the temptation to make the "building block" assumption. Here, we assume that the human "lifeworld" is made up, or *concatenated* of complicated combinations of simple factors. Our job is to find the simple building blocks. Some of the more traditionally oriented branches of qualitative science tend to follow this path. These efforts are all about finding the simple keys in nature that determine our complex actions and cultures. Furthermore, these simple keys operate on the basis of principles that are independent of us, and therefore beyond our control.

There are two basic problems with adopting this approach as a guiding vision for all of qualitative research. First of all, actions like the search for the elementary building blocks of culture lead researchers away from an appreciation of the complexity of culture on its own terms. Second, by assuming that we are determined by these sorts of independent forces, we are taking away the critical examination of our ways of understanding the world as a key goal for qualitative research. In short, this vision is too impoverished to capture the inherent richness of the qualitative approach.

But we cannot allow ourselves the compensatory temptation of assuming that the human lifeworld is therefore completely artificial and constructed. This is to hold the conceptual error that because reality is not created from simple pieces, reality is therefore not natural. It is true that we can create meaningful constructs within culture, but ultimately those constructs have to be grounded in aspects independent of our designations. That is, even the most fanciful creation of meaning within a culture has to obey certain rules of reality.

For instance, some cultures celebrate gender-bending costumes and activities during Carnival, but those actions are symbolic and cultural rather than "natural." That is, the celebrants may don gear of the other sex, and pantomime stereotypical behaviors of the other sex, but they do not shift physiologically from male to female and vice versa at will. They simply cannot do so within the rules of reality. At best, they can approximate such changes surgically, but they will never achieve the ease of physical gender shifting of, say, an earthworm.

Yet we, as human beings, perform a vast and fascinating repertoire of actions in the presence of "reality" restraints, and this allows us to create great patterns of variations within such restraints. But these restraints do not vanish, and the basic rules of reality do not change when cultural rules change.

This discussion of reality seems to be at odds with much that has been written about the nature of reality in qualitative research. This other position seems to be best reflected in a second traditional assumption, although it comes from a different tradition than the first. We will look at that assumption next.

Many qualitative researchers seem to make what we might call the "personal" assumption about reality. With this assumption, there is the notion that reality is not outside of us. It *is* us. That is, reality is what we, individually or collectively, say it is. Reality is therefore a matter of discussion, negotiation, and convention.

One of the most common positions that arises in certain branches of qualitative inquiry is derived from this assumption. It is the notion that there are many realities, and that each of us lives in our own reality. Taken at face value, this is nothing more than solipsism, and really does not represent anything more than trying to make the results of our inquiry align with the dictates of our will.

But if the notion of multiple realities is so theoretically sterile, why is it such a popular idea? There are a number of reasons.

Often when someone is talking about "multiple realities," what he or she is really talking about is multiple interpretations of reality. But there is a vast difference between interpreting reality and creating reality. We simply do not have the kind of omnipotent power we would need to truly create a reality. But we can, and do, *constitute* important, lasting, and broadly social patterns of interpretations that are so real to us that they might as well be part of reality proper. Identifying and sorting out these sorts of constitutions is an important part of what qualitative research does.

In short, we have to be aware of a false dichotomy around the nature of reality that seems to be a part of our superficial understanding. We seem to think that we either have to sit back and allow all our actions and institutions to be determined by the forces of some independent reality, or else that reality is whatever we want to make it to be. Neither choice seems to be correct.

First of all, we are not independent of reality. We are part of it, and as part of it, we contribute to its changing nature. Therefore, because we do play a role as creatures who are part of reality, we cannot be totally determined by external forces. But our ability to make an impact in guiding the changing nature of reality seems to depend on what we want to change. The more that something is constituted by its physical or noncultural nature, the harder it is for us to change.

For instance, we can take a body of land and designate it as a national park, or the continent of Asia, or the future site of our new vegetable garden; then we have changed the way that we might speak about and interact with these various parcels of land. But we have not changed the forests in the new park from pine to maple, nor have we gotten rid of the Ural Mountains just because we would rather have them in Africa, nor have we made our patch of ground less acidic by designating it as a garden plot.

There are other aspects of reality that are much more amenable to my efforts to change them. Suppose I want my neighborhood to be cleaner. One way that this can happen is for me to go out and pick up trash every day. I cannot control the source of the trash, but I can help affect its lingering presence. Here I can change the nature of my setting quite a bit.

One way to look at this issue is to step back and make a more abstract pronouncement. Reality is the sum of all that is. Because it is the sum of all that is, we are a part of it. Because we are a part of it, we can impart change within it. This is called the principle of recursion, or feedback. Some aspects of reality are quite resistant to our feedback, and so recursion is negligible. Here, we are fairly safe in saying that these particular aspects, though not actually independent of us, might as well be. We are not going to have any real impact on them. Therefore, they are for all intents and purposes independent of us, and any changes they impart on us will look deterministic. On the other hand, there are other aspects of reality that are quite sensitive to our feedback, and so any actions we do along these lines seem to make immediate and real changes. In these cases, our feedback is so powerful it is as if we were actually making the reality that we are dealing with.

Most of the time in qualitative research, we are dealing with areas where recursion and feedback is real, but moderate. The best example of such a state of affairs is a familiar cultural setting.

Therefore, let us look at an example of the recursive nature of reality in cultural settings. Currently, I am writing these words as a resident of the state of Pennsylvania. Until recently, though, I was a resident of the state of Illinois. "Pennsylvania" and "Illinois" are in one sense merely cultural creations. But these cultural creations have taken on an extended and rich constituted existence. I had to exchange my Illinois driver's license for a Pennsylvania driver's license. Some acts are legal in Pennsylvania and illegal in Illinois, and vice versa. For these and many more reasons, I have to take seriously the fact that I now live in Pennsylvania. In order to participate in the process of "Pennsylvania" I had to sign on to accept its rules. But Pennsylvania has changed because of the fact that I have moved here. Perhaps in this case the changes are fairly trivial, but they need not be. Suppose I wanted to run for the Senate from Pennsylvania. Now I can do so. And if I win, I can have a genuine impact on the rules of the state.

In summary, because qualitative research does not tend to address issues like the role of physical laws of nature, the deterministic perspective on reality is of limited use at best. When we zero in on a particular individual, and the profound impact that person does or could have in that setting, then we might talk about a "constructed" or "multiple" reality domain to indicate that we are in a high-feedback and high-recursive territory. But we have to be extremely careful not to extend the bounds of that territory beyond the limits of influence of the individual. Most of the time, we are on much safer ground by assuming that reality changes us and that we change reality, and that there is some kind of balance or equilibrium in place. Locating the balance point of that equilibrium nearer or further from us gives us a sense of how much potential impact or control we might have. If I am drawing a personal portrait of a remarkable individual, then I can talk about how he or she has molded reality in some fashion. If I am talking about trading in my driver's license, then my role is far more humble but potentially no less interesting to study.

CREATING A CONTINUUM FOR INTERPRETATION

The task of any and every type of interpretation is to make meaning clear. How do we proceed with this larger and more comprehensive task of making meaning clear? As we might suspect, there are a number of ways to do this. But we cannot proceed without some framework for dealing with types and forms of interpretation.

Garrick (1999) suggests a useful framework to look at all forms of interpretation in qualitative research. We can think of description as the starting point of all interpretive actions. As such, we can also think of description as being the end point of a continuum of interpretation in qualitative research.

As we move away from description toward the other end of the continuum, we come upon a series of interpretive goals. These goals come with their own sets of rules and procedures. In addition, these goals also start out being more grounded in a qualitative science worldview and then move into areas more relevant to those who practice qualitative inquiry.

However, it is important for us to realize that there is no hard and fast line of demarcation between forms of interpretation used by qualitative science or qualitative inquiry. Furthermore, it is not unusual to find examples of both qualitative science and qualitative inquiry research that cut across these dimensions of interpretation. In general, though, the continuum is a rough guide to some of the differences in interpretive goals and practices between these two dimensions of qualitative research.

In order, these goals are based on *prediction, understanding, critical awareness,* and *postmodern awareness* (roughly following Garrick, 1999, p. 154). We will examine each of these interpretive dimensions in turn.

PREDICTION

Prediction has long been the goal of science in general, so it is no surprise to find prediction being an important interpretive goal of qualitative science. The primary tool for prediction is a sound theory. That is, if we have a sound theory, then we have the basis for making predictions. Therefore, theory building is our first step in looking at interpretive systems dealing primarily with prediction.

Qualitative research in general, and qualitative science in particular, takes a much different approach to theory and theory building than quantitative research. The goals of prediction and theory building are based on a framework of interpretation that emphasizes settings and situations where you, the researcher, can go in with as few preconceptions and presuppositions as possible. The idea is to build a theoretical understanding starting with descriptions and then moving into concepts based on our understandings of those descriptions. All of this eventually comes together to form theory. As we have mentioned, Grounded Theory is the epitome of this process (Glaser, 2003; Glaser & Strauss, 1967; Strauss & Corbin, 1998).

Grounded Theory works best for those situations in which your understanding can truly grow from the ground up. Sometimes, this is because you know next to nothing about what you are about to study. Sometimes, it is because you truly have the ability to set aside what you already know, and can allow the situation to "speak" to you as if you had never been in a situation like that before, nor had heard a message like that. If you can actually do this, then you can have a great future ahead of you as a Ground Theorist. Many researchers find the task to be a formidable challenge, however, and one that requires years of effort to refine.

Closely related to the notion of theory building is the concept of interpretive analysis. Thorne, Kirkham, and O'Flynn-Magee (2004) look at interpretive analysis in clinical and practical settings as a form inductive analysis. In this fashion, researchers can make applied clinical predictions based upon these analyses.

More details on Grounded Theory and other qualitative science methods based on prediction and theory building are found in Chapter 7.

UNDERSTANDING

Many qualitative researchers feel that understanding is one of the primary goals of any form of qualitative research (Schwandt, 1999). For this reason, we find a variety of ideas about understanding in the field, and a variety of interpretive techniques targeted toward the goal of understanding.

Qualitative Science and Understanding

We will first turn to qualitative science to see how it envisions understanding. The concept of understanding in qualitative science is similar to the concept of understanding in science in general.

For science, all knowledge is based in the empirical world. Through our senses and our ability to abstract and refine sensory data, we come up with a set of truths. These truths are the bedrock of our knowledge. At the same time, these truths are the bedrock of our understanding of the world. In science, knowing takes precedence over understanding. Finding truth is the aim and goal of science. We then reason about true things to see if we can understand how they might fit together. This is the essence of theory.

In qualitative science, as in science in general, theories are provisional systems of understanding. Theories are provisional because new knowledge and new truths could invalidate a theory at any time. Our confidence in our theories is grounded in how useful they are. Do they explain things simply? Do they allow us to control certain empirical processes? Do they show us where to look for new knowledge? Do they allow us to make predictions? In short, the pursuit of understanding and the pursuit of theory are most often equivalent practices in qualitative science.

Phenomenology and Understanding

Scientific understanding has always been important in empirical inquiry, but it is not the only kind of understanding. During the rise of science in the late-19th and early-20th centuries, Husserl felt that there were other types of knowledge that were geared toward human experience. Following the lead of psychologists like Brentano, Husserl reminded us that experience was always an experience of something. For instance, people were not afraid—they were afraid of something.

In order to understand these sorts of experiences, Husserl invented the form of inquiry we know as *phenomenology*. Phenomenology was an empirical form of inquiry; it was grounded in experiences. But it did not try to reduce these experiences to states that could be studied by such sciences as physics, chemistry, or biology. Instead, Husserl developed procedures for us to "bracket" or set aside our impressions of our experiences, and focus instead on the process of experiencing per se.

The phenomenological process always begins, in some fashion, with the individual person and that person's awareness of the world. When we do a phenomenological study, we attempt to "get inside" the meanings and the world of that person. If this personal and individual focus is both fruitful and appropriate for your research purposes, the phenomenological approach can yield rich and insightful patterns of interpretation for you.

More details on phenomenological processes, and details of specific current phenomenological research methods, are found in Chapter 7.

Hermeneutics and Understanding

Traditional phenomenologists believe that meaning is a property of the world, and that many meanings can be discovered like any other phenomena. Later thinkers, starting with Heidegger, questioned the idea that meaning can ever be independent of the interpreter (Heidegger, 1927). Meaning, for those thinkers, occurs as we try to make sense of a world that comes with no rules or instruction manuals. The world is less like a source of meaning, and more like a text to be read. Drawing upon notions of reading and interpretation, this branch of phenomenological research became known as *Hermeneutics.*

Hermeneutics in particular, and Heidegger's ideas in general, have had a profound impact on qualitative research. For instance, such areas as social interactionism, ethnomethodology, and many if not most postmodern methods of qualitative research owe a debt to the hermeneutics of Heidegger. His ideas of "throwness" and "being in the world" led to many of the relativistic and interpretivist models and approaches in qualitative research. Finally, Heidegger's thought helped ground the existential movement, which was a precursor to many of today's explorative approaches to meaning.

More details on hermeneutic processes, and details of specific current hermeneutic research methods, are found in Chapter 7.

CRITICAL AWARENESS

In addition to seeking understanding, a number of qualitative approaches are designed to go beyond understanding per se to seek *critical* awareness. Critical awareness aims not only to show us some of the things that are going on, but also to show us ways to make things better.

Ideology and Critical Theory

Critical theory is not just about finding and fixing complex problems. It also has a comprehensive theoretical component (see Kemnis & McTaggart, 2000; McTaggart, 1991). One of the most important influences in critical theory and its use in the social sciences can be found in the work of Habermas (1971). Geuss (1981) summarizes Habermas's theory as it relates explicitly to social science research.

The most important notion for a critical theorist is the concept of ideology. An ideology is an organized set of beliefs that guides social action. More often than not, ideologies are implicit rather than explicit. That is, people are more likely to "live out" their ideologies than they are likely to be able to express or describe them.

All of us have ideologies, and according to Habermas, ideologies per se are neutral. The real culprits are false ideologies. A false ideology is some belief about the world that is simply not true. False ideologies lead to false consciousness. And when a person or a group suffers from false consciousness, then they cannot see what is really true. Often, they are unaware of the impact of their beliefs on others. And, more often than not, their false understanding of the situation leads them to think and act in ways that are against their own self-interests.

It is the job of critical theory to first help those identified as suffering from false consciousness to understand what is really going on, and then to work with these people to consider what action they should take. If the persons involved seek to change things, then the action researcher should serve as a resource for such change.

Consider the following example of false consciousness in action. Suppose you have a financially distressed person who believes the only way that he can get any extra income in his life is to win the lottery. He is not greedy, and so he only plays the "daily three" game. In the typical daily three game, he bets one dollar on a single number between 1 and 999. If he wins, he claims a prize of $500. He plays each and every day, hoping to win that single large jackpot.

What our poor gambler does not realize is that his belief in the lottery is working against his own best interests. Look at the payoff structure. He makes a daily bet at 1000:1 odds. If he wins, the lottery pays off at 500:1 odds. In short, he stands to win at half the rate that he bets. He fails to realize that he is being "cheated" by the lottery each time he lays down a dollar and picks a number to bet. Over the long run, he and his betting comrades will win back only half of what they have bet, with the lottery keeping the rest. Most likely, he personally will not win anything at all.

In the case of the daily gambler, a bit of knowledge about probability is needed in order to raise his awareness of what is really going on. Once his awareness has been raised, and he understands what is happening, what should an action researcher do? It all depends on what the gambler thinks, once he knows the score.

If he has been trying to win big, then he has only been deluding himself. He may of course stop, but what else should he do? Should he warn others who may be thinking along the same lines? Should he lead a protest action against the lottery, to make them stop paying such low odds? Should he seek to get some of his past wagers returned to him?

Once you, as critical theorist, have intervened in a situation like this, then you are obligated to see it through. You must help the people involved make the best choices they can. It is also important that these choices be theirs. Your place is not to tell them what to do. You are there to help them clarify their choices, to support their decisions if possible, and to help them secure the resources they need to pursue their desired outcomes. Of course, if you feel that the people involved are making wrong choices, you do not have to support those choices. But you must make it clear to everyone involved why you feel these choices are wrong.

On the other hand, suppose our gambler is not poor at all but looks at the whole situation as a form of entertainment, with the occasional win as a windfall to perk up the process. In this case, he has a more realistic understanding of what he has been doing. Even if you might not approve of gambling, or even if you feel that he is still being foolish, your involvement is over. The gambler has made a realistic choice and understands the consequences. He is aware that his odds are too low, but his gambling is not really about winning. He enjoys the act for its own sake. If he is not hurting anyone else, then he is free to pursue this hobby. In other words, sometimes no action is the best action for a researcher to pursue.

The Scope of Critical Theory

Ideologies are powerful, and so any theory that deals with ideology has to be able to address a wide and comprehensive range of applications. Geuss (1981) points out that there are few comprehensive critical theories that can be used to guide social science research. Marxism, for example, is cited as a form of consciousness-raising in terms of the role of economics in power struggles between classes and also in the way that economic issues affect the operation of everyday life in capitalist cultures. In addition, the Freudian position that the unconscious mind plays a pervasive role in the lives of individuals and in the operation of society as a whole is yet another historical example of a comprehensive critical theory.

Though Marxism has continued to play a theoretical role in critical theory, particularly in more radical liberation models (some of the models to be addressed later on in this chapter, for example, are explicitly Marxist in nature), Freud's influence has been on the wane. Instead, we see the emergence of a powerful new form of comprehensive critical theory—namely, feminist thought.

The Nature of Feminist Critical Theory

One of the clearest uses of critical theory in the social sciences can be seen in the growing awareness and emphasis on feminist ideology as a major form of critical theory. The essence of feminism as a critical theory is simple: Feminism represents a form of consciousness-raising not only for society in general, but for social science research in particular. We need not model traditional male values or perspectives when we do our research, so long as we are aware of how we are explicitly incorporating feminist values and perspectives. This alters the language we use, the criteria we use to evaluate the quality of research, our choices of what to study, and how we go about seeking to bring about positive change.

Gilligan's (1982/1993) study of moral judgment among women is considered by many to be the groundbreaking feminist work in social science research. A former student of Kohlberg's, Gilligan challenged Kohlberg's model of moral development. Kohlberg, she claimed, put too much emphasis on male values and male perspectives. Gilligan set out to collect a diverse body of moral judgements by women, finding in these judgements a strong emphasis on consensus, sharing, and harmony.

Lather (1991) is another strong voice for the feminist perspective in the social sciences. In particular, Lather seeks to blend feminist and postmodern perspectives in an insightful and seamless look at both cultural and political issues. Lather is also a strong advocate of gender issues as part of the overall qualitative research agenda.

There is certainly no shortage of good work for students to use as models of feminist inquiry in the social sciences. Horney (1967) and Mead (1949) are important "ancestors" for any feminist social science researcher to explore. hooks (1984) combines racial and gender perspectives in a provocative and skilled fashion. Along more traditional lines, Maher and Tetreault (1993) are representative of a feminist approach to ethnography within an educational setting. Madriz (2000) discusses how feminist research uses and transforms focus group methods.

The list of feminist researchers is impressive and continues to grow each day. As Denzin (1997) and Crotty (1998), both of whom are male, note, feminist perspectives are a central component of contemporary qualitative research.

Critical Race Theory and Postcolonial Thinking

Other forms of critical theory have arisen to address issues of race and oppression. Critical Race Theory, or CRT, first arose in the legal profession (Parker & Lynn, 2002). It first attempted to show that legal decisions often mask racist goals, and that advancement by certain Blacks only occurred when White self-interests were also served. CRT also focused on the power of informal narratives and storytelling to maintain racism in society. Often, these stories appear to be innocent on the surface, yet they mask a racist ideology.

CRT has been incorporated in qualitative research as a mode of consciousness-raising. Ladson-Billings (2003) in particular has been active in the use of CRT to address Self and Other dynamics from a racial perspective. Also, she has been involved in the use of alternative storytelling to counter existing racist informal narratives.

Postcolonial work seeks to free the study of culture from the lingering bonds of colonial thought. Early thinkers like Fanon (1968) and Freire (1968/1983) spoke out on colonial suppression and oppression. In recent years, thinkers like Spivak (1988) have advocated awareness of colonial oppression and thought patterns in everyday settings. Bannerji (2003) points out that such concepts as "traditional" are masks for oppressive systems of thought and action.

In some ways, all of these critical approaches are related. There are many examples of multiple oppression. For instance, a woman of color in a third-world setting often has to deal with racist, feminist, and postcolonial issues. The point is not so much to isolate and examine . . . , as it is to understand how consciousness in general might be raised in productive and affirming ways.

POSTMODERN AWARENESS

At the far edge of interpretation is a process designed to cast doubt on the very process of interpretation in the first place.

We cannot understand the key issues of Poststructural and Postmodern thought unless we understand how they subvert deeply held ideas in our culture on the nature and roles of subjectivity and objectivity. Therefore, we need to spend a bit of time examining these key concepts.

Structural and Poststructural Thought

Poststructural thought grounds much interpretive effort in qualitative inquiry, and thus is important to understand. We cannot address Poststructural thought, however, without first addressing Structural thought.

Structuralism

Structuralism has had a long and distinguished pattern of influence on theory and research. Structuralism traces its roots to the work of Saussure (1959). Saussure was a Swiss linguist from the early 20th century who explored the use of language as a general modeling system for all kinds of codes and systems within culture. As researchers like Jacobson (1976) explored the complexities of language as a coding system, social researchers like Levi-Strauss (1966) and Barthes (1957) applied these ideas and findings to anthropology and popular culture, respectively.

The basic idea of Structuralism is that there are abstract and formal structures that underlie all complex systems in culture. As such, Structuralism was part of a larger movement in Western thought known as Modernism. Modernism was born in the era of industrial progressivism in the Western world of the late 19th century. It rejected notions such as history and culture as the foundation of society. Instead, it sought to discover the pure essences of things, and to champion those pure essences as the true foundation for knowledge and culture. These ideas are seen in such movements as Modern Architecture and Modern Art. In both of these movements, details are stripped away and things are taken to their essences. This search for essences and universals were also found in the social sciences as well. Skinner boxes in psychology and behavioral objectives in education are examples of the spirit of Modernism.

Poststructuralism

Poststructuralism is a particular form of Postmodernism that takes Structuralism as its point of departure. The basic idea of Poststructuralism is that there is no single set of universal codes that underlay culture. Instead, we have a process that leads us to uncover and evaluate these events not as languages but as situational discussions. We will look at the ideas of Poststructuralists in more detail during our discussion of postmodern styles of investigation. In the meantime, we will focus instead on the work of Eco (1976, 1984).

Eco is an important transition figure between a pure Structural model and a more freeform Poststructural approach. He argues that interpretation is a tension between more universal, language-like codes on one hand, and the production of specific meanings in specific settings on the other hand. He suggests that we turn to linguistics as our basic model of semiotics (Eco, 1984) but insists that interpretation is not just a matter of "reading" circumstances as if they were texts (see Eco, 1990). Eco is a formidable thinker, and he will most often be using ideas that you are not used to thinking about, but his work can be rewarding to the careful and patient reader.

Because Structuralism and Modernism are so intimately related to each other, most qualitative researchers tend to combine Poststructural theory and practice into the larger domain of Postmodern thought.

Postmodern Thought

What is Postmodernism? There is no easy answer to this question. The Postmodern world is a world where fundamental meaning is no longer the privilege and responsibility of universal structures or essences. Grand and sweeping theories have been replaced by local accounts. Cultural and historical sensibilities, once swept under the rug by Modernism, have reemerged to assert their power to shape meaning in the world.

Another way to understand Postmodernism is to look at the ideas of people who call themselves Postmodernists. There are a number of these important postmodern thinkers. There are also a number of postmodern initiatives that have had a major impact on qualitative research theory and practice. We will look at key examples in each area in turn.

From the practical and critical side, Michel Foucault (1984) has been extremely influential. Foucault is best known for his critical examination of the role of power in the formation and operation of social systems.

Foucault is best understood as a disciple of Neitzsche. Neitzsche said "might is right." By this, Neitzsche meant that power is the most important force in culture, and that those who have power decide on the rules. Foucault extended these ideas to our understanding of the relationship of history and culture. History, for Foucault, was just another form of coercion. When we have the power, then we write history to suit our needs. Furthermore, this is fundamentally okay. This is because there really is no such thing as "history' in the absolute sense, any more than there are such things as "morals" and "ethics" and "rules." In Foucault's eyes, all of these systems of cultural understanding and regulation boil down to exercises in power.

By studying institutions like prisons and hospitals, and by looking at such fundamental human mores as sexuality and its legitimate and illegitimate forms, Foucault hoped to show that we cannot resolve our differences through appeals to reason. Reason requires a grand vision that we all can buy into, and in our postmodern era we have no such grand visions anymore. Therefore, all differences are struggles of power, and all resolutions involve subjugation and domination.

Foucault does not paint a pretty picture of culture or humanity, but his followers insist that, if we accept his honest appraisal of the role of power at all levels of culture, we can seek mutual self-interest instead of drawing moral battle lines. Within a Postmodern world, how could we ever expect to find any battle lines in the first place, and how could we expect them to stand still long enough for us to defend them?

Another critical dimension in many forms of postmodern thought is the question of relativism. The most important document in the rise of relativism in postmodern thought is Rorty's (1979) book *Philosophy and the Mirror of Nature*. Rorty called for a fundamental change in the nature of epistemology, or the study of how things can be said to be true. Ever since the ancient Greeks, claimed Rorty, we have embraced a correspondence theory of truth. That is, we accept something to be true if it corresponds to some aspect of the world as we perceive it.

Rorty argues that this seemingly innocent idea is actually fraught with peril. There are few, if any, things in the real world we understand well enough to say that we can set up the kind of correspondence we would need to properly prove the correspondence theory. What we do instead is take our perspectives on things and elevate them to the level of complete accounts. But our perspectives will be necessarily incomplete. They also will most likely be different from the perspectives of members of other cultures, who have different vantage points from ours. Besides, being able to find a complete perspective would require us to buy into comprehensive worldviews that we have learned to mistrust due to the harsh lessons of history.

If we cannot buy into the correspondence theory of truth, does that mean we have to abandon the notion of truth? Not exactly, said Rorty. We cannot aspire to or claim universal truth anymore. But we can embrace relative truths. Relative truths are those claims that are true from our perspective and for our particular cultures. Our criterion for truth is no longer correspondence to reality, but a concept Rorty calls "coherence." The coherence theory of truth says that all of our little truths have to make sense in relation to each other. That is, we need to be able to take all of these useful little truths and put them together to form a coherent picture of our world.

The coherence model not only works within our culture, says Rorty, but also across cultures. When two cultures must coexist, we can expect them to differ in their views of truth.

Such differences can lead to conflicts. How can we live together? Rorty suggests that we re-think the pursuit of truth, not as a task, but as a conversation. If we can continue the conver-sation, both within and across cultures, on what to accept as truth, then it can only be to our mutual benefit.

Relativism has had a significant impact on social science theory and practice in general, and on qualitative research in particular. One of the most comprehensive source books for the relativistic perspective is Anderson's (1995) compellingly titled *The Truth About Truth*. An-derson collects a series of excerpts from key postmodern writers and thinkers to illustrate their basic points. Along with Lechte (1994), it is a good entry point into contemporary post-modern thought.

We have examined only a few of numerous important and influential postmodern thinkers. Lechte (1994) is a clear and concise source for the basic ideas of many of these thinkers. From these thumbnail sketches, you can then pursue avenues that are particularly interesting or useful to you.

Deconstruction and Other Postmodern Methods

From a theoretical perspective, one of the most important Postmodern thinkers is Jacques Derrida. Derrida is the architect of a postmodern technique known as deconstruction (1981). Deconstruction was originally used as a tool to read texts, but it has since been expanded into other areas of inquiry. But, for simplicity's sake, we will describe it as a tool for examining the meaning of texts.

The essential assumption of deconstruction is that every reading of a text first privileges some viewpoint, and then that self-same reading eventually subverts itself. That is, when we construct a meaning of a text, our construction will eventually deconstruct itself. Another way to say this is to say that any interpretation sows the seeds of its own destruction.

Let us look at an example of deconstruction in action; I will take one of Derrida's basic examples and modify it for our use. Suppose there are two researchers out in the "wild" doing fieldwork. One of them decides to tape all field conversations, and the other decides to rely on fieldnotes alone. We might immediately assume that the person using the tape recorder is doing a better job in collecting conversational data. She walks away from the setting with a more accurate record on the experience, whereas her colleague can only depend on his field-notes to the extent that they can jog his memory of the actual experiences.

Not so fast, says Derrida. What happens when you tape record a field conversation? We cre-ate an exact record of the words that were said, and the tone of voice used to say them. Therefore, at one level, you have an account that is superior to the fieldnotes of the second researcher. But what happens when the second researcher sits down to look over his notes? He is forced to re-construct the setting over and over again, as he struggles to understand the meaning of the words, gestures, and deeds that he has observed. Is his record on paper, then? No. His record of the field events is a living, rich, vivid set of recollections within his own memories. His notes are simply an aid to help him sustain access to these mental recordings. Furthermore, these mental record-ings are multimodal. Not only do we have the words that were spoken, and their intonations, but we have gesture and setting details as well. As he pulls out his recollections, guided by his notes, he remembers sounds and smells and any number of vivid aspects of a rich field setting.

In the case of the first researcher, however, the recorded interviews take on a life of their own. First of all, they are sent out to be transcribed. These transcriptions are an exact replica, on paper, of the words spoken during the field interviews. Before long, the transcripts become the objects of study. The words are coded, and then the coded phrases are analyzed for themes and patterns. With each step, the researcher moves further and further away from the field setting. Because she has an exact record of the words spoken, she does not have to depend on her recollections. Soon, she may lose personal contact with these recollections.

So now, from Derrida's perspective, we have a deconstructive moment. The first researcher recorded her interviews because she wanted an exact record. But the very exactness of the record made it an object in itself, which was then analyzed as such. She ended up with a less exact record than the second researcher was able to sustain, using his inexact fieldnotes to help him retain critical details in memory. Therefore, our intent to be exact has backfired on us, leading us to a stance that is less exact than what we sought to replace. At this point, our efforts have deconstructed themselves.

For many people, deconstruction looks like nothing more than word play. To a degree, Derrida would agree. He would say that we no longer have foundations grounded in, universal assumptions. We only have word play. But deconstruction must be exploratory word play instead of mere rhetorical word play. If you are willing to deconstruct the field recording example just given to explore the basic assumptions of gathering data in the field, then deconstruction is a positive and useful tool. If, on the other hand, you are already convinced that we need to go back to using fieldnotes alone, then you are merely wielding deconstruction as a rhetorical weapon. The techniques will often look the same, but the intents will be greatly different. Therefore, when we look at examples of deconstruction, issues of "why" are just as important as issues of "how."

Another major Postmodern trend that has impacted social science research and practice to a large degree is known as Constructivism. Constructivism is the brainchild of von Glasersfeld (1984), who calls his strong version *Radical Constructivism*.

Radical Constructivism is similar to Relativism, in that it holds that there is no absolute knowledge "out there." Instead, all living creatures "construct" the knowledge they need in order to survive and thrive. Human beings are no different. When we acknowledge, says Radical Constructivism, that all knowledge is constructed instead of just simply existing in the world, then we realize that we are in control of what we know. Our standards for judging knowledge are no longer abstract absolutes, but instead the criteria of what we need in order to go about our lives, learning and growing.

Radical Constructivism is distinct from *Social Constructivism*. Social Constructivism is based on the ideas of Vygotsky (1962, 1978). Vygotsky believed that all human thought was grounded in social, historical, and cultural dimensions. Like the Radical Constructivists, Social Constructivists believe that knowledge and knowledge systems are constructed. That is, they believe that knowledge and truth are not just found in the world, and most important, are not absolute and independent of human experience. However, the Social Constructivist believes that these systems of knowledge are first constructed at the social and cultural level, and are then reconstructed and tweaked by individual learners and inquirers. As a result, you and I might differ somewhat in our knowledge and understanding of key concepts and ideas, but at heart we can work together because our individual "takes" on knowledge are ultimately grounded in similar social and cultural concepts and models.

Constructivism, particularly in its Social Constructivist form, has had a significant impact on social science theory and practice, and on qualitative research in particular. For instance, Duffy and Cunningham (1996) talk about the nature of Constructivist educational practices.

From this perspective, it is no longer the role of the teacher to deliver knowledge to students who then passively consume that knowledge. Instead, the teacher becomes a facilitator for helping students construct their own knowledge. This theory holds that constructed knowledge, actively made instead of passively acquired, is much more interesting and meaningful to students than knowledge acquired the old-fashioned way.

One final set of Postmodern methodological notions comes directly from the work of Foucault (1984). In his earlier works, Foucault was interested in digging into the strange patterns and assumptions that can be found under the facade of apparently simple and stable cultural institutions. He called this approach an *archaeology of knowledge,* because it resembled the digging process that archaeologists engage in at their sites.

In a later and more refined version of this process, Foucault was interested in the *genealogy* of the key ideas and assumptions underlying various cultural institutions and phenomena. Genealogy targets unique and critical events in historical settings where prevailing thought and power seem to tangle and bring about changes in the way we envision aspects of both history and culture. Quite often, these events might appear to be modest and even insignificant on the surface. It is the job of the genealogist to discover and explore these sorts of events. Meadmore, Hatcher, and McWilliam (2000) provide a useful introduction and set of examples of genealogical research for qualitative researchers.

The Postmodern approach to meaning and research is complex and influential. Therefore, we cannot ignore its presence. Whether we choose to embrace it or turn away from it in a quest for yet another from of narrating, we must first understand it. Following some of the sources previously described is a good place to start. In addition, Manning (1995) lays out many of the critical issues that Postmodernism raises for the qualitative research community.

BALANCING INTERPRETIVE FRAMEWORKS

We have spent some time looking at frameworks for performing interpretative research. Which framework should we use? Should we use only one? Should we move back and forth, depending on the research task?

I think the safest strategy is to start by using the interpretative framework that is best suited to the way that you look at the world and the process of qualitative research you are most comfortable with. You should then stay with that approach until it no longer allows you to ask the sorts of research questions you want to ask. Then, and only then, you are ready to explore new approaches toward interpretation.

So what does each of these frameworks have to say about the world and the task of doing research? Perhaps the best way for us to summarize these ideas is by looking at how interpretation operates within both qualitative science and qualitative inquiry.

Interpretation in Qualitative Science and Qualitative Inquiry

The differences between qualitative science and qualitative inquiry are often grounded in the realm of interpretation. Each field looks upon interpretation in fundamentally different ways.

Interpretation and qualitative science.
Qualitative science tends to favor those aspects of interpretation that deal with objective phenomena and theory building. Prediction and understanding based on theory predominate in

these areas. When qualitative science does venture into subjective territory, it feels most comfortable with such notions as intersubjectivity. Structuralist ideas also show up in certain forms of qualitative science research.

Interpretation and qualitative inquiry.
Qualitative inquiry seems much more comfortable with the interpretive tenets of critical theory and postmodern thought. Subjectivity, in a variety of forms, also surfaces quite often in qualitative inquiry research. We should not downplay the importance of phenomenology or hermeneutics or even thick description in qualitative inquiry, however.

INTERPRETATION AND THE MIRROR, WINDOW, AND LANTERN

If we return again to our three technologies of looking from Chapter 1, we can use them to help sort out some of the basic interpretative issues that confront us as qualitative researchers. In this case, we see that each approach represents a dimension we might adopt toward the task of making meaning clear.

Interpretation and the Mirror.   The first major dimension toward meaning involves how we go about making new meaning part of our understanding of the world. That is, how can we make *this* meaning *our* meaning? This dimension involves the act of reflection.

The great truth we find in this dimension is the awareness that meaning never stands alone. It cries out to be integrated into what we already know, and how we already understand the world. By looking on the process in a reflective manner, we take control of this need to integrate.

The great danger of mirror strategies for the resolution of meaning is that they invite the potential for privatization of meaning. That is, the world comes to mean what I want it to mean. You can make the world mean what you want it to mean if you want to, and we can all go along our merry ways creating meanings and truths and realities to suit our purposes or even our moods.

The notion of creating relative meanings and relative truths and relative realities is quite appealing to some people who do qualitative research. Their work does remind us that meanings are not like stones, just lying around waiting for us to pick them up. But they lose sight of the fact that human beings are social creatures and that inquiry is a collective process. No society could have any kind of coherence if everyone made their own meanings and their own realities. We are compelled to work together.

Interpretation and the Window.   When we are concerned with window issues in interpretation, we are saying that we are seeking interpretation that is "not just an opinion" or an interpretation that is "more than just my interpretation." We want an interpretation that anyone would agree with. We tend to feel that this sort of interpretation is our best strategy in capturing what is really present at the scene. If everyone can agree, then we are more likely correct.

Window strategies are our best source of collective interpretations that converge on a set of commonly held points. They allow us to create resolutions of meaning that everyone can live with, and that can then guide both practical actions and further research.

We need to remember, however, that these interpretations, no matter how commonly held and no matter how much data has been collected to support them, are still provisional. They are subject to change. That change may come from either new data or from a new way to look at existing data.

Interpretation and the Lantern.   The lantern approach is a sort of balance point between the mirror approach and the window approach. It shares the window view that meaning is collective, and that how we interpret is framed by what our culture holds as meaningful. Like the mirror approach, it holds that meaning resolution has an inescapably personal dimension. So how does it reconcile these two apparently contradictory dimensions?

The essence of the lantern approach is to treat the issue of meaning as an ongoing process. The problem is not so much that we hold wrong meanings, as it is the fact that we do not ever have enough meaning. That is, our understanding of anything is always too simple, too incomplete. We need to pick up and move the light so that we can see something that we have not seen before.

Therefore, there is always the pull between personal and collective interpretation. We start with collective interpretation as our map of what we think things already mean. This is our roadmap of presuppositions and cultural understandings. Our task is not so much to attack these, but to move beyond them. And we can only do so as individual inquirers (or a part of a small team of investigators). We deliberately look for those boundary conditions and those margins where current understandings are inadequate or where they break down. Can we reconcile our findings from the edges and margins with what we already know? Or do we have to rethink our basic understandings? These are empirical questions. That is, the answers depend on what we actually find.

BACK TO THE MUSIC

The most important lesson to learn from the music listening exercise is this: Interpreting is *not* making up meaning. The beauty of music is that it is always and every time meaningful, even if we do not know or understanding that meaning.

"But," you might argue, "I read all the time about how qualitative and other interpretative researchers are in the business of making meaning. Doesn't that contradict what you just said?"

Not quite. If you look carefully at what is being said, the phrase *making meaning* almost always means *making meaning clear.* It does not mean, *making something mean anything I want it to mean.* On the other hand, it also does not mean, *any meaning that I find has to be true.* Remember that meaning and truth are not the same concepts; they may be related, but they also can be independent of each other.

Good interpretative research is all about walking the tightrope between creating meaning out of thin air versus insisting that just because some interpretation is meaningful it has to be true. In between these two poles lies the target—the ability to make meaning clear.

The frameworks discussed in this chapter are ways to attempt to make meaning clear. But they are not the only ways. Sometimes, you just have to interpret your findings in the best way you can. When this is the case, remember that there is no virtue in interpreting quickly. You are better off taking your time, even though every instinct you have says to go ahead and resolve ambiguities and murky areas of meaning as quickly as possible. This is one of the hardest things to do as a qualitative researcher—to live with the feeling that you do not understand the situation yet. But the longer you can live with this feeling, the greater the chance that you will see those subtle nuances in meaning that make the difference between ordinary and great qualitative research. And that is the name of that tune!

PLANNING YOUR RESEARCH PROPOSAL: FIRST THEORETICAL MODEL

Are you doing qualitative science or qualitative inquiry? Or does this question even matter for your research? At this point in time, Albert and Carol need to weigh these sorts of issues. The theoretical direction they choose to take will affect the form and nature of their research questions, the concerns they will have to address about their data and findings, and their choices of methods.

Carol

Carol is committed to a qualitative science approach. She will attempt to create a theory to explain how young, poor, urban women balance their career and love needs. She wants to make sure that her sample is well chosen and at least somewhat representative. She wants to make sure that her findings can generalize to other young, single, urban women. She is concerned with reliability and validity. She wants to make sure that she has collected data properly, and that her major findings have been triangulated using a variety of data sources.

Albert

Albert is taking a qualitative inquiry approach. Because he has uncovered a potentially new and undiscovered group of math anxious students, he wants to make sure that their voices are heard. For now, his plan is to interview the students, their teachers, and their parents. He wants to understand how these students feel about their anxiety, how they try to cope with it, and what he or others might be able to do to lessen it. At this time, he is wavering between taking a critical theoretical approach or a participatory action research approach. Though he wants to help these students, and plans to do so eventually, for now he is thinking that it might be best to simply sit back and let the students tell him what their conditions and feelings are like.

Ourselves

Theoretical perspectives are important. At some stage, we must make at least some initial commitment to the theoretical framework that we are going to pursue. As you can see from this example, qualitative science frameworks tend to be more structured and formal at the outset. Ask yourself the following questions:

- Do you see your work going in a qualitative science direction? Which form of qualitative science best describes your current thinking?
- Do you see your work going in a qualitative inquiry direction? Which form of qualitative inquiry best describes your current thinking?

CHAPTER 6

Questioning

Exercise Five—*Stalking the Wild Research Question*

Where do good research questions come from? The simple answer is—*everywhere!* Qualitative researchers do not have to depend on theory to find areas of research to pursue, nor do they have to depend on previous research as much as other forms of empirical inquiry. They can find research questions just about anywhere.

Quite often, the world of experience will offer myriad problems if you are careful and observant. You can never tell where you might first find a potential research question—in the newspaper, in a magazine, in a conversation you overhear on the street, on a TV show or on the Internet, or even as you drive by a familiar spot in your neighborhood. You can never tell what might trigger your attention, and eventually your desire to conduct research. Research questions are everywhere. You just have to learn to harvest them.

In this exercise, you will practice "harvesting" research questions from the world at large:

- Start by tapping into your natural curiosity. Make a list of four or five target areas. A target area is an area where you have some interest. Keep these target areas very broad for now.
- Gather a set of resources. For this exercise, you will want to collect popular and general types of resources. For now, avoid technical or specialized materials.
- Newspapers are good resources. You might also want to include news magazines and popular magazines on a variety of topics. Movie and TV reviews, popular CDs, and even web pages are acceptable.
- Now, start examining your resources for stories and examples that fit within your target areas. How are the writers or artists addressing these target areas? As you examine their stances, think about how well these points are illustrated or validated in the "real world."
- For each target area, try to find at least one point raised in your resources that would benefit from closer examination. You now have the bare bones of a research question.
- Practice putting each of these questions into a form that could be addressed by a researcher. You can read a variety of qualitative articles to see how those researchers identified and stated their research questions.
- Try to generate a list of four or five research questions from different sources, and share them with your classmates. In addition, do not forget to bring in your original sources.

Research questions come from a variety of sources, including practice and theory. But the world itself is also a good source of research questions and target areas for research.

REFLECTING ON THE ROLE OF QUESTIONING

Questioning is a diverse and complex process in qualitative research. It can be as simple as finding a straightforward research question, and as complicated as hanging around a setting and waiting to see if a research target area will come into focus.

We will start by looking at the notion of a qualitative research question proper. Though it is true that many qualitative research projects start with a research question, this is not always the case. There has been a long history of qualitative research based on the efforts of researchers to find a target area, put themselves in contact with that area in one form or another, and see and report what happens. Therefore, we will also look at research target areas as part of the questioning process.

After we look at the specifics of target areas and questions, we will then draw back to look at the questioning process in a more global fashion. Qualitative research understands and uses the concepts of strategies and tactics in a unique way, and so we need to look at these topics more closely.

The questioning process, by itself, does not guarantee that we will put ourselves in the position to do good research. Therefore, we need to consider how to evaluate our efforts. The issue of quality, in terms of reliability, validity, trustworthiness, and other concepts, will be examined.

Questioning is never done in a vacuum. In traditional research, the review of the research literature plays a key role in helping frame and contextualize research questions. We will examine the role of the literature review in qualitative research briefly, to reveal how it might impact different sorts of qualitative studies.

Finally, we will look at one final and important form of questioning—ethical questioning. We will note some of the basic ethical guidelines in qualitative research, and some of the ethical challenges and dilemmas qualitative researchers have actually encountered in their works.

ASKING THE QUALITATIVE RESEARCH QUESTION

What kinds of questions do qualitative researchers ask? Do they differ from the sorts of questions other researchers ask? Do they differ from each other?

First of all, let us look at the things all research questions have in common. Every genuine research question ever pursued was asked out of curiosity. What was the first research question you ever asked? Mine was—*I wonder what is under that rock?* If you have a point to prove, or an axe to grind, or an old wound to salve, or a message to deliver, then there are other legitimate ways to pursue these ends. Do not disguise them as research. This is not to say that research cannot prove a point, or grind an axe, or salve a wound, or deliver a message. But these secondary and incidental effects should only occur along the way toward resolving a matter of curiosity.

What one thing makes qualitative research questions, in general, distinct from other sorts of research questions? Simply, the fact that qualitative research questions direct their curiosity focus on the area of meaning.

The prototypical qualitative research question is—*What does it mean to be X?* Variants include—*What does X mean? What does it mean for X to be present? For X to be absent? What do we currently understand X to mean, and in what ways is that current understanding incomplete? What way of understanding X, if brought to light and explored in detail, would change the way we look at or use X in our ordinary lives?*

In addition, quantitative research questions are oriented toward verification or prediction. Qualitative research questions, on the other hand, lead us in the direction of gaining a deeper understanding. Some ways of gaining that deeper understanding include but are not limited to: (1) exploring unexamined aspects of X; (2) making our picture of X more complex in a manageable and empirically driven way; and (3) seeking unusual or unexplored perspectives on X, usually from persons who are not part of the current discourse on X. It is not so much that case that we have the wrong understanding of X. Rather, it is that our understanding of X is incomplete or superficial.

The use of "X" is admittedly abstract, but it has been a useful tool for us to use in order to make some general comments about qualitative research questions. We will take a look at some more specific kinds of "X"s next, when we consider the nature of general categories, or types, of research questions in qualitative research.

TYPES OF QUALITATIVE QUESTIONS

There are a number of ways to ask questions about meaning. Therefore, there are a number of different types of qualitative research questions. In recent years, there have been some efforts to create frameworks for asking qualitative research questions. For instance, McCaslin and Scott (2003) advocate a five-question protocol for developing qualitative studies. More often than not, though, qualitative research questions are grounded in more specific goals or agendas. These goals and agendas usually lead to a wide variety of research question types.

The easiest way to look at various types of qualitative questions is to put them along a continuum. At one end of the continuum we find those questions that are most similar to typical quantitative questions. As we move away from this pole, the questions take on a more personalized and interpretative character.

Hypothesis Testing

Some people would argue that qualitative research should avoid the notion of hypotheses altogether. But hypotheses can play important roles in any sort of research if used properly. In qualitative research, hypotheses are appropriate if they lead us in the direction of expanding our understanding of the situation. Also, more often than not, if qualitative researchers are testing hypotheses, they are doing qualitative science.

What would a hypothesis look like in a qualitative research study? For instance, suppose you are interested in doing research in how homeless mothers educate their preschool children. You might hypothesize that any such education will be informal, as homeless mothers are not likely to have the resources to place their children into preschool programs. This is a sort of hypothesis based upon your initial understanding of the lives of homeless mothers and their young children. But you are doing your research in the first place because you are aware that your understanding of these circumstances, and the understanding of society in general, is sketchy at best.

Our relation to hypotheses is different from the relation we find in most quantitative research. In quantitative research, we make every effort to state our hypotheses as clearly as possible, and to derive testable claims from them. When we are able to verify those claims, then we have further support for our hypotheses and the theories behind them. When our claims are not verified, then we must change our hypotheses or even our theories as a result.

In qualitative research, however, we look at a hypothesis as a sort of filter. When we use this filter to look at the data, we see certain things. But we must remain open to the possibility that we need to fine-tune or even change our filters once we are on site and gathering information. That is, we are not testing hypotheses so much as we are seeing how effective they are in letting our information flow. If we find, for instance, that our informal education hypothesis in the earlier example is not very useful in helping homeless mothers and children open up and give us information, then we might need to modify or abandon it for another approach. We have not tested the hypothesis per se; instead, we have tried it out as a tool. If it does the job in getting us information, then we can keep it. If not, we just might need another tool.

Exploration

This is one of the most common types of research questions in qualitative research. It is an especially popular sort of question for beginning researchers. But genuine exploration is not a matter of your own personal lack of knowledge. Exploration is necessary when the research community as a whole has absolutely no clear picture of what is going on. Are we dealing with a setting that has never been studied before? Are we dealing with a set of ideas that have never been applied to field settings? Are we talking to and observing people who are so unique that we have no previous models to draw from? These are the sorts of issues that invite exploration.

At the heart of exploration is the notion of the unique opportunity. Let us return to the question of homeless mothers and the education of their children. You have been reading up on research on homelessness. One of your classmates happens to mention that she had been raised in a series of shelters by a homeless mother. You casually ask your classmate about her mother's current status. When, you ask, was she able to get out of homelessness? Your classmate replies, in an equally casual tone, that her mother had been homeless by choice, and was indeed still homeless. This is the epitome of the unique opportunity. Why did this mother make her choice? Why did she continue to live the homeless life? What could her unique situation tell us about homelessness that goes beyond our current models?

Exegesis into Empirical Meaning

All qualitative research questions at some level take on the following basic form—*What does it mean to be X?* Exegetical questions address this sort of issue most directly, and are most often found in qualitative inquiry approaches.

Exegesis means "to draw out." It was first used by Biblical scholars as a tool to draw out deep and hidden meanings from the Bible and other religious texts. But it soon became a popular tool for literary critics who wanted to go beyond surface meanings in their analyses of works of literature. Finally, it entered the social science research world. Exegesis in social science research centers on the idea that words, deeds, and settings can be understood as if they were texts, and thereby "read" for deeper or hidden meanings.

Let us return to the project of homeless mothers and the education of their preschool children. What does it mean to be a homeless mother? We have all sorts of standard understandings on this topic. But if we looked more carefully at the words of these mothers as they talked about their children, what would we hear? If we talked to the children themselves, how do they look at the world? What does it say about society that homeless mothers are allowed to raise their children in shelters or on the streets? What are the artifacts that homeless mothers and their children possess, and what meanings do these things have for them?

As we pursue these sorts of questions, we need to do so with the full realization that our culture already has "acceptable" answers for many of them. But we cannot escape the fact that we still do not understand this phenomenon very well. When we interact with homeless mothers and their children, we are constantly surprised by what they say or do. Our surprise is based on our overall lack of understanding, and that overall lack of understanding is based on the fact that we have not "read" the meaning of this situation well enough. It is the task and challenge of exegetical research questions to help set up these more complex and more in-depth cultural and psychological readings.

Critical Examination and Action

Some qualitative research questions go beyond the task of gathering information. They call for social change as well. Here, we are talking about the kinds of questions that action researchers raise. We have already discussed action research in some detail in Chapter 4. Now let us look at our homeless mother example from an action research perspective.

Our efforts are twofold. First of all, we need to take a look at the assumptions and ideological beliefs that are held by homeless mothers. How have they come to accept a set of circumstances that are against their own best interests and the best interests of their children? Do they willingly accept their status as something they somehow deserve (which of course they do not!), or do they feel actively oppressed? How can we raise the consciousness of society as a whole, so that it seeks out ways to help these homeless women and children? In short, what is a proper critical theoretical understanding of this situation?

From our initial critical understanding we can next build an action plan. We are no longer committed to simply understanding the plight of these people. We cannot leave the scene until we improve it. But we must improve it on its own terms. It is not our job to go in and make these people into cultural replicas of ourselves. To prevent this from happening, we need to seek constantly to understand their needs and their motives. We need to understand them from their own perspectives and on their own terms. The surest way for an action research project to succeed is to make sure the people involved take charge of their own circumstances. When they have identified the problems and planned the solutions, then they can continue the process that you have started. When this happens, you have answered your questions and you are free to leave the setting with a clear conscience.

FINDING AND DEVELOPING A QUALITATIVE RESEARCH TARGET AREA

Not all forms of questioning in qualitative research lead to asking specific research questions. For instance, ethnographers have showed up in order to mingle with and study unfamiliar cultures. Participant observers have infiltrated various strata of society to find out what is going on there. Critical researchers have used their sensitivities to language and their fieldwork skills to try to understand complex patterns of behaviors. Participatory researchers have taken their leads from the marginalized people whom they are trying to help. The list goes on and on.

The key to identifying a good research target area depends on your ability to realize whether or not a given setting or situation can tell you anything new about your larger area of interest. Unlike quantitative research, qualitative research is rarely interested in the ordinary or typical per se. Instead, we seek those settings and conditions where things are not operating as usual. Are there strange and baffling little cultural quirks that might be masking larger and deeper variations in the way their advocates look at the world? Are things unusually bad? Are they unusually good? Are there other sorts of unexpected results or practices that call out for a closer look? These little ruptures or advances or declines in the ordinary are often fertile soil for further qualitative research. As such, they stand out as potential research target areas.

In cases where qualitative researchers are trying to find good target areas, it can actually be counterproductive to be too systematic in the initial stages. Instead, as Kincheloe (2001) argues, we need to be more like bricoleurs. Bricoleurs are those who practice the art of bricolage in social science research.

Bricolage is a concept in qualitative research that goes back to the pioneering work of Levi-Strauss (1966). Bricolage is the skilled practice of putting together those things we find at the scene in order to craft a keen and insightful understanding of what we find. The bricoleur is much less concerned with bringing in ideas and techniques, and much more concerned with working with whatever is on hand. This is because those things and ideas that are on hand are often the most authentic aspects of the phenomena we are trying to study.

In short, qualitative target areas are more often than not discovered on-scene and in the practice of trying to come to understand complex settings in their natural forms and on their own terms. As such, the discovery and development of research target areas is a paramount example of the overall dependence of all forms of qualitative research on the use of tactical techniques and skills. Because the role and nature of tactical thinking is so important in the process of questioning in qualitative research, we will look at it in some depth.

THE TACTICAL BACKDROP OF QUALITATIVE QUESTIONING

Regardless of the kinds of questions you ask and the type of research methods you use, there is one fundamental stance that all qualitative approaches share. They know at times that it is important to take a tactical approach toward the object of their research. That is, qualitative research is often much more tactical than strategic, and doing good qualitative research can depend on understanding and using tactical perspectives (Shank, 1994). Therefore, we need to spend some time making sure our understanding of the difference between strategic and tactical approaches to research is clear.

The Nature of Strategies

Strategy is at the heart of all quantitative research efforts. Strategies are plans we draw out to help us reach some goal. If we are going to war, then our battle plans are strategies for winning those battles and eventually the war. If we are going to build a house, then our blueprints are strategies we use to decide how to assemble and put together the various materials we want, eventually, to turn into a house. If we want to test the effects of wearing a uniform on being able to get street directions from strangers in a big city, then developing an adequate research design is our basic strategy.

A good research design, like a good strategy, is all about anticipation. If we read a blueprint and we see that we will have to secure thousands of wood screws, we might anticipate buying or renting an electric drill. If we are going to war in the dead of winter, we might want to make sure our soldiers have warm coats. Attention to these sorts of details is just as much a part of the strategy of building a house or waging war as the basic blueprints or the terrain models in the war room. All of these aspects are anticipations in their own ways, and a good overall strategy addresses as many of these layers of anticipation as it can.

We can see the workings of anticipation in research design as well. Take our example of a direction-asking study. We start with a basic quasi-experimental design. We know that we actually have to go out into the streets and ask for directions from real people. If we tried to simulate these circumstances in a more controlled laboratory setting, then our critics could rightly challenge our findings. How would we know, they might say, that our subjects in the laboratory are not just trying to help us get the experimental results that we want? So, in anticipation of these criticisms, we move the study into a real-world setting where we ask questions of people who do not know that this is a social science experiment. Because we are ethical researchers, we will let these people know afterwards that we have been conducting a study, and then ask their permission to use our findings.

Now we need a basic decision point. Here is where the research question comes in. Let us suppose we have good reason to believe (from theory and prior evidence) that people will be more likely to give directions to a stranger in uniform than to a stranger dressed in casual clothes. But we need to turn to the world of experience to get a more definitive answer.

Strategy and Anticipation

Our first task is to strategize just exactly how our research question gets translated into action. Again, we are guided by anticipation. We have to create two sets of nearly identical circumstances, where there is a direction asker and a potential helper. As near as we can make it, the only difference between the circumstances is the presence or absence of a uniform.

The answer is simple, you might say. Have the same person ask directions of strangers, sometimes in uniform and sometimes in street clothes. Use a set script with a set number of prompts. Pick the people to ask at random, and make the choice of "uniform vs. no uniform" condition random with each person as well. Ask enough people under each condition to get a large enough sample to "wash out" weird people and weird answers. Then compare the average number of helping responses between the two conditions. If the uniform condition has a greater number of significant helping responses than the casual condition, then you have provided a type of inductive and empirical "proof" of your original claim.

But our strategic anticipations are far from being over at this point. As we continue to strategize, we will see cycles of anticipations developing and interweaving with each other. Does the particular type of uniform matter? Does the destination of the direction-asker matter? How casual should the casual clothes be? Should the direction-asker be male or female? Does it matter if we do this study on a weekday or a weekend? Does the time of day matter? There is no definitive answer to the question of just how many anticipations a research design needs to incorporate—that is why good quantitative research is no more mechanical than good qualitative research. Statistical designs, for example, help us instantiate our judgments. There are no statistical procedures, however, than can substitute for our own good judgments.

Tactical Research

There is a temptation to think that qualitative research deals with some of these more peripheral strategic issues, or serves to chart out the lay of the land so that we can get down to the business of doing real research. In other words, there is at least some covert sentiment among social science researchers that qualitative research in general is the refinement and ultimate development of the fine art of the pilot study.

But qualitative research is a completely different type of beast. It is the type of social science research that steps away from a strategic approach in favor of a more tactical approach. What do we mean, though, by *tactics?*

Tactics are those questions and decisions made on the spot, in the field, because circumstances dictate that those questions be asked and those decisions be made. For instance, when we are building the house from the earlier example, we had planned to set out shrubs along the front of the house. As we start digging our foundation, however, we discover that our soil is too acidic for shrubs. We need to shift from shrubbery to ground cover to achieve our goals. In our war example, we have the generals at field headquarters who make decisions about when and how to move troops. But we also have field generals who can change the whole plan, if need be, based on the actual circumstances in the field.

Qualitative research is not just about using tactical designs to adjust for unanticipated circumstances, however. Qualitative research embraces tactical methods because these methods allow for creativity and flexibility in field settings without sacrificing our commitment to finding true and useful findings.

Because qualitative research tends to put tactical matters ahead of strategic matters, we can say that it has a more tactical vision of research. But how does it manifest this vision?

First of all, being tactical does not mean being a *tabula rasa*. We do not, because we cannot, go into a setting with no preconceptions. When we are out and about in a setting, we are always balancing "what corresponds with what goes beyond." We want to keep a light touch on the "correspond" because we already know what that path pretty much looks like.

Being really good and really natural at "going beyond" is at the very heart of the tactical dimension of qualitative research. One good source of information that "goes beyond" can be found in marginal people. Although marginal people are sometimes "weirdoes" and cranks and can frankly be a waste of time, sometimes they are people who just happen to see things differently. When we find someone with a truly different but really interesting and potentially useful viewpoint, our best tactic is to follow where they lead us. But we cannot anticipate, or strategize, finding these people. That is, there is no good way to tell a genius from a skilled weirdo beforehand. Also, ethical researchers are commited to treating all persons with respect and dignity.

Even more tactically important than marginal people are those inevitable "sidetracks" we find in the research process. But it can be very hard for us to realize how valuable certain sidetracks are, and for us to learn the skill of dropping what we were doing and pursuing those sudden opportunities instead. I find this skill particularly hard for professional education scholars to learn. Something about the makeup of many of them makes them extraordinarily task oriented. If you are setting out to interview someone as a task, and you have a clearly articulated set of questions and goals (maybe that you eventually hope to code using your actual transcript data) then you are almost certainly flirting with disaster. I call these "elephant" interviews. The task oriented interview, like a bull elephant heading for its watering hole, relentlessly tramps toward its goal. By and large, the stuff that gets pushed aside is often more interesting and more important than the set of preconceived findings for which the interview was nothing but another task.

An Example of Making a Quick Tactical Turn

A skilled tactical interviewer is capable of turning on a dime. Here is one example from a case study from a class long ago. The student had chosen as her expert the head of a major construction company in the region. She wanted to know how he decided that he wanted to start his own company. She had an entire set of follow-up questions based on what she expected him to say.

Instead, he threw her a curve. He had started out as an electrician. She had known that fact, and expected him to say that he went into general contracting as a way of expanding this earlier area of interest. The real truth is that he loved being an electrician. But one day, when he was on a remote job, he reached into a box to get a section of wiring. The site was so remote that they brought along Portajohns to take care of their biological needs. Anyway, apparently one of the workers was too lazy to walk all the way to a Portajohn, and so used an empty wire box as his makeshift version. It was into this box that her expert thrust his hand, and he did not come out with a handful of wire. At that moment, he lost all desire to be an electrician, and set out to be a general contractor instead.

Nothing could be more off task than this unpleasant little anecdote. But the student realized that it carried powerful meaning for her expert. So she threw away the rest of her prepared questions, and pursued this issue. Her expert himself was particularly struck at the lack of control he had had as an electrician, but had not realized that personal epiphany until this event. He swore that neither he nor anyone who ever worked for him would ever have an experience like that again, and he built his entire company around that unwritten and unstated rule. Note that there was no way that the student could have strategized to make sure that this information would have surfaced. But once the information was there, she had enough tactical savvy to know that it was time to change course and go down a road she did not even know was going to be there.

EVALUATING RESEARCH QUESTIONS AND TARGET AREAS

Once we have a set of research questions, or a well-articulated target area, then we have to ask ourselves if these questions or targets are any good. Will they allow us to get somewhere? Are they flawed? How will we know if we have addressed them? If we have addressed them, have we done so adequately?

In order to help us address these sorts of issues, there are a variety of research concepts that we use to see if we are on the right track or not. Not all of these tools are useful for all forms of research. The following sections describe a few of the key areas where qualitative researchers have turned for ongoing guidance as they pursue questions and targets.

Reliability, Validity, and Generalizability in Qualitative Research

Few ideas have played more important roles in the formulation and evaluation of research questions in the social sciences than the following triumvirate: reliability, validity, and generalizability. In fact, at least as far as traditional quantitative research is concerned, we might call them "the Big Three." That is, if a quantitative researcher in the social sciences does not take a clear position on the role of each of these factors in his or her research, then that research is in trouble at the outset. Are these same circumstances true, however, for qualitative research? Let us look at each factor in turn to try to answer this question.

Reliability

We start with reliability. Reliability is one of the cornerstones of conventional social science research. Does it play a necessary role in qualitative research? That is a controversial question. Let us start by looking at the "job" that reliability is expected to play in research.

Briefly put, reliability, in its various manifestations, is usually about the matter of accuracy (Golafshani, 2003). There are a number of ways to look at accuracy. There is an accuracy of effort—*Is my attempt to measure what is happening here accurate?* In other words, if I measured the same thing again, would I get the same results? These concerns deal with the question of the reliability of measurement. Traditionally, we do things like retest our samples to make sure we have an accurate system. If we keep measuring the same thing and keep getting the same results, then chances are we are measuring accurately.

Next, there is accuracy of type—*Is the thing that I am using to make my measurements giving me unique readings, or is it just one of a whole type of things that I could be using to make my measurements?* If the thing we are trying to measure is pretty ordinary, then we should be able to find a variety of measuring instruments. Traditionally, we might develop two or more measuring instruments. If we measure the same thing using these different instruments and keep getting the same results, then chances are we are measuring something that is not unique to our measuring instruments.

Finally, we have to acknowledge that there is often no simple way to measure what we are trying to measure. More often than not, we have to ask several, if not many, different questions to get at what we are trying to find. Are all of these questions working together to give us a picture of one complex concept, or are they measuring different things? Here we are dealing with the role of consistency within accuracy. Traditionally, we do things like compare each measurement item to the process as a whole. If we find that each and every item acts like a miniature version of the whole measuring program, then chances are we are measuring consistently. Consistency is often measured when tests are used to collect data. In this situation, each question is treated as if it were a tiny little version of the test, and consistency is measured in that fashion.

We have described systems within quantitative research that help ensure accuracy. What are accuracy issues in qualitative research, and do we have the same sorts of systems to draw upon? It depends on the type of qualitative research you are doing. If you are doing Grounded Theory or some other type of coding system, then you have to make sure that your codes accurately reflect your observational or archival data. If you are interviewing, then you need to ask for clarification or follow up information if you are not sure you understand what you are being told. If you are doing field observation, it doesn't hurt to check with informants to see if you have your facts straight. If you are doing interpretative analysis, you need to move back and forth between your sources and your insights to make sure they are in sync.

At the moment, though, there is not one single good set of policies or concepts that can ensure qualitative accuracy. Some concepts, like trustworthiness or triangulation, work well in some settings but not so well in others. For now, the best approach toward accuracy is to take a method-by-method position. That is, how do you ensure accuracy within this particular qualitative design?

Validity

Validity deals with the notion that what you say you have observed is, in fact, what really happened (Golafshani, 2003). In the final analysis, validity is always about truth. Is your observational record true?

The concept of truth is a complex issue in qualitative research. There are some researchers who deny that there is anything such as truth, and that all matters of truth are really matters of personal opinion. Other researchers say that there are many truths, and each is grounded in its own context and personal perspective.

Though I think that such debates are critically important, is it possible to say something about validity that all qualitative researchers, from the most relativistic to the most scientific, can agree on? All qualitative researchers would agree, I think, that the stance of the observer needs to be made explicit. At the risk of leaning too heavily in the direction of traditional science, let us call those issues a matter of *observer effects*.

At the far end of the discussion are those researchers who are practicing qualitative science at its most stringent levels. For these researchers, the job of the observer is to be transparent and to observe only those things that are really there. At the other end of the discussion is the relativist, who says that the observer is busy creating his or her own record of the truth, and in fact his or her own reality. In the middle are those researchers who think that settings and observer perspectives interact in complex ways.

Regardless of position, it is critical for the observer to be honest about his or her perspective. Whether you want to call that perspective a "bias" or the "basis for creating reality," it has to be out in the open. What are your predilections? How did you feel about what you have observed, especially if those feelings are strong? Upon reflection, what might you have missed because you would not normally look for such things? All of these, and related, issues need to be a part of the explicit record. It does not matter what your particular theory of truth is. As long as you are open and honest about it, and its possible impact on you as an observer, you can participate in both the ongoing discussion and the process of research.

Qualitative science often pays particular attention to standard notions of validity, as validity is such a key concept in the conduct of science in general. Morse (Morse, Barrett, Mayan, Olson, & Spiers, 2002; Morse & Mitcham, 2002; Morse & Pooler, 2002) in particular has been active in seeking to link analytic modes of induction with rigorous methods for ensuring validity in qualitative fieldwork. Her model starts with an analysis of relevant concepts, with the idea of building a skeletal framework. The concept is then studied inductively, where experiences are scaffolded into the skeletal framework. As the research matures with more and more field data, the scaffold eventually grows into a field-based theoretical framework. Morse and her colleagues (Hupcey, 2002; Penrod, 2002; Spiers, 2002) continue to test and refine this model for creating theory while establishing validity.

Other researchers continue to explore other specialized aspects of the search for validity in qualitative research. Beach (2003) looks at the political dimensions of validity in qualitative research by comparing and contrasting democratic and capitalist perspectives toward qualitative research in general. Koro-Ljungberg (2004) examines the negotiation of both validity and truth claims in general in studies where a number of theoretical perspectives are

mixed together. Aguinaldo (2004) reevaluates the notion of validity from a social constructionist perspective. In his view, a shift to a constructionist perspective moves the notion of validity from the task of making sure the research is true, toward the task of making sure the
research is useful.

As we can see, the concept of validity in qualitative research is neither simple nor static.
Qualitative research seems to be committed to the notion of making sure its research efforts
are true, but as we find in most forms of qualitative research, the very concept of truth takes
on many nuances and shades in the process.

Generalizability

Finally, there is the issue of the target—Do the people I am using in my study constitute a representative sample? Would I find what I found if I measured any other similar group of persons under such conditions? Traditionally, we use procedures such as taking several samples
to make sure we have an accurate picture of how typical persons would respond under such
settings. If we keep sampling different groups of people and keep getting the same results, then
chances are we can extend our findings beyond our samples to the population at large.

In other words, the issue here is one of generalizability (see Schofield, 1990 for an example of how some qualitative researchers have sought to ground generalizability from a theoretical perspective). More often than not, standard generalizability concerns can get in the way
of doing good qualitative research. We can see this happening in two different ways.

First of all, traditional issues of generalizability are rooted in the "typical" case and the
"typical" situation. That is why such strategies as random sampling are important. If we can
establish that it does not matter who our sample members are, then there is a better chance
that our sample findings can be applied, or generalized, to some larger population. Understanding "what the typical is like" matters because we are usually trying to verify some theory,
and the strongest theories are the ones that hold true for the most people. Therefore, if we can
show that our theory holds for the typical person and/or the typical situation, then we have a
broad-ranging theory.

But in qualitative research, we are just as likely to be interested in the special and the unusual. We might know what average people might do in ordinary settings. But if we take average people and put them in extraordinary settings, or talk to extraordinary people about
ordinary topics, then we have a chance to shed light on perspectives and actions that might
never have been studied before. To try to "tame" these findings by turning them back toward
the mainstream does more harm than good. At best, profound insights tend to be watered
down. In summary, we are more often interested in samples that are more fertile than typical.
We have no qualms in looking at exemplary persons or truly unique circumstances. More often than not, these are the dark corners of our world, where the light of research and understanding too rarely shine.

Finally, generalization is often an effort toward simplifying our understanding of some
phenomenon. If we can generalize an abstract claim and show how it holds under a variety of
conditions, then we have a firmer grasp on the basic dynamics of the situation. It is simpler to
understand and apply a few basic principles than to have to learn complex rules for each and
every situation.

But in qualitative research, we are not always interested in simplifying our understandings. We usually believe that our current understanding is too simplistic as it stands. We are

not in favor of gratuitous complexity, but it is just as wrong to try to make something too simple so that key aspects for understanding are lost. Generalizability is most often a push towards breadth, and qualitative research is much more concerned with depth. More often than not, these two fundamental dynamics just do not coordinate all that well.

Finally, we need to realize that not all forms of generalizability deal with data and demographics. Generalization is an important logical concept as well. The methodological understanding of induction most often used in qualitative research argues that we move from the specific to the general. Though this is most often used to represent scientific thinking in general, this sort of practical induction can also play a role in certain forms of qualitative research as well (especially qualitative science efforts).

Smaling (2003) builds upon simple models of inductive generalization to develop a variety of new conceptual forms of generalization that are particularly relevant to qualitative research. Specifically, he feels that generalization via analogy is particularly apt for qualitative research, given its dependence on meaning. Analogical generalizations allow for comparisons based on degree of plausibility, and are grounded in analogical reasoning. Analogical reasoning, for Smaling, is grounded in six key criteria: (1) the degree of similarity between your target and your example; (2) the relevance of the analogy for your final conclusions; (3) support by other similar cases; (4) support by the lack of evidence of any other systematic sources of variation between target and example; (5) the relative plausibility of your conclusions without the support of the analogy; and (6) the amount of empirical and theoretical support for the analogy (pp. 13–16).

In summary, we should embrace generalizability only when it seems to fit our aims and purposes, and not as some necessary precondition for doing qualitative research. For instance, Levin-Rozalis (2004) advocates a move away from induction per se toward abduction, particularly when projective techniques are also used. But, if you find that you must turn away from standard generalizability, be prepared to defend your choice to an audience that is used to generalizability as part of the equation.

Triangulation

One of the most popular validation strategies is called *triangulation*. Triangulation is the process of converging upon a particular finding by using different sorts of data and data-gathering strategies. Each set of data or each strategic finding on its own might not be strong enough to support the finding. But when these different "strands" are taken together, there is stronger evidence for the finding.

Triangulation can be used with different methods, different researchers, different sources of data, and even different theories. For instance, we may suspect that poor nutrition is having a severe impact on the children in a small and isolated community. We gather information about their nutritional intake by looking at what the schools serve for lunch, what meals are served at home, and what food items are commonly sold at the general store. We measure nutrition with reports, medical tests, and observational studies. We have several persons collecting similar data. And we research the theoretical role of nutrition on learning from both a biochemical and a sociocultural perspective. When all of these efforts converge to support our hunches, then we have pretty strong evidence that nutritional intervention is needed in this case.

Triangulation can be used by any empirical study, and it has been around for many years and in many settings. In qualitative settings, however, triangulation often takes on its own character. Seale (1999) reviews the history and use of triangulation in qualitative settings. Noting that triangulation had its start in measurement paradigms in quantitative research, Seale points out that many recent qualitative researchers are using triangulation not just to pinpoint effects but also as a means to create a common point of view. This common point of view can be forged by looking at how knowledge might be constructed from differing perspectives and by using different methods. In this fashion, triangulation can be used effectively not only in qualitative science studies that treat data in a more objective fashion, but also in qualitative inquiry studies in which data and findings are often negotiated and even debated. Triangulation, in these settings, allows for a public inspection of the process, and helps add validity and confidence as well.

In qualitative research, triangulation is also often called upon to help establish and maintain *rigor* in a given study. A rigorous study is one that was designed carefully, conducted properly, and analyzed correctly. Furthermore, its findings are robust and important. In a sense, a rigorous study is one you can count on. As studies grow more complex, rigor becomes harder to establish and maintain. For instance, Crawford, Leybourne, and Arnott (2000) describe the complex process they used to ensure rigor in a particularly complicated study involving multiple sites, disciplines, and researchers.

Qualitative science in particular emphasizes rigor, but rigor is also considered important for most kinds of qualitative research efforts.

ALTERNATIVES TO RELIABILITY, VALIDITY, AND GENERALIZABILITY IN QUALITATIVE RESEARCH

A number of qualitative researchers have explored alternatives to reliability, validity, and generalizability. Much of this work was first developed by Lincoln and Guba (1985, 2000). The first four concepts—dependability, credibility, transferability, and confirmability—reflect some of their earlier thinking.

Dependability

Dependability refers to our ability to know where the data in a given study comes from, how it was collected, and how it was used. Lincoln and Guba (1985) saw dependability as the qualitative correlate of the traditional notion of reliability. The key strategy for ensuring dependability is an audit trail. With an audit trail, there is a clear and constant path between the collection of the data and its use. Furthermore, qualitative researchers can increase dependability through member checks. A member check occurs when outsiders examine the notes and data of the researchers to make sure these data are saying what the researchers claim they say.

Credibility

Credibility, for Lincoln and Guba (1985) deals with the degree of believability of the research findings. In credible research, the data is consistent and cohesive rather than scattered and contradictory. Credibility can be established through maintaining an extended contact with the respondents, in order to get to really know them and how they act. Triangulation in data collection is also an important tool because credibility is improved if multiple data sources tell you the same thing.

Transferability

Lincoln and Guba (1985) saw transferability as the degree to which the results of a given qualitative study can be transferred to a different setting, or used with a different population. The primary tool for establishing transferability is the use of adequate and detailed description in laying out all the relevant details of the research process. With this information at hand, the diligent reader can then decide whether or not the process can be transferred to another setting or population.

Confirmability

Confirmability deals with the details of the methodologies used. Have the researchers given us enough detail so that we can evaluate their data gathering and analysis? Confirmability is determined via its own audit trail. This methodological audit trail addresses such issues as the type and nature of the raw data, how the data was analyzed, and how categories and themes were formed. If available, notes and instrument development information can also be involved. The end result is not only a clear picture of the methodology, but also a clear map for creating a similar study.

Trustworthiness

The four concepts just described represent the qualitative approach to validity, when validity is viewed in a traditional way. Taken together, they comprise the qualitative validity concept of *trustworthiness*. In their earlier vision, Lincoln and Guba (1985) saw trustworthiness more or less as the sum of dependability, credibility, transferability, and confirmability. In their more mature model (Lincoln & Guba, 2000), trustworthiness is seen as a more unitary concept, with its four aspects acting as facets that complement each other.

In summary, trustworthiness is simply the degree to which we can depend on and trust given research findings. Trust is not really established; it is built up and nurtured. By rejecting the more traditional methods of establishing validity in empirical research, Lincoln and Guba (1985, 2000) sought to give qualitative researchers their own sets of tools by which to evaluate the quality and effectiveness of their work. Trustworthiness preserves many of the criteria of traditional models of validity, but the implementations of those criteria have a far different character and flavor.

It has also become common to see qualitative researchers extend this quest for understanding trustworthiness by applying its processes to different sorts of qualitative methods. For instance, Harrison, MacGibbon, and Morton (2003) have explored the relationships between reciprocity, particularly in feminist models of research, and trustworthiness. In a similar fashion, Moss (2004) looked at trustworthiness in critical narrative research.

Authenticity

Over the years, Lincoln and Guba (2000) sought to refine and expand their thinking on validity in qualitative research. In particular, they set out to address the question of validity when research is conducted in a more constructivist and more interpretivist manner. Issues of trustworthiness do matter in these forms of research, but they saw the need for an additional kind of validity that was directly relevant to the aims and natures of their particular research efforts. Many of these concepts of validity are now addressed by the concept of *authenticity*. Lincoln and Guba (2000) argued that rigorous and valid qualitative research is authentic in five senses of the term.

First of all, authentic research is *fair*. It presents as many points of view as necessary, and does so in a calm and balanced manner. If it advocates a point, it does so right up front and as soon as possible.

Second of all, it is *ontologically authentic*. That is, it seeks to raise awareness in a genuine and legitimate fashion. As part of this process, cultural and historical insights are used with their proper emphases and in their proper settings and perspectives.

Third, it is *educatively authentic*. By this, Lincoln and Guba mean that research should be able to offer us the chance to apply critical thinking to propose strong moral and ethical stances. Furthermore, these stances should be clearly stated.

Fourth, it is *catalytically authentic*. As such, the research directs us to action that is appropriate to and matches its findings. The researchers neither go too far nor not far enough in their call to action, based on their data and research.

Finally, it is *tactically authentic*. Tactically authentic research serves as the foundation for training others to take certain kinds of action. Again, this training cannot be the result of underextending or overextending the actual research findings (Lincoln & Guba, 2000, pp. 180–181).

In short, authenticity is a plan for evaluating the potential impact of a piece of research in the world at large. Is it as free as possible of defects that might affect its ability to be understood or implemented? What are its potential practical or moral implications? Is it general enough to guide a wide variety of potential interpretations, insights, or calls to action?

QUESTIONING AND THE LITERATURE REVIEW

What is the role of the literature review in qualitative research? Do we need to do a literature review to find or refine a research question, much as we do in many forms of qualitative research? Once we find a research question or a target area, do we turn to the literature to help refine our questions or frame our approach? Or do we avoid the literature altogether, and let the world of experience lead us directly? These and similar questions are important to address.

How do you take the information that you have gotten from other researchers and theorists and use this information to set up your own research questions? That is, how do you use the literature to support your research? Whether we realize it or not, a literature review is an argument, and every argument is built by the use of reasoning. But we know that qualitative research emphasizes different reasoning skills and strategies. How does this affect the nature of the literature review in qualitative research?

Every time we do a literature review, we are also doing an exercise in applied logic and argumentation. As we will see, this is an extremely complex and controversial topic within qualitative research. Again, we need to start by drawing back and looking at the bigger picture. What is the purpose of doing a literature review? It all depends on the type of research you are pursuing.

The Role of the Literature Review in Quantitative Research

In the case of quantitative research, the literature review is the basic tool we use to ground our claims, our theories, and eventually our hypotheses. To be more precise, we review the literature in quantitative research for three primary reasons.

First of all, the traditional literature review in quantitative research shows that we are not working in a vacuum. By pulling in the findings of other researchers, and the claims of other theories and theorists, we can show how our work fits into a larger frame. When we can demonstrate that we are not working in isolation, this lends credence to the importance and relevance of our own work.

Second of all, the traditional literature review lays out the findings and arguments of those who do not agree with us, so that we can make a case for our approach being more correct. If we give opposing views a fair hearing, and then we show how these views can be reinterpreted from our perspective without our perspective being reduced to theirs, then we have a powerful case for our perspective being more correct. Too often, we ignore opposing views, or reduce those views to simplistic and inaccurate versions instead of looking at them as they really are. This process of putting forth inadequate versions of a position just to make it easy to refute that position is called "the straw man argument" or "setting up a straw man just to knock it down." The straw man is a vivid way of describing an oversimplified position; it has about as much life, when compared to the original theory, as a straw man has when compared to a real person. When we avoid the straw man approach, we ultimately benefit by having a more powerful and plausible theory.

Finally, the traditional literature review is used to demonstrate the uniqueness of our own research. By looking at the research on your topic, you can demonstrate that no one else has done this particular piece of research. Given that research often involves a tremendous expenditure of time and money, it is important to demonstrate that you are not simply repeating another piece of research. Instead, you are using your time and money and effort to break new ground.

The Role of the Literature Review in Qualitative Research

An effective literature review is an important part of the process of doing qualitative research. Like literature reviews in more traditional research models, it is an argument. But is it the same kind of argument? And how should it be conducted? There are two schools of thought on the nature of the literature review in qualitative research. We will consider each in turn.

The first school of thought holds that "ignorance is bliss." That is, it is the job of qualitative researchers to treat field data on its own terms. One way to make sure that you can give your field data its proper weight is to set aside your own biases and preconceptions. Therefore, it is the job of qualitative researchers to set aside their preconceptions and let the data speak for itself. This is certainly a hard thing to do. One way to make this job harder is to go out and do a lot of reading on the topic beforehand. In this fashion, you are just adding more stuff that you will have to set aside.

From this perspective, the literature review is broken into two stages. At the outset, you need to read only enough research and theory to make sure that you are not doing research that has already been done. Once you are well into your research, or perhaps at the end of your data collection, then you return to the literature and review it, based on what you have learned from your field experiences. So, it is not the case that you are avoiding a literature review. You are simply altering its timing, because of your need for having as fresh a perspective as possible when you do your data collection.

The second school of thought acknowledges the importance of reading and reviewing and understanding the literature on your topic prior to your data collection. The more you know about your topic, the better job you will do on setting up your research. In this case, the literature review is not used to show why the research is needed to answer some question. Instead, the literature is reviewed to demonstrate that our understanding of the topic in question is somehow incomplete. Again, it is not the case that we have a wrong understanding of some phenomenon; it is the case that we do not understand it well enough. But it is important to document the understanding that we do have, and that is the role of the literature review. Metcalfe (2003), for example, looks at the literature review as analogous to the testimony of expert witnesses. By seeking the counsel of these experts, then, you are better informed on your topic and how to proceed.

How you choose to do your literature review will depend upon both your topic and your approach. If you are looking to build data-driven theory, then you need to be able to go into the data-collection process as fresh as you possibly can. If you are looking for neglected angles and nuances and patterns that will enhance and complexify our current understanding of some phenomenon or issue, then you need to gain and document as complete an understanding of that phenomenon or issue as you can. In that fashion, you will have built the "standard" picture that you eventually hope to modify.

ETHICS AND QUALITATIVE RESEARCH

A good researcher is an ethical researcher. Ethical issues pervade all of qualitative research (see Christians, 2000; Soltis, 1990). Furthermore, becoming an ethical researcher is a lifelong learning process. That is, we can never say that we have no more to learn or understand about the ethical implications of our actions (Roth, 2004).

General Ethical Guidelines

Fortunately, we can begin the complex process of mastering the ethics of qualitative research by concentrating and building on a few simple phrases. Here are four notions I try to build into all of my own work, and I invite you to consider them for your work as well.

First of all, *do no harm*. Make sure you have permission to observe. Make sure the people you are working with do not suffer in any way from your research. Make sure that if you are working with children or other special populations, others know what you are doing and agree that you are likely to do no harm. Informed consent is the keystone of ethical conduct in qualitative research. Embrace it, instead of treating it as some nuisance that has to be dealt with in order for you to get about doing your work.

When you are asking questions, try to put yourself in the place of the people you are asking. Are these questions hurtful in any way? Do they bring up painful issues that you are not prepared or qualified to deal with? Are they really necessary, or are they just satisfying some idle curiosity of yours?

When you are participating in some field setting, are you welcome? Are you setting people up for getting into trouble later? Are you making promises that you cannot keep? Are you walking away from settings where you have raised peoples' expectations and given them false hope? Are things better, or at least no worse, than they were before you got there?

When you interpret and analyze your data, are you being fair to all parties concerned? Are you careful to protect identities? Are you making claims or laying out interpretations that could eventually get other people on the scene in trouble? Have you shared your interpretations with others to make sure they are comfortable that they can live with your claims and conclusions?

Second, *be open*. Do not observe people without their knowledge. Do not tell people you are doing one thing when you are really doing something else. If someone asks you what you are doing, tell him or her the truth. If your informants want to know what you have written about them, show them. If they do not like what you have said, remember that the data always belongs to them. They are not allowed to edit your work, but they are certainly allowed to remove their thoughts or words from your research. After all, you are only borrowing them for your work. If you do not want someone to remove his or her words or thoughts, then talk to them and tell them why you have used the material in the way that you have. But be willing to accept their point of view and their decisions.

Third, *be honest*. Do not lie to people. Do not use material without permission. Just as importantly, be honest to yourself. Do not delude or deceive yourself. If you were wrong, or you have changed your mind, say so.

Finally, *be careful*. Make sure that you have documented your work so that others can follow what you have done. In some forms of qualitative research, and in qualitative evaluation in particular, it is most important to be able to create an audit trail through your work. When you have made claims and conclusions, can these be traced to your data? It is important to leave not only a final record of your work, but also a working record. You will often not publish your working records, but it is important to hold onto them. You never know when current or future researchers will feel the need to take a closer look at your work, and you need to make that task as easy for them as possible. All of this documentation, of course, should not compromise the confidentiality of your sources or settings.

Ethics and Qualitative Practice

How have qualitative researchers addressed specific ethical issues in their own practices? A number of recent examples are provided in the following subsections.

Confidentiality.
Baez (2002) examines the dilemma that confidentiality often raises in qualitative research. First of all, confidentiality is designed to protect the privacy of the individual and protect that individual from harm. Often, researchers have to discard findings because reporting those findings might reveal the identity of the informant. However, when the research has important political implications, how important is the secrecy of the informant? If the informant is working in an oppressive situation, and the research could offer the potential for resistance or reform, should the researcher protect the privacy of the informant? Does the chance for greater good outweigh the need to protect the individual? Baez discusses these issues in terms of secrets and openness, and the roles these ideas play in certain forms of transformative qualitative research.

Informed consent and power dynamics.
Knight, Bentley, Norton, and Dixon (2004) explored the perception of consent forms by minority parents. In their study, none of the parents of Latino/Latina children were willing to sign a consent form. Part of their problem was the fact that their Institutional Review Board (IRB) had advocated the use of a standardized consent form. Although this standardized consent form guaranteed consistent rights across all participants, its language conveyed a substantially

different meaning to the minority parents. These authors argue that we need to reexamine the need to contextualize consent forms, especially in those cases where groups with less social power might feel threatened by the wording and format of a standard consent form.

Informed consent at your home institution.

Malone (2003) set out to do what she thought would be a fairly simple and straightforward study—she attempted to collect data at her home institution. She soon found out that "familiarity breeds complication." In particular, she warns us that academic institutions are often contentious places. People who agree to do research in their home settings may unintentionally place their participants at greater risk. Identities are often harder to conceal in these settings, and people with lesser power, such as graduate students and nontenured faculty, may well find themselves at risk if they go against prevailing patterns and currents. Malone recommends that researchers working in their own backyards need to hold themselves to a higher standard of confidentiality and protection.

Collaborative research.

Goldstein (2000) describes some of the ethical dilemmas she encountered in her collaborative research efforts with a classroom teacher. These dilemmas covered a wide range of topics. First of all, there was a lack of clarity over what constitutes collaboration in the first place, coupled with a narrow range of examples of collaboration from educational settings only. This inadequacy of focus was soon coupled with real-world problems dealing with power, privilege, and roles. Paradoxically, the fact that Goldstein and her collaborator were friends only seemed to heighten these power conflicts. In the end, it took enormous amounts of soul searching and good faith work to make the collaboration successful. Goldstein warns us that good faith and good intentions are not enough when dealing with complex tactical research issues.

Ethically important moments.

Guillemin and Gillam (2004) point out that ethical tensions are to be expected in qualitative research. Going into the field and dealing with things as you find them will always be complex, and some of that complexity will be ethical. Day to day issues, or "ethics in practice" are particularly important. In order to go beyond the standard protections that we seek through consent forms and other devices, Guillemin and Gillam recommend that we be ethically sensitive as well. By being reflexive over our practice, and by being alert to ethical issues as they arise in everyday practice, or ethically important moments, we can better perform our ethical responsibilities as researchers. Given that qualitative research deals with more complex settings, it only follows that our ethical responsibilities will be equally more complex.

QUESTIONING IN QUALITATIVE SCIENCE AND QUALITATIVE INQUIRY

Questioning is a multifaceted and complex process. Some aspects of questioning are relevant for all forms of qualitative research.

First of all, all forms of qualitative research need to be ethical. When we raise our questions, we need to make sure we do not hurt anyone in the process. Sometimes, the correct ethical choice is obvious. Other times, making the correct ethical choice can be subtle and elusive. We are nonetheless committed to making those choices as correctly as we can.

Next, all forms of qualitative research should be honest and truthful in their designs and discussions of findings. We need to make sure that others understand what we have done, and that they would reach many of the same conclusions that we do, based on our analyses.

Finally, all qualitative research studies must earn the trust and respect of their readers. We need to make sure our findings are trustworthy for ourselves and for others. Our results should speak to ourselves and to our readers in authentic ways, and should guide legitimate action and even reform. Beyond these universal points, different forms of qualitative research deal with questioning issues in different ways.

Questioning and Qualitative Science

Many forms of qualitative science depend upon the research question as the guideline and basis for conducting research. They may start with a specific question, or that question might arise after they have been doing research on-site. Sometimes, hypotheses are raised and tested. Conceptual frameworks are built. Qualitative science, like all forms of science, pursues systematic sources of knowledge, and the questioning process is seen as an important part of that systematic process. Tactics are important, but strategies also play a key role in these forms of research.

Questioning and Qualitative Inquiry

Qualitative inquiry is often based upon finding a target and approaching that target with a particular tactically-based research agenda. Sometimes, that agenda is to understand the situation better. Participants and researchers share experiences and stories, and rich and thick accounts and descriptions are forged. The nature of the particular target comes into clearer focus. Insights and interpretive illuminations are often the results.

Other times, the agenda is more critical. Key ideas and notions are often deconstructed, or efforts to raise awareness are conducted as part of the research effort. In some cases, actual change is advocated and pursued. More than anything else, the question that guides most qualitative inquiry is a simple "why?" But, as we often come to find out, "why" is usually anything but simple.

QUESTIONING AND THE MIRROR, WINDOW, AND LANTERN

If we return to our three technologies of looking from Chapter 1, we can examine them in light of how they might guide our questioning processes. How do these different perspectives address issues like reliability, validity, and generalizability? What sorts of research questions or target areas are foregrounded by each approach? And how would each perspective deal with the matter of tactical adjustment?

Questioning and the Mirror.   The basic question that we ask when we look into a mirror is always a variant of the following—*Who am I?* If the rest of society is looking over our shoulders then we can expand the question to—*Who are we?*

The mirror is at the heart of all exegesis. When we want to know what certain things mean, we do so to learn more about ourselves and our cultures. Validity is an important notion in mirror-based questioning. Is our reflection clear and true? Or has it been distorted by the mirror? We need to keep the issue of truth front and center to prevent the temptation of allowing our research questions to focus too much on ourselves, our thoughts, and our feelings. There is a confessional tone within much good qualitative research, but those confessional aspects are always a means to a larger end. After all, we are interested in the world at large. We are part of that world, and therefore a valid part of our inquiry into its nature, but we are not the whole world. Keeping our eye on the larger issue of validity can help us stay on track here.

Questioning and the Window.   When we walk the path of the window, we need to take care that our efforts are unbiased and representative of the world in general. Therefore, reliability and generalizability are more important issues for window-based forms of questioning.

When we adhere to the window approach, we are committed to making sure our research addresses as broad an audience as possible. Therefore, we need to make sure we are asking questions that not only give us accurate information, but also information that has broad applicability. When qualitative research turns its questioning focus on the typical person or the typical setting, then we are also saying that our work needs to be as reliable and as general as possible.

The question any qualitative researcher should ask, given this need for reliability and generalizability, is this—*Should I handle this research from a quantitative perspective instead?* The tools for ensuring reliability and generalizability are much more refined from a quantitative perspective; so you must make a good case for taking the qualitative path. Quite frankly, a desire to avoid measurement and statistical issues is not good enough. All qualitative researchers should have at least a basic mastery of these quantitative procedures, just in case they need to change methodological direction due to the changing nature of their conceptualization of the research question.

Questioning and the Lantern.   Of all forms of questioning in qualitative research, the path of the lantern is most suited to the concept of tactical adjustment. Armed with the basic realization that we do not understand our phenomenon well enough, the researcher asks his or her question not to predict some final answer, but to set us off along some fruitful path. Not all paths will be equally valuable. Some dark corners lead to dead ends, and sometimes we have to backtrack conceptually as well as physically. But every dead end is another alternative that can be scratched off the master list. Therefore, tactical adjustment is not just about awareness and flexibility. Like all other forms of research, there is a dimension of persistence as well.

PLANNING YOUR RESEARCH PROPOSAL: FIRST DRAFT OF THE RESEARCH QUESTION

Actually, neither Albert nor Carol has a full-fledged research question so far. Carol has a goal to develop a grounded theoretical understanding, and Albert has a target area and a specific population to examine.

Carol

Carol realizes that her research question is about interactions. She wants to know how such things as the search for a good education, the search for a good career, and the search for a good life partner all interact. Do they work together? Do they conflict with each other? How do single women with limited means find the energy and the money to address all three issues?

Albert

For Albert, his research question came from a surprise in his everyday life. This is not unusual—qualitative research is often driven by the power of surprise. Once he became aware of these unusual students, he wanted to study them closer. What are they like? What can they tell us about math anxiety that is new and illuminating? How can we help them?

Ourselves

Research questions and target areas come from all sorts of places and experiences.

Try this process to help sharpen your own potential research questions:

- Write out a general research area that interests you.
- Now, without too much thought, generate a list of potential research questions or topics. Do not worry whether or not they are well written or well formed. Just get your list on paper.
- Rank these questions and topics.
- Take a look at your top three choices. What do they have in common? How are they different?
- Finally, rewrite your top choices in your best possible form. These are now a set of potentially good research questions.

CHAPTER 7

Data Gathering

Exercise Six—*Metaphor Repair*

One of the most powerful and natural conceptual tools that we possess is the ability to create and understand metaphors. In fact, Lakoff and Johnson (1980) argue that all concepts are metaphorical at heart. One reason for the power of metaphor is that we generally use them to move from the familiar to the unfamiliar.

Metaphors can literally change the way we understand things. Consider the following famous example. Atoms were once thought to be hard little balls of matter. When the nucleus and electron theory of the atom first emerged, it was hard for people to think of atoms as being made of parts. This unfamiliar notion was clarified by the use of a metaphor—the atom is like a solar system. The nucleus is like the sun and the electrons are like planets. In this fashion, a strange and novel view was rendered more common and ordinary. People became comfortable with the solar system metaphor of the atom. They expected electrons to orbit nuclei along carefully determined paths.

But then quantum theory came along, and described the position of electrons not by their orbits, but by the probability of them being at a certain spot at a certain time. So the metaphor shifted again. Now electrons were seen not as planets in an orbit, but as "clouds" of probable locations (known as orbitals) around the nucleus. As our understanding of subatomic particles continues to change, our metaphors are hard pressed to keep pace.

In our atom example, we see that metaphors are far from perfect. The problem with all metaphors, as Homer so correctly pointed out several millennia ago, is that they limp. In other words, though metaphors get some things right, they inevitably get other things wrong. As we have seen, the atom-as-solar-system metaphor itself made it hard for some people later on to grasp the quantum nature of the orbital. So in essence, the cloud metaphor was introduced to "repair" the earlier planetary metaphor.

This exercise will focus on metaphor repair in an area of your personal interest. Unlike the more difficult task of using one metaphor to modify an existing metaphor (like the cloud metaphor being used to modify the solar system metaphor of the atom), we will use a more simple replacement method:

- With the replacement method, an underlying metaphor is first identified within an area of interest. This is actually easier than it seems although we rarely if ever do it. Take a common example. Schools have often been compared to factories. How does a "school as factory" metaphor work? Well, factories produce goods, and schools produce educated students. Instruction becomes the school "manufacturing" process, and teachers are the workers. The curriculum is the blueprint, or manufacturing specifications. Principals and superintendents are the management team, and the school board is the board of directors. Tests and other forms of assessment are quality control devices to assure that the products—that is, the educated students—are within acceptable ranges of tolerance.

- Once we have identified our working metaphor, we then evaluate it. For example, there are both positive and negative consequences of the factory metaphor of schooling. On the positive side, clarity and unity of purpose are brought to the foreground, along with an emphasis on efficiency and accountability and an ongoing desire to sustain quality control. But students are active learners, and products in a factory are just passive "stuff" that await shaping and manipulation, so the metaphor breaks down fairly quickly. Therefore, it is in need of metaphor repair.

- Finally, we set about to find an alternative metaphor. One replacement strategy is to find an alternate metaphor that has been used with success in the past. If we go to early models of schooling for small children in Germany, we find the concept of the kindergarten, or garden of children. In the garden metaphor, children are seen as active, growing things that need nurturing, cultivating, and pruning.

- A more interesting strategy is to apply a metaphor that, to your knowledge, has never been used before. What sorts of fresh things can you find out about schooling when you juxtapose this concept with, say, the concept of air traffic control? Or a rodeo? Or, as I discussed in one of my own pieces (Shank, 1996), how are teachers and school kids like the O-ring booster seals that failed to operate in the doomed *Challenger* shuttle flight of 1986?

- You are now ready to pick a topic of your choice. What is the prevailing metaphor that society uses to look at this topic? How does this prevailing metaphor fall short? What might be one or more metaphors you could use to rethink our understanding of this concept?

- Write a brief report of your thoughts to share with your instructor and your classmates.

REFLECTING ON THE DATA-GATHERING PROCESS

You do not have any form of empirical inquiry without data. Therefore, data gathering is a crucial part of any form of empirical research. Each form of research collects data in its own way. This is no different for qualitative research.

We need to start by thinking about some of the basic aspects of data. As Miller and Fredericks (2003) point out, data are, first of all, evidence. Furthermore, qualitative data can be evidence *of* a claim, or *for* a claim (p. 10). Therefore, unlike some other forms of empirical inquiry, we can be collecting data to shed light on a variety of points at the same time.

Second, data collection in qualitative research, more often than not, involves a certain amount of effort spread over a substantial amount of time. This is particularly true in many of the participative forms of research like ethnography and action research. Although there are some forms of qualitative research that are designed to take place over a short period of time, such as microethnography (Erickson & Mohatt, 1982) and critical incident analysis (Angelides, 2001), most of the time we can expect data gathering to involve a good deal of time and effort.

Third, qualitative data is used to address a variety of concerns for a variety of audiences. Jacob (2001) points out that the distinction between theory-oriented and practice-oriented qualitative research is often blurred. We rarely collect data just to make a theoretical point or just to bring about improvements. Theory and practice often interpenetrate in qualitative research, and this interpenetration affects data-gathering techniques and strategies.

Finally, qualitative research is constantly examining its own methods and techniques, and so data collection is often turned back on itself to help us understand the growth and development of the field as a whole. Jones (2004) argues that data-collection methods reflect upon the basic assumptions and standards of the field, and so need to be included in our ongoing attempts to refine and improve qualitative research as a whole.

Our review of data gathering proper will focus on the skills needed to implement certain models and aspects of data gathering. We will start by looking at means and methods for handling qualitative data.

QUALITATIVE DATA-GATHERING METHODS

Data gathering and method go hand in hand. We have already discussed some of the ways to collect data using fieldnotes and interviews and the like. In this chapter, we will look at some of the most important systematic approaches for gathering data. We will start with the relatively simple process of doing case studies, and work from there into some of the conceptual and procedural details of doing a grounded theory study. After that, we explore some of the more interpretively based approaches to data gathering. These approaches include phenomenology, hermeneutics, gender-based approaches (including feminism and queer theory), and semiotics. We will conclude this review with a look at the role and power of metaphors to help us find and understand qualitative data.

CASE STUDY

The simplest form of fieldwork is the individual case study. Case study research only requires a single informant and you, the researcher. In other words, case study research is based upon the participatory relationship between you and another person. Most often, participation on your part involves you as a listener and an observer. Occasionally, you may be invited to try some activity, but that tends to be the exception rather than the rule.

Early models of case study research in qualitative research, such as Yin (1994), emphasized a more structured approach to information gathering from the case informants. Current thinking seems to favor less structured and more narrative approaches. At heart, though, the notion of a case study remains a simple idea. What can we find from a given individual that leads us toward seeing the world in different terms?

Case study, by its nature, turns as away from the typical and toward the unique. To understand the "typical," you really should do survey research. To understand an individual in depth, regardless of why, you need to sit down and talk and listen to that person (and observe if that is also feasible). Three approaches toward performing a case study predominate within the current qualitative research literature.

Stake (1995) has outlined a case study model and a set of techniques that emphasize the skills and insights that he personally has developed over his long and distinguished career as an evaluator. As such, it involves the strong use of field observation as a critical part of the case study process. But Stake is clear that the basic purpose of the single case study is not to evaluate or generalize to a larger population. The single case has to make its own case, as it were:

> A case study is expected to catch the complexity of a single case. A single leaf, even a single toothpick, has unique complexities—but rarely do we care enough to submit it to case study.

We study a case when it itself is of very special interest. We look at the detail of interaction with its contexts. Case study is the study of the peculiarity and complexity of a single case, coming to understand its activity within important circumstances. (p. xi)

For Stake, and for other case study theorists as well, a "case" is often not just a single individual. A single classroom, or a single school, or a single office setting, for example, all qualify as cases. Just because we use the language of the individual person does not rule out the use of these methods to look at single social cases as well.

Merriam (1998) lays out a set of procedures that are more general and reflect her orientation toward naturalistic inquiry. Her approach emphasizes the following criteria:

Qualitative case studies can be characterized as being particularistic, descriptive, and heuristic. *Particularistic* means that case studies focus on a particular situation, program, or phenomenon. The case itself is important for what it reveals about the phenomenon and for what it might represent. This specificity of focus makes it an especially good design for practical problems—for questions, situations, or puzzling occurrences arising from everyday practice. . . . *Descriptive* means that the end product of a case study is a rich, "thick" description of the phenomenon under study . . . *Heuristic* means that case studies illuminate the reader's understanding of the phenomenon under study. They can bring about the discovery of new meaning, extend the reader's experience, or confirm what is known. (pp. 29–30)

A third variant on the basic notion of the case study is *portraiture*. Lawrence-Lightfoot and Davis (1997) have moved beyond the simple notion of documenting a case toward the richer and more complex notion of portraiture. In their model, creating an illuminating case is as much an artistic task as it is a piece of scientific reporting:

A sure intention in the methodology of portraiture is capturing—from an outsider's purview—an insider's understanding of the scene . . . portraitists try to feel as the subject feels and to represent that understanding in a portrayal that exceeds the level of literal depiction found in a map or plan. (p. 25)

Recent work in portraiture has sought to extend the basic boundaries laid out by Lawrence-Lightfoot and Davis (1997). For example, Bloom and Erlandson (2003) expand the range of portraiture to look at how an audience of such research reviews and reacts to this material.

Alternative Case Study Types

Some of the best guides for the student of case study methodology can also be found outside the traditional social science research literature. In the best of these alternative sources, the researcher goes beyond the mere documentation of cases to make them rich sources for insight and reflection. For instance, Sacks (1985, 1990) is a wonderful example of skilled reworking of cases taken from the technical medical literature and recast for a broader audience. His cases deal with some of his more unusual neurology patients. By looking, for example, at a man in the full heat of Korsakov's Syndrome (pp. 108–115) who is driven to narrate his immediate and ongoing life in order to sustain his identity; or the brain lesion victim who tried to place his wife on his head, mistaking her for his hat (pp. 8–22); Sacks shows us something fundamental about the depth and complexity of the human mind that can only be seen in marginal psychic shadows like these. No survey of so-called "normal" people, no matter how extensive, could reveal these sorts of things to the researcher. Only in the mirror of these cases where things have changed so drastically, where the people involved navigate through the world so much differently than we do, can we see just how complex our apparently normal functioning really is.

Some of our alternative examples are exceptional for their astuteness and care. For example, Fadiman (1997) provides us with a perfect example of balanced yet personal involvement in an extended case study setting. Her case covers several years in the lives of a Hmong refugee family in California. She focuses on the doctors who seek to save this family's youngest daughter using Western ideas of medicine, the case workers who try to help the family become enculturated, and the family itself that seeks to preserve its way of being in the world and tries to save their child on their own cultural terms. Fadiman resists the notion of making either side look too saintly or too wrongheaded, and yet she allows us to see how people of good faith and goodwill can clash on such a fundamental level with such tragic results.

Cumulative Case Study

Although it is usually beyond the scope of a beginning researcher, it also makes sense to be aware of the cumulative case study. In the cumulative case study, a single topic is examined through the perspectives of many different case samplings. A single complex case is built by selecting and ordering individual cases.

Two of the best (and most famous) cumulative case studies are an enduring part of not only the social science literature, but of contemporary popular thought as well. Terkel's (1975) *Working* is the older of the two. This journalist from Chicago tackled what is seemingly a simple topic: What do people's jobs mean to them? In this cumulative case study, each respondent is sampled briefly but succinctly; Terkel rarely spends more than a page or two on any given person. The craft of the study is in the weaving and texturing of these tales, in their positioning and their flow. Personal account seems to build upon personal account, to give us a rich and complex picture of American working life.

Pipher (1994) spends a bit more time describing each of her case informants in her influential study of the toxic impact of contemporary American culture on adolescent girls. A counselor and therapist who specializes in the treatment of adolescent girls, Pipher paints a compelling and intricate case through the words and images of the girls themselves. Each account seems to build on the last, to make her arguments more and more credible. Like Fadiman, Pipher is not looking for villains. She does what any good researcher would do; she is trying to get to the truth instead.

Like Terkel's work, Pipher's study has a cumulative impact that no single case study could have. In this fashion, they are a bit like survey research. These cumulative case studies differ from surveys, though, in the fact that each new case is deliberately added to make the overall picture richer, deeper, and more complex. In a survey, we would look for patterns of how people might typically react. In the cumulative case study, we have instead an exploration of options. This work is too time consuming, and too demanding, for a novice researcher to tackle. That does not mean that they should not be read and appreciated, however.

It is also true that there are important and significant cumulative case studies within the traditional social science research tradition as well. While such studies as Gilligan (1982-1993) and Heath (1983) fall within the *general* framework of the cumulative case study, they will be discussed in depth later on for different reasons.

GROUNDED THEORY

One of the most venerable approaches to qualitative research in general is the process of Grounded Theory. Grounded Theory was first articulated in 1967 by Barney Glaser and Anselm Strauss in their landmark work, *The Discovery of Grounded Theory*.

Glaser and Strauss were sociologists engaged in the examination of complex interpersonal and social dynamics within the domain of medical sociology. Medicine is one area in contemporary life that is rife with meaning. Quite literally, medical practices and medical understandings are often matters of life and death.

As Glaser and Strauss sought to apply the sociological theories of the time to their observations in the field, they realized that existing theory was not rich enough to capture the dynamics of the situations they were finding. But at the same time, they were committed to the notion that empirical inquiry should conform to basic scientific tenets and principles, and one of the key principles was that, sooner or later, scientists create and test theories.

So, here was the bind that Glaser and Strauss uncovered—more complex theories were needed to capture the richness of meaning in social settings, but proper sociological research insisted upon having at least some theoretical position before engaging in research. Glaser and Strauss addressed this bind by insisting that the building of theory was just as much a part of the empirical tradition as testing theory. Furthermore, a piece of research could be valid if it were used to build theory, without having to go on and test that theory.

Grounded Theory, then, is a method of building theory from the ground up, so to speak. Why do we consider it an interpretative method? Simply put, theories are organized meaning claims. The role of any theory is to make sense of what is happening in a particular setting, and what is this act other than a restatement of the principle of "making meaning?"

A standard meaning-making strategy for human beings is to move from the known into the unknown. This was precisely the strategy that Glaser and Strauss sought to augment, if not replace. Instead, they argued that complex settings are best understood by starting at "ground zero" and letting the data themselves guide the growth and development of the theory.

The Evolution of Grounded Theory

Over the years, the two founders of Grounded Theory drifted away from each other, as they pursued different approaches toward extending the ideas and methods of the original theory.

The Glaser Approach to Grounded Theory

Glaser (1978) felt that Grounded Theory was in danger of becoming too mechanical. His later work was based on his desire to make sure that the approach remained sensitive to the need to treat the creation of grounded theory as an organic, ongoing process. He rejected the use of rules for data gathering and manipulation in favor of procedures to keep the researcher open and aware of new possibilities of meaning within the emerging data record.

In his later work, Glaser takes great pains to distinguish the philosophical and conceptual underpinnings of Grounded Theory from such current modes of thought as Constructivism (2002b September) and Naturalistic Inquiry (2004, January). In his current thinking, he stresses the role of creating concepts. Glaser feels that approaches such as Constructivism and Naturalistic Inquiry provide too many received concepts and ways of looking at the world.

Rather than bringing a set of preconceived ideas into a setting, Glaser says that we must bring a clearly delineated process of interacting with the setting in order to raise our conceptualizations from the setting itself. This clearly delineated process is at the heart of Grounded Theory. His most recent set of prescriptions and descriptions of the process can be found online at Strauss (2004, May). Because these processes are somewhat similar to the more familiar details of Strauss and Corbin (1998), we will not lay them out here.

The Strauss and Corbin Approach to Grounded Theory

Strauss (1988, 1995) was more concerned with standardizing the process and making it available to more and more researchers. Strauss and Corbin (1998) have produced the definitive practical guide to Grounded Theory. In their model, Strauss and Corbin emphasize a balance between taking an objective stance as a researcher while being sensitive and aware of subtle issues and possibilities to extend the research in creative ways.

The heart of Strauss and Corbin's approach to Grounded Theory is an awareness and understanding of the systematic uses and potentials of coding data. From their perspective, the coding process is based on the following stages (based on the original processes developed by Glaser and Strauss):

1. The first step is a *microscopic examination of the data.* Strauss and Corbin (1998) define microanalysis as: "The detailed line-by-line analysis necessary to generate initial categories (with their properties and dimensions) and to suggest relationships among categories . . . " (p. 57).
2. The next stage of the process is called *open coding.* During open coding " . . . data are broken down into discrete parts, closely examined, and compared for similarities and differences . . . . Closely examining data for both differences and similarities allows for fine discrimination and differentiation among categories" (Strauss & Corbin, 1998, p. 103).
3. After open coding, the researcher moves on to *axial coding.* Strauss and Corbin (1998) define axial coding as " . . . the act of relating categories to subcategories along the lines of their properties and dimensions. It looks at how categories crosscut and link" (p. 124).
4. In the *selective coding process,* we see the move from coding systems to actual grounded theory. Strauss and Corbin (1998) see this as an integrative process. It starts with the selection of a central category from the data, and then the integration of existing categories in relation to this central category as a first approximation of theory generation (pp. 143–160).
5. *Coding for process* is also a necessary step to help lay out the dynamics of the emerging theory. This process, according to Strauss and Corbin (1998), adds a dynamic dimension to our understanding of the emerging structure of the phenomena in question. That is, the structure is the snapshot of our theory, and the process is our moving picture of the theory as it operates in the world (p. 179).
6. Finally, we have the creation of the *conditional/consequential matrix.* This is defined as "An analytic device to stimulate analysts' thinking about the relationships between macro and micro conditions/consequences both to each other and to

process" (Strauss & Corbin, 1998, p. 181). This stage was the major point of departure from the earlier approach laid out by Glaser and Strauss.

At this juncture, the emergent Grounded Theory can go in a number of directions. For example, the researcher can engage in theoretical sampling to take a look at specific types of persons or situations to clarify "fuzzy" aspects of the theory. At some point, eventually, the researcher finally engages in the process of writing up the first version of the theory. It is now ready to present to the larger research community for evaluation, modification, and extension.

Grounded Theory, by its nature, moves from the specific to the general. In some cases, the research needs to stay rooted and grounded in the specifics of the particular case. In these situations, research from a phenomenological framework can be a very useful way to gain and build interpretative understanding.

Further Resources for Grounded Theory

Grounded Theory is much more involved and detailed than the outline we have sketched out here. If you find such an analytic procedure potentially useful or intriguing, then you should look at the entire process as laid out within Strauss and Corbin (1998) and Glaser (2004, May). Charmaz (2000) looks into the differences between taking an "objectivist" stance versus taking a more "constructivist" stance when doing Grounded Theory. Glaser himself (2002, September) rejects the notion of a constructivist approach to Grounded Theory, but Bryant (2003, January) argues in turn that Glaser is being too protective of the approach. Whether or not Grounded Theory stays close to its founding principles and methods, or whether it evolves, is an ongoing discussion. In the meantime, researchers like Scott (2004) continue to explore how some of its current tools can and should be used in qualitative data gathering and theory development.

PHENOMENOLOGICAL AND HERMENEUTIC DATA-GATHERING METHODS

Another major framework for interpretation is a family of diverse theories and methods that are often collected under the single label of *phenomenology*. If you are confused about phenomenology, don't be alarmed. You are not alone. There are at least two major branches of phenomenology, with a whole series of practical variants.

Phenomenology

At its most general level, phenomenology is a fairly simple notion. As human beings, we do not experience anything directly. Instead, we come to know things by the impact those things have upon our consciousness. In other words, what we really know are the effects of things on our awareness, and not the things themselves.

By carefully examining our conscious processes, however, early phenomenologists thought it was possible to be able to look through those effects, and to become aware of things as they really are. In other words, the task of phenomenology was to move past, or transcend, our conscious awareness of the nature of things, to an eventual awareness of the things themselves as they really are. Husserl (1960) laid out a series of introspective procedures designed to help us get past our conscious images of things, to the things themselves.

As a consequence, we have the empirical branch of phenomenology that is most relevant to our concerns as qualitative researchers. Most forms of phenomenological inquiry in qualitative research follow the empirical approach. We are interested in seeing how people interpret their worlds, and how we can in turn interpret their interpretations. When we start working with these sorts of systems of meaning, then we are very close to our final interpretative framework.

Over the years, there have been a number of researchers and theorists who have explored the use of phenomenology as a form of research in the social sciences (see Cohen & Omery, 1994; Ray, 1994). Alfred Schutz (1932/1967) was perhaps the first social scientist to incorporate phenomenology into his work in a systematic way. For Schutz, the goal of the social sciences was to understand the ways that people understand and function in the everyday world. Contemporary thinkers like Berger and Luckmann (1966) and Gergen (1994) have made important contributions in developing these and other ideas of Schutz and other early phenomenological thinkers.

One of the most practical forms of phenomenological research is the Interpretative Phenomenological Analysis (IPA) approach. Smith (2004) points out its basic characteristics. First of all, IPA is *idiographic*. By this, Smith means that IPA researchers work with a small number of cases, which they explore in great depth and detail. Second, IPA is *inductive*. Techniques are designed to be flexible enough to allow new and unanticipated themes and understandings to emerge in the process of doing the research. Finally, IPA is *interrogative*. It seeks to take a questioning stance toward its participants, to allow for greater depth of insight and illumination. Through an interplay of these three dynamics, the IPA researcher comes up with a multilayered analysis of the target concepts of the research.

Similar to IPA is the phenomenological approach used by Groenewald (2004). In this fairly representative study of traditional phenomenological analysis in the social sciences, Groenewald is looking at a phenomenological understanding of the concept of talent in cooperative educational programs.

Groenewald uses a five-step process to conduct his study. First of all, he identifies a topic that is appropriate for phenomenological inquiry. In this case, the concept of talent, and how it interacts with cooperative education, is his focus. From there, he then seeks to locate his participants. This sampling process starts out in a purposive fashion; Groenewald is looking for people who have something important and informed to say on these topics. Once he finds a few carefully selected participants, he asks those participants to lead him to other relevant potential contributors. This is known as the snowball technique, where leads from early participants "snowball" into greater and greater numbers of participants.

Once he has his participants, Groenewald is ready to interview them. He uses in-depth unstructured interviews. He and his participants seek to explore their beliefs and feelings toward their target concepts. Groenewald is careful to bracket his own thoughts and interpretations, and to aid his participants in bracketing theirs. To this end, he helps them move away from specifics and personal details toward a more global and abstract consideration of their experiences.

Groenewald also uses fieldnotes to help him gather data. He uses four types of notes: (1) *observational notes*, which record all important events that happened during the interview process; (2) *theoretical notes,* where he reflects initially on the meaning of certain things; (3) *methodological notes,* to remind him to do certain things at certain times; and (4) *analytical memos,* which were abstract summaries generated at the end of the day or of a set of sessions.

Finally, he analyzed, or rather explicated, his data, using the following five steps:

1. *Bracketing and Phenomenological reduction.* Here, Groenewald listened to his tapes extensively to get the gestalt, or the holistic sense, of what was being said. He paid particular attention to unique utterances and points of view, and was careful to try to filter out his own point of view when representing his participants.

2. *Delineating units of meaning.* At this point, Groenewald generated a list of meaning units. When forming these units, issues of relevance, frequency of occurrence, and manner of statement all play a key role. Ambiguities and redundancies are discarded, leaving the researcher with a manageable list of clear and meaningful concepts.

3. *Clustering of meaning units to form themes.* When meaning units are put together properly, areas of significance come into focus. By rigorously examining these pairs to make sure the right units are put together, these areas of significance serve as the bases for emerging themes.

4. *Summarizing each interview.* Once the themes are done, it is time to go back to the data once again. By summarizing each interview, he now sees how well the themes address the issues and concerns of the interviews themselves. If need be, deletions and modifications are made.

5. *Making a composite summary.* Now it is time to bring all the data together. Each interview is examined for its own unique set of themes. Common themes are discerned across all the interviews. By reflecting upon and playing off these unique and general dimensions, a composite summary was generated that illustrates both the unique and general dynamics.

Hermeneutics

Later phenomenologists, led by Heidegger (1927), declared that it was impossible to sort out the role of interpretation in our understanding and awareness of the world. We are tossed into the world as it is, and we must make our way through it as best we can, learning how to interpret and how to guide our lives based on our ability to interpret. Here we find an emphasis on hermeneutics.

Hermeneutics is the science of interpreting texts (Grondin, 1990/1994). It was first crafted by scholars who were interested in unlocking all the possible and potential meanings hidden in the books of the Bible. Later, it came to mean the art of interpreting any text, particularly when subtle or hidden meanings are the target. In the hands of a phenomenologist like Heidegger, Hermeneutic Phenomenology was all about treating our awareness of the world as if it were some complex text, with phenomenology being the art of reading and interpreting that awareness.

Moustakas (1990, 1994) has been instrumental in the growth and development of Phenomenological and Hermeneutic methods in the social sciences. His work in both Heuristic and Phenomenological research methods has built on the earlier work of the Empirical Phenomenological school that started at Duquesne University in the early 1960s. Moustakas

(1994) notes that there are seven key principles that ground all hermeneutic research in the social sciences. These seven principles are (p. 21): (1) a commitment to the use of qualitative methods; (2) a primary focus on the whole experience, rather than on its parts; (3) a search for meaning over a search for rules; (4) primary use of first-person accounts as main data sources; (5) insisting that accounts of experiences are a necessary part of any scientific understanding of any social phenomenon; (6) performing research that is guided by the personal interests and commitments of the researcher; and (7) the necessity of treating experiences and behavior as integrated parts of a single whole.

One of the most important ideas in hermeneutic research is the concept of the *Hermeneutic Circle* (Heidegger, 1927). This idea says that interpretation is self-contained. Unlike the idea of Bracketing in traditional phenomenology, the process of interpretation never ends. It continues to cycle, with each new cycle hopefully adding new depths and nuances of understanding. Also, because it is a circle, it is never grounded in anything outside of itself. In a sense, hermeneutics argues that the end product of interpretation is more interpretation.

Comparing and Contrasting Phenomenological and Hermeneutic Methods

In summary, phenomenology is that form of interpretation that says that human consciousness is the key to understanding the world. Husserl and his followers felt that we have to start with conscious awareness and then move to transcend consciousness by putting aside our presuppositions and learning to see the world as it really is. Heidegger and his followers felt that phenomenology is a form of interpretation that allows us to pursue the meanings that we hold and form about the world and our place in it. The Empirical Phenomenologists believed that we could not only examine our own consciousness to see the workings of meaning and interpretation in our perception of the world, but by careful and skilled questioning, we could come to see how others tackle those same tasks.

Laverty (2003) looks at the similarities and differences between traditional phenomenological and hermeneutic research models and strategies. In short, phenomenology is more transcendental and ahistorical. It is searching for a new type of knowledge that has its roots in the knowing subject. By being careful in its application of techniques like bracketing, it can come up with data that are valid and reliable.

On the other hand, Hermeneutic methods take an entirely different perspective. They focus on the individual not so much as a knower, but as an interpreter who is struggling to make sense of the world as he or she finds it. Hermeneutic analyses are historically and culturally grounded. Meaning is based not on the discovery of a new form of knowledge, but upon the shared understanding and interpretation of culture, history, language, and practice. Interpretations lead to other interpretations, via the Hermeneutic Circle. In the final analysis, the result of hermeneutic research is shared understanding that can allow us to navigate better in a complex and subtle world.

GENDER-BASED ASPECTS OF DATA GATHERING

Over the years, a growing number of qualitative researchers have argued that the act of gathering data is not an abstract or context-free process. Instead, who we are often influences what we see, how we act, and what we consider important. Nowhere have these issues been more important than in examining the role of gender in data gathering.

The two most important dimensions of gendered data gathering involve feminist approaches to qualitative research and the role and impact of queer theory.

Feminist Approach to Data Gathering

Ever since the landmark 1986 book by Belenky and her colleagues on women's ways of knowing, feminist thinking has played a key role in data gathering in qualitative research (Belenky, Clinchy, Goldberger, & Tarule, 1986). In this work, they conducted 135 in-depth interviews with women, exploring the ways that women looked at the world and at patterns of growth and development as women become more refined and more empowered as thinkers.

Based on the findings of their interviews, Belenky and her colleagues developed the following five-stage model of growth in feminist epistemology. The first and most primitive stage is the *silent* stage. In this stage, women simply keep quiet and follow the lead of others around them.

From this stage, women then can develop into the *received knowledge* stage. In this stage, women actively look outside themselves for guidance in understanding themselves and the world.

From the received knowledge stage, women can then grow into the *subjective knowledge* stage. Here, women start paying attention to their intuitions and inner voices as a source of knowledge and wisdom.

Once women are comfortable with themselves as sources of knowledge, they can start incorporating knowledge from the outside once again into their epistemological frameworks. This *procedural knowledge* stage starts off with a skeptical sort of awareness that puts everything into doubt and works from there. This separated aspect of procedural knowledge then involves into a more connected form of procedural knowledge, where women start to connect with worldviews that support and nurture them.

Finally, there is the *constructed knowledge* stage, where women not only construct personal understandings but they also seek to construct mutual patterns of knowledge and understanding with others. In this stage, there is a sense that all knowledge and truth is constructed and embodied. Knowledge is situated in particular circumstances, and subjectivity plays an integral in pulling together a cohesive understanding of the world.

Building upon these basic ideas about the growth and evolution of knowing among women, other researchers began to develop feminist approaches to doing qualitative research. Stanley and Wise (1993) list the following seven key principles of doing feminist qualitative research, based upon feminist models of knowing:

1. The researcher/research relationship should not be a hierarchical relationship.
2. Emotions should be seen as valuable aspects of the research process.
3. The conceptualizations of "objectivity" and "subjectivity" as binaries or dichotomies must not occur in research.
4. The researchers' intellectual autobiography must be taken into consideration when viewing their conclusions.
5. The researcher must consider the existence and management of the different "realities" or versions held by the researchers and the researched.
6. The researcher must be aware of issues surrounding authority and power in research.
7. The researcher must recognize that there is authority and power in the written representation of research. (p. 189)

Feminist research continues to play an important role in qualitative research, and its perspectives continue to evolve. For instance, Pillow (2002) examines the notion of whether or not a man can conduct a proper feminist study.

One of the key areas of examination of feminist thought by feminist researchers involves its philosophical grounding. St. Pierre (2000) argues that feminist research is importantly related to current poststructural movements in philosophy. She sees feminism as part of a larger countermovement against classical humanism and the Enlightenment. Poststructural thinking subverts and critiques such cherished humanist domains as the ability of language and discourse to clarify our rational understanding of the world. In its place, poststructural thought offers an ongoing examination and conversation of such dynamics as power and repression, and the relation of these dynamics to issues of truth and identity. Feminism, in many of its forms, shares the same concerns and focuses on the same issues. These concerns also shape what counts as data, and how one goes about collecting and analyzing data.

Queer Theory

Queer theory is another mode of gendered interpretation and data gathering (see Jagose, 1996 and Pinar, 1998 for an introduction to queer theory). Queer theory is sometimes difficult to pin down, but its basic premise is that gender and sexual identities are representational in nature (Butler, 1990). Because there is nothing that is intrinsically male or female, or straight or gay, our embodiments in the world are largely determined by cultural dynamics.

Queer theory makes extensive use of the concept of reading. As Bloom (1999) points out, "For qualitative researchers, interpreting gender, sexuality, and sexual desires in the lives of respondents is crucial as a means to make visible the ways that the social constructions of intelligibility and unintelligibility are lived" (p. 331).

In her study, Bloom (1999) makes this point by rereading an older piece of research. This particular piece of research was a feminist analysis of an individual she called Sandy. In her original analysis, Bloom had not focused on the role of sexual preference and desire in Sandy's life and life history. However, because Sandy professed to be straight, Bloom failed to take proper note of various lesbian recollections and reflections. By rereading the data from a queer perspective, Bloom was able to see that she had missed key dynamics in Sandy's motives and patterns of interactions with the world.

Bloom concludes her study with the following salient recommendation:

> Feminist postmodern psychoanalytic theories, lesbian theories, and feminist theories all encourage us to reframe the epistemological standpoints from which we interpret what it means for each of us and those we study to be gendered, sexual beings in a particular cultural/social milieu. By gaining an understanding of the many interpretive theories and epistemological standpoints available that do not force individuals into false intelligibility according to linear scripts of sex, gender, and sexual desire, we have a tool that can be used to dismantle epistemological structures that seek to stabilize individuals repressively. (p. 343)

SEMIOTIC APPROACHES TO DATA GATHERING

The least prevalent, but in some ways the most powerful, framework of data gathering for qualitative research is grounded on semiotic theory, or semiotics.

Semiotics is the general science of signs. What is a sign? A sign is anything that can stand for anything else. Eco (1976) likes to say that a sign is anything you can use to tell a lie. Signs tend not to stand alone in the world. Instead, we find systems of signs. Semiotic research is about learning to discover and use such systems.

Semiotics seems to occupy a middle ground between grounded theory and phenomenology. Like grounded theory, it seeks to map out formal systems and relationships. Like phenomenology, it focuses on the operation of meaning in everyday life and experiences. In other words, it is more situational than grounded theory, but more formal than empirical phenomenology.

The Language of Signs

Semiotic research models usually take one of two different forms. The first model is based on Saussure's (1959) initial linguistic insights into the nature of the sign. This form of semiotics, called *semiology,* took its nature from a declaration by Saussure (1959) that language is a special form of a more generalized code process known as semiotics, and that semiotics proper is the science of studying language and other codes as they function in societies and cultures (Hawkes, 1977).

Two of the most famous examples of a semiological approach to semiotic data gathering are found in the works of Barthes (1957, 1967) and Levi-Strauss (1966, 1978). Barthes began as a cultural critic who was interested in looking for codes and patterns that underlay the form and function of apparently ordinary and simple popular cultural trends and artifacts. He turned that research toward a more formal model (Barthes, 1967) that laid out the framework for a semiological theory of popular culture. Barthes was particularly important to literary critics who were interested in looking toward literature as a guide for understanding culture, instead of the more usual move of using culture as a way to understand literature.

Levi-Strauss was one of the most empirical of the structuralist semioticians. He established the discipline of structural anthropology (Levi-Strauss, 1966, 1978), which sought to understand culture as if it were a language. Levi-Strauss was particularly adept at the analysis of myth, showing how the key components of myths were actually markers of deep and often unexamined cultural patterns and traditions.

Within structures of kinship and myth, and whether or not food is cooked or eaten raw, or whether or not the flesh of a given animal is considered food, Levi-Strauss was able to unravel remarkably precise rules that cut across particular cultures. It was his goal to uncover the universal structures that undergird any and all cultures, and to show how myths, rituals, and practices are ways that a given culture handles those universal rules and structures.

In short, semiology was a strategy that sought to use the "languages" and codes of culture, those that transcend any and all given actual cultural practices, to collect data on culture. Gilgun (1999) illustrates the use of these techniques in qualitative research. In her study, she treats the narrative account of her participant, a confessed serial killer, as a complex interplay of data creating an overall "text." Using many of Barthes's methods and insights, she is able to pull these aspects of her data together to create an insightful and cohesive picture of the thoughts and motives of her participant.

The Logic of Signs

The second, and far less prevalent, semiotic approach within the social sciences attempts to implement the logically based insights of C. S. Peirce.

As difficult and unusual as the ideas of Saussure and the structuralists are, the ideas of Peirce are even more unfamiliar and difficult. Peirce is considered by many to be the greatest mind produced in American culture, but he demands precision and commitment from his readers. Be aware of this if you turn to reading of Peirce directly (Peirce, 1992 and Peirce, 1998 are an excellent introduction to Peirce's own writings).

Peirce's model of semiotics is tied directly to his foundational work in the philosophical school known as Pragmatism (see Peirce 1903/1992 for his mature thoughts on the nature and basis of Pragmatic thinking). For Peirce, Pragmatism is first and foremost a theory of meaning. How do we determine the meaning of things? Peirce asked. He decided that for an empirical researcher, the meaning of a concept is based on the impact of that concept on our practices in the world.

The impact of a concept on the world is rarely direct, however. Therefore, we seldom find meaning directly. More often than not, the meaning of a concept is embedded in the relation of that concept to other things in the world. Another way to say this is to say that the meaning of a concept is found in the signs of the presence or absence of the concept in the world. That is, we do not have the concepts or their meanings readily available. What we have instead are the signs. What we need to do is to reason from those signs to their meanings (see Peirce, 1898/1992 for his most comprehensive statement about the relation of logic and reasoning to empirical inquiry).

Therefore, for Peirce, semiotics is a way of thinking and reasoning about what we find in the world, so that we can infer deeper or covert or hidden principles or properties in action. Deely (1990) provides a challenging but comprehensive picture of the scope of Peircean semiotics and semiotic thinking in his attempt to understand the nature of the world.

There are relatively few people working on explicit Peircean semiotic methods for the social sciences. Don Cunningham and myself (Cunningham & Shank, 1984; Shank & Cunningham, 1992) have been looking at how semiotics can change the vision and practice of empirical researchers. I have been interested in how this way of reasoning can impact qualitative research in particular (Shank, 1994).

Let me illustrate how a Peircean semiotic approach might allow us to conduct a fundamentally different type of qualitative inquiry by focusing on a particular example of my own research. In 1996, I decided to work on a piece to explore some possible implications of the *Challenger* disaster for us in research (Shank, 1996). Ten years earlier, the space shuttle *Challenger* exploded shortly after liftoff. After careful analysis, it was found that its O-rings had failed to seal.

The O-rings were a set of soft, rubbery seals that were supposed to create a seal for the solid rocket boosters of the *Challenger*. Because the launch had occurred on a cold January morning, the seals were stiff from the cold and therefore not pliable enough to work properly. The rest is tragic history.

The essence of the semiotic approach is to treat matters in the empirical world as signs for real or possible meanings. How do we apply these ideas in this particular case? First of all, we can say that this particular inquiry started out with conjecture, which then was formed into a metaphorical understanding of the world. That newly created metaphorical understanding, teased out of the details of the *Challenger* case and our conjecture, was then given to a community of thinkers to reflect upon and modify. Let us look at each step in turn.

We start with our conjecture. We know that the O-ring boosters on the Challenger failed because the temperature at launch time was too cold and they failed to be pliable enough to make a proper seal. But suppose, for the sake of looking deeper into the nature of the problem, those O-ring seals had not been mere inanimate objects. What, we might conjecture, would have happened if the O-ring seals had been alive?

The most likely answer to the question just raised is this—if the O-ring seals were really alive, then most likely they would have found some way to seal, cold or not. After all, their own survival would have depended on their ability to form such a seal. And as a consequence, the launch would have been deemed a "success" and the launch conditions would have been deemed "acceptable."

The heart of the article is the application of this notion of a living O-ring as a metaphor for American public schools. What would happen if teachers and students were like actual O-rings, and just responded to conditions as given? How much of the very survival of the American educational system depends on heroic efforts of teachers who love to teach and students who love and need to learn?

These ideas were transmitted electronically to various discussion groups, and input and dialogue from these groups were added to the final version of the paper. In this fashion, a framework of meaning grounded in experience was both formed and applied. Efforts such as these are the strong points of the semiotic interpretative framework.

USING METAPHORS TO GATHER DATA

Many data-gathering methods in qualitative research are grounded in particular philosophical positions. Sometimes, we need ways to approach data that are less shaped by the belief systems we either bring in or find in place. This is where the use of metaphors to find and gather data can come in handy. In recent years, qualitative researchers have advocated the use of metaphors to explore data (Koro-Ljungberg, 2001). Procedures for analyzing metaphors (Schmitt, 2000, January) and using metaphor to build theory in qualitative research (Aubusson, 2002) have also been developed.

Metaphors are just one of the tools that we can use to reorient our thinking to come up with new insights to pursue as researchers. These sorts of creative tools have always been available for researchers, and the best researchers have always used them. But, in moving from quantitative to qualitative research, these tools shift from playing an implicit role to playing a more explicit role. To see this we can look at the role played by metaphor (one of the most creative thinking tools within research) within both quantitative and qualitative research.

Metaphors in Quantitative Research

As we stated in the exercise, metaphors have always played a role in research. But in quantitative research, metaphors have been used to give explanatory clarity to theoretical positions. That is, while metaphors were used to understand scientific theory, and in some cases to even create theory, they were always replaced by scientific theory eventually. In other words, metaphors are like maps used to describe and contextualize scientific theory; but as we well know, the map is not the territory.

For these reasons, metaphor is always subservient to scientific theory in quantitative research. Another way to look it is as follows: metaphor is one way to get at meaning in quantitative research, but a major role of scientific theory is to settle matters of meaning in order to get on to the business of testing hypotheses. In quantitative research, there is no meaning without scientific theory.

In short, metaphor can play a guiding and descriptive role in quantitative research, but not a fundamental role. This is because the fundamental nature of quantitative research is verification. We addressed this issue briefly when we talked about the shortcomings of induction for empirical researchers. We now need to look at it a bit closer.

Is a certain claim true or not? Before we can verify a claim, we first have to make sure that it is meaningful. Once we are sure that a claim is meaningful, or in other words, we have settled the matter of the meaning of a particular claim, then we can go about trying to determine if it is true or not. But there is no point in trying to verify either a meaningless or ambiguous claim, as we would not understand what the claim is really saying to us even if we knew that somehow it was true.

In quantitative research, the meaning of a claim is settled in two ways. First of all, the claim is usually grounded in some scientific theory. The best case is when the claim is a hypothesis that can be formally derived from the scientific theory and then tested empirically to see if it is true in the world of experience. The second form of meaning settlement is in terms of the conditions for identifying the presence of the claim in the world of experience. Claims are made up of terms, and these terms have a presence in the world.

Suppose, as a scientist, I say that my theory predicts that hungry people are more likely to steal than people who are not hungry. First of all, I need to show how my claim is derivable from a larger theory of behavior and society. But then I need to pin down the meaning of my key terms. What do I mean by *hungry?* What do I mean by *steal?* In familiar parlance, I am required to provide operational definitions for each of these key terms. *Hungry* and *steal* need to be defined in terms of public and observable actions or conditions. In this fashion, the question of the meaning of these terms is settled along the way to verification.

In summary, the issue of meaning in quantitative research is handled strategically, in terms of scientific theory, and operationally, in terms of defining key concepts. In this fashion, meaning is a matter to be settled and resolved prior to any empirical test of verification. Therefore, the effects of a meaning-exploratory notion like metaphor have to be either resolved or assimilated before any empirical test can be performed.

Metaphors in Qualitative Research

Metaphor can play a much more fundamental role in qualitative research. Because qualitative research is the systematic empirical inquiry into meaning, metaphors are natural tools for leading us toward previously undiscovered modes of meaning. Meaning, for qualitative research, is not a puzzle to be solved before the real work of verification can commence. Meaning is instead an integral part of reality. It is not the wholly concocted product of researchers and other people. It is a form of order that helps keep the complex fabric of reality together.

Meaning reveals itself via things like metaphors, and part of our job as researchers is to pay attention to the signals that metaphors and other things give us, and to see how they fit into our current understanding of things. If there is an existing theory that fits the meaning patterns, well and good. If not, then it is our theories, and not the world, which are lacking in meaning.

Let us now go back and consider our exercise from the beginning of this chapter. We started thinking about schools. One way to look at the original example is to say—*What do schools mean?* When we tackle issues of meaning, more often than not we move from the familiar to the unfamiliar. Our first attempt dealt with the comparison of schools to factories. We might not be all that familiar with schools, but we do understand how factories work. And so we use our understanding of factories to help increase our understanding of schools.

When we choose our metaphors for expanding our understanding, we are also no longer solely at the mercy of the situation. We can bring in other systems of understanding to compare and contrast. Why should we do this? For one thing, this procedure allows us to find ourselves in a state of surprise. If there is no surprise, then there is no "opening" for abductive reasoning. We already are quite comfortable with the understanding we already have because that understanding allows us to move smoothly along. But as researchers, we are committed to the notion that there is always more to understand. If the situation does not present us with surprises naturally, we can use metaphors to create these surprises for ourselves.

There are dangers involved in metaphor use, and indeed with all forms of abductive reasoning. Three pitfalls in particular loom large for the qualitative researcher.

The first danger is the cliché pitfall. Here, we have decided that we are going to replace an old, worn-out metaphor with a brand new metaphor that we expect will serve us well as a source of new insights. Earlier, we had suggested that we might want to replace the "school as factory" metaphor with, say, a "school as rodeo" metaphor. But now we have a problem. We just do not know very much about rodeos. Our knowledge and experience with rodeos is superficial. Therefore, we run the risk of replacing one cliché with another.

To avoid the cliché pitfall, we must be careful to choose metaphors of which we do have some in-depth understanding, or where we can turn to the world of experience to give us that understanding and knowledge base. If you are determined to go with the rodeo metaphor, then take some time to learn about rodeos. Go to as many rodeos as you can, for as long as you can. Talk to as many rodeo people as you can. Observe and participate as much as you can. The more you know and experience, the richer will be your use of the metaphor.

The second danger is the commitment pitfall. Here, we expect that any metaphor we choose will pay off for us. All we have to do is to select a metaphor, stay with it, and the insights will just come rolling in. But there is a problem here. We are, after all, doing research in the empirical world. And whether we like it or not, the empirical world is ordered on its own terms, and not ours. Therefore, we have to expect that some metaphors will be more fertile than others. We also have to expect that sometimes a metaphor will lead us down a dead end. If we persist with a sterile metaphor, then at best we will force it to yield some very peripheral insights.

The commitment pitfall is actually fairly easy to avoid. All we need is a clear head and the ability to swallow our pride. So the rodeo metaphor is not proving to be very fruitful after all. Just like the quantitative researcher who derives a hypothesis that just does not pan out under test, we have to admit failure and move on. There are plenty of other avenues to explore.

The third and final danger is the completeness pitfall. Here, we expect our metaphor to give us a complete understanding of what we are studying. This is the most fundamental and most dangerous pitfall of all. Sometimes, we are more than willing to assert that what we have indeed found is a complete understanding. To continue our example, we might claim that by using the rodeo metaphor, we now finally understand the nature and functioning of schools.

We avoid the completeness pitfall by admitting that no understanding is complete. The reason we began this metaphor exercise in the first place was not because our understanding of school was wrong—it was incomplete. When we are done, we have a richer but still incomplete understanding of schools. As long as we avoid the temptation to replace understanding, and instead stick with the task of building a richer base of understanding, then we should avoid trouble.

One of the most powerful metaphors in qualitative research is the concept of the rhizome. First laid out in the work of Deleuze and Guattari (1987), the rhizome gives us a model and pattern of complex conceptual frameworks. Rejecting older hierarchical models, Deleuze and

Guattari argued that concepts are organized like the spreads and nodules of plant roots. These weblike structures called rhizomes allow for complex and nonhierarchical interactions of concepts. Jackson (2003) has extended these ideas into our examination not just of concepts, but of voices intermingled in complex settings. She calls this phenomenon *rhizovocality*. By using this metaphor, she argues that we can better collect and organize and understand the complex interdynamics of voices that often characterize qualitative data.

QUALITATIVE DATA HANDLING

Once you have gathered your data, regardless of the methods you have used, you need to handle it properly. Data handling involves three key dimensions: data access, data storage, and data retrieval.

In the earliest days of qualitative research, there were limited forms of data. Qualitative researchers were able to collect artifacts that illustrated key points about culture and society, or they generated fieldnotes to describe their experiences, findings, insights, and reflections. When we confine ourselves to artifacts and fieldnotes, then our access, storage, and retrieval issues are fairly simple.

As data-recording technologies improved, and as data-gathering methods became more complex and more standardized, data-handling issues also became more complicated. More often than not, qualitative researchers do not deal directly with much of their data. Artifacts are accessed and stored via various representation methods, including photographs, video records, and computers. Verbal materials are often taped or recorded via digital technology. Data storage and retrieval has become a varied and flexible process in qualitative research. New methods for recording and storing data literally seem to evolve overnight. Which systems should you use? My suggestion is to pay attention to both reliability and cost. If the method for recording data has proven to be reliable for long-term use, and its cost is affordable to you, then that is the method I would use to gather my data.

Perhaps the most important issue of qualitative data handling and retrieval examines the creation and use of transcripts of verbal material. There are varying opinions in qualitative research regarding transcripts. Should you hire someone to do them for you? Should you do your own transcripts? How much information is lost by transcribing? How does transcription help you organize your data better?

There are no hard and fast answers to any of these questions. Some qualitative researchers prefer others to transcribe their verbal data because it can help the researcher establish some objective distance from the data. Other researchers feel it is critical to transcribe your own data, as the very process of transcribing often allows you to garner new and fresh insights into the data. Lapadat and Lindsay (1999) and Tilley (2003a, 2003b) explore these and other dimensions within transcription.

DATA GATHERING IN QUALITATIVE SCIENCE AND QUALITATIVE INQUIRY

Data gathering is not a simple or straightforward process in qualitative research. Very often, your stance toward research, and the type of research paradigm you adopt, will affect data gathering at every level. These issues can be illustrated clearly across qualitative science and qualitative inquiry dimensions.

Data Gathering and Qualitative Science

Qualitative science favors those data-gathering methods that are publicly verifiable and objective in nature. Early models of case studies, like those proposed by Yin (1994), are a good example of these sorts of aspects of data gathering. Grounded Theory methods are also excellent examples of a qualitative science approach toward gathering data. Semiological forms of research, in their search for underlying structures, often seek external validation of their data-patterning efforts. Finally, some of the more traditional forms of phenomenological research strive, via bracketing, to get objective and verifiable types of data.

Data Gathering and Qualitative Inquiry

For qualitative inquiry, the acts of data gathering and interpretation are often intermingled. Also, there are often critical and artistic dimensions to data-gathering efforts as well. In many forms of phenomenological and particularly in hermeneutic research, the researcher's stance and perspective becomes an important part of the data-gathering effort. This can also be seen in most gender-based modes of research, and to a lesser degree in the semiotic modes of data gathering. The idea of innocent, independent, exterior data is often rejected by those doing qualitative inquiry. Instead, all data is seen as situated, as contextualized, and as personalized to some degree.

DATA GATHERING AND THE MIRROR, WINDOW, AND LANTERN

Research methods, data gathering, and analysis are often interconnected in complex ways in qualitative research. Some of these interconnections can be illustrated nicely by considering our three forms of vision in qualitative research.

Data Gathering and the Mirror.   Some approaches to qualitative data gathering are highly reflective in nature. In particular, the notions of Heidegger are quite relevant. Heidegger saw human beings as creatures that were thrown into a world that makes no sense. Part of our ongoing struggle to be human is to take our experiences and our perceptions of things in the day-to-day world and understand them. Although this effort requires a great deal of personal reflection, it also calls upon a collective sharing at all levels of culture, from history to language. This situated type of reflection permeates other sorts of qualitative data-gathering efforts as well, especially those efforts that are critical in nature or those that seek to understand the world from a particular position, be it race, gender, sexual orientation, or whatever.

Data Gathering and the Window.   Those who advocate a window position tend to look at data as building blocks. Individual sets of data are important, but more important are the theoretical structures that we can build from good data. Therefore, the window approach is very much concerned with the quality of data as data. It is like an analogy to using bricks—you can only build a good brick house if you use good bricks.

Data Gathering and the Lantern.   Illumination is often sudden and usually unexpected. Those forms of data gathering that emphasize putting ourselves in places where the unusual and unexpected can be expected are the most pure advocates of the lantern perspective. And of all the data-gathering methods we have examined in this chapter, the use of metaphor to generate new ways of looking at the world is the best example of this search for the unexpected place to stand. Furthermore, this appeal to unusual and unexpected sources of data is one of the things that makes qualitative research a unique form of inquiry.

PLANNING YOUR RESEARCH PROPOSAL: SORTING AND RANKING POTENTIAL METHODS

Every proposal must address the notion of data gathering. In this chapter we look at how our participants are thinking about their potential methods at this stage of the process.

Carol

From the beginning, Carol knew that she would be using Grounded Theory in her study. She also knew that it was important for her to keep an open mind about methods, as well. Perhaps, as she explored qualitative methods in greater detail, another method that she did not previously know would suggest itself as a better alternative.

In fact, at one point of her methods review, she did entertain the notion of switching methods. The idea of using a memory-work strategy appealed to her because of its feminist learnings and its insistence on creating systematic collective biographies. In the end, however, she decided that she really wanted to hear each of her informants' voices on their own terms. She felt that she could develop a sounder theory if common points emerged from separate discussions, and if the same points were crafted in a collective fashion.

Albert

Albert has actually decided to move away from a critical approach for now and to adopt a more traditional phenomenological stance. He realizes that his main interest is in understanding this concept of " first-time math anxiety in formerly successful middle school students" on its own terms and at its own level. Once he has a firm grasp of this notion, then further research can be conducted from a critical perspective.

Ourselves

By now, you should have a clear idea of your methodological plan. It is not necessary for you to have decided on any specific method, but you should have a good sense of the "ball park." If you are unsure about what specific method you might choose, then you might follow Richard's example for now and list a family of related methods.

CHAPTER 8

Analyzing

Exercise Seven—*Twenty Questions*

Analyzing qualitative data can be quite different from analyzing quantitative data. To highlight some of these differences, we will engage in the following exercise:

- The focus in qualitative data analysis, in spite of appearances, is not so much on coding, categorizing, sorting, testing, and similar procedures. Underlying all of these sorts of activities is the basic notion of engaging in a dialogue with your data. Even those forms of qualitative research that do not create codes, find themes, or test hypotheses nonetheless engage with their data in meaningful ways.
- One of the best ways to engage your data is to ask it questions. Think back on the old childhood game of 20 questions. One player gets to think of an item or topic, and the other players get to ask 20 questions in order to help identify that item or topic.
- In this exercise, we will develop a list of 20 questions that you might use to engage your data in a variety of areas or settings. Therefore, these questions will be fairly general in nature. Their value is that they allow you to orient yourself toward some of the major topics and issues in qualitative data analysis.
- In order to get the ball rolling, I will offer five questions. Next, you should develop five questions of your own that you might find personally useful. These questions can take a variety of forms and address a variety of topics and areas. You might take a reflective stance with some questions, a theoretical stance with other questions, and a practical stance with yet other questions. The nature and variety of these questions are up to you and your own needs and creativity.
- Ideally, each member of your class will develop five questions, and the class as a whole can examine and debate these various lists to come up with a set of the best 20 questions. Even if you do not do this in a class exercise, you will nonetheless have at least 10 questions you can use in the future.
- Good luck in your efforts to ask interesting and useful questions. Here are five questions that I often ask of my own data:
    1. What sorts of findings did you get that you expected to get?
    2. How can you best organize these expected findings?
    3. What sorts of findings did you get that you did not expect to get?
    4. How can you best organize these unexpected findings?
    5. Which three findings do you feel are the most important?

REFLECTING ON ANALYSIS

This chapter is designed to help you address one of the scariest parts of qualitative research for the beginning qualitative researcher. You have gathered your raw data. As a matter of fact, you probably had a pretty good time gathering these data. Now, what the heck are you supposed to do with all this information?

The answer to this question will depend on what you are trying to accomplish in your research. However, all answers are directed toward one simple objective—we need to turn data into research findings. We will therefore look at a variety of ways to turn data into research findings.

Before we look at the variety of analytic approaches and techniques at our disposal, we need to reflect a bit on how we as researchers view our data. In qualitative research, we consider data to be more than collections of facts or the building blocks of theory. Our relation to data is more active and more interactive. In a sense, qualitative researchers are always in "conversation" with their data. We want to hear what it has to tell us and see what it has to show us. We engage with our data, back and forth, much as we would with any other informant. For these reasons, qualitative data analysis is rarely prescriptive and never mechanical in nature.

COMMON PHASES OF QUALITATIVE ANALYSIS

Baptiste (2001 September) argues that there are four common phases for all forms of qualitative data analysis. Beyond these common phases are a wide variety of strategies that different forms of qualitative research use to execute those phases. These four phases (or tasks, or goals) are: (1) defining the type of analysis to use, (2) classifying the data, (3) making connections among different classes of data, and (4) presenting the results of the analysis.

In the first phase, researchers make decisions about what general approach to use. Each approach comes with its own assumptions about reality, knowledge, and values. Researchers who take a qualitative science approach to data analysis, for example, are making far different assumptions than qualitative inquiry researchers, even if they are looking at the same kinds of data.

The second phase deals with ways that researchers choose to organize their data. First of all, they need to choose which data to pay most attention to, and which data, if any, to ignore. These are not simple or innocent choices. Once researchers have sorted their data, then it is time to organize the remaining data into groups or categories. Again, the different assumptions of different fields will determine which kinds of grouping and classifying strategies to use. For instance, qualitative science researchers might be looking for more abstract classifying strategies, whereas some qualitative inquiry researchers might adopt a more situated and contextualized approach. Regardless of approach, however, all qualitative researchers need to be alert to certain basic categorical issues. Do I have too many categories? Too few? Have I captured all the "important" data? Are there things being left unsaid?

The third phase goes beyond the organization of data to see what our data are "telling" us at some larger level. In many cases, those larger levels deal with the creation of themes and/or theories. These larger levels can also include patterns and even stories that we can then use to understand others or even model their behaviors. It can also include practical recommendations, warnings, deep and rich insights, and even theories. Of course, different types of qualitative research will aim for different sorts of larger accounts. It should be no surprise, for example, that qualitative science per se values theory building more than qualitative inquiry. On the other hand, we should not be surprised to see more rich and detailed telling of stories and accounts in qualitative inquiry analyses than in qualitative science analyses. The final phase deals with issues of writing and communication. These topics will be addressed in detail in Chapter 10.

Once we realize that we need to "converse" with our data in certain systematic ways, the choice then falls on which approaches to use to analyze our data. We will look at a few major categories of data analysis. These categories address issues of coding, thematic analysis, meaning verification and generalization, and synthetic and illuminative approaches to data. Finally, we will look at a variety of data sources, including artifacts, visual data, and data generated from or analyzed by computers. The relation between analysis and evaluation is also important in qualitative research, and needs to be examined as well.

Before we begin, we need to get one other matter straight. The discussions to follow will not teach you how to code or analyze qualitative data. Those are technical skills that are constantly being refined, and there are also a number of different approaches within each of these basic areas. We are looking instead at the more basic personal skills that underlie each analytic method we will discuss.

You will be pointed toward more comprehensive technical sources when they are available. Your instructor will also be an invaluable resource as well. The purpose of this chapter is to draw the map, so you can gain a sense of where you want to go and how you might proceed to get there. Once we understand the aims and goals of these various approaches, then we are well on the way of knowing how to learn the technical aspects in a more meaningful fashion.

CODING AND ANALYSIS

Some approaches to qualitative analysis start the "conversational" process by coding the data. Coding, however, should not be viewed as an automatic or a prescriptive process. It requires a great deal of skill, and that skill can only be developed through practice. Fortunately, however, the sorts of things we do as coders are related to the sorts of things we do already in ordinary life. All you are doing, when you code, is making note of the same sorts of things you pick up, either implicitly or explicitly, when you pay attention to unfolding events in the world.

Let me make my point in the following way. Consider how complex our ordinary experience of the world really is. We perceive the world through an interconnected series of perceptual modalities. We simultaneously see it, hear it, taste it, smell it, and feel it while we orient these experiences spatially, temporally, culturally, and personally. It is remarkable that we are able to combine all of our sensory modalities (in this case, visual, auditory, gustatory, tactile, and motile), and many others, so naturally and so effortlessly in everyday life. Given that we can do all of the above, the task of learning how to code and analyze experiences in a qualitative manner should be a breeze! In fact, however, coding and analyzing is a difficult and complex set of skills to learn and master. But they are not unfamiliar skills.

Coding, in the final analysis, is an act of selective attention. When we code, we mark those things in our data that we need to revisit. Not only are we going to revisit them, but we are also going to reconsider these pieces of data from a particular perspective.

Quantitative researchers tend to use predetermined coding categories, and coding in this case is the application of those categories to the data proper. Though this is sometimes the case in qualitative research as well, more often than not we are building our coding categories as we go along. We let important and intriguing items within our data lead us to crafting and creating these evolving codes. As these codes take more determinate shape and form, we often call them *themes*. The formation and analysis of themes can be a major part of many forms of qualitative research.

THEMATIC ANALYSIS

A major task in the process of understanding qualitative data analysis is to explore the art and practice of coding and analyzing from a more traditionally "scientific" perspective. For many researchers, this form of coding and analysis represents what qualitative research is really about. Rather than to continue using the rather awkward "coding and analyzing" phrase, though, we will describe this process as *thematic analysis,* or TA coding for short.

We will base most of our examination of TA coding methods on Grounded Theory. We looked at Grounded Theory in Chapters 5 and 7, as both a popular interpretation strategy and a data-gathering strategy in qualitative research. Here, we will concentrate on how Grounded Theory actually goes about coding and analyzing data. There are, of course, other forms of TA, but given the prevalence of Grounded Theory in qualitative research, it is important that we consider it first. We will use the Strauss and Corbin (1998) approach, as it provides the most commonly used set of detailed and explicit procedures for coding and analysis from a Grounded Theory perspective.

Themes, Emergent or Otherwise

We will start by taking a closer look at both the idea of a theme and the process of creating themes from coding. Thematic analysis, first and foremost, is about searching for patterns in data. When we find a pattern, then we have good reason to suppose that something systematic is creating that pattern. Another name for such a pattern is, of course, a theme. When observations pile up, and a theme seems to suggest itself to the researcher, thematic analysts say that these themes seem to "emerge from the data." This is a particularly important notion in Grounded Theory.

The notion that themes emerge from data is one of the most misunderstood concepts in qualitative research, let alone Grounded Theory. Morse (1994) helps us understand what researchers mean when they say that themes emerge from the data. As she states with great eloquence and insight:

> Doing qualitative research is not a passive endeavor. Despite current perceptions and students' prayers, theory does not magically emerge from data. Nor is it true that, if one is only patient enough, insight wondrously enlightens the researcher. Rather, data analysis is a process that requires astute questioning, a relentless search for answers, active observation, and accurate recall. It is a process of piecing together data, of making the invisible obvious, of recognizing the significant from the insignificant, of linking seemingly unrelated facts logically, of fitting categories one with another, and attributing consequences to antecedents. It is a process of conjecture and verification, of correction and modification, of suggestion and defense. It is a creative process of organizing data so that the analytic scheme will appear obvious." (p. 25)

In short, themes do not really emerge from the data. What emerges, after much hard work and creative thought, is an awareness in the mind of the researcher that there are patterns of order that seem to cut across various aspects of the data. When these patterns become organizational, and when they characterize different segments of data, then we can call them *themes*.

The Key Characteristics of Thematic Analysis

Thematic analysis, then, is the main route for researchers to take when they are looking for themes to arise as a result of their active inspections of the welter of confusions that often characterizes "raw data." What are the key characteristics we can expect to find in any thematic analysis? There are three fundamental aspects to any TA project. We will examine each in turn.

The Inductive Approach

First of all, most examples of TA will employ some variant of what is known as the *inductive approach*. There are several different meanings for the term *inductive* in the world of ideas, so we must be careful not to confuse these possible meanings when we look at how the term is used in TA.

First of all, there is the notion of *induction*, as it is used in logic. To review briefly, induction is about reasoning to a probable conclusion. So, from a technical logical standpoint, inductive reasoning is about creating and testing probability claims. At the heart of inductive proof in logic is the notion of falsifiability. In practice, we most often test falsifiability using the null hypothesis method. That is, we make the claim that no matter how much data we test, there will not be a relation between two variables. Then we test the likelihood that this claim, or null hypothesis, is likely. We seek to turn away from our earlier claim, so that we can accept the notion that a relation is highly probable after all. This is the logic of the null hypothesis, and it is fundamentally inductive in nature.

In qualitative research, the term "inductive" has often taken on a related but different meaning. Here, we see a variant understanding of "inductive" to indicate the process of moving from the specific to the general. As specifics are collected and gathered, they tend to suggest a more general pattern of order. It is important for the qualitative researcher to be open to the possibility of such an order taking shape. As you can see, qualitative researchers employ a much different understanding of the concept of induction than the one used by researchers interested in hypothesis testing. Therefore, it is important at the outset to at least be able to keep these two uses straight. Strauss and Corbin (1998, p. 136) do go on to note that any sort of theme or code is at heart an interpretation by the researcher, and they consider such interpretations as deductive. Therefore, they state that there is no pure induction of any themes from the data; interpretation does and must play some role.

Perhaps we ought to consider eventually abandoning the use of the term *inductive* in qualitative research altogether, as the process of studying patterns for themes is much more abductive in character (see Shank, 1994 for a discussion of abduction in qualitative research). I personally think that this should be the case because there is much to be gained by adopting the terms and concepts of abductive reasoning. But this is not a matter for us alone; it will take some time for the field of qualitative research to evaluate and assimilate these issues. In the meantime, we need to understand the language as it is currently used, and to understand terms as they are currently meant. The use of *inductive* is one the best examples of this situation in action.

Feedback and Comparison

Second, any thematic analysis will employ a feedback system to allow for the refinement or change of emergent themes. Strauss and Corbin (1998) call this the comparative method.

There are two basic types of comparisons made by the comparative method. The first kind of comparison allows for the comparison of incidents to each other. This process of incident comparison allows later incidents to serve as feedback for categories and conclusions drawn from earlier incidents. By looking at the similarities and differences among these sorts of incidents, the researcher can start putting together both the beginnings of theory as well as a more refined coding process.

Sometimes, however, new incidents do not lend themselves easily to comparison with previous incidents. In this case, Strauss and Corbin (1998) talk about theoretical comparison. Here, the researcher is not interested in incidents per se, but in the categories that incidents might belong to. Sometimes these categories are straightforward, but often they are metaphorical or abstract.

To illustrate these two comparison processes in action, suppose we decide to work on a theory of what factors guide young men to choose certain types of blue jeans. First, we look for incident data. We notice that young men try on jeans. We also note the body types of the young men. Are certain brands of jeans chosen more often by slim men? By husky men? By muscular men? As we watch, we might see these sorts of comparisons unfolding in front of us. But we also notice that one brand of blue jeans seems to sell to all body types. Is there something more abstract than good fit going on here?

We begin to suspect that there are certain cultural advantages for young men in owning one brand over another. To support this notion, we realize that all the jeans on sale are sporting prominent brand logos, which can be seen and read easily by others. In summary, when we are dealing with data relating to body type, we are doing incident comparisons. When we shift to the more abstract focus of brand name desirability, then we are doing theoretical comparisons. For Strauss and Corbin (1998), both types of comparisons are often necessary.

Saturation

Finally, any thematic analysis will reach saturation. We looked at saturation earlier, in relation to observation. But saturation involves both theoretical as well as observational issues.

Saturation is related to the notion of convergence. When we are doing Grounded Theory, we are seeking themes that will eventually serve as the bases for theory. Theories are always larger in scope and more abstract than the phenomena they seek to explain. Another way to look at this is to say that theories are like the "kernels" of abstract truth that we then can build elaborate patterns of phenomena upon. So, there is a commitment to the notion that theories are somehow more abstract, and their pieces more simple, than any other sort of attempt to explain phenomena.

There are two ways to get at the abstractness and simplicity you need in a good theory. The first and time-honored way is to create the theory first. Take what little you need of the ways and workings of the world, and craft a theory from these observations. Then, establish the validity of the theory by using it to predict and control other phenomena.

Grounded Theory follows the other available path. Stay focused on the nuts and bolts of ordinary everyday life, and start looking for regularities. As you pile data upon data, you begin to see what you can live without. Carefully trim away the excess, and sooner or later a viable theory will emerge from this process. But how will you know that your theory has any validity? You have gathered so much data that it would be hard to trim it down and set up any real predictive tests anytime soon. What you have instead is a growing awareness that you have collected so much data that there are no real surprises lurking out there for you. As you look at more and more data, you start seeing the same old patterns over and over. When this starts to be the case, then you can say that you are closing in on saturation. It is time to start shutting down the data-collection process, and start making sure that you can find a place for each and every piece of data you have collected to date. In other words, you are free to begin the microanalysis of your data because you have made sure that you have staked out all the macro boundaries.

Other Forms of Thematic Analysis

A number of analytic procedures in qualitative research, apart from grounded theory, make extensive use of thematic coding strategies. Boyatzis (1998) lays out a program that integrates themes and codes. Boyatzis (1998) acknowledges that themes can be derived from an "inductive" look at the data and also by appeal to theory. But he goes on to emphasize the importance of prior research and prior data. This is a sharp contrast to grounded theory, which advocates being as free as possible from the influence of past research when setting out to discern themes from data.

Boyatzis (1998) also lays out criteria for good codes. A good code, from his perspective, has each of the following five elements:

1. "A label
2. A definition of what the theme concerns (i.e., the characteristic or issue constituting the theme)
3. A description of how to know when the theme occurs (i.e., how to "flag" the theme)
4. A description of any qualifications or exclusions to the identification of the theme
5. Examples, both positive and negative, to eliminate possible confusion when looking for the theme (pp. x–xi)"

Ryan and Bernard (2000) emphasize data organization as a necessary part of the coding process. In their use of hierarchical structures and cognitive mapping as part of code development and use, their approach serves as a bridge between more traditional coding and thematic analysis models and the types of analyses described in the next section.

Attride-Stirling (2001) advocates the use of thematic networks for analyzing complex qualitative settings. She argues that systems of themes often take on hierarchical characteristics. Briefly, in her approach she identifies three levels of themes. Basic themes are found by looking at examples in the actual data. These basic themes can then be gathered into organizing themes, which integrate various basic themes into clusters that capture similar points and issues. Finally, within most systems of data that capture the basic organizing principles there are themes that connect the organizing themes. Attride-Stirling calls these global themes. Because the patterns of formation are systematic, once you are through delineating basic, organizing, and global themes, you have also delineated a network that links them all together. These sorts of networks can be very useful in organizing and understanding large or complex sets of data.

Finally, Kluge (2000, January) argues for the extension beyond themes and thematic networks into the formation of types and typologies in qualitative analysis. Kluge sees the process of creating these sorts of empirically grounded types as a four-stage process. First of all, there is the development of relevant analyzing dimensions. In this stage, critical properties are identified for the coding and sorting process. In the second stage, empirical regularities in the data are used as the basis for grouping cases and starting analysis. Analysis continues in the third stage, where meaningful relations are identified and then used as the basic for creating more abstract and general types. Finally, in the fourth and final stage, these types are characterized, labeled, and described for further use and application. In this way, Kluge hopes we can add new types to our theoretical understanding of the world, as fueled by our qualitative approach to examining that same world.

Whether we are dealing with matters as simple as coding data to see how often certain things happen, or a complex as creating theories, networks, and typologies, coding and themes often play a role. Beyond the creation of patterns of meaning, however, some qualitative analyses strive to address issues of meaning in a more direct fashion. Researchers often use meaning generation and confirmation approaches to create analyses that are clearly formed and rigorously grounded.

MEANING GENERATION AND CONFIRMATION

One of the most comprehensive sources for learning and using techniques of meaning generation and confirmation comes from Miles and Huberman (1994). In short, they see qualitative research as a two-stage process. The first stage involves the creation of meaning. Given our data, how can we make sense of it? Once we are comfortable that we have created viable meaning, then we need to move to the second stage of the process. How can we confirm that our newly created meanings are true?

Procedures for Making Meaning

Miles and Huberman (1994) have laid out a hierarchy of meaning-making strategies that range from studying simple interactions in the environment to building complex theoretical claims.

At the lower end of their model is the *search for basic themes*, as well as looking for clustering or patterns in the data. They also suggest that the simple act of counting can provide the researcher with a good deal of information about how common these various instances really are.

Moving away from simple interaction with data, they then suggest a number of *psychological operations*. The simplest of these is the search for plausible explanations, but more complex operations include the use of metaphors and making comparisons and contrasts.

The next level of meaning making focuses in on the *search for variables*. Do we have all the important variables identified, or might we suspect the presence of intervening variables? Are our variables too complex, and should they be partitioned into simpler variables? Are our variables too simple, and should they be subsumed into larger principles? Are there important connections among variables, and are there larger factors of variables to be discovered?

At the top of their meaning-making hierarchy is the set of *coherence-making strategies*. How can all these various meanings be brought together into a coherent whole? Two methods for doing so include the formation of logical chains of evidence and the creation of theoretical and conceptual models of coherence.

It is not enough just to make meaning from one's data, argue Miles and Huberman (1994). A good researcher must be able to stand behind those meaning-making efforts, and see how they play out in understanding the phenomena in question. In other words, qualitative researchers need to be able to go on and verify if these meanings are true or not.

Procedures for Verifying Meaning

Verification is an important concept for traditional quantitative research, and Miles and Huberman (1994) borrow heavily from those traditions in their own treatment of verification.

Miles and Huberman (1994) start by recommending that we deal with issues of *reliability, validity, and generalizability*. The biggest threat to reliability in qualitative research, from their perspective, is researcher bias. Have you become too involved with the site? Are your personal interests making it more likely that you are seeing one kind of data and overlooking another kind? Do you have something you really want to prove in this research? All of these factors, and others, might influence your research in a negative way.

In order to make sure your research is generalizable, they recommend that it be evaluated in terms of its representativeness. Have you sampled a broad enough spectrum of informants? Have you gone to a variety of settings? Are your conclusions supported by a large enough body of data? They also suggest replicating your research. In the case of qualitative research, repeating your study is less straightforward than replicating an experiment. But if sites or cases are selected carefully, they can add breadth to your earlier findings.

Validity is a more complex matter, and Miles and Huberman (1994) suggest several approaches to validity. One key procedure is to weight your evidence properly. Some data, they suggest, are stronger than other data. Firsthand data are stronger than secondhand data. Data that have been observed are stronger than data retrieved from reports or statements. Data collected in informal settings are often more trustworthy than data from more formal settings. This is due to the fact that formal settings often control the flow of information and behaviors, whereas such information and behaviors tend to unfold more naturally in informal settings. Data from trusted informants are stronger than data from untrustworthy or marginal informants. When data are collected one on one, the informants are also more likely to be open and honest than they might be if others are present. Finally, Miles and Huberman (1994) feel that data collected later in the process are often stronger than data collected earlier on. They do warn about making sure that you have not gone too "native" later in the data-gathering process, thereby setting up the possibility of researcher bias.

Another area of verification that Miles and Huberman (1994) suggest is the area of *logical verification*. First of all, they suggest that we begin to set up *if-then* tests as we gather our data. If-then tests allow for the preliminary linking up of variables that are emerging within the data. Suppose we find that very few people in a tiny village go to Sunday services at the village church. We observe the few people who actually go, and they act passively. Do we have the beginnings of a relationship here? If the villagers are passive, then they will go to church?

Preliminary if-then statements are not enough. Miles and Huberman (1994) suggest two further logical strategies. First, you need to rule out spurious relationships. Are passivity and church attendance only coincidentally related? Are they related, but indirectly? Are there other variables affecting the relationship, variables you have not observed or tracked? Then, you need to look for negative evidence and rival explanations. Are all of these people passive, or only some subset? What other factors might be keeping the rest of the village from attending services, other than their lack of passivity?

Finally, Miles and Huberman (1994) suggest a number of *tactical strategies* for verification. For instance, they recommend that you should check the meaning of outliers. Outliers are persons or things that seem to be acting differently than the rest of the population. Why are they different, and what does that difference mean? Don't be afraid to look at extreme cases. Extreme cases often give us a particularly clear look at what we are studying. As we have repeated over and over again here—*follow up on surprises*.

The final tactical strategy takes place after you have written the first draft of your report or study. It is usually a good idea to take a copy of this study and use it to get feedback from informants. Did you describe events accurately? Did you grasp the meaning of what the informants were trying to tell you? How do you need to modify your results, based on this feedback?

"Research Displays" That Incorporate Meaning and Verification

It has already been noted that Mile and Huberman (1994) import many notions from quantitative research into their processes for making meaning and verifying those meanings. The link to more traditional quantitative forms of research also is evident when their basic research designs are considered. These designs are most clearly seen in what they call *research displays*. They present two basic displays: within-case displays and cross-case displays.

Before we look at data displays in particular, we need to consider what they are intended to do. Data displays are intended to allow us to move from merely describing our data toward explaining patterns and variables within the data. Data displays allow us to see those patterns, find the variables, and map out possible relationships. In other words, by organizing our data, we make meanings easier to find.

Miles and Huberman (1994) break this process into two main phases. The first phase of data display deals with exploring and describing the data. This phase is concerned with organizing the data and starting the task of creating what they call the *analytic text*. The analytic text is the results of the research in process; it is our first attempt at capturing the data. As the displays build, they impact the analytic text, and as the analytic text becomes richer and more textured, it provides feedback and guidance for the growth of the data display. Therefore, these two processes become interdependent.

In the second phase of data display development, we move beyond exploration and description. We seek to explain, order, and predict. Causal modeling and causal networks become an important part of this process.

One more word of caution. We will be sketching out a great number of displays, and their differences are often complex and technical. The following descriptions are far too sketchy to serve as the basis for creating and using these displays. We are only interested in drawing a broad map of the territory. You need to turn to Miles and Huberman (1994) or some other similar source if you actually want to make some of these displays with your own data.

Within-Case Displays

The first research display is the within-case display. The within-case display is used to help sort out the order found within a given case, or its internal order. Another way to look at this is to say that we are interested in finding variables, and so we use cases as sources of variables. That is, we seek order by finding those variables that are responsible for the order.

The least intrusive ordering strategy is called a *context chart*. A context chart consists of a list of key behaviors observed within the case, where context information is used to create a network showing the impact of these context factors on the behaviors. Context factors can range from setting factors to rank and status social factors. Obviously, you cannot identify and map out all the context factors that impact behaviors. But if you can display the factors that you do know, then you are farther ahead in the process of creating a systematic understanding of why these behaviors occurred.

Another relatively unobtrusive within-case data display process is the *checklist matrix*. Here, you have determined which variables are important ahead of time. You break each variable down into its components and then use your list to create a checklist. You make no effort to rank or weight or order the components; you are merely interested in seeing if they are present. These observations can then be cross-listed to other dimensions that might be important to you. Does it matter who engaged in the components that you observed? Does it matter when they were observed? How do your participants feel about these components?

Sometimes, you will need to be more structured in your data-description process. There will be key dynamics that will need to serve as the organizing focus of your data display. Miles and Huberman (1994) identify three main organizing categories for within-case displays:

- The displays can be time-ordered, in which events, activities, decisions, critical incidents, and similar phenomena, are mapped out along a time continuum.
- With role-ordered displays, we organize our data around the people involved and the roles that they fill within the setting.
- When we use conceptually ordered displays, we create displays that are organized in terms of the variables we seek to understand. Cognitive maps are common examples of conceptually ordered displays.

Within-case displays are not just used for description and exploration. We can create displays for within-case research that will allow us to explain and predict phenomena. The two primary tools for this work, according to Miles and Huberman (1994), are the *case dynamics matrix* and the *causal network*.

A case dynamics matrix is a map of the changes that have occurred within the case over time, and these changes are seen as outcomes or consequences of certain forces or efforts.

A causal network is a visual map of independent and dependent variables in their cause-effect states. Arrows are used to link variables in directional ways. On the surface, causal networks resemble path analysis models from quantitative research. With their emphases on causal relationships, both of these tools can be used to make predictions and therefore to test hypotheses.

Cross-Case Displays

The second research display is the cross-case display. Cross-case displays allow us to dig into the particular and historical character of cases. We try to keep data from any given case together, and then use these cases as our focus for seeking order. In this fashion, we preserve our picture of individual cases, while using a number of cases to build a larger picture.

Like the within-case design, we have first a set of exploration and description displays, and then a set of ordering and explanation displays. We will examine each category in turn.

Description and Exploration in Cross-Case Displays

The basic description and exploration tools for cross-case displays are similar to the ones used for within-case displays.

Again, we find *time-ordered* and *conceptually ordered* displays. Instead of using variables as our organizing scheme as we did in within-case displays, here we treat each case as a source of data. Time markers are used to label columns in the time-ordered display, with cases serving as row markers.

For the conceptually ordered display, we have the same model, except we substitute concept markers for time markers. We also develop a *case-ordered display*. In a case-ordered display, we identify a main variable of interest. We then rank each case as high, medium, or low on the variable. All the high-ranked cases are then grouped together, as are the medium- and low-ranked cases. This grouping allows us to see patterns within each ranking group, as well as patterns across groups.

Ordering and Explanation in Cross-Case Displays

Cross-case displays can be used to order and explain data. Our choice of matrix to use for cross-case displays is determined by what sort of relation we are interested in finding.

If we are interested in finding out the effects that our cases can bring about, then we need to create a *case-ordered effects matrix*. Here, we assume our cases act as causes, and we explain the sorts of effects that we get via each particular case.

If, instead, we want to look at our cases as being effects of some prior causal system, then we need to organize our data using a *case-ordered predictor-outcome matrix*. Here, we try to explain our cases by appealing to predictor variables of interest. That is, we lay out our predictor variables first. Then we try to fit our cases in as outcomes of these variables in action.

We can also build *causal networks* for cross-case displays, but they tend to be more complex than the networks we build for within-case displays. First, we have to map out all our variables on a case-by-case basis. Some cases will have most if not all of our variables of interest, whereas other cases might have fewer. We begin to build a case for our strongest variables, or those variables that seem to show up in the most cases. Now we have our variable set for making multiple-case models. We can now use the same causal modeling techniques we used for within-case displays to build multiple-case networks.

Other Approaches to Meaning Generation and Verification

Over the years, a number of researchers have updated the basic work in meaning generation and verification. One area that has grown in importance and popularity is the method of *content analysis*. Silverman (2000) provides a recent overview of content analysis in particular, and the task of tackling meaning and truth in texts and transcripts in general.

Similar to the notion of content analysis is *conversation analysis*. Long an important part of ethnomethodology, conversation analysis looks at verbal, nonverbal, and formal properties of conversations. Psathas (1995) provides a brief and useful summary of basic techniques in conversation analysis. We will look at conversation analysis in more depth in Chapter 9.

SYNTHESIS AND ILLUMINATION

We are now at the other end of the continuum. Here, we are no longer interested in coding per se. Our analysis of the data takes on a more anecdotal, a more personalized, and a more interpretative character. This mode of analysis seems less familiar than either thematic analysis or meaning generation and confirmation, but it is in fact the method that many qualitative researchers actually use. More often than not, they will not use such terminology as *synthesis* and *illumination*. But we will adopt this common set of terms so that we can compare and contrast these various efforts. First of all, let us map out what all forms of synthetic analysis have in common. There are three key components to any such analysis.

The first component is a deliberate focus on what we might call *facet*. The notion of *facet* is similar to the more familiar concept of *theme*, but with a few key differences. We must be careful, as the differences between themes and facets are often quite subtle on the surface. When we get to the heart of each concept, however, we can see that they are truly different in nature.

The key difference between a facet and a theme is the holistic nature of a facet. Let us go back a second to think about the nature of themes. In most cases, we tend to think of themes as the building blocks of understanding. That is, if I can determine the 5 or 10, key themes that seem to be in place for a particular social function, then I can characterize that function in terms of those themes.

A facet is a much different concept. Think of the facets we see in a perfectly cut diamond. Each facet provides an angle to look at and understand the diamond, but it retains the nature of the diamond as a whole. That is, diamonds are built of facets. Facets are the sides and angles that they turn to the world. With diamonds, facets tend to be symmetrical. In real life, phenomena often show us unique characteristics when they shift and show us different facets. Each new facet reveals some new dimension or nature of the whole. We all have heard about, say, the cold-blooded killer on death row who keeps a pet canary, or the kind and sweet person who suddenly shows us a ruthless side that we would not have ever suspected. People and phenomena are complex, and we can only see parts of them at any given time. But these parts inform the whole, much as a facet cut heightens the sheen of a diamond. We must be careful not to mistake facets for themes. This mistake could lead us on the trail for causes, when what we need instead are new angles for seeing.

The second component is the deliberate use of a perspective on the part of the researcher. Here, we return to the notion of interpretation as a basic skill in qualitative research. We need to remember that interpretation is a basic skill of life. But, whether we want to admit it or not, we have to take a particular stance before we can interpret anything.

We can see the power of taking a stance on interpretation in the following classic experiment from the early days of cognitive psychology. Pichert and Anderson (1977) wrote a straightforward description of a house. They then asked subjects to read the description from one of two perspectives. In the first perspective, they were asked to imagine that they were potential homebuyers. In the second perspective, they pretended to be burglars casing the place as a potential robbery site. After each reading, they were asked to recall as many features as they could. When they shifted perspective (it didn't matter if they shifted from buyer to burglar or vice versa), their subjects were able to remember things they could not previously recall, and they also forgot to recall things they had previously remembered.

Most often in quantitative research, perspective and interpretation are seen as liabilities. They bias the researcher and filter the results through these lenses. But qualitative researchers not only acknowledge that interpretation is inevitable, we advocate the deliberate and public selection of interpretative stances. Far and away the most common perspective is adopted in qualitative research is autobiographical. Taking an autobiographical stance can be useful if done deliberately and reflectively. We must always admit at the outset what our stances are, why we chose them, and what impact they have on what we can see and cannot see. So long as we keep our stances out in the open, we can be assured that our readers have been properly informed. We start to get in trouble when we assume that our given interpretative stance is somehow universal and exhaustive. That is, when we assume that anyone would see what we see, and that we have seen everything important to see, we have crossed the line from interpretation into self-indulgence.

The third component is the identification of those aspects of the case or the situation that are unique and special. More often than not, this focus is implied and covert, but with careful inspection we can usually find its presence. Why are unique and special things so important? First of all, they require us to expand our understanding of the concepts we use to study the original targets of our research. If we find that we cannot fit all of our cases into neat little boxes or matrices, then we have to acknowledge that our original models were too simplistic and superficial. But we are fortunate in that we have these special and unique cases right in front of us.

Part of any process of dealing with the examination and exploration of data is the presentation of findings. For many of these synthetic and illuminative approaches, data are examined, organized, and presented in some sort of narrative fashion. Given the importance of narrative and narrating in qualitative research, this topic will be handled in its own chapter. These issues will be explored in depth in Chapter 9.

ANALYZING ARTIFACTS AND DOCUMENTS

When we go into the field, we often find informants who are willing to tell us things we need to know. But there are other types of "informants." For instance, every culture makes things for its use. Some of those things are tools; others are buildings and dwellings. They make toys and treasures, gifts and weapons. They shape natural objects into more useful shapes, and they invent gizmos that no one else has ever seen. Many cultures also take some of their words and put them on paper or other forms of permanent storage. Some of these words are stored for official reasons, and other sets of words are preserved by individuals for their own uses. When we talk of material culture, we are talking about all of these sorts of things, and many others (Hodder, 2000). Material culture is the sum of artifacts that we find in any particular culture or society. An artifact is nothing more than something that someone has made in order to transform nature. That transformation can be material, intellectual, emotional, spiritual, ideological, or any combination thereof.

Artifacts also tell us quite a bit about the persons who made them and used them. Those artifacts that are most directly involved in communication are written words. Though the analysis of nonwritten artifacts is a fascinating and worthwhile topic, we will concentrate instead on written artifacts. These artifacts are known as documents, and their study is called document analysis.

Merriam (1998) reminds us that documents are either formal or informal. Formal documents are called records. Records are stored in places called archives. For most of us, the image of an archive is stuffy and boring. Hill (1993) disagrees sharply:

> Archival work appears bookish and commonplace to the uninitiated, but this mundane simplicity is deceptive. It bears repeating that events and materials in archives are not always what they seem on the surface. There are perpetual surprises, intrigues, and apprehensions. Archival research holds the power to confirm as well as disturb our collective legitimations. Archival discoveries are, as often as not, threatening to established reputations and the hegemony of the status quo. Archival work is never the safe road, because we know not where it leads—or who may want to lead us in one direction rather than another. (pp. 6–7)

What are some examples of these perpetually exciting places known as archives? Webb, Campbell, Schwartz, and Sechrest (2000) label public archives as sources of "the running record." Actuarial records are the most accessed public records in our culture. Actuarial records record birth, marriage, and death data. Beyond their obvious genealogical value, these archives can tell us much about the patterns of life for people in the culture.

Similar to actuarial records are political and judicial records. Here we can find voting data for the public and for public representatives. We can also study the sale and transfer of land and other forms of property. We can look at tax rates and their changes, and shifts in representational districts. The records of school boards and their voting patterns are also part of the public record. And finally, we have a substantial record of criminal activity and legal responses to criminal behavior. With the advent of freedom of information laws, the public record has never been more accessible to researchers.

The other great public archive is the mass media. Mass media used to consist solely of newspapers. Newspaper archives are still an outstanding source of information, particularly of information from more than a few years ago. Although newspaper archives are often the largest and the most comprehensive, other forms of mass media have developed archives as well. Motion picture and television archives are becoming more extensive and more common. The Library of Congress and the Smithsonian have extensive archives of music, spoken word, and interviews. And the Internet promises to be a nearly limitless archive for all sorts of information, from the erudite to the esoteric to the exotic.

Some documents are not part of the public record. Webb et al. (2000) call these "episodic and personal records." Some of the more common episodic records are generated by business and commerce. Sales records, industrial data, union records, and records by schools and other institutions fall into this category. These records are much more private and much less accessible than public archives. It may take some persistence and persuasion to get access to some of these records, but they often prove to be worth the effort. It is never allowable, however, to bend the rules of ethics to get access to these data.

The final type of document data consists of personal documents. These are documents created by individuals for personal reasons. Some types of personal documents include diaries, letters, drawings, and notes. Diaries are often the most private of all documents, and should not be read without clear and explicit permission. Letters can be as personal as love letters, and as political as protest letters or letters to the editor. Two-way correspondence is much more valuable, but much harder to get. Drawings can consist of portraits, marginal sketches, and sketchbooks. Some people communicate much better with images than with words, so we need to be aware of and alert to these types of data. Finally, we have notes. Notes can range all the way from shopping lists to suicide notes. With the exception of suicide notes, they are also usually more relaxed and less formally structured. More often than not, notes are immediate and informal, and can give us a rare glimpse into the day-to-day actions of the people involved.

There is no one right way to analyze document data. Your treatment of these data will depend upon a number of things. How public are these data? How structured are they? Where do they fit in your overall cache of data? The main thing to remember about documents is the fact that they exist. Do not overlook documents as you conduct your fieldwork. Very often, they will give you a richer picture of your topic.

ANALYZING VISUAL DATA

In recent years, there has been a growing trend in qualitative research to move beyond a strict dependence on the written and spoken word as the primary source of data. Visual data has long played a role in qualitative research, particularly in sociology. Harper (2000) reviews the extensive role of photographs and other forms of visual representation in qualitative research. With the advent of cheap and portable videotaping systems, video has also played an increasing role in qualitative research (Elderkin-Thompson, & Waitzkin, 1999). In particular, Goldman-Segall (1998) has been doing exciting and pioneering work by blending video ethnography and the Internet to expand our practices and perceptions into using both mediums within qualitative research.

COMPUTERS AND QUALITATIVE DATA

Before we move away from this discussion of technology and research, we have to talk about a growing dimension in the coding and analysis of qualitative data: the use of computers and computer programs. First of all, we will look at some of the ways that qualitative researchers have explored changes in culture brought about by the use of computers and particularly the Internet. Then we will examine the use of computers and computer software to analyze qualitative data. Another word of caution is warranted—because computers and computer culture changes so quickly, do not take these sections as the last word. Make sure you explore current dimensions and sources of information to be up to date.

Using Computers for Qualitative Research

One of the most exciting trends in qualitative research has been the exploration of cyberspace. Whether we realize it or not, there is an emerging and evolving Internet culture consisting of people and groups whose thinking and practices have been fundamentally shaped and changed as a result of being active members of this culture. This culture continues to grow at an exponential rate, and it has already pervaded and affected nearly every aspect of contemporary life. Furthermore, qualitative research may be the best, and perhaps the only valid, way to build a genuine understanding of Internet culture.

We are now just starting the task of trying to understand the Internet per se. Its earliest histories are just now being documented. For instance, Salus (1995) lays out the history of the formation and early days of the Internet. Early on, the Internet expanded from its first home in the Department of Defense toward becoming a tool for a select few research centers and universities. Once the Internet began to take hold in the scientific and academic community, it eventually became a haven for avant-garde (and in some cases extreme) views as well. Some of these avant-garde ideas became the basis of the Internet culture of today.

One of the most intriguing early perspectives on Internet culture was a treatise by a professor writing under the pseudonym of "Hakim Bey." Bey (1985) is most noted for his concept of the TAZ, or temporary autonomous zone. To understand the concept of a TAZ, we have to look at the nature of Internet communities.

From the very beginning, people who were connected through the Internet began to use the medium to form communication channels. Two particular types of communication delivery began to prevail. In the first case, shared email messages turned into listservs. A listserv is a delivery system where messages were automatically routed to everyone on the distribution list. As long as your computer was connected to the Internet, and your name was on the routing list, you received every message sent to the listserv address.

Listservs branched out and evolved very rapidly. We now see four major kinds of listservs. First of all, there is the open listserv. Anyone can join an open listserv, and all messages are sent along without inspection or editing. There is also moderated listserv. Membership is again open, but the messages are perused by a moderator, or more often a moderator will step into an ongoing discussion and modify or end it. Open and moderated listservs are quite common, and these terms are familiar to most Internet users. The next two kinds of listservs are much less common, and so I have coined terms to describe them.

The third kind of listserv I call the *semiporous* listserv. Here, membership is not exactly open, but it is not hidden. People usually hear about semiporous listservs by word of mouth, or pick them up from web pages or the like. The rule is that if you know enough to find the listserv, you can usually join. Sometimes, you will have to apply for membership to the moderator, who then decides if you can join or not. Finally, we have the last kind of listserv, the *clandestine* listserv. Membership in clandestine listservs is by invitation only. Semiporous and clandestine listservs are used to create homogenous discussion communities.

Not every communal message was sent via listservs. Many messages were posted on newsgroup servers, where anyone who plugged into that particular subset of the server could read the messages and respond in kind if they so chose. Whereas listservs are like discussion groups, newsgroups are like bulletin boards, You do not have to join a newsgroup to post a message—you just metaphorically stroll over to the message board and electronically tack up your note.

The most common newsgroup source is Usenet. There are two basic kinds of Usenet groups—moderated groups and alternative groups. A moderated group is a group founded by people who have petitioned the overall Usenet community for the right to create that group. Every user of Usenet has the right to vote, and if there are enough yes votes, the moderated group gets a spot on the Usenet hierarchy. Moderated Usenet groups are numerous, and range from computer programming bulletin boards (such as comp.language.java .programmer and comp.bugs.misc) to hangouts for sports and music fans (such as net.sport.hockey or rec.music.phish).

What if you cannot get a moderated group accepted, or you just don't want to bother? Then you can set up an alternative (or alt.) group if you know how. Some alt groups have been around for a long time (such as alt.tasteless and alt.chinchilla), whereas other alt groups are just silly examples of computer folks playing around (like the hopefully nonexistent alt.shank.clueless.about.qualitative.research).

Why all the detail on listservs and newsgroups? Because they were the first sites where Internet culture began to take form. These information delivery modes, which look fairly pedestrian on paper, became the vehicles for a dizzying array of tiny communities and enclaves. For instance, the folks who posted and replied to posts on alt.chinchilla were chinchilla raisers. But the group began to take on its own personality. The tone of posts became universally humane, helping, and civil. These norms defined the "alt.chinchilla" experience. On the other hand, the early folklore listserv became so contentious that it was converted from a single open listserv into two moderated listservs.

These enclaves of communication, conduct, and identity were TAZs. A TAZ, or temporary autonomous zone, is a community that knows it is ephemeral and constantly mutating. Not only does it lack the stability of a "normal" culture, it shuns such stability. Instead, people cycle in and out of its membership list or clientele. Passions can run high, and sometimes people get flamed (a flame is a particularly nasty or hostile message). Topics also tend to cycle. Qualitative listservs, for example, tend to bring up the topic of computer coding of data about every six weeks or so. Sometimes, listservs and groups become the home of various Internet personalities. These personalities hold court for months or years, and then fade into the background or vanish.

In short, the Internet is the home for temporary culture after temporary culture. And we have only scratched the surface. Cultures thrive in the richness of Internet Relay Chat, or IRC. Hackers and crackers and phreaks have their own networks and codes of conducts and the like. Traditional social science is not well situated to understand these shifting and emerging cultures. Instead, we find efforts to "tame" the Internet, treating it like a massive shopping mall or yet another delivery system for distance learning. But even mundane activities like commerce and educational delivery get changed by the shifting structures and codes of meaning that proliferate and mutate along the Internet. All of this change is driven by meaning, and so qualitative research is the perfect medium for studying it.

The Internet is not just a place where temporary cultures can mutate and thrive. The Internet has set up its own communication modes. For instance, I (Shank, 1993) coined the terms *multilogue* and *multiloguing* to describe unique Internet communicative acts and their dynamics, respectively. *Multilogue* is a concept built up from earlier notions of monologues and dialogues. A multilogue is simply a conversation where more than two people are participating simultaneously. On listservs and newsgroups, these multilogues unfold as *threads*, or strings of related messages. On IRC, conversations pile on top of other conversations, and IRC participants might be carrying on a dozen conversations simultaneoulsy with each conversation having six or seven participants. Standard communication theory and straightforward research strategies simply cannot capture the dynamics of such fascinating interchanges, particularly those that unfold on IRC. Again, Internet culture is inventing its own ways of handling meaning, and qualitative research is the perfect vehicle to tackle these meanings.

When we look at dynamics like TAZs and multiloguing, we realize that we are looking at a culture that structures consciousness in fundamentally new ways. The linking of qualitative research and Internet culture seems to be a natural move.

Most important, the Internet is just one place and its study is just one way where qualitative research can thrive on its own terms. Endless arrays of questions wait for us to ask them. But we must never be afraid to ask questions that make no sense from other perspectives. How else are we going to know that we are on our own ground?

On a more practical level, some qualitative researchers have found the Internet to be an ideal tool for doing particular sorts of research with particular audiences. As we saw in Chapter 3, the Internet is an easy and effective way to conduct data gathering in dangerous or inaccessible places, or to get participants from all over the world.

McAuliffe (2003) developed a more formal version of this sort of Internet-based data-gathering process. She called it *Email-Facilitated Reflective Dialogue*. Data were collected using asynchronous email. Her subjects were able to adjust their participation to fit around their lives and needs. In a similar vein, Seymour (2001) used online procedures to conduct her research with people with disabilities and their usage of computer technologies.

Whether we are using computers to solve practical problems in data gathering, method, or analysis, or whether we are looking at how the online world has changed our culture, computers, the Internet, and online environments will provide topics for qualitative researchers for years to come.

Using Computers for Qualitative Analysis

Most of us are much more familiar with the use of computers to analyze qualitative data. By now, most of us have at least heard of the growing use of computer programs for thematic analysis in qualitative research. It is impossible to stay up to date on which programs are currently in use, which version is most recent, and which features are allowed. Weitzman (2000) provides a comprehensive review of some of the most popular software programs. To date, there are a growing number of programs being used for qualitative research, including but not limited to NUDIST, N-VIVO, Atlas-TI, Ethnograph, Hyperresearch, and more. For the most up to date and comprehensive comparison of these methods, and for much more information and helpful tips, you can hardly do better than the website of the Computer Assisted Qualitative Data Analysis (CAQDAS) Networking Project at the University of Surrey. The home page for that website is *http://caqdas.soc.surrey.ac.uk*. I particularly recommend a working paper by Ann Lewins and Christina Silver that is free to download. This paper is an exhaustive guide for comparing various software packages for qualitative data analysis.

There is a growing literature of advocates of the use of computers for qualitative data analysis. Bong (2002) details use of computer analysis in her grounded theory study, and argues that computerizing such processes as the constant comparative method extends the power and range of grounded theory efforts. Bourdon (2002, May) notes that researchers, in spite of resistance and difficulties that often accompany computer use of any kind, are becoming more skilled and adventurous in their computer data analysis efforts. Spiers (2004) reviews current links between computer analysis and the use of video data. Finally, Walsh (2003) describes her novel efforts to use Nvivo, a popular qualitative data analysis program, in teaching an introductory qualitative research course.

Fielding and Lee (1998), while advocating computers, also raise a number of important questions about the role and use of computer software and hardware in the day-to-day practice of qualitative research. They ask such questions as—*Do researchers take advantage of the full capacities of most software programs, or do they settle for low-level use of these programs? Is there a move in the field toward more "researcher-proof" software, and do such moves create important conceptual limitations for researchers who use these programs? Do computer programs sometimes inadvertently bury important data because the algorithms of the programs do not easily handle these data?* These and other such issues are matters that need to be constantly considered as the role of computers and computer programs continue to grow within qualitative research.

MOVING FROM ANALYSIS TO EVALUATION

Analysis is not the only process that is involved in the qualitative approach to studying empirical questions. There has been a substantial history of the use of qualitative methods, for example, in the field of evaluation. In fact, many of the pioneers of qualitative research, including Egon Guba and Yvonna Lincoln, Michael Patton, and Robert Stake, are best known for their work in evaluation research and theory.

Qualitative Evaluation Models

Evaluation is not the same thing as research, but it is definitely a related concept. The major difference between research and evaluation is in terms of intent. Research always boils down to curiosity, whereas evaluation always boils down to accountability. In research, we want to know why something is the way it is. In evaluation, we want to know if what someone said they would do was actually done.

Another key aspect of evaluation involves the timing of the process. When we have a summative evaluation, the evaluators come in after the fact and seek to determine if all deeds were done and all promises were kept. In the case of a formative evaluation, the evaluators are often part of the process. Evaluation is used not to make some final judgement, but to set up and sustain an ongoing assessment of the projects, the goals, and the methods used to try to reach those goals.

Qualitative evaluation methods were an early part of the qualitative movement. It became apparent to many evaluators that a strictly quantitative look at a program or a setting often missed many of the key dynamics that were a part of the setting. This was particularly true when it came to the evaluation of many social programs (Greene, 1994, 2000). By taking a qualitative approach, evaluators were free to look for changes and improvements and effects that could not easily be translated into numbers and measured. Qualitative evaluation reports, once considered radical, have now become much more accepted. There has also been a trend, again first substantiated in evaluation efforts, to blend qualitative and quantitative approaches in an effort to achieve a broader and richer picture of the actual impact of settings, services, and interventions. These mixed model efforts will be considered in more depth in the final chapter.

Certain qualitative evaluation models have also been adapted for broader use as research models. For instance, Stake (1995) deals with the extension of evaluation-derived case study techniques into the broader area of qualitative research proper. Fetterman (Fetterman, Kaftarian and Wandersman, 1996) has been involved in the linkages between evaluation and participatory action research. And Patton (2002) has served as a mainstay for many researchers looking for an evaluation-based understanding of qualitative research in general. Patton also goes beyond evaluation to address a number of crucial issues in the area of research models and skills.

ANALYZING IN QUALITATIVE SCIENCE AND QUALITATIVE INQUIRY

When we do analysis in qualitative research we are asking our data to tell us things—truthful things, honest things, things that we can count on, things that we did not expect, things that we did not know, things that help us understand. In other words, we engage with our data. This process of engagement can be quite different for qualitative science and qualitative inquiry.

Analysis and Qualitative Science

Qualitative science tends to put its trust in the principles of analysis that have dominated scientific thinking. Those principles are truth testing, objectivity, and standardization.

First of all, qualitative science demands that its data tell the truth. Truth is the number one goal of scientific inquiry, and as a result is the number one goal of qualitative science as well. Furthermore, qualitative science uses analytic techniques and processes that are designed to lead toward objective truth. Objective truth is truth that is not bound by context, situation, culture, history, or any other modifying agents. Qualitative science acknowledges that there are historical truths, cultural truths, contextual truths, and even situational truths. But qualitative science believes that underneath these provisional sorts of truth, there is still objective truth to be found.

The number one strategy for pursuing objective truth, from a qualitative science perspective, is the notion of standardization. Standardized methods, from classic ethnography to conversation analysis to grounded theory, allow us to be sure that these methods are being used properly. There is also the sense that when we use standardized methods, we have to accept the results they give us. If they happen to give us what we are looking for, then we can trust our findings more than if we might modify our methods to make sure we find what we are looking for.

Analysis and Qualitative Inquiry

Qualitative inquiry is not at all sure that there are universal truths lurking under cultural, historical, and contextual truths. Some qualitative inquirers argue that we need to focus on these more provisional forms of truth because they are much closer to the lived world. Other qualitative inquirers reject the notion of objective truth in the first place.

If situated and contextualized truth is your goal, then you have little use for standardized methods. Qualitative inquirers depend instead upon the power of illumination and correct practice. Their analytic efforts are often more critical in nature, and often focus on what people will actually do with the knowledge they find. For qualitative inquirers, the documentation of their engagement is the most important part of the analytic process. They acknowledge that they are an important part of the research process, and their analyses often include their reflective thoughts and impressions.

A FINAL LOOK AT ANALYSIS

The term *analysis* comes from the Greek verb *analyein*, which means "to break apart" or "to resolve into its elements" (Reese, 1996, p. 18). When we are looking at analysis in terms of coding and meaning generation, this is a particularly apt term. What is coding, other than the breaking down of data into its relevant parts or elements? But we have also seen data handling and synthesis that strives to keep the data whole. Here, we are interested in seeing how phenomena can be understood on their own terms, and at their own levels. We can use our three modes of looking to help us get a more systematic look at this complex and subtle set of circumstances.

ANALYSIS AND THE MIRROR, WINDOW, AND LANTERN

Analysis and the mirror.   Analysis, from the mirror perspective, is an additive and categorical process. It is additive because we are adding a look at ourselves to the analysis of the world. But this look at ourselves is just one of a number of categories that mirror analysis insists upon. When we speculate, we are looking to the past to try to understand the future. If we can sort out and isolate the primary categories that we have found, over and over again, then we can use those categories to calibrate our mirror. Therefore, when we do mirror analysis, we are looking simultaneously at ourselves and at our history. Document analysis, particularly analysis of public records, is the most mirror-like of our current analysis strategies. Another way to look at this is to say that mirror aspects of analysis lead us closer to historical analysis than any other form of analysis we use.

Analysis and the Window.   The window perspective is the default understanding of analysis for most researchers. That is, when we talk about analysis per se, we do so from the window perspective. When we look at analysis models like grounded theory, and the myriad of design and verification models laid out by Miles and Huberman (1994), we are closest to the traditional window spirit of empirical research in the social sciences. Is this a bad thing? No, but it will become a bad thing if it prevails as the *only* legitimate way to do qualitative analysis.

Analysis and the Lantern.   Illumination and synthesis are the coin of the realm for lantern analysis. Here we have the opportunity to pick up our efforts and move to where the conceptual light is the weakest. We do not have the luxury of well-developed theories. We often have to craft our methods as we go. But in the end, this is one of the most promising and exciting areas for further development in qualitative research. We just have to remember to acknowledge its presence and make room for it to grow.

PLANNING YOUR RESEARCH PROPOSAL: CREATING A RESEARCH PROPOSAL OUTLINE

Each of our researchers has created an outline of their formal research proposals. Each outline addresses the title of the research proposal, a statement of the problem, a review of key information sources, an explication of their theoretical frameworks, and a discussion of the methods to be used. Like the first informal outline, responses will be no more than one sentence long.

Carol

   I. *Title:* Struggling with Love and Life: Examining the Interactional Dynamics Among School, Work, and Love for the Young, Aspiring, Single, Career Woman.
  II. *Problem Statement:* We know a lot about how young women deal with each of these issues singly, but very little about how they deal with all these issues at the same time.
 III. *Important Information:* For now, I will be staying away from the literature I have collected. I will use it later on, as part of the theory-building process.
  IV. *Theoretical Framework:* Grounded Theory.
   V. *Proposed Methods:* Grounded Theory. I have identified 16 potential participants so far.

Albert

   I. *Title:* Math Anxiety on the Heels of Success: How Math Anxiety Is Understood by Formerly Successful Middle School Students.

II. *Problem Statement:* Math anxiety is unfortunately common in middle school, and we know a lot about it. What we have never studied, however, are those students who are used to being successful and then develop math anxiety in middle school. What are these students like?

III. *Literature Review:* I will review literature on math anxiety in middle school and high-achieving middle school students.

IV. *Theoretical Framework:* I will be conducting a phenomenological study to try to see how these formerly high-achieving students understand their math anxiety.

V. *Proposed Methods:* I will observe and interview the students, their parents, and their teachers. So far, I have identified five potential participants.

Ourselves

Take a few moments to lay out your own research proposal outline. Try to keep your responses no longer than one sentence each. Compare this outline with your first informal outline. In what ways has your thinking changed? What things have remained unchanged?

CHAPTER 9

Narrating

Exercise Eight—_Once upon a Time . . ._

In 1947, Raymond Queneau wrote a curious little book called _Exercises in Style._ This book is still in print and still exerts a certain degree of influence in literary circles. In this work, Queneau purportedly observes a confrontation on a bus, and later sees one of the antagonists talking to a friend and getting advice about sewing on a new button for his overcoat. Queneau takes this minor incident and retells it 99 different ways!

Your efforts in this exercise will not be as ambitious, but the results should be eye opening, nonetheless. Pick some minor episode from your own life—perhaps the time you first learned to ride a bike, or your 10th birthday, or even just an incident from last week. This incident will be your "raw material," so to speak.

- First of all, write up your account of the incident as plainly as possible. Use as many one-syllable words as you can. Also, keep it short; less than one page is ideal.
- Now, rewrite the incident as if it were a piece of gossip about you that someone else had overheard and was describing. Think of a particular person who is doing the gossiping, and try as hard as possible to use his or her voice.
- Next, rewrite the original incident again. This time, write the account as if you were a field researcher observing yourself and taking notes. Remember, a field observer cannot get inside anyone else's head. Make your account as factual and objective as possible.
- Finally, treat the original incident as if it were a fable, such as an Aesop's fable. Don't forget the moral!
- What things stayed the same through the various tellings and retellings? What things changed?

REFLECTING ON NARRATING

This chapter is on narrating skills, and the next chapter is on writing skills. You may be a bit confused. Aren't writing and narrating the same thing? Not at all. Narrating is the art and skill of taking different experiences and events and putting them together into a single, coherent story. For countless millennia, we have been telling stories to each other. From campfires to castles to radio and television, we have listened as others told us stories. Only in the last few millennia have we perfected the skill of converting words to writing. Thus, narrating has been around far longer than writing, and even now writing has not replaced narrating.

But the differences between narrating and writing go well beyond this oral–written dimension. Even if every story we told in this culture were written down, there would still be a fundamental difference between narrating and writing. In the next chapter we will look at the skills of writing on its own terms. For now, we will strive to become better receivers and tellers of stories. There is an art to creating narratives, and there is an art to listening to and properly understanding narratives. We need to pay attention to both of these skill areas.

It is almost impossible to do qualitative research without listening to, and often creating, stories. Why are stories so important to qualitative research? The answer is simple: Stories often play a fundamental role in every sort of human interaction. So of course they are important for qualitative research. Furthermore, stories are about meaning, and qualitative research is a systematic empirical inquiry into meaning. Finally, when we look for meaning, we are often looking for different sources of order than we might use if we did other forms of empirical inquiry. Narratives are an important source or order for qualitative research.

NARRATIVE AND HUMAN UNDERSTANDING

What are the most important things that stories do for us as humans to help us understand and deal with our world? We will look at two of the most critical functions in turn.

Our insight into the first function comes from an unusual place. Empirical researchers almost never look toward religious practices for methodological guidance. But David Buttrick (1987), in his groundbreaking book on homiletics, addresses the role of language in preaching (itself a time honored and important type of story), and thereby shows us something very important about narrating. He concludes a short section on language and story as follows: "We have put together a slapdash phenomenology of language. Language constitutes our world by *naming,* and confers identity in the world by *story*" (p. 11, italics his).

How do we know who we are? That is, how do we establish our ongoing identities? We tell ourselves—and other people—our stories. When we gather field information, information on identity is critical. And most if not all of that information will be conveyed to us in story form. Therefore, we need to know how to listen to these stories and understand how identities are conferred and then conveyed within the rules and nuances of the story forms used. What may seem to be a straightforward type of story in one culture may well sound convoluted and labyrinthine to outside ears. We must learn to follow stories that are structured differently from those stories we are used to hearing, so that we can understand what we are being told. In this fashion, we will have an inside track on the task of understanding our target culture on its own terms.

The second function deals with our ongoing search for order. Suppose we start writing down a record of incidents as they occur. How do we know if these incidents are related, or just coincidental? One of the best ways to make this decision is to see if these incidents can be brought together into a story. If they do form a story, then it is highly unlikely that they just happened to occur, one after the other. In other words, story is the enemy of chance. If we can create a story out of incidents, then we have found at least another plausible source of order in our setting.

STORY GENRES

Understanding and creating stories is a powerful process, and like all such powerful processes, it is prone to pitfalls. The most serious pitfall is to fail to understand the complex and varied natures of stories. We tend to act as if there were only one type of story, and then we look at all accounts from that perspective. But, as we will see, stories come in a variety of types and forms. Each type allows the teller and the listener access to a different sort of information and order. That is, each different type of story performs a different type of "job."

The formal name for story type is *genre*. Genre is an important concept in postmodern thought in particular, and several important postmodern notions about genre have played a role in certain forms of qualitative research. For instance, Rockwell (2000) discusses the influence of Bakhtin's theory of genre on both qualitative research and teaching. Going back even further, Oliva (2000) looks at the impact of Saussure's notions of langue and parole on understanding critical aspects of qualitative research from a genre perspective.

Our aims here, however, will be much more modest and informal. We will set out a basic typology of story genres. As you read about each genre, think about whether or not you have seen these stories played out in the real world. Chances are, you have. There is no single and absolute list of story genres. Therefore, we will look at four common genres of story that show up in many forms of qualitative research. These genres are in no particular order.

Myth

A myth is a story we use to explain why something is the way that it is. Another version of this definition is to say that a myth is a story that is primarily about the meaning of something. Yet a third way to say the same thing: Myth is an account whose historical veracity is irrelevant.

During that period of the 20th century when Western empirical inquiry was busy trying to redefine all issues of meaning as acts of verification, myth fell into deep disrepute. As a term, *myth* on one level was synonymous with *superstition* and on a more day-to-day level was synonymous with *misconception* or *lie*. As we gradually felt more and more uncomfortable talking about the myths of "ignorant savages" we talked instead about the superstitions that formed the misunderstandings of our own everyday lives. We can see vestiges of this thinking today when we read about, say, the nine myths of air travel or the four myths that destroy marriages.

We can take comfort in the fact that the low point for myth has been reached and passed, and we are seeing a gradual restoration of respectability and understanding for myth.

It is easy to see the power and potential of myth in culture. How can we access this power as cultural and social researchers? Part of the key to appreciating the potential role of myth in qualitative inquiry is based on the ability to develop, in the words of Moore (1996), a "mythic sensibility." As Moore explains:

> Myth is one of the genres of experience, a way that imagination wraps us in fantasy even as we dream or live out a day. It accounts for the deepest level of emotion, understanding, and valuing in experience. Because it is so deep, it is collective in tone, full of memory that goes back so far as to feel antecedent to personal life and even to human life. In it, unfamiliar plants, animals, geographies, and notable events may take their place regardless of any connection to actual experience. Perhaps because myth is so much larger than personality, we tend to mystify it, and although we want to see daily experience in relation to myth, we may juxtapose a mythic theme with an event in life and miss the deep story that is suggested within the event. (p. 20)

This beckoning sense of depth that we find in myth is akin to the longing for a depth of understanding that brought us to qualitative research in the first place. If, as Moore warns us, we simply get in the habit of labeling events as myth, then we risk missing other aspects of depth that remain unexplored in these events.

So, the notion of a mythic sensibility is the ability to step away from myth and see events with fresh eyes. Eliade (1954/1959) was one of the first important scholars to look at myth beyond either literature or so-called "primitive mythologizing" to examine the impact of mythic thinking on everyday life. For Eliade, the key to myth was its cyclical nature. One of the great powers of myth is its ability to take us from some beginning through a cycle and then back to another beginning. Many early myths were undoubtedly patterned on the cycles of nature, such as the passage and return of the seasons. But myth soon extended into other, more cultural cycles. A mythic perspective takes such historical events as births, marriages, and deaths, and translates them into an intergenerational and trans-historical look at the rhythms and cycles of human life within culture.

If Eliade and others restored myth to social science scholarship, then Joseph Campbell (1972) reclaimed the concept of myth for our culture at large. More than anyone else, Campbell helped popular consciousness move beyond the notion that myths were merely misconceptions or lies. He called our attention to myths throughout history, and in every major culture. But in the end, he brought all this mythic wisdom back to our everyday lives. In myth, we can see the clear distinction between knowledge and wisdom. History often makes us knowledgeable, but myth more often than not makes us wise.

As we listen to the stories that we hear others tell us on site, are we listening to accounts that can be deemed, in some fashion, to be mythic? The answer, more often than we might suspect, is yes. Though we currently live in a culture where historical consciousness is held to be dominant, mythic thinking can play a surprisingly large role. For one thing, we are great consumers of myth. For instance, when we look at the *Star Wars* saga, what is this story cycle other than a myth of what we treasure and fear in our own culture?

More importantly, we can feel confident that we are in the presence of mythic thinking when we see cyclic patterns and variations of the great mythic themes in the accounts we gather from the field. We must pay attention to these accounts as historical records and tangible accounts. But in doing so, we must not forget to look for any mythic aspects in these tales. More often than not, the mythic awareness is the superstructure that we use to build our seemingly mundane and ordinary accounts. Who knows whether or not the Wounded Healer is lurking in the tale of the housewife and her trip to the butcher shop, or if the Dying God is sitting beside you on the bus as you head to work.

Myth has not been the object of much qualitative research to date, but there are notable and interesting exceptions. Patton (1999) argues that myths can serve as both norms and frameworks for interpreting life stories and oral histories. Kamberelis (2003) explores the use of the Trickster, one of the most universal and perplexing of all myths, as a model for the qualitative postmodern bricoleur described in Chapter 7.

Fable

A fable is a realistic or imaginary account that is supposed to teach us a moral lesson. Fables range all the way from the animal stories of Aesop to the parables of Jesus Christ.

How do you know, when you read your notes of some account from the field, that you are in the presence of a fable and not some other type of story? There is a simple test you can perform. Read or listen to that account from the field one more time. When you have reached the end, say to yourself: *And the moral of this story is* . . . . If you can finish this sentence, then you are dealing with a fable.

You will find fables over and over in your fieldwork. Human beings seem to have an instinct to teach (Shank, 1994), and through fable we can make our teachings both vivid and clear. Furthermore, fables are characterized by their enormous depth of meaning. Just because you can find one moral to your fable does not mean that you have exhausted its potential meaning. Far from it.

Parables, in particular, are essentially endless sources of meaning (Scott, 1989). Consider the famous parable of the prodigal son from the New Testament. At one level, its meaning is fairly clear. When you deal with a loving presence, you will always be forgiven. But does the story stop there? What about the other workers? What about the dutiful older son? How do they figure in the meaning of this fable? These and many other avenues of interpretation lay open to the careful and skilled interpreter of this and other parables.

Folktale

A folktale is an account from the lives of, usually, ordinary folk, and its purpose is to show us how things really are and what things really mean in a given cultural setting. Unlike a myth, however, a folktale goes beyond the explication of meaning to validate some aspect of the identity of the culture in question. In other words, a folktale often tells us something about why our tribe or nation or race is the unique way that it is. As such, it often plays the important role of being a vehicle or delivery system for enculturation of the young. Thompson (1946) was an early pioneer in the effort to collect, document, and categorize folktales. Hamer (1999) has explored the use of folklore as a tool for understanding the storytelling aspect of teaching.

Stepping out of the ordinary into the fantastic is the basic move we find in the type of folktale known as a fairy tale. The fairy tale focuses on the extraordinary to give us a fresh look on the more ordinary. We just need to listen or read with careful eyes and ears.

Children have never had a problem learning complex lessons from fairy tales. One reason, perhaps, is the fact that they do not bother to reflect on how or why they are learning. They merely gravitate to the lessons laid out by the tales. When a fairy tale strikes a powerful chord with them, they want to hear it or read it over and over. When the issue is resolved, they set aside that particular tale and move on (Bettelheim, 1975).

Another reason for the power of fairy tales is that the traditional fairy tale did not pull its punches. A quick look through Grimm's fairy tales (Grimm & Grimm, 1815/1993) will clarify this point. In this famed collection of tales, we have people chopping off parts of their feet, wild animals devouring human beings, witches threatening to cook children, and general killing and mayhem everywhere. Many fairy tales are dark and foreboding. They deliver their life lessons straight, with no chaser.

Fairy tales, like folktales in general, are wonderful windows into authentic cultural differences. For instance, in many cultures the boundary between the natural and the supernatural is just not that important, and so our effort to sort their accounts into either folktales or fairy tales is often pointless and arbitrary. Even if the tales we find are accounts of ordinary and mundane things, we will often be struck by differences we note in tales from cultures other than our own. Details we might think to be trivial will be magnified, and key issues from our perspective might be simply passed over. The order of telling and the structures and mannerisms of the story telling art might seem quite strange to us. These and many other differences can serve collectively as a guidebook into the nature of meaning in those cultures, when taken on their own terms.

Legend

A legend is supposedly an historical account, but its meaning and purpose goes well beyond the recording of that historical event.

When we think of legend, we might recall the heroes and epic events from ancient Greece. Or we might turn instead to one of the many great medieval romances. But it might be more useful for us to look instead at a more contemporary and more modest form of legend known as the urban legend.

Urban legends bear many resemblances to their older and grander cousins. For one thing, there is the insistence that these legends are based on true occurrences. Tellers of these legends claim that someone told them that they saw the story on TV, or that it was in the newspaper somewhere, or that they heard it secondhand via that ubiquitous presence in the urban landscape, the FOAF—"Friend of a Friend." These transmitters of urban legends are convinced that these stories are true, and will often be offended if you suggest that they are "mere" legend.

But, as you might suspect, legends are anything but "mere." These urban legends would not exist if they did not play some important role in culture. In one sense, it is just as important that they *could* be true as it is whether or not they are *actually* true.

Once you start looking for urban legends, you can find them almost anywhere. Jan Brunvand, the primary researcher in this area, filled five books with them (Brunvand 1981, 1984, 1986, 1989, 1993). They also cover just about every area of human life within our culture. Most of us have heard versions of these tales, from the Neiman-Marcus cookie recipe supposedly circulated to spite the greedy store, to the Mexican sewer rat raised as a pet Chihuahua, to the jealous husband who filled his new convertible by mistake with fresh wet concrete. Police departments have put out warnings about killers who lie beneath cars in shopping center parking lots and slash the tendons of unwary drivers, and they have been alerted to gang initiation stunts where innocent drivers who flash their headlights to remind other motorists are stalked down and slain. Of course, all these incidents are urban legends. But they do speak to the deepest concerns and fears of our culture, and they are a ripe topic for qualitative research exegesis.

NARRATIVE

The four story genres just described have a long and venerable history. Today, however, they are subsumed in qualitative research by the larger and more formal concept of the *narrative*. A narrative is a story created during the age of literacy, and thus is governed by the rules of literary creation. Because narrative is such a large and amorphous concept, we are better served by making a distinction between formal and informal narratives.

Formal narratives are an important part of any literate culture. Examples of formal narratives include, among other things, books, plays, recordings, poems, stories, and the like. Literary critics perform the important task of delving into these formal narratives and bringing new insights and understandings to the culture at large.

For those of us who do research in the social sciences, though, most of our work into the nature and meaning of narratives tends to center on the examination of informal narratives. Therefore, when we talk about narrative from now on, we will mean "informal narratives."

What are informal narratives? Informal narratives are accounts, often oral, that describe certain events or circumstances or affairs without trying to adhere to any of the structural components we might find in more formal stories. Eyewitness accounts and oral histories fall in this domain. Rarely are informal narratives just simply an accounting of factual information. Instead, we find the teller often, consciously or unconsciously, shaping the account according to narrative principles. But the chief intent of the teller is to convey information and/or a set of impressions. Anytime we interview anyone in the field, it is highly likely we will end up with an informal narrative or a string of such narratives.

One of the most important kinds of informal narratives are the stories people tell about themselves. These sorts of life histories are an important source of qualitative data and qualitative research efforts in general (see Cary, 1999 for a recent review and discussion of issues). Tenni, Smyth, and Boucher (2003) explore similar issues with autobiographical data treated in narrative and life history fashion. Of course, whether we are doing biographical or autobiographical research, we have to be careful to make sure our accounts are as truthful and accurate as possible. In particular, Gardner (2001) warns about unreliable memories and their potential impact on biographical research.

Narratives are powerful beyond their particular types and manifestations, however. To that end, researchers have been interested in understanding how narratives of all shapes and sizes might be described by common terms and understood using common methods. Underlying all of these efforts is the search for narrative universals.

Narrative Universals

Even though most of the narratives we look at in qualitative research are informal accounts, they still share certain principles with all forms of narrative. Bruner (1996) has taken a careful look at the concept of narrative universals, particularly as they apply to social science research. He argues that there are nine narrative universals that help us construe the realities of our human affairs. The following are Bruner's narrative universals (pp. 133–147). I have taken the liberty of condensing and relabeling a bit for the sake of saving time and space.

The first principle is that narrative unfolds according to its own, and not absolute, time. This is similar to what Crosby (1997) called the difference between *venerable time* (linked to the patterns of the sun and the seasons) and *clock time*. We must understand the flow of time in narrative on its own terms, and not try to impose some temporal metric on it.

The second principle states that narratives deal with particulars, but that these particulars most often fall into more inclusive genres. We have already been examining the notion of genres in story. Bruner goes on to argue that narrative genres not only organize particulars, but in a sense generate them. In the literary world, we have genres like the mystery story, the science fiction story, the romance novel, and so on. With informal narratives, we find genres that are closer to lived experience. That is, we have work stories, marriage stories, coming of age stories, and so on. Also, the forms we considered earlier, such as myth, legend, folktale, and the like, can also be considered genres.

The third principle, according to Bruner, is that actions have reasons. The impact of co-incidence and chance is minimized in favor of the roles of purpose and choice. This is another way to say that story is the enemy of chance.

The fourth principle says that narratives are both composed and meant to be understood in terms of hermeneutic dimensions. This shifts our focus as ordinary consumers of narrative away from issues of structure, or how a narrative is put together, toward issues of function, such as why certain events happened they way they did.

Fifth on Bruner's list is his insistence that narratives are sensitive to ordinary and conventional rules of society, or canons, and that they invariably break those same rules. In other words, if a hero is warned not to do something, then the hero will invariably violate that warning.

The sixth universal narrative in Bruner's model deals with the essential role of ambiguity of reference within narratives. This ambiguity is not due to poor storytelling technique, but reflects the notion that reference in narrative needs to be loose enough to allow for constant and liberal substitution of elements and events. This openness will create the sort of necessary ambiguity of reference needed to shuffle around events and characters as needed.

Universal principle number seven deals with norms. Just like rules, norms seem to exist explicitly in narratives in order to be violated. In fact, the only functional difference in narratives between rules and norms is that norms are always more implicit. Those norms that we follow will be assumed, rather than mentioned. In other words, if a norm is not mentioned, then it will be followed. But if it is mentioned by name, then it will be violated.

Bruner's penultimate principle deals with the inescapable role of negotiation between the narrative creator and the narrative consumer. We hold each other accountable to certain narrative conditions, and we feel angry or anxious if those conventions are violated. This is particularly true of genre understanding. If, for instance, the murderer in a murder mystery is introduced only at the time of the solution of the crime, we are furious with the author. Part of the deal is that we get to guess "whodunit." In a similar fashion, when Alfred Hitchcock killed off Janet Leigh's character in the movie *Psycho* (who was apparently going to be the heroine of this movie), some moviegoers were so frightened and upset by this violation of narrative rules that they actually refused to ever take a shower again without locking the bathroom door.

Bruner's final narrative principle is the fact that narratives not only unfold in time, but also in history. Every event in a narrative has an historical antecedent, both for the creator and the consumer of the narrative. And there is no rule that says these two histories have to be exactly the same.

Bruner is, of course, not the first person to tackle the issue of narrative universals, even psychologically. But for those of us in the social sciences, there does seem to be a focus in Bruner's list that turns the study of narrative away from the composed literary text. We now have a tool to look at the role of day-to-day narratives as part of our social lives. This principle is drawn even more in focus when phenomenological concerns are added to the mix.

Phenomenology and Narrative

Many of those who emphasize the role of narrative in qualitative research also take a phenomenological perspective. It should therefore come as no surprise that the link between phenomenology and narrative knowing is extensive. Polkinghorne (1988), in particular, has explored those dimensions. In his work, he builds explicitly on Merleau-Ponty's understanding of the relation of language to human experience:

> Merleau-Ponty held that in whatever part of our lived experience that has not been spoken of, there is a raw meaning, a "wild logos." This raw meaning calls out for thematic expression . . . . Even though we bring the "call" of reality into language, Merleau-Ponty believed that we are not prisoners of language, making up and projecting ideas into the world. Merleau-Ponty recognized the existence of an inspiration prior to expression. However, he said, this inspiration does not fully exist before it has been interpreted in speech . . . . The meaning of our world and of our existence is not given in advance, and the task of knowledge is not merely to discover this given. Rather, the perceived world imposes a task to be accomplished, which is to make out of what is given something meaningful . . . . Merleau-Ponty arrived at the position that is central to my position—namely, that language takes up the contingencies of existence, and the perceptual openness of life to the natural and intersubjective worlds, and molds them into a meaningfulness that is greater than the meaningfulness they originally held. One of the ways language does this is to configure these givens into a narrative form in which desires and aspirations are used to transform the passing of life into an adventure of significance and drama. (pp. 30–31)

Postmodernism and Narrative

Narrative plays an important role in postmodern thought and research, and postmodern thought has radically altered many of the ways we look at narrative. Tierney (2002) points this out clearly:

> Over the last generation there has been a shift in qualitative methods away from producing the static narrative forms found in traditional, science-oriented research, and toward a more dynamic representational strategy that explicitly locates the author in the text. (p. 385)

This postmodern approach to the use and creation of narrative has resulted in the development of a number of new tools and perspectives. Sondergaard (2002) illustrates a few of them. Inclusive and exclusive discourses are one such perspective. Every discourse has its boundaries. Sometimes, those boundaries are quite stylized and explicit. Other times, these boundaries are informal and can often be subtle. As we look at larger discourses in culture, we realize that these discourses often include certain groups of people and exclude others. For instance, women and minorities in business have complained about the "old boy's" networks. These networks are sites of discourses that have traditionally excluded women and minorities. Even when the excluded parties gain access to such sites, narrative boundaries of exclusion are sometimes still maintained.

A second powerful postmodern narrative concept is the notion of the storyline. Sondergaard (2002) defines a storyline as follows:

> The term storyline refers to a course of events, a sequence of actions that, just as with categories, creates identities through inclusive and exclusive discursive movements. A storyline is a condensed version of a naturalized and conventional cultural narrative, one that is often used as the explanatory framework of one's own and others' practices and sequences of actions. (p. 191)

Some people see themselves as alienated and separated from others. Others feel like they are golden children. Every organization seems to have its working-class hero, and its fair-haired boy. Some people are applauded for being a credit to their race. We are confused when the good neighbor or the friendly coworker goes amok. All of these identities are grounded in discursive storylines. As you can see, the identification and study of storylines is an important part of qualitative research from a narrative perspective.

Another important postmodern approach to narrative research has been the development of memory work. Onyx and Small (2001) provide a brief introduction and review of this method. Memory work is grounded in both social constructivist thought and feminist research perspectives. It is a three-phase method (pp. 775–777):

- In the first phase, individuals construct memories on a relevant topic. They start by writing one or two pages on some event that serves as a trigger for their memories on the larger topic. They write in the third person, using a pseudonym to disguise their identities. Though they try to write in as much detail as possible, they actively avoid engaging in any form of interpretation or explanation.
- In the second phase, all the members of the memory-work team read these written accounts and offer their opinions and thoughts. Working together, the team seeks to find areas of similarity and difference in these accounts. They look for contradictions, cliches, cultural markers, and even pay attention to what is not said. The group explores the written records from popular and theoretical perspectives, and members are invited to rewrite their memories if they wish.
- The third phase seeks to bring together the written accounts and discussions into a single collective understanding of the memory topic. Although all the members of the team contribute their insights and analyses, it is usually produced in final form by a single member of the team. In these ways, memory work seeks to go beyond the notion that single narratives from informants is the best, or even the only, way to explore and analyze complex cultural and historical topics.

Finally, narrative thinking also shows up in postmodern versions of participatory action research. New ways of understanding narrative and story allow us new ways to understand the marginalized and oppressed, and to intervene on their behalf. Arnett (2002) illustrates this process in his analysis of the development of the thought of Freire along narrative lines.

Metanarratives and Postmodern Genres

We will leave the realm of postmodern aspects of narrative by considering the possibility of the death of the metanarrative and the birth of postmodern genres.

First of all, what is a metanarrative? *Metanarrative* is a concept drawn from the work of Lyotard (1979). In this groundbreaking work on the postmodern condition, Lyotard declared that cultures in the past were governed by metanarratives. A metanarrative is a complex and comprehensive narrative that an entire culture accepts as its grounding "myth." Metanarratives are so engrained in the warp and woof of a particular culture's understanding that the members of the culture often accept the metanarrative as the "natural" way to look at the world. Cultures therefore often have trouble seeing beyond the basic assumptions of their metanarratives. These basic assumptions shape and constrain all aspects of culture, including the topics and procedures for doing empirical research.

What are some examples of metanarratives throughout history? We will take a brief look at three powerful and influential metanarratives from the history of Western civilization, from one of the earliest to the most current.

One of the most important metanarratives in Western civilization was the vision known as Christendom. Christendom held sway as a metanarrative from the time of the edict of Constantine, in which Christianity became the official religion of the Roman Empire, until the Renaissance helped spark the split between formal religion and other cultural domains. Christendom, therefore, is roughly equivalent to the historical period we call the Middle Ages. Christendom's basic story was that the world was the book of God. Every thing and every action in the world was a symbol of the power and nature of God. Therefore, religious understanding was applied to every other cultural system, from politics to economics, from art to music, from natural science to practical arts. Not only was the power of the church supreme, but the view of the church was universal. Contrary to current propaganda, Christendom was not an era of ignorance and superstition. It was an era when all accounts about the nature of things had to be "reduced" to their fundamental natures within religious doctrine and dogma. This worldview allowed for all sorts of sophisticated philosophical and artistic works that still remain as an important part of our intellectual and artistic heritage. But Christendom eventually grew old and stale, and newer narratives were needed to help us understand aspects of reality that were not accessed easily from the Christendom metanarrative.

Our second metanarrative played an important role in building Western industrial society. It is a complex account that evolved from revolutionary and pioneering roots, and served as the basis upon which the values of bourgeois capitalism were built. We are talking, of course, of the Protestant *work ethic*.

The Protestant work ethic was a discovery of late 19th-century social science, but it had been around for some time in Western society. The basic tale of the Protestant work ethic is this: Persons are no longer prisoners of their birth status. Anyone, whether or not they were born rich or poor, can work hard and thrive. So if you are poor, then it is probably your own fault. And if I am rich, then I have worked harder than you have. In fact, being rich is part of my reward, from God, for being such a virtuous hard worker. This ethic allowed individuals and their companies to amass great fortunes and control vast amounts of resources with the blessing of society. Struggles for economic reform not only had to work against the power of the wealthy; they also had to work against the pervasive acceptance of the Protestant work ethic at all levels of society.

The final, and most contemporary, metanarrative on our list is modernism. Modernism was born in the Enlightenment and reached its full flourishing in the first half of the 20th century. Modernism was a very scientific and ahistorical worldview. The essence of modernism is the idea that, underneath any and all historical and cultural phenomena, there are underlying basic principles to be found and followed.

The search for the basic universals lurking underneath any and all phenomena was the rallying cry of modernism. Modern architecture stripped buildings to their geometrical basics, and a modern building could be built anywhere in the world and still be recognized as modern. Modern art stripped away all aspects of art deemed to be situational, and focused instead on such universal basics as form, color, and shape. Modern politics sought to set aside historical quarrels and build the United Nations. What Newtonian physics had done for science, modernism strove to deliver to culture as a whole.

Lyotard (1979) noted that all metanarratives, and in particular modernism, had eroded by the late 20th century. With globalization and instantaneous communication, we no longer had the luxury of metanarratives to give us perspective on the world and its nature. Starting with the Cuban missile crisis and the Kennedy assassination, the major events of our world were experienced immediately by nearly everyone in Western culture as they were happening. Metanarratives began to fragment, and we now face the world as members of multiple narrative communities. The disintegration of all metanarratives and the rise of a myriad of "special interest" narratives was, to Lyotard, the keystone of postmodernism.

Postmodern narratives are different in form from more traditional narratives. Many of these fragmented narratives are mixed and matched to create forms of expression and meaning that could not have existed under the reign of metanarratives. For example, the film *Blade Runner* is a curious but effective mix of the apocalyptic science fictional vision of novelist Philip K. Dick combined with classic film noir sensibilities straight from 1940s Hollywood.

ANALYZING NARRATIVE DATA

There are two qualitative data-management strategies that help us to juggle information load and narrative structures when studying informal narratives: conversation analysis and narrative analysis proper. We will look at each in turn.

Conversation Analysis

We mentioned conversation analysis in passing in Chapter 8, but we need to take a more comprehensive look. Conversation analysis developed out of the need to capture the critical nonverbal aspects of field conversations. Such aspects of conversation as pauses, intonations, cut-offs, changes in breathing, and the like were systematized by various models of conversation analysis, so that this sort of data could be incorporated into the analysis process. Equally important is the discovery and documentation of patterns and sequencing in conversation that frame larger systems of communication.

Erving Goffman, Harold Garfinkel, and Harvey Sacks are three of the key researchers who have developed and refined systems of conversation analysis. If you are interested in looking at a readily available and fairly simple transcription system, Psathas (1995) lays out a variant of one of the more common approaches as an appendix to his monograph.

It is also useful to look at actual examples of conversation analysis. Roulston (2001) provides an outstanding recent example of the use of conversation analysis in qualitative research. In this work, she reexamines data from an earlier study on personal practical knowledge of music teachers. By performing conversation analysis on these data, she is able to gain a richer and more detailed picture of many of the key issues.

Over the years, qualitative researchers have developed a variety of modifications and extensions of conversation analysis. We will look at two such examples: membership categorization analysis and positioning analysis.

Membership categorization analysis is an extension of ethnomethodology. Housley and Fitzgerald (2002) note that categorization analysis currently has fallen into a degree of disuse. However, they feel that its emphasis on social and cultural aspects of narration allow for an expansion of the close and detailed work that often characterizes conversation analysis. By adding these dimensions back into the general ethnomethodological mix, they feel that narrative analysis is strengthened:

> The normative power of categorization and the sociology of inference, assessment, moral evaluation, prejudice and identification represents an extremely rich vein of enquiry to which the

reconsidered model of membership categorization can make a positive contribution. Indeed, membership categorization provides a method for analyzing wider conceptions of social structure in a way that draws attention to members' methods and the local accomplishment of social organization without falling into the dualism of micro versus macro perspectivism. . . . (p. 80)

Positioning analysis is an attempt by Korobov (2001) to reconcile conversation analysis and discourse analysis. These forms of analysis often overlap, but there are many points of contention as well. Because most of these points are fairly technical, we will not discuss them. Instead, we will look at the three levels of positioning analysis, and how they guide the process:

- Level one looks at the how conversational units are positioned in relation to each other. Here we are looking at the interaction of such things as characters, events, and topics.
- Level two is concerned with how speakers position themselves in relation to their real or perceived audiences, and how they are also positioned by those same audiences. These social and cultural dynamics are critically important in the production and understanding of narratives.
- Finally, level three deals with issues of identity. Narrators position themselves with respect to such questions as, *Who am I? Why is this important to me? How would I like to be understood?*

In summary, conversation analysis and its variants have played an important role in the analysis of narratives in qualitative research. As times goes on, it is clear that we can expect both more studies using these methods and more variants to these methods arising out of more and more research efforts.

Narrative Analysis

Narrative analysis, for a lack of a better explanation, is a family of techniques for turning informal narratives into more formal accounts, or, perhaps more precisely, for discovering these more formal principles as they are embedded in those same informal accounts. For instance, Riessman (1993) and Lieblich, Tuval-Mashiach, and Zilber (1998) are two fairly recent summaries that lay out some of the more common strategies.

Narrative analysis strategies can range all the way from coding activities that look like grounded theory in action to the use of formal linguistic and semantic principles to restructure transcribed text and highlight the presence of those same principles in action. But the crucial issue for any narrative analysis is the set of assumptions that the researchers make about the nature and use of narrative materials.

Riessman (1993) approaches narrative analysis as primarily the task of rendering what are often large and complex oral accounts into narrative research reports. The approach she outlines is driven more by the specific needs and insights of the researcher than trying to conform to some analytic model. Nevertheless, she sees the following three issues as fundamental to all such efforts, regardless of any particular methodological bent:

1. "How is talk transformed into a written text and how are narrative segments determined?
2. What aspects of the narrative constitute the basis for interpretation?
3. Who determines what the narrative means and are alternative readings possible? (p. 25)"

Lieblich et al. (1998) lay out a much more prescriptive and directive approach to narrative analysis. They start with an explicit definition:

Narrative research, according to our definition, refers to any study that uses or analyzes narrative materials. The data can be collected as a story (a life story provided in an interview or a literary work) or in a different manner (field notes of an anthropologist who writes up his or her observations as a narrative or in personal letters). It can be the object of the research or a means for the study of another question. It may be used for comparison among groups, to learn about a social phenomenon or historical period, or to explore a personality. (pp. 2–3)

In their approach, Lieblich et al. (1998) go on to lay out two poles for defining the critical issues for narrative analysis: a holistic versus categorical dimension and a content versus form dimension. Because these two dimensions are orthogonal, they create four working spaces, or reading strategies, within which different forms of narrative analyses can be performed—a holistic-content type of analysis, a holistic-form type of analysis, a categorical-content type of analysis, and finally a categorical-form type of analysis. It is worth noting that Riessman's (1993) three questions are relevant for all four of the analytic models proposed by Lieblich et al.

Several recent modes of narrative analysis have also emerged. For example, Nygren and Blom (2001) offer a set of procedures for reading and analyzing short reflective narratives. This method combines narrative analysis and coding to yield short analyses that can easily be compared with each other and brought together to form a larger theoretical picture of the areas of reflection.

Other recent models try to address a larger scope. For instance, Mello (2002) argues that coding and related forms of analysis do not capture narrative understandings very well. She argues instead for what she calls *collocation analysis*. In collocation analysis, narrative data is examined by using four operations (pp. 236–240). First of all, we need to examine narratives in terms of their textual operations. These operations describe both how factual information is conveyed and which basic story motifs and plot devices are present. Transactional operations make up the second dimension of analysis. These operations describe how speakers and audience interact, and describe physical and other setting characteristics. Next are sociocultural operations. These operations deal with culturally specific information, social functions, and ceremonial dimensions of the narrative and the act of narration. The fourth and final dimension for collocation analysis is the educative operation. Here is where we look at the narrative and the narrative act as a teaching and learning phenomena. In short, collocation analysis helps us bridge the gulf between the narrative as a communicative act and as an act within the general framework of culture.

Finally, not every narrative analytic approach is so formally structured. For instance, Clandenin and Connelly (1994) outline methods that, while narrative at heart, are still grounded in the concepts of personal experiences. Smeyers and Verhesschen (2001) argue that narrative analysis is not just empirical but can also be philosophical in nature. By this, they mean that the study of narrative can lead us to insights into our deepest philosophical issues in qualitative research.

NARRATIVE INFLUENCES ON RESEARCH THINKING

Narrative has not just served as a tool for doing social science research. There have been a number of researchers who have looked into the nature of narrative as a guide for understanding the nature of social science research. These works have had a varying impact on qualitative research. We will look at several of these initiatives.

Spence (1982) was one of the earliest explorers into the theoretical realm of narrative in the social sciences. Even though his contrasting of narrative and historical truth was laid primarily in relation to psychotherapy, his work has had a more far-reaching impact. Richardson (1995, 2000) has had a tremendous impact on the awareness of the importance of narrative in qualitative research. Her perspective is that writing and narrative are not just tools for doing research—effective narration and effective writing are a fundamental and irreplaceable parts of the research process itself. Bal (1997) summarizes the extensive body of work in the field of narratology. Narratology is a discipline that seeks to lay out the structural and functional dynamics of narratives on an abstract level, whether or not the narratives are formal or informal. And finally, Paulos (1998) is a popular example of the use of mathematical and other logical tools to explicate the nature of ordinary stories.

All of these directions share one common theme: Though it is important to use research to understand the nature of research, it is equally important to keep in mind that our growing understanding of narrative can also be used to expand our understanding of the research process per se.

NARRATING AND THE MIRROR, WINDOW, AND LANTERN

We live in a narrative-saturated world. As a result, the telling and understanding of stories is an integral part of qualitative research. We have examined a variety of narrative types, along with ways of analyzing and interpreting them. What can our three forms of looking tell us further to help put our narrative understandings into practice?

Narrating and the Mirror.   What sorts of stories help us see ourselves, and the world, in fresh and new ways? The simple answer is *all of them*. Each and every story has a mirror function built in. The sort of order that stories convey is necessarily reflective. It is rare, if not impossible, to find a story that does not tell us something about ourselves. Story is one of the most powerful "glues" we have to hold cultures together, and reflection is an intergral part of the operation of that glue. If we fail to look for and understand the mirror aspects of any narrative we find, then we run the risk of missing the fundamental meaning of that narrative.

Narrating and the Window.   Here is where the ideas of qualitative science come to play in the field of narratives. When we move from the task of deciphering and understanding the significance of narratives to the question of what makes them tick, then we have moved into the window perspective. As we have seen, stories fall into categories, and each category lends itself to story that does unique sorts of cultural work. So, the task of categorizing and ordering narrative types is not a sterile exercise. Think of it as a form of tool ordering. If we set out to do a task, more often than not we will need to use some tools. We have to take a close look at both the task and the tools we have in order to know what to use to do the job correctly. There is a science of story, and we would be foolish not to learn it and use it.

Narrating and the Lantern.   The essence of the lantern is to move into the dark corners and to shed light where no light has been shed before. The dark corners in narrative are interpretative. How can we dig deeper into this story, to discern legitimate meaning that no one has seen before? What collateral information do we possess, no matter how seemingly trivial or peripheral, that we can use to wrestle deep and subtle meaning from our tale? Along with reflection and awareness of process, illumination is the third crucial and indispensable aspect of narrative interpretation.

PLANNING YOUR RESEARCH PROPOSAL:
FIRST DRAFT OF THE RESEARCH PROPOSAL

For the first draft of the research proposal, Carol and Albert return to their outlines. Now, instead of making a simple statement they elaborate wherever necessary. Following are some of the key points they address in their proposals.

Carol

I. *Title:* Struggling with Love and Life: Examining the Interactional Dynamics Among School, Work, and Love for the Young Aspiring Single Career Woman.

II. *Problem Statement:* Carol explains that young women often struggle with career issues, school issues, or relationship issues. How do some of these women manage to balance the struggle among all three issues, especially when they are in the lower financial echelon for their age and gender groups? We have a good amount of data on each of these issues, and some anecdotal evidence on how they interact. What we lack, and what this study seeks to address, is the need for a good theoretical understanding of these interactional dynamics.

III. *Important Information:* Carol lays out the demographic characteristics of her proposed sample. She informs us that she has a preliminary agreement with 16 potential participants who have examined her proposed consent form and who understand her research goals and aims. Carol also tells us that there is a body of research findings related to her topic. In keeping with the tenets of Grounded Theory, she has not explored that literature in any great depth, but she makes us aware of the fact that she is ready to access that literature at the appropriate time in her theory-building process.

IV. *Theoretical Framework:* Carol explains the basic tenets of Grounded Theory and her rationale for choosing this approach for her study.

V. *Proposed Methods:* Carol reminds us that she is using Grounded Theory and takes some time to explain both her sample and the sorts of data she will actually be gathering. She also shares with us some of her initial questions for her participants and some of her initial observational strategies.

Albert

I. *Title:* Math Anxiety on the Heels of Success: How Math Anxiety Is Understood by Formerly Successful Middle School Students.

II. *Problem Statement:* Albert tells us that his research area came from his own personal experience as a middle school math teacher. Though the phenomenon of the math anxious student is not uncommon, the first-time math anxious middle school student with a prior record of success is much more rare. Furthermore, such students can shed light on previously unexplored aspects of math anxiety.

III. *Literature Review:* Albert has reviewed a fairly extensive body of literature for his study. First of all, he outlines major research findings and theoretical issues on the general topic of math anxiety. Then, he focuses on recent qualitative research on this topic. What areas have been explored? What methods were used? He then reviews the literature on high-achieving middle school students. What do we know about these students when they struggle in some areas? Through this extensive review, Albert builds a clear picture of our current state of understanding and our current assumptions and presuppositions as well.

IV. *Theoretical Framework:* Albert is committed to two issues here. First of all, he wants to explicate the notion of math anxiety among first-time math anxious, former high-achieving middle school students. He wants to see how this concept is both related to other forms of math anxiety and how it is unique. Second of all, he wants this concept expressed in the voices of those concerned—the students, their parents, and their teachers.

V. *Proposed Methods:* Albert plans to interview and observe students, teachers, and parents. From these data, he hopes to build a phenomenological picture of this complex concept. To that end, he has identified five potential participants. He has presented his consent materials to these students, their parents, and their teachers, and has received preliminary permission from all three groups. Albert realizes that because some of his participants are minors the review process will need to be thorough and that he needs to be prepared to alter aspects of his proposal to reflect possible calls for change by the Institutional Review Board.

Ourselves

As you get close to the point of writing your own proposal, you need to start gathering your thoughts and approaches together. Are there any holes in your current drafts? How can you fill them? Are they minor, or do you need to rethink parts or all of your proposal to address them?

Do not forget to ask for help if you need it. At this stage of the game, another set of eyes can be invaluable.

CHAPTER 10

Writing

Exercise Nine—*Focusing the Expert Case Study Report*

We set off in Exercise 3 to do our expert case study project. Since then, we have looked at field methods, interpretation models, how to ask good questions, how to gather and analyze data, and how to find and understand stories from others. In addition, we have followed Carol and Albert through their proposal preparations. We have not said much about this project since Exercise 3 because there is no guarantee that each and every thing we studied along the way would be of direct relevance to your expert case study project. I hope, though, that you have been able to use much of what we have talked about and practiced to bring your expert case study project along nicely. At this time, we can all get together and go back to the project to talk about how to start writing up the final report.

By now, you should have collected most (if not all) of the data you need in order to complete your expert case study. You have found your expert, talked to him or her, perhaps observed him or her practicing his or her expertise, and analyzed and organized your observations and findings. All that remains is to actually write the case study report.

If you are a practiced and skilled writer, then this step should be familiar to you (although it is rarely ever easy). But for the rest of us, the job of creating the final written product seems like a daunting task.

This exercise will help you use the aspects of qualitative research you have learned so far to create a focus for the expert case study report. Once you have achieved such a focus, then we can concentrate on the art and craft of writing itself, and how you can best use that art and craft for your own purposes.

Your focus should consist of the following:

- First, you need to write down your goal. In this case, it is fairly simple: What does it mean to be an expert in the area you have chosen? Write your goal in capital letters on a single sheet of paper. This will be your anchor. Everything else you do in this exercise should help answer this single question in some way.
- Now, you need to sort out your findings. The following is a set of categories that are often useful. Feel free to modify, change, or delete categories based on your actual case study:

    Category 1: What did I believe, or think I knew, about this area of expertise before I started? Which of my preconceptions, if any, were confirmed? How did my expert confirm these preconceptions?

    Category 2: What surprised me the most? How did this surprise inform my current understanding of this area of expertise? What other surprises did I find? How did they change my current understanding?

Category 3: Did I find it necessary to actually observe my expert in action? If not, why not? Were there good reasons that I could not observe my expert? Did actual observation just not make sense, or was it not necessary? If I did actual observation, what did I observe about my expert that caught my eye?

Category 4: Does my expert have a unique voice, or way of looking at and speaking about the world? If so, how can I capture the texture and nature of that voice in my report?

Category 5: How does my expert compare to other experts in the area? How do I know this information? How unique is my expert among other experts in the field in question? What can we learn from this uniqueness?

Category 6: What have I learned about myself as part of this assignment? How relevant is that learning to the task at hand of writing the case study report?

This list of categories is not a checklist that has to be addressed, point by point, in order to write good case study reports. Instead, think of it as a crude map of the terrain. A crude map does not lay out all that many details, and some of its territory may not be relevant to you. But it is a sketch based on the actions of previous explorers of the same terrain, and in that fashion it can be useful.

Good luck on finishing the final expert case study report. The rest is up to you!

REFLECTING ON RESEARCH WRITING

One thing is immediately apparent from the focus you have just created—it will not write the case study report for you. Even though you have a goal and a set of insights and observations and findings, they are not a report.

In this chapter, we will explore some of the ins and outs of writing up qualitative research. Unlike most examples of quantitative research, writing is actually one of the key aspects of qualitative research analysis. More often than not, the project itself is not complete until it is in final written form.

RHETORIC AND RESEARCH WRITING

In order to write, you need to delve into a realm that is rarely addressed explicitly in qualitative research—the realm of rhetoric. We will start with basic rhetorical devices per se, and then move along to genres of research writing, and then conclude with a smattering of practical tips for writing qualitatively within the social science tradition.

You may be a bit surprised that we are starting with rhetoric. *Rhetoric* is one of those words that have taken on a negative connotation over the years. Who has not heard the expression "mere rhetoric" used to describe a statement? What does this expression usually mean? More often than not, something is described as "mere rhetoric" if it is intended simply to persuade you without being all that concerned with the truth.

When couched in these terms, rhetoric seems to be the enemy of empirical research. No wonder that research prose has traditionally been simple and objective and transparent. It is as if we seek to squeeze out all overt references to persuasion so that the mere facts can be free to speak for themselves.

We will not dwell on the idea that even the most apparently innocent piece of scientific prose is trying, deep down, to persuade you. We will leave that train of thought for another day and time. Instead, we want to take a more positive turn. Is there a way to understand rhetoric as a more positive force in empirical research writing?

Let us go back several centuries and look at rhetoric as it once was understood. The master rhetorician, in medieval times in particular, was concerned with persuasion. But more importantly, rhetoric was seen to be the art of being able to convey as precise a set of impressions as possible from one person to another. Furthermore, this aspect of "elegant communication" can be expanded to target not only our colleagues, but our critics and even whole communities of interest (deMarrais, 2004).

If we move toward the goal of clarity and precision and place less emphasis on the goal of persuasion, then we can begin the process of mastering the rhetoric of qualitative research writing.

A Quick List of Important Rhetorical Devices

Skilled writers make use of a wide variety of rhetorical devices, regardless of the type of tale they are trying to tell. These devices are also called tropes. Some tropes are quite familiar and remain part of the common legacy of writing. Similes, metaphors, and personifications are examples of more common tropes. But there are also two other classes of tropes: (1) implicit tropes, or those tropes we know from use but not by their names or formal characteristics; and (2) specialized tropes, or those tropes we use when we are trying to craft an exact representation that proves to be hard to capture using the ordinary rules of prose. Espy (1983) is a delightful and comprehensive source for all three types of tropes. As you may suspect, there are scores (if not hundreds) of common, implicit, and specialized tropes. We cannot examine all of them, but we will look at a few examples of the two more uncommon types.

Perhaps the most often used implicit trope is *metonymy*. Metonymy is when we try to evoke one idea by using an associated idea. For instance, when we say, "The pen is mightier than the sword," we mean "the press" when we say "pen," we mean "exerts more influence" when we say "is mightier," and we mean "the military" when we say "the sword." So why don't we just say, "The press exerts more influence than the military" in the first place? Because we want to show that when the press exerts its influence, it is capable of standing up to the physical power of the military. So instead of talking about influence, which is an intellectual term, we use might, which is a physical term. So the essence of the metonymy is the association of "might" to stand for "influence."

The pen is mightier than the sword. This apparently simple statement has a complex rhetorical structure. This fact becomes clearer when we realize that, within this overall metonymy, there is a second more specialized form of metonymy called *synecdoche*.

Synecdoche is a type of metonymy where the association is part-for-the-whole. In other words, we talk about the part when we mean the whole. Synecdoche may be the single most common implicit trope. Not only do we use "pen" for "the press" and "sword" for "the military," but we also talk about our "wheels" when we mean our "car" and we say that Pittsburgh won the Super Bowl when we mean the Steelers football team. Even though we use synecdoches all the time, we don't know all that much about the term and especially its formal properties. Our grasp of its properties is from usage, not from any formal understanding. But once we become more aware of the formal properties of terms like metonymy and synecdoche, we can use them more deliberately and reflectively. We do not have to depend upon our instincts alone.

Specialized Rhetorical Tropes

A grasp of formal properties becomes even more important when we consider how and when to use specialized rhetorical tropes. As an illustration, we will look at one of these tropes in some detail as it might actually be used.

Suppose that you once did research in and among the poor homeless and parentless children in, say, the Trenchtown slums of Kingston, Jamaica. These children faced the real possibility of starvation on a daily basis, and so they often turned to theft and other crimes just to survive. But you were studying the work of a small but dedicated community of volunteers who came to the government square each and every evening with cooking pots, bowls, and sacks of cornmeal porridge. Without any funding and without any formal support, these volunteers built simple fires and cooked porridge and fed as many of these starving children as they could.

Before too long, you left the island and began work on writing up your findings. Some of your writing was fairly straightforward. You described the number of children you worked with, the number of volunteers, their stated motives, responses of the children, governmental responses, and the like. But you get stuck on one point. You want to highlight the impact of the charitable acts of the volunteers, but you don't want to simplify or sentimentalize your conclusions. At the same time, though, you don't want to over-intellectualize the situation. You want your readers to see the real human dynamics of the situation.

You write the following sentence: "The outpouring of love by the volunteers was only topped by the regular outpouring of food into the bowls of the children." Blessedly, you stop writing. This will never do. The volunteers deliberately maintained a low-key presence. The streetwise children would have met any "outpouring" of love with justified suspicion. So not only was your first try too sentimental, it was also incorrect.

You try again: "By providing a constant source of food, these volunteers were able to help the children maintain good nutrition. With their nutritional needs met, the children were far less likely to steal for food and get in trouble." Okay, these sentences are true but this argument is too linear. It implies some sort of straightforward causality that misses the true significance of the situation. But it is a much better statement than the mawkish sentence you discarded earlier. Can you fix it up a bit?

You settle on the following: "By providing a constant source of food, the volunteers were able to help the children stay out of trouble and maintain good nutrition." This sentence meets your needs, and so you finally move on.

Whether you realize it or not, you have turned to a rhetorical trope known as *hysteron proteron* to solve your problem. *Hysteron proteron* is Greek for "last one first." It occurs when you take a sequence and reverse the order of occurrence. In the previous example, the volunteers were first providing good nutrition and as a result of that good nutrition, they were then providing the children with a chance to stay out of trouble. Why do we reverse the order? Because we feel that the chance to stay out of trouble will have a more wide-ranging, long-term impact on the lives of these children, and so we want to highlight it. But the provision of good nutrition is also critically important, so we don't want to lose that observation as well. And we don't want to run the risk of our readers thinking that there was a simple correlation between providing food and helping the children stay out of trouble.

By using hysteron proteron, we make the exact point we want to make. These volunteers were helping the kids stay out of trouble, but in a complex and holistic way that involved food, modeling, and love. But these kids were also getting the nutrition they needed to stay alive. By shifting the sequence from a temporal to a significance order, we achieve our goal without drawing undue attention to our solution. Mission accomplished.

By being more rhetorically sophisticated, you have managed to create a report that conveys what you really want to say. But if you want to see an account of this situation elevated to the rank of true genius, seek out the Bob Marley song "No Woman No Cry." In this song, Marley describes his early life as one of these homeless children in Trenchtown, and how "Georgie" would feed the children every evening. Marley generously shared writing credit (and royalties) with one of these "street chefs" to help supply funds to keep the work going.

Rhetorical Trope Awareness

How can you go about the task of building your rhetorical trope awareness? The best strategy is to proceed slowly and steadily over time. Get a good sourcebook of tropes, and check out one or two new ones every now and then. Start out with those tropes that seem to draw you to them. They are probably already a part of your own reading and writing.

Once you have settled on a trope to explore, the rest is easy. Make sure your sourcebook gives you plenty of examples of the trope in use. Write down a few examples of your own. Make it a point to look for this trope as you read. After some time, you will start to feel comfortable with this trope, and you can now consider it part of your rhetorical inventory. This will help you avoid using the trope in your own writing in a mechanical or superficial way. A good trope should blend seamlessly into the rest of your writing, pointing toward the point you want to make without drawing undue attention to itself.

Mastery of rhetorical skills takes time and patience. You must allow yourself the time to become a better writer. No one becomes a skilled writer overnight. What should you do in the meantime? Make sure you have something important and interesting to say. Your readers will forgive an occasional lapse into clumsy writing if you are telling them something they want or need to know.

FROM RHETORIC TO THE RESEARCH TALE

Rhetoric consists of a bag of tricks we can use to hone and craft our writing to make it do what we want it to do. But good writing is not just attention to these sorts of details. Good writing is also well organized. Our first foray into the realm of exploring good research writing will deal with looking at which sort of research tale we might choose to tell.

The Research Tale

The most important guide to the notion of the research tale is van Maanen's (1988) *Tales of the Field*. In this highly influential work, van Maanen lays out three fundamental categories of field reporting. Each of these categories is labeled as a different sort of research tale. We will examine each tale in the order he lays out.

The Realist Tale

van Maanen's (1988) first category is the *realist* tale. In this category:

> . . . a single author typically narrates the realist tale in a dispassionate, third-person voice. On display are the comings and goings of members of a culture, and usually a hesitant account of why the work was undertaken in the first place. The result is an author-proclaimed description and something of an explanation for certain specific, bounded, observed (or nearly observed) cultural practices. (p. 45)

van Maanen uses the notion of conventions to discriminate among the three primary kinds of field tales. He identifies four primary conventions in the creation of the realist tale.

The first convention deals with the absence of the author in the account. In the realist tale, the fieldworker's/author's voice is submerged by a focus on the words, deeds, and thoughts of the culture under study. At the same time, however, the author of the realist tale must take care to make sure the audience can trust what the author has to say. So, while the author per se is not present in the work, his or her credentials are often on display. This appeal to authority is also seen in the way accounts are written. If we do not say "I saw the islanders plant crops by the light of the full moon" we must say instead "the islanders plant crops by the light of the full moon." By removing our presence, we give a sense of institutionalized authority to our claims. That is, we are not stating our perceptions, but we are telling it like it is.

The second primary convention we find in the realist tale is ". . . a documentary style focused on minute, sometimes precious, but thoroughly mundane details of everyday life among the people studied" (van Maanen, 1988, p. 48). That is, when we write realist tales, we focus on the ordinary instead of the dramatic. We are trying to inform our readers, not entertain them. If the exploits we witness prove to be entertaining, then so be it. But our commitment is always first and foremost to the task of chronicling everyday life.

The third convention of realist tale writing is a commitment to the perspectives and points of view of the members of the culture themselves, and not those of the researcher. One of the best ways to convey these native points of view is by using their own words. van Maanen (1988) notes: "Extensive, closely edited quotations characterize realist tales, conveying to readers that the views put forward are not those of the fieldworker but are rather authentic and representative remarks transcribed straight from the horse's mouth" (p. 49).

The fourth and final condition that helps define the nature of realist tales and our accounts of them is a concept that van Maanen labels *interpretive omnipotence*. By interpretive omnipotence, we mean that the fieldworker has the right to claim the final word as to the selection and interpretation of his or her findings, representations, and accounts. Most often, writers support their position by appealing to theory to justify their claims. Other times, they may support their work by appealing to the members of the culture under study. But in the end, the only voice that finally comes through on these matters is the voice of the writer. That is, we may pull in all the support we want or need, but when we write, we write in our voice alone.

Realist tales are the most traditional of all field-writing accounts. For decades, they dominated the writing scene. Over the years, however, we have seen the gradual emergence of the other two types of tales.

The Confessional Tale

Van Maanen's second category is the *confessional* tale. van Maanen (1988) defines the confessional tale as follows: "The distinguishing characteristic of confessional tales are their highly personalized styles and their self-absorbed mandates" (p. 73).

Like the realist tale, the confessional tale has its own set of conventions. The first convention addresses the matter of authority. In the realist tale, the author minimizes his or her own voice and creates a sense of institutional authority to legitimize the claims put forth in the account. In the confessional tale, the tables are reversed. Authority becomes the personal responsibility of the author. It is up to him or her to establish a sense of presence and intimacy with the reader, so that the reader will then come to trust the author's words.

The second convention deals with point of view. Unlike the realist tale, where the point of view of the members of the culture predominates, the confessional tale always foregrounds the researcher's point of view. There is always something autobiographical about a confessional tale. It is not an account of "life among the natives." It is always instead "my account of the time that I spent among the natives." Quite often, much of the confessional material centers around the task of learning how to be a field researcher. A good confessional account will chronicle failures and blunders and lucky accidents, in addition to standard descriptions of successful field efforts and initiatives.

The final convention of the confessional tale is that of naturalness. Naturalness is not only a matter of capturing ordinary events and behaviors in proper context. It is also about the seeming inevitability that well-done fieldwork will bear fruit. That is, if you go about acting and interacting in a natural way, then all will turn out well. Or, as van Maanen (1988) concludes: "The implied story line of many a confessional tale is that of a fieldworker and a culture finding each other, and, despite some initial spats and misunderstanding, in the end, making a match" (p. 79).

We can readily see that confessional tales are more personal, more dramatic, and in some senses more romantic than realist tales. Though there is always the danger of excess, a well-done confessional tale can breathe life into a field account. van Maanen (1988) notes that confessional tales usually do not replace but instead supplement realist tales.

The Impressionist Tale

van Maanen's (1988) third and final category is the *impressionist* tale. van Maanen draws the name for these sorts of tales from the Impressionist movement in art. He notes that Impressionist painters set out to dazzle and startle their audiences with their masterful and novel techniques and styles:

> The impressionists of ethnography are also out to startle their audience. But striking stories, not luminous paintings, are their stock-in-trade. Their materials are words, metaphors, phrasings, imagery, and most critically, the expansive recall of fieldwork experience. When these are put together and told in the first person as a tightly focused, vibrant, exact, but necessarily imaginative rendering of fieldwork, an impressionist tale of the field results. (pp. 101–102)

Like the other two tale motifs, impressionist tales have their own conventions. The first convention van Maanen calls *textual identity*. Textual identity always has a purpose: "The form of an impressionist tale is dramatic recall . . . . The idea is to draw an audience into an unfamiliar story world and allow it, as far as possible, to see, hear, and feel as the fieldworker saw, heard, and felt. Such tales seek to imaginatively place the audience in the fieldwork situation . . . " (van Maanen, 1988, p. 103). In short, field accounts take on the textual characteristics of a story told, rather than a set of events documented and chronicled.

The second convention noted for impressionist tales is the use of fragmented knowledge. Information unfolds in the telling, instead of being described and documented. Impressionist tales take on the character of stories and novels, where understanding on the part of the reader evolves as a result of the skillful manipulation and delivery of information on the part of the author. All this is seen as part of the process of helping the reader learn about the culture: "The audience cannot know in advance what matters will prove instructive, and thus by trying to hang on to the little details of the tale, they experience something akin to what the fieldworker might have experienced during the narrated events" (van Maanen, 1988, p. 104).

The final two impressionist tale conventions are characterization and dramatic control. Characterization is self-explanatory. In order for an impressionist tale to work, we have to be able to recognize and empathize with the people involved. The author often works carefully on his or her own portrayal, seeking a balanced pose between humble apprentice of the culture and shrewd interpreter of seemingly trivial details. But the author must bring the other key informants to life as well.

Dramatic control implies that a field account is not just a chronicle, but a story moving along toward some dramatic resolution. The impressionist tale writer must understand how to create this sort of literary tension in what is ostensibly a research report:

> The author must not give away the ending before it is time. A degree of tension must be allowed to build and then be released. . . . Artistic nerve is required of the teller. Literary standards are of more interest to the impressionist than scientific ones. A general audience unfamiliar with the studied scene can judge the tale only on the basis of its plausibility or believability, not on the basis of accuracy or representativeness . . . . The audience cannot be concerned with the story's correctness, since they were not there and cannot know if it is correct. The standards are largely those of interest (does it attract?), coherence (does it hang together?), and fidelity (does it seem true?). (p. 105)

What sort of tale should you adopt as you set out to write up your case study report? That will depend on your prior level of skill as a writer. Confessional tales can be tricky to write without lapsing into self-indulgence, and impressionist tales require a basic level of mastery of the art of writing. Your safest strategy is to outline your report as a realist tale. If that outline captures the essence of what you want to say, then proceed. If you feel that you need to take a more confessional or impressionistic stance, then by all means do so. Actual writing is the best way to improve writing skills. If your direction does not work out, you can always erase and start again.

The Less Common Tales

van Maanen (1988) briefly notes the presence of four less common types of field tales. We will mention them briefly, although each of these tales deserve careful consideration for possible use as a guide for writing.

The first of these less common tales van Maanen calls the "critical tale." This is the sort of tale that you might tell, for instance, if you were reporting on action research. There is an inescapable political edge to the critical tale, as van Maanen notes: "Critical tales often have a Marxist edge and a concern for representing social structure through the eyes of disadvantaged groups in advanced (and not-so-advanced) capitalist countries" (1988, p. 128).

The second tale van Maanen calls the "formal tale." These are the field tales that blend applied theory and ethnographic accounts. They are very much guided by bringing a particular theoretical position into the research setting, as van Maanen points out:

> . . . the tellers of formal tales push a much narrower view of ethnography under labels such as ethnomethodology, semiotics, symbolic interactionism, conversational analysis, ethnosemantics, sociolignuistics, ethnoscience, various forms of structuralism, and so forth. The analytic goals, while many and diverse, include the derivation of generalizations through inductive and inferential logic. (1988, p. 130)

As van Maanen seems to suggest, these tales are the most "scientific sounding" of all field tales.

The third less commonly used type is actually becoming a very common type. van Maanen called it the "literary type." These are much more emotional in content, and resemble more popular works of fiction or creative journalism. There are two primary devices used in literary tales. The author either tries to tell the tale as a story being narrated by a native of the culture, or the author moves entirely to the other end of the spectrum and tells the tale as an autobiography. We can see many similarities between the literary tale from an autobiographical perspective and the autoethnography.

The final less common field type van Maanen (1988) calls the *jointly told tale*. Here, the field report is a collaboration between the researcher and one or more people from the native culture. Though there is growing interest in the inclusion of more voices in field reports, actual cases of jointly told tales are still rather rare.

van Maanen's advice on creating fieldwork tales is valuable, but it is no substitute for basic principles of writing per se. We will take a look at the practice of research writing next.

THE PRACTICE OF RESEARCH WRITING

Most advice about writing is excruciatingly practical: In order to write, you must first sit down and write. Do not write and edit at the same time. Clear writing usually sounds clear and smooth when read aloud. The only way to improve your writing is to keep writing. And on and on and on . . . .

Are there crucial issues particular to qualitative research writing as a form? Wolcott (1990, 2003) addresses several major issues. We will cover a few of them here.

Get into a Routine

Wolcott's first suggestion is that you adopt as any routines as possible in your writing life. How might you apply his advice? Find your most comfortable place to write, and do most of your writing there. Find your best time of day to write, and write then whenever possible. Find your comfortable writing length, for one sitting, and write that much. Even the most creative and unorthodox writer is usually a creature of routine. Routine adds a level of comfort to a complex and challenging practice.

Find Your Focus

The next suggestion is to get and keep a focus. This focus is first reflected in your plan, or your problem statement. If people ask you what you are trying to say, can you tell them in one sentence? The longer your explanation, the less clear and focused your plan and your problem. In your exercise for this chapter, you worked on the focus for your expert case study. Can you take all your category statements and your goal and create a one-sentence plan?

Don't Duck the Details

When putting your report into writing, it is tempting to skip over details in order to get to your main points. However, qualitative research writing depends on details. Wolcott advises us to put in the details as they arise, and to get them right the first time. Nothing is more perplexing and demoralizing than trying to figure out how to go back and "fix" sketchy or incorrect details. If you put them in right at the outset, then you can always go back and tighten your report.

Know When and How to Get Feedback

Wolcott advises on waiting for feedback until your work has started to take shape. While we often desire praise and support, we often impede our progress when we seek this support too early. Choose your early readers with care, and limit them to a handful of people. Feedback can be a demanding and difficult process, as Wolcott (1990) notes:

> Timely and useful feedback on writing is hard to give and hard to take. The problem is compounded in qualitative research because there are so many dimensions on which feedback can be offered: whether one has identified the right story to tell, how well it has been told, and how well it has been analyzed and interpreted. And as with any writing, it is easier to identify problems, difficult sentences, and alternative explanations than to know what to say about particularly well-conceived studies, particularly well-turned phrases, or particularly insightful interpretations, other than a cliched "I really liked this" or "Great!" Even gentle reviewer-critics are more likely to fault weaknesses in a manuscript than to applaud strengths, unless they render only a global reaction and leave the nitty-gritty to others. Thus, regardless of intent, feedback tends to be disproportionately critical and negative. Your only consolation may be that the more painstaking the critique, the more you may assume that your critic has taken your effort seriously. (pp. 43–44)

Follow Accepted Conventions

It is important to develop and nurture your own style as a writer and qualitative researcher. It is equally important to realize that you are participating in a process with existing procedures, conventions, and rules. Your final writing must reflect your knowledge and awareness of these rules and conventions.

First and foremost, you must learn and follow the rules for manuscript preparation. What are the rules for titles? Headers? Margins? What citation style should you follow? How should footnotes be handled? Page numbers? There are any number of authoritative guides for proper manuscript preparation in the style you need to use. Sometimes, it is handy to use what I call *double-entry* style checking. Secure a manuscript that is in proper form. As you prepare your manuscript, compare your work first to this correctly formatted manuscript. Often, it is easier to learn rules by imitation. Once you are done, check your style manual to reinforce or refine your formatting choices.

Other rules and conventions are less straightforward. Make sure you target your work to the proper audience. For instance, if you are doing research on criminology, do not send your findings to a health science journal. What about conceptual and theoretical rules and conventions? Do you accept them, or push against the standards and conventional thinking of the field? Here you are on muddy ground. I am reluctant to tell you to read what is already published and then try to make your work conform to these ideas and findings. On the one hand, if you try to make your work fit in, it will be accepted more readily. But if we all do this, then we will eventually all be writing the same thing. In short, there are power and political dimensions to research writing, and you should at least be aware of them. If the familiar ideas of the field fit your work, then there is no problem. If you are going in a different direction, then you have some hard decisions to make.

OTHER GUIDES TO GOOD RESEARCH WRITING

There are a number of other recent guides for good writing in qualitative research. Ely, Vinz, Downing, and Anzul (1997) address the notion of qualitative research writing from a number of perspectives. Ely and Vinz are professors, and Downing and Anzul are learning specialists and librarians in public school settings. Unlike Wolcott, who is speaking to the individual working writer, Ely et al. focus on the act of writing as a social and collective process. Writing, in their view, transforms the society being described and discussed, but the act of writing also transforms the writer as well.

Woods (1999), on the other hand, is more of an example of the "how to" approach to writing. This work concentrates on issues of style, organization, and revision and editing. It also includes an extensive section on writing for publication.

EXPLORING ALTERNATIVE MODELS FOR QUALITATIVE RESEARCH WRITING

Most qualitative researchers have turned to earlier examples of published qualitative research for guidance in writing up their own studies. Though this is a useful and effective strategy, it is also important to remember that there are any number of other appropriate writing models and styles to draw from. Janesick (1999) reminds us that journals are not only important sources of data and reflection, they can also serve as the base for our research writing as well. Harrington (2003) offers a wealth of practical information and examples of how journalistic writing can inform qualitative writing, particularly in the area of ethnography. And finally, Smaling (2002) reminds us that every research report is, at heart, a logical argument. His approach combines reasoning and dialogue in a way that can be particularly useful for qualitative writers.

EVALUATING QUALITATIVE WRITING

We can evaluate how accurate, how important, and how meaningful a given qualitative study is. We can also evaluate it in terms of style. Is it well written? Is it clear? Is the writing style appropriate?

Zeller and Farmer (1999) examine the long and fascinating debates over style in research writing. Until recently, there was an emphasis on the use of scientific writing in all forms of empirical research. Such emphases included the exclusive use of the third-person voice, the use of simple and objective prose and sentence structures, and the avoidance of all forms of figurative language. With the advent of qualitative research in the social studies, there has been a subsequent loosening of these restrictions in all forms of writing, including quantitative research writing. Personal writing styles have become more acceptable as well. Hanrahan, Cooper, and Burroughs-Lange (1999) document the use of such personal writing styles in qualitative dissertations.

As qualitative writing has grown more experimental, the need has arisen for criteria designed to specifically evaluate these sorts of writings. Clough (2000) has outlined some of the key criteria that have emerged in this area. First of all, she suggests that we be open to ongoing experimentation and avoid the rush to closure of style. Second, she opposes trends that pit writing and theory against each other. Both writing and theory will continue to develop and evolve, and they need to stay in touch with each other. Finally, she advocates that we not engage in "methodological policing." Researchers should be free to experiment as writers, as well as researchers. If we try to valorize and elevate certain forms of new and experimental writing prematurely, we run the risk of cutting off the growth of new and exciting forms of expression.

Finally, as qualitative research has become more global and more multicultural, the role of multiple language use has become more problematic in qualitative research writing. For example, Temple and Young (2002) discuss the problems that arise when data are collected in multiple languages, and all facets of the study from data gathering to writing are permeated by translation concerns. The authors address a number of key issues: Should the researchers also act as translators? If translators are used, how should they interact with researchers? How should researchers handle concepts that do not translate well across languages? We can no longer afford to be naive about language, especially in qualitative research.

WRITING AS QUALITATIVE RESEARCH

Sometimes, writing is more than a means to an end. The act of writing itself can become an integral part of the qualitative research processes. Here we are looking at the boundaries and edges between narrating and writing. Brady (2000) reviews the long history of writing in anthropology, and how a growing sensitivity to poetics has changed the nature of the ethnographic writing. Writing has become less invisible, and a more active partner in the research process.

Richardson (2000) pushes the process even further with her consideration of writing as an act of inquiry in itself. The following are some examples of writing extended as a research tool into a number of areas that are critically important to qualitative research as a whole.

Collective Biography

Davies, Browne, Gannon, Honan, Laws, Mueller-Rockstroh and Petersen (2004) created a collective biography on the topic of reflexivity and ambiguity and their effects on research practices. Following a memory-work design, they explored their own personal ideas about language and their awareness of the power of language. In particular, they examined writing in their lives:

> We also turned our reflexive gaze on writing, on seeing writing as a way of coming to know. Writing is a significant everyday practice in the lives of all the women in our group, all academic workers. We write in our professional lives and in our personal lives, each of which

bleed into one another in our writing as they do in our living. Yet despite our high levels of literacy and comfort with writing practices, the stories we recalled about self-writing did not celebrate this practice or suggest that it was easy or readily accessible. (p. 380)

As they explored writing as a process of their lives, this group of women used their collective biography to document their feelings of, ". . . drowning, spewing, poisoning, blockages: the words as abject, the practice of writing as a practice of abjecting ourselves. The words—out there in the world—became risky" (Davies et al., 2004, p. 381).

In this experimental form of collective biography, the researchers were able to understand writing not only as a way to capture research findings, but also as a reflexive and powerful part of their research efforts.

Literary Analysis and Ethnography

Meiners (1999) uses the boundaries between fact and fiction to craft an ethnographic study on trauma from a postmodern, and specifically critical race and queer, perspective. She offers the following rationale for her approach:

The relationship, between the potential intimacy of ethnographic fictions and the implied (and seemingly required) rigour of ethnography, interests me, and in my own fieldwork experiences I found the two to be incompatible, yet equally desirable. In my research, my want to convey affect and my desire to be rigourous and professional, while not totally compatible, raised questions about research methodology and about the placement (and displacement) of truth and fictions in research. (p. 351)

This desire to create an interplay between affect and rigor permeates many qualitative studies, and the use of the tensions between truth and fictions to illuminate that interplay is a good example of the writing process coming front and center in a given piece of qualitative research.

Poetry

Poetry has become an increasingly important tool in qualitative research. Langer and Furman (2004) compare and contrast the use of research poems and interpretive poems. A research poem occurs when a researcher takes a piece of transcript from an informant and puts that information verbatim into poetic form. In this way, the research poem is a writing device used to bring possibly subtle points into sharper focus, and to foreground important issues that might be left underexamined.

Langer and Furman (2004) also talk about interpretive poems. Interpretive poems are original compositions written by qualitative researchers to present their data in a certain light. In the research poem, researchers are working and crafting words of others. In the interpretive poem, researchers are entering the process itself with their own words and insights.

Piirto (2002) warns us about the use of poetry in qualitative research writing. As a published poet of some repute, she reminds us that writing poetry is hard. Using some of her own work to illustrate what she calls "inferior poetry" she shows us how mastery of the poetic craft allows a true poet to take a mediocre piece of work and raise it to the level of authentic poetry. She concludes by welcoming poetry into qualitative research, so long as it is crafted by those who know what they are doing:

To learn the essence of the domain's educational implications at the feet of the artist/teachers who are seeking to synthesize the expression of their work in both domains—the domain of the art and the domain of education—is an exciting possibility. They will create new forms, new expressions, new ways of thinking that bridge domains. Let us welcome our artist-educators, as well as our self-exploring novices. But let us not confuse the quality of and their qualifications for rendering, making marks, embodying, and distilling. Let us not confuse the seekers for the masters. Let us not confuse the poetasters for the poets. (p. 444)

WRITING AND THE MIRROR, WINDOW, AND LANTERN

We saved the art and skill of writing for last for several reasons. First of all, writing is often the last thing we do when we perform a piece of qualitative research. Second, writing by its very nature draws upon the other skills to meet its own goals. And finally, for many of us, writing is the hardest and most intimidating skill we have to learn as qualitative researchers.

One thing we need to remember is this: There is no one good way to be a writer. The material in this chapter should serve as helpful hints and guidelines, rather than hard and fast rules to use in order to write. Some books suggest that you start writing first thing in the morning when you are fresh and rested. But what if you are a night person? Others suggest that you write something each and every day. But what if you are more comfortable with mentally gestating for several days, and then producing a burst of writing all at once? Another standard suggestion is to let the words flow freely, and then trim back and edit later. But suppose you are more comfortable in writing brief outlines at first and then fleshing in the details later? In short, write in the manner that is most comfortable for you. Listen carefully to all the advice you can get, but only use what is truly helpful.

Finally, writing is as much about perspective as it is about technique. How can we make use of our three familiar visions in our task to become better writers? Let us take a brief look at each in turn.

Writing and the Mirror.   Here we are looking at eyewitness, confessional, and apologetic writing. For much of recorded history, these three modes of writing dominated our accounts of the world and our place in it. The earliest histories were eyewitness accounts of famed battles and marvelous, far-off lands. The task of the writing was to bring us readers to those clashes and inside those exotic lands, so that we might feel that we had actually been there. This same kind of eyewitness immediacy, judiciously used and carefully crafted, often enlivens the very best of contemporary qualitative research accounts.

Not all exploration is external. Starting with Augustine, there has also been a strong confessional streak in Western writing. We have covered this confessional aspect earlier. All we need say here is that confessional writing is a form of psychic exploration. As such, it can be as fascinating and as lively as any traveler's tale.

Our first reflective dimension was experiential, and our second dimension was internal. Our third and final reflective dimension is communal. Apologetics deals with the ability to describe and explain some functioning system or culture on its own terms. We do not have to justify a culture to create an apologetic description of it. We do have to be able to show why the people in the culture value the things and deeds that they value, whether we agree with them or not. Apologetics is the least understood and often the most valuable writing skill that a qualitative researcher may need to use. It behooves us all to pay more attention to this dimension of qualitative writing in the future.

Eyewitness, confession, and apologia are three dimensions of writing that often occur in qualitative writing. However we seek to communicate what we have found and what we have come to understand, we must always remain open to the reflective possibilities in our writing. Whether or not our pieces are primarily eyewitness, confessional, or apologetic, these dimensions more often than not at least play some part, large or small, in any piece of qualitative writing.

Writing and the Window.   Window writing encompasses old, familiar territory. When van Maanen was talking about the realist tale, he was talking about window writing. Clean, clear, crisp objective prose is window writing. Any time the writer steps completely aside, takes an invisible stance, and strives to allow the data and conclusions to speak for themselves, then we are seeing window writing.

There are two mistakes that qualitative research needs to avoid in relation to the window perspective of qualitative writing. First of all, we must not strive to minimize or eliminate its presence. Just because we feel that we have been freed up to use first person, or present tense, or autobiographical collage, or what have you, does not mean that we have to consign window writing to oblivion within qualitative research. Sometimes, the best way to describe something is to make a clear and straightforward account. You do not need to insert your presence into every scene or every account, and you do not have to use experimental modes of communication or composition just to be using them. Part of the freedom of good qualitative writing is the freedom to write conservatively if it serves your purposes.

We must also be careful not to make the mistake of severing all ties between qualitative window writing and other forms of research writing. This mistake would involve going in the opposite direction of the first mistake. Here, we run the risk of trying to reinsert the virtues of standard scientific writing as the primary virtues of all qualitative writing. We are most likely to see this mistake made by researchers adopting a mixed methods approach. Though many qualitative issues can be captured from a window approach, many others will simply not fit the window mold. We must allow our writing, even in mixed methods designs, to seek its best level of explication. If that means that we must suddenly shift into first person, or take a confessional or postmodern stance, then so be it.

Writing and the Lantern.   The lantern approach to writing is that approach most akin to skilled rhetorical practice on one hand, and postmodern sensibilities on the other hand. Like the rhetoricians of old, we are first and foremost concerned with our ability to convey a precise understanding. Did I choose just exactly the right word? Do I need one more example to make my point clear? These issues are important when we are doing any type of writing, but when we are striving to communicate new and unique insights they are absolutely necessary.

One of the hallmarks of lantern vision is its affinity to exploration and experimentation with new forms and structures. This affinity draws the lantern perspective and postmodern thought toward each other. Is this because postmodern thought is genuinely new, or is it because it is merely novel? Time will tell, but in the meantime, the systematic search for meaning on its own terms and postmodern sensibilities seem to complement each other quite nicely.

GOING BEYOND THE SKILLS

With writing, we finish our modest list of basic and advanced skills for qualitative research. Does this mean that we have covered everything we need to cover in order to build personal skills as qualitative researchers? Of course not. We have barely begun the process. It takes a lifetime to become truly skilled at anything. But we have taken the important first steps along the path, and that is certainly an accomplishment in anyone's book.

The last two chapters are designed to help us put our emerging personal skills in perspective. Chapter 11 deals with the issue of evaluating qualitative research and being able to tell good research from bad. And in the final chapter, we take a look at where we might want to go as a field by looking at where we are and how we got here.

PLANNING YOUR RESEARCH PROPOSAL: FINAL DRAFT OF THE RESEARCH PROPOSAL

Albert and Carol have finally gotten their research proposals into proper shape. We have asked each of them to tell us about their finished proposals.

Carol

"Putting together a proposal was both harder and easier than I thought. Since I was using Grounded Theory from the outset, I suspected that this process would drive my thinking more than it did. I was surprised by the fact that I had to think out some of the aspects of my proposal, like my sampling strategy and the sorts of questions I might ask at the outset. Once the proposal began to take shape, though, I was surprised how easy it was to build on my momentum and get it down. I am eager to start observing and talking with my participants, and seeing the data collected and coming together."

Albert

"I was very excited to discover this line of research, and now I am equally excited to get going. Doing the proposal was hard work, but it is just a means to an end. The actual research is my target and the whole point of my effort. Nonetheless, I am glad that I took the time to craft a good proposal. It is good to have some of those issues behind me, so that I can now move forward. I am a bit worried about my review board, since I am going to interview and observe some minors, but I hope I did a good enough job in laying out my plans and my protections, so that the board will let me go forward pretty soon."

Ourselves

What have you learned about the proposal process by looking at and thinking about these two examples? Do you feel more prepared to tackle the process? What sorts of things still bother you? Where can you find help to address your concerns?

Remember, a research proposal is nothing more than a guide for doing a piece of research. Do not feel that you have to be bound by every single word and concept—after all, qualitative research more often than not is tactical. On the other hand, a good proposal solves a lot of potential problems before they get to be real problems. Good luck on your own proposals, and on your research efforts in this wonderful and exciting field.

CHAPTER 11

The Seven Deadly Sins
of Qualitative Research

STANDARDS, VIRTUES, AND PITFALLS

Now that we have looked at some of the most important skills needed to be good qualitative researchers, we have to think about what makes for good qualitative research. This often leads to the question of how to set standards. In recent years, Miles and Huberman (1994), Fraenkel (1999), Breuer and Reichertz (2001), and Sandelowski and Barroso (2002), among others, have all set forth standards for conducting qualitative research.

We will take a more informal and process-oriented approach here. We also want to take a positive approach. If we talk about fostering the sorts of "virtues" that characterize good qualitative research, then we can start building both a positive and a flexible outlook. We are more interested in the notion of quality per se (see Lincoln, 1995 for an alternative discussion on the topic of quality in qualitative research) than the task of setting strict guidelines for evaluating research.

Although we want to stay as positive as possible in this task of fostering virtues, it will be necessary to deal with the sorts of errors and pitfalls that often befall qualitative work. So, at least part of our effort will involve naming and illustrating some of these errors and pitfalls. Furthermore, these pitfalls and errors are far from rare and so will probably ring true within your own experiences as a reader and possibly even as a doer of qualitative research. I know that they have shadowed my own past work. But I did want my intent to be clear: I am not out to condemn certain qualitative researchers or qualitative studies, but to attempt to advance the art of evaluating qualitative research in certain very practical ways.

One way to begin the process of evaluating the process of qualitative research is to take a moment to talk about key issues in the evaluation of empirical research in general. From this vantage point, we can then examine those concerns that seem to be shared by both qualitative and quantitative research. Finally, we can then move on to those problems that seem to be unique within each mode of research.

Murphy's Law

Many of the methodological errors and pitfalls that mess up research in general can be derived from that ubiquitous piece of folk wisdom known as Murphy's Law—anything that can go wrong, will. Murphy's Law, however, functions in different ways for quantitative and qualitative research.

At the heart of the quantitative researcher's understanding of Murphy's Law is the belief that any phenomenon that can be studied is made up of simpler components and factors, and that as many of these "pieces" as possible have to be identified and controlled. If you do not control the actions and processes that are involved with these components and factors, they will inevitably come back to haunt you. Forget to control for initial group differences? They will end up being significant. Not sure whether your sample is too specialized or too extreme in some fashion to generalize? It will be. Did you assume that extraneous variables not identified would cancel each other out? They won't.

As a quantitative researcher, you must take things apart carefully, label the pieces meticulously, and remember where you put them. You must also know what you are doing, because actions like taking things apart and recombining them are rule-bound activities, and you really need to understand how these rules work and where they apply. If you make a wrong assumption or use a wrong tool, you mess up everything.

Many beginning qualitative researchers start their careers just as wary of Murphy's Law as their quantitative counterparts. But alas, this concern usually does more harm than good. First of all, it pushes them into a control mind-set, which can be disastrous in qualitative research for reasons that will be highlighted in a bit. Second, it puts them into the "component and factor" mind-set, which mistakenly heightens more specific scientific concerns over and above more holistic and potentially more useful empirical concerns. In other words, where is it carved in stone that the only way to be systematic and empirical is to be scientific?

Finally, it leads them into trying to make sure their work is free of the sorts of errors that primarily plague quantitative research. These errors usually deal with issues of reliability and validity, and deal with matters such as making sure your facts are straight and that you are truly measuring what you set out to measure. But these sorts of concerns can actually impede qualitative research.

Let me be clear here. I am not saying that qualitative researchers should not worry about making errors of fact, or should discard the notion of truth. Far from it. But I am saying that the safeguards built into scientific inquiry to protect against errors of fact and against false claims do not work very well from a qualitative perspective. Our errors of fact and our false claims tend to arise from different sources.

So how does Murphy's Law haunt qualitative research? Our trepidations are more often based not on strategic blunders, but on lack of tactical preparation. If we are not prepared to deal with the tactical shifts often required by the very richness of our research conditions, then we are forced to go along with our original plans. Did you forget to cancel your afternoon meeting? Too bad, because your informant was willing to spend the entire afternoon with you, helping you secure entry into a tricky site. Did you forget to pack an extra cassette tape? Too bad, because you have already filled two tapes and there is much more to record. Did you wear your nice shoes? Too bad, because we need to tromp through the mud to get to a particularly important place. Do you have extra consent forms? If not, how can you use the information you are getting from this unexpected informant? In short, you cannot anticipate everything, but you must be prepared to make these sorts of fundamental adjustments.

The Primacy of the Research Question

Though it is true that Murphy's Law does address many of the methodological errors and pitfalls that can befall research, it does not illuminate the single most important source of error—the error of asking a bad question. Bad questions are signs of bad judgement. But bad judgement has its quantitative and its qualitative sides.

All quantitative research starts with a question or series of questions that have been explicated by a combination of clear thinking and prior knowledge on the topic, but whose ultimate answer can only be verified by an appeal to the world of experience. How can such a question go bad?

First of all, it can contradict prior knowledge, usually as a consequence of a lack of awareness on the part of the quantitative researcher that such knowledge exists. This is the sort of error that comes from not doing your homework beforehand.

Secondly, the research can ask a question that has already been answered. This is an even more grievous example of ignoring your homework. The only time it can be justified is when you have the bad luck of doing a piece of quantitative research just behind some other researcher. By the time you are finally aware that this slightly earlier research is going on, it is too late to change or modify what you are doing. I have known graduate students who have had actual nightmares of picking up the latest issue of their field's flagship journal and seeing an article that exactly duplicates their dissertation research. But if these students and their mentors have been paying attention to the trends in the field, and going to conferences, and logging into the Internet, this nightmare will most likely never be realized in the light of day.

Third, the quantitative research question can be so ambiguous or unclear, as a result of poor reasoning or poor articulation of the question, that it really cannot be properly answered. In the most advanced cases, the question is simply incoherent, such that it is not really a question after all but a series of claims that are not genuinely related. These are errors of logical laziness. Lack of logical skills is no defense, as most logical arguments in quantitative research have to be fairly basic and straightforward if we expect trends in the data to support them. Correcting these sorts of errors by rethinking and rewriting is far less costly than throwing away a whole bunch of hard-earned data because the findings don't make any sort of sense at all.

Bad Judgement in Qualitative Research

One of the oldest notions in empirical research in the social sciences is the idea that the type of research to be used depends not on the method of choice of the researcher, but on the question raised. Though this is partially true, it is ultimately a misleading way to couch the situation for qualitative research. As we saw in Chapter 6, qualitative research is not strictly question driven. Instead, it starts with a basic formulation of a question, which then evolves tactically based on the actual circumstances at hand.

In other words, what we start with in qualitative research instead of a formal question is an awareness of a need for deeper understanding. Therefore, instead of reasoning through a set of claims about prior knowledge and pertinent consequences to build questions that need empirical verification, qualitative research deals with opening up areas where a departure from current preconceptions promises the potential for new insight and understanding.

Therefore, if we insist on using the "question criterion" as a sorting device for qualitative and quantitative approaches, we must be aware that these different types of questions are not readily translatable into each other. This leads us to the conclusion that we cannot use one type of question and one standard of evaluation for both qualitative and quantitative research.

THE SEVEN DEADLY SINS

We have seen that Murphy's Law works pretty well in helping quantitative researchers address strategic concerns when doing research. If, however, Murphy's Law and the primacy of the research question per se are not all that useful as guides for qualitative researchers to use to avoid errors and pitfalls and to build our virtues as researchers, then what is? Can we devise a working metaphor that seems more akin to the nature and functioning of qualitative research at its heart?

For reasons that I hope will grow clearer as we proceed, I invite you to explore with me the use of the ancient and venerable model of the seven deadly sins as our metaphor of illumination. It is my hope that the idea of the seven deadly sins can be modified and recast as our guide along the path of exploring the weaknesses in others' qualitative research with the goal of improving our own work.

The Wisdom of the Seven Deadly Sins

Where did the seven deadly sins come from? Fairlie (1978) gives us a useful picture of the deadly sins, then and now. They were first developed as a part of Eastern Christian monasticism, and were brought into the consciousness of Western monasticism during the late 4th century A.D. as part of the Conferences of Saint John Cassian. But it was Saint Gregory the Great, in the late 6th century, who created the list we acknowledge today: In alphabetical order they are anger, envy, gluttony, greed, lust, pride, and sloth.

When we first look at the seven deadly sins, we are a bit surprised. Certainly these are not the worst sins that we could commit. Where is murder? Cruelty? Deceit? Exploitation of the innocent? Genocide?

Though the deadly sins are serious, they do not seem to be the great crimes and transgressions that destroy life and culture. But when we talk about the seven deadly sins, we are talking about those sins that kill the spirit of those who commit these sins. And, as the spirit dies, there becomes room for the heinous and the selfish and the cruel, because we are less human now.

Another way to look at this matter is to realize that the seven deadly sins are at the heart of all the other supposedly more serious sins. Why do we kill? Why do we exploit others? Why are we cruel? Why do we mislead and deceive? Because we have followed a path that has led us to value these acts. We have turned away from our fundamental nature, and the surest way to do this is to follow one or more of the deadly sins to its fruition.

It is tempting to try to map out qualitative errors and pitfalls directly into the deadly sins, but this is nothing more than misunderstanding the nature and purpose of the metaphor we are using. We are using the model of the seven deadly sins not to talk about pride and anger and the other deadly sins and their roles in qualitative research; we are tapping into the principle that a deadly sin is a fundamental sin that cripples or kills the spirit of the sinner. Often as not, it can start as a small, almost trivial digression or concession toward something less than ideal. But, because it is fundamental, it will eventually lead us to more and more serious transgressions and errors. And most importantly, these sins unchecked will eventually rob us of the ability to be good qualitative researchers.

This is the sense of the notion of a deadly sin that I would like to employ here. Why is this a more useful approach for us to take? Simply put, bad qualitative research is usually not a case of something going wrong, Murphy-style. More often than not, bad qualitative research is qualitative research that is just not good. And this is a very different matter than simply making mistakes and not properly controlling variables or even asking bad questions. It is a matter of making bad decisions for apparently good reasons—which is also at the heart of the original deadly sins, by the way.

In other words, what are the seven worst methodological decisions that a qualitative researcher can make? And how do these bad decisions cripple qualitative research and eventually the researchers making them? I will lay out these "deadly sins" in no particular order. Each sin does its own violence to the spirit of qualitative research, and therefore it is hard to say which is the worst or the most serious. I will also talk about virtues that we can develop in order to move away from each deadly sin.

The Sin of Competitiveness, or "One Size Does Not Fit All"

The first bad decision, or qualitative deadly sin, is to engage in the "sin" of *competitiveness*. Here we have the case where we think it is a necessary part of our research efforts to establish the "fact" that our work is just as good as, if not better, than a quantitative study on the same topic. This sin manifests itself in a number of ways.

First of all, competitiveness sufferers tend to go to great lengths to show how their research design is "just as valid" and "just as rigorous" as any quantitative study. No detail is too small to report, and no observation is too minor to ignore. Every piece of data can be defended by some reference to the research design.

Because these studies want to compete head-to-head with quantitative research, we often find extensive usage of such quantitative-looking procedures as *a priori* data-gathering and computerized analysis strategies. As we might expect, these procedures are often described and justified in painstaking detail. These researchers will not get caught looking less scientific than any quantitative researcher.

Finally, we usually have a set of findings and conclusions that, though they might not be very interesting or original, are certainly based on an exhaustive and totally thorough look at the data. No one could look at this work and accuse it of being less complex, or less rigorous, than any given quantitative study.

Competitiveness is, ironically enough, a manifestation of the original deadly sin of envy. When we try to prove that our work is just as scientific as a study that uses the scientific method of making observations and creating and testing hypotheses, we are as good as admitting that we must employ the tools and concepts of science for any form of empirical study. But, in order to make the scientific method work, we have to clear up ambiguities of meaning before we can actually test our hypotheses. So we have painted ourselves into a pretty little corner in our attempt to resolve our envy of the scientific process. In order to make our work rigorous and precise in a scientific way, we have to resolve issues of meaning prior to serious data collection. But if we are doing qualitative research, we are in fact interested in exploring issues and consequences of meaning. In other words, we can specify meaning or explore previously unexamined domains of meaning, but we cannot do both at the same time. However, in our heart of hearts, we do not really believe that an empirical examination of meaning on its own terms is good enough. It is just not scientific enough. So, just as the envious person turns away from his or her own nature out of a false sense of shame and self-loathing, so does the competitive qualitative researcher turn away from the sorts of decisions he or she needs to make in order to study meaning on its own terms.

Qualitative research that is contaminated by the sin of competitiveness takes on a certain character. There is an inordinate emphasis on coding strategies; the use of computerized coding and data sorting programs is often put into play to add another layer of legitimacy to this complex coding endeavor. The poor qualitative researcher is often concerned with making sure that he or she can account for each and every piece of information in the transcripts, and can assign each and every content piece to an appropriate category. But this exercise in pseudo-completeness more often than not actually buries the few really interesting and surprising and significant points that by all rights should shine forth in the data like diamonds buried in the muck. In the process, we are well on the way to a thoroughly pedestrian study, even if it does have an extensive methodology section, and its coding systems are clearly defended, and all the data has been put into one neat coding container or another.

If we wish to avoid the sin of competitiveness, then we need to foster the virtue of *confidence*. Confidence occurs in qualitative research when we are relaxed and comfortable with our choice of method, and we feel that the use of the method explains its own presence. We quit trying to defend our methods, and get on with the process of doing our research.

The Sin of Appropriation, or "Qualitative Research Is Not an Envelope"

The second fundamentally bad decision in qualitative research is the sin of *appropriation*. Appropriation occurs when we are doing our research not to be doing research, but to further some other agenda we have. The actual research is just a means to an end.

Qualitative research is not an envelope that you use to deliver a message. One of the worst things we can do as a qualitative researcher is to be convinced that we are right about something before we begin. Even worse is the belief that doing the actual research is the best way to make sure that you were correct in the first place.

The essence of qualitative research is the search for that fresh insight, that new understanding. So what if you have to reorient some of your precious beliefs? If your belief system is any good, it will only improve as a result of these adjustments. Qualitative research, like any other form of research, involves risk. The sin of appropriation says that some beliefs are too important to risk testing in the world of experience. All that appropriation will do, in the end, is ossify a belief system at a static level. At best, your research will be stale. At the worst, it will retard the natural growth and evolution and maturity of genuinely beneficial beliefs. Such is the self-defeating nature of appropriation in the final analysis.

If we wish to avoid the sin of appropriation, then we need to foster the virtue of *trust*. Trust occurs in qualitative research when we are willing to allow our data to guide our findings. We also need to trust our fellow human beings more. Most of the evil deeds in this world are performed by people who do not fully realize the impact and consequences of their actions. Their understanding of the world is too sketchy, and so they do not know how much damage they are really doing.

If we trust in the world to show us truth, and we trust others to be educated from our findings and to change their practices when they see a better way, then we do not have to convert our research efforts into crusades. We can then allow research to be research; the activity we perform ultimately out of curiosity and not to slay dragons.

The Sin of Rigidity, or "You Cannot Tame Everything"

The third fundamentally bad decision in qualitative research is the sin of *rigidity*. This is another example of misunderstanding the goals of science as being the goals of empirical inquiry in general. But this sin is grounded in mistakenly thinking qualitative research is conducted according to the same principles that quantitative studies are conducted.

When we set out to test and hopefully verify a research question from a quantitative perspective, we need to know just exactly what we are asking and what we expect to find. As we said earlier, a poorly stated or poorly argued research question will sink a quantitative study. So it becomes necessary to develop a clear focus on what the question should be, a clear means for developing and articulating that question, and a clear set of empirical consequences that will answer the question with a minimum of ambiguity. All of these skills are strategic decision-making skills, and they are vital for quantitative research. Research design from a quantitative perspective is essentially a strategic exercise, where procedures and controls are mapped out in advance so that they can be executed smoothly in the field.

As we said earlier, research design in qualitative research is minimally strategic. Instead, it is all about creating space for tactical decisions that may take you not in the direction that you had anticipated, but in the direction that ongoing circumstances suggest is actually the most fruitful line of inquiry to pursue. This skill actually runs counter to most training that researchers get from a quantitative perspective. Instead, it emphasizes flexibility and a clear-headed and tactical sense of fluidity of direction. Control is carefully given over to participants or circumstances, so that they can guide you in the appropriate direction.

We can recognize rigid qualitative research by its adherence to finding the points that had been determined *a priori* and strategically to be of the most value. In these studies, we see fact after fact, incident after incident, piled together to substantiate the correctness of the initial assumptions. And, ironically enough, those assumptions might indeed be valid. But we have no sense of their relative importance in relation to other unexamined issues, because these other issues were relentlessly filtered out by the single-mindedness of the research process. Perhaps there is nothing further to be understood in a given study, but we have no way of determining that.

If we wish to avoid the sin of rigidity, then we need to foster the virtue of *flexibility*. Flexibility occurs in qualitative research when we are capable of making the tactical adjustments we need, on the spot. We are prepared to take what the setting gives us, on the assumption that it will be richer and more complex than anything we could have anticipated.

A useful model for the kind of tactical flexibility needed in qualitative research is white-water rafting. Unlike a rigid approach, where the stream has been dredged and the channel straightened, the flexible approach accepts the river as it is, with its drops and twists and rapids and placid pools. The task is not to try to seize control of the river. In rafting, that strategy will land you in the drink in no time. Instead, there is a constant interplay between the rafter and the river. The rafter works with the river, allowing it to do most of the work, and yet is always alert and mindful of potential problems and sources of trouble. Occasionally, the rafter must paddle furiously to avoid overturning, but if the raft is guided with skill, these exertions can be kept to a minimum. In one sense, the rafter is always in control, but rarely in charge. It is this sort of delicate and flexible balance that yields the best results in qualitative research.

The Sin of Superficiality, or "A Comfortable Idea Is Probably Wrong"

The fourth fundamentally bad decision in qualitative research is the sin of *superficiality*. Superficiality in this case is often just another name for mediocrity. What constitutes mediocre qualitative research? We have mediocre research in those cases where the researcher needs to take further steps, to dig deeper, to draw out more extensive and subtle consequences, and yet chooses not to do so.

This is arguably one of the most serious of all transgressions within the practice of qualitative research. When a researcher stops short of something truly significant and instead produces a superficial piece of work, then he or she is going against the basic grain of the qualitative approach. That is, superficial qualitative research sacrifices the search for depth of understanding that justifies a qualitative approach in the first place.

One of the hidden reasons for superficiality is the overdependence by some qualitative researchers on causality as an explanatory device. As qualitative researchers, we believe that the world of experience is both ordered and intelligible. But that does not mean that we think that the order that permeates existence was designed to our human specifications, or that "intelligible" means "moldable to ordinary human understanding." We have to be open to the possibility that the order we see around us cannot be completely explained in causal terms. Sometimes, what we need to do is to find that order, and leave the explanation for later. Suppose, for example, you decided that you wanted to marry someone. And then, for the next week, every day you happen to meet a different long-lost and long-forgotten lover. Is this mere coincidence, or is it part of a more complex pattern of order? We will never know if we brush these experiences away without exploring them in more depth.

You might argue that causality is the best way to reveal what is actually going on. In a sense, you are right. Causality is the best way to reveal the causal nature, if there is any, of the event or phenomenon in question. But remember, anything that does not reveal, conceals! In our effort to find causes, what forms of order are we burying or ignoring?

We are learning more and more each day about other patterns and types of order in the world of experience, from fractal models (Mandelbrot, 1983) to chaos theory (Gleick, 1987) to fuzzy logic (Kosko, 1993), and others either newly found or perhaps waiting to be discovered. Causality is actually one of the least interesting forms of order. Its rules are so stringent and its scope is so narrow that more often than not it is not quite the ordering tool we want or need. Right now, we ought to be cautious, and be content in documenting these alternate experiences of order, taking care to make sure we have a case for them being more than just coincidence.

If we wish to avoid the sin of superficiality, then we need to foster the virtue of *curiosity*. The more curious we are, the less likely we are to settle for superficial results. We are driven to find out more, to dig deeper, and to bring to light that mysterious insight that helps bring the whole field into a new sense of clarity.

The Sin of Sentimentality, or "The World Is Not for Your Entertainment"

The fifth fundamentally bad decision in qualitative research is the sin of *sentimentality*. This sin represents a misunderstanding of the spiritual aspect of qualitative research. Too often, we conflate spiritual and emotional issues. We feel that if we write our work with a lot of emotion, and we try to stir the emotions of our readers, then were are getting into the spiritual domain of our work.

The problem with this approach is that it is inherently manipulative. We are trying to direct our readers to feel a certain way. If we are more concerned with their emotional response than we are with them reaching a new level of insight and understanding, then we are being sentimental. In sentimentality, you have the feeling and yet you keep your insight level where it was.

This is not to say that every account from the world that has an emotional impact upon us is sentimental. It is sentimental if it *only* has an emotional impact. Authentic accounts, wherever we find them, show us a new way of understanding.

Let me illustrate with an example from my own experience. For years, my daughter Morgan was a huge Tori Amos fan (she still likes Tori's music, but with less of the hero worship of her early teens). Every evening, it seemed, I would walk past her tightly closed bedroom door and hear the strains of Tori's music leaking under the doorjamb. Morgan was particularly drawn to songs that documented the awkwardness and poignancy of being a young female in this culture, songs like (Amos, 1992) "Silent All These Years" and "Happy Phantom" and "Winter."

At her invitation, I sat down one evening and listened to the CD *Little Earthquakes* (Amos, 1992). One song in particular struck me profoundly—it was called "Me and a Gun." I asked Morgan about the song, and my daughter told me that it was a documentation of a stranger rape that had happened to Tori Amos a number of years ago. The experience had almost led to Tori's death, but somehow she managed to get away alive.

Here is the chorus. Tori sings the song a cappella:

> "Me and a gun and a man on my back
> But I haven't seen Barbados so I must get out of this."

As a male, I have no direct sense of what it must be like to be a woman and to have to deal with something as savage as rape. I also cannot imagine how any man who had a shred of human dignity could perform such a degraded and cowardly act. But in the honest authenticity of this song, I came as close as I ever have to understanding just how invasive and how vicious an act of rape really is.

Tori was not trying to pull any emotional strings with me; to cite a cliché, she was telling it like it was. At times, her words turned harsh and bitter and defiant:

> "Yes I wore a slinky red thing
> Does that mean I should spread?
> For you, your friends,
> Your father, Mr. Ed?"

Let me say that I have never read any account of rape that I thought was sentimental, so I am not comparing what Tori Amos is saying to other unauthentic accounts. There are complex issues about femininity and its role in culture and research, some of which we have already explored a bit.

The point I am trying to make here is this: One of our tasks as qualitative researchers is to convey as rich and accurate and nuanced a picture of what we find as we possibly can. And there will be a number of aspects to this task. If there are emotional aspects, then they must be laid out and addressed authentically. If we take the easy way, and go for an emotional response rather than a deeper and richer understanding, then we are being sentimental.

If we wish to avoid the sin of sentimentality, then we need to foster the virtue of *empathy*. Empathy is not a matter of feeling sorry for someone, or living vicariously through another's triumphs. It is something far deeper. It is the ability to place yourself in another person's perspective. When we can do that, then the shallow and inauthentic trappings of sentimentality fall away and we can then find the deeper and richer wisdom that we seek. Ultimately, we have to return to our perspective as researcher. But when we have established genuine empathy, we return to our research world much wiser for our foray into the life world of someone else.

The Sin of Narcissism, or "Life Will Go on Without You"

The sixth fundamentally bad decision in qualitative research is the sin of *narcissism*. This sin is a perversion of the human tendency to look upon the world as a source of reflection and contemplation. We have been talking about the metaphor of the mirror as an abiding and useful image for speculative empirical inquiry. Isn't this, you might ask, a form of narcissicism?

There is a fundamental difference between speculative insight and narcissism. With speculative insight, we look carefully at what the world is telling us about ourselves, our culture, and our world. In genuine speculative work, these three aspects are all present and all linked.

Furthermore, we are seeing something new and important as a result of our speculative work. For example, we might discover, in looking closely at, say, a particular oppressive situation, that the oppressors are acting out of a deep and unconscious fear of the people they are oppressing. What does this tell us upon reflection? For one, we might recognize in our own personal areas of fear the seeds or even the unrealized fruits of our own acts of oppression. What was once unsuspected in us rises suddenly into the realm of plausibility.

When we then push out into the culture at large, we might also see a previously unrealized interconnected patterning between oppression and fear in places and situations where we may never have looked before. These findings and insights might also play a role in the way we look at and appreciate and work with and within the complexities of the human spirit. Perhaps oppression can be relieved not just by freeing the victims themselves, but by also freeing their oppressors from their fears. When we treat these acts of oppression as a mirror, we must look carefully, broadly, objectively, creatively, humanely, and critically for the insights that they will bear.

A narcissistic act is much different. If we go back to the Greek myth of Narcissus, we find a young man who is so taken with his own image that he cannot pry his eyes away from a reflected image of himself. When we extend this metaphorical circumstance into empirical research, it yields research that is ultimately only about the researcher. I need to make a careful distinction here. I am not claiming that autobiographical inquiry is, prima facie, narcissistic. For instance, if we look at the first great autobiography in Western thought, the *Confessions* of Saint Augustine, we see a work that is intensely autobiographical without being self-absorbed. How did Augustine pull off this feat? By using his experiences as a map for others. We need to follow suit in our own research efforts. Do these experiences ring true with your experiences? Are these central concerns that resonate with broad human goals and desires? Am I concerned not just with myself and my own well being and growth, but with humanity as a whole? Have I changed for the better or worse, and in my change, have I shown a path for others to follow or avoid?

It is most particularly in the last question that we see the authentic use of autobiography in qualitative research. No one is really interested in who the researcher is, but in who he or she has become. And furthermore, this change in the researcher is important only to the degree that it can be used as a guide for others. This is particularly tricky when there is a strong emotional content to the research. That emotional content must reveal something previously unknown from the realm of understanding if it is to be of any value as a piece of research. Otherwise, the research becomes nothing more than a piece of self-congratulatory propaganda at one extreme or a pointless mea culpa at the other extreme.

Another aspect of narcissism is its tendency to make us voyeuristic. Voyeurism is the consequence of a mistaken sense of a need for detachment between the researcher and that which he or she attempts to study. So, we find ourselves staring at our subjects. There is a barrier between us. If we are careful, that barrier is transparent and unobtrusive, and so we have established a classic piece of window research. And in fact, some cultural settings are best examined from a window. But that is not the purpose of qualitative research. We are there to discover, and simply looking and remaining detached does not allow us the depth we need. At the same time, we run the risk of becoming absorbed in what we are doing, and so losing our ability to make objective judgements. It is the fear of losing this objective power that is at the heart of voyeurism in qualitative research.

The worst type of voyeurism is to adopt an intellectualized affectation of objectivity in place of authentic human contact. This affectation is most often motivated by a desire to be "scientific" and so not to "spoil" a field setting by interjecting your own judgments and values. But this can lead to some very unfortunate confrontations and dilemmas. A former colleague of mine was once working as an anthropologist and a physician in New Guinea. One day, he stopped a young mother rushing with her newborn daughter to a nearby waterfall. When he asked her what she was doing, she calmly told him that she was going to toss her child into the waterfall because it had been born a witch. How was he to react? There is no clear-cut answer to this question. It is not an intellectual exercise. It is not simply an issue of culture or research, but one of humanity. Though he has no right to impose his own cultural mores on another, it is equally wrong for him to pretend that his stance as a human being is irrelevant in this situation either. And, even on a cold-blooded level, being a mere voyeuristic observer deprives him of the chance to open a deeper channel of communication between himself and this culture. In short, there is no requirement that we sacrifice our humanity to be qualitative researchers. So long as we remember to not be rigid, and so long as we respect and come to the values and mores of others with a sense of good faith, we can both understand and draw wisdom from other cultures.

Before I leave the sin of narcissism, I want to say a word about what I have been doing all along in this book. Perhaps you are tempted to charge that I have been narcissistic myself. Haven't I been talking an awful lot about myself? How is this different from narcissism?

In my own defense, I have been using my own accounts because these are concrete areas where I can be sure that something actually happened, and that I am on solid ground when I reflect on how these experiences can be used as sources of insight. It becomes important if I can use these experiences as a legitimate jumping off point to make hard points clear. At some point in the account, the "me" fades away, but the point keeps on going until we get a good clear picture of what is being represented. Or at least, that is my intent.

If we wish to avoid the sin of narcissism, then we need to foster the virtue of *compassion*. Unlike narcissism, compassion is always directed outwards. We are no longer absorbed with our views and our needs. We need to be careful not to confuse compassion with sentimentality. In fact, sentimentality and narcissism are first cousins. They both direct you back into yourself, and allow you to preserve views and understandings that you want to keep because they make you feel good. This is not to say that research should not make you feel good. But it should be a good feeling based on accomplishment and change, not one based on stroking your ego.

The Sin of Timidity, or "A Good Idea Is Worth Defending"

The seventh fundamentally bad decision in qualitative research is the sin of *timidity*. Simply put, timid research is work that makes no breakthroughs, provides no new insights, nor discovers or discerns previously unknown or unexplored aspects of meaning, and yet within its own framework affords no criticism or methodological challenge. That is, it is research that is first and foremost safe. All conclusions are defensible, all methods are careful, and all arguments are sound. But nothing is learned, and nothing is really being served.

Timidity is most often the sin of the beginning qualitative researcher. The beginning researcher is often afraid of failure, but his or her most common failure is a failure of nerve. There are a number of dynamics that lead to timidity. One of the most common reasons is that the researcher is directed toward timid conclusions by mentors, or in the case of students, by their research advisors. It is a sad fact that mentors and advisors are too often concerned with how a piece of student research will reflect on their adequacy as advisors. So, if students produce safe and careful research that is difficult to challenge, then the advisor is validated as a successful mentor. Sometimes, too, if the student is working with multiple advisors, then simple and safe and timid results are the only results that can be brought to consensus.

As often as not, though, timidity in research is the fault of the researcher and not any advisor or mentor. It is a form of "failure of nerve," and often it occurs at an unconscious level. The researcher in this case is burdened with a set of unexamined assumptions and caveats about research, and the work is guided and directed in such a way so as not to upset or challenge any of these unexamined assumptions. Unfortunately, many if not most of these assumptions are either naive or just plain wrong. We have uncovered a number of such assumptions in this textbook; it is one of my hopes that by exposing these assumptions explicitly, it will embolden timid researchers to look for them in their own work and to move beyond them.

It might appear that, of all the sins that we have discussed, timidity is the most minor and the most benign. But this is simply not the case. Though timidity is not as dramatic as some of the other sins, it can be just as deadly not only to the work, but also to the growth and development of researchers themselves. For no other reason, timidity shuns surprise, and surprise is the lifeblood of qualitative research.

If we wish to avoid the sin of timidity, then we need to foster the virtue of *courage*. Courage is an integral part of any kind of research, but it is often easier championed than lived. How, you might ask, can I be courageous in settings where others control whether or not I get a degree, whether or not I keep my job, or whether or not I keep getting the funding I need? Isn't it safer to tell others what they want to hear, or to deliver results that no one can challenge? I understand and empathize with (and in some cases have lived) many of these issues, so I know that these questions are real. All I can offer in response is the following (probably apocryphal) old Russian proverb: People who take big chances in life never miss a meal.

Dealing with the Deadly Sins

As you can see, the metaphor of the seven deadly sins has led us to confront directly the issues of the nature and responsibilities of the qualitative researcher. These issues have not been clearly articulated. In the early days of qualitative research theory, one prevalent but unfortunate slogan was that "the researcher is the instrument." It is hoped that as a result of our considerations in this chapter, we can put this phrase to rest and explicate what really seems to be at issue in this matter.

We are not instruments in the sense that we are data-recording devices. But we are not mere storytellers either, free to pick and choose what we find in order to make whatever points we wish to make. We are something completely different, much harder and much more rewarding. We are the translators of the human condition. We translate between the expected and the unexpected, the known and the unknown, the ordinary and the wondrous. We believe that the world is meaning-rich, but that our understanding of this meaning-rich world is not only too sparse, but that the pursuit of such meaning is a valuable goal in itself and on its own terms. Each of the seven deadly sins we have described work to cripple our efforts to translate the masterpieces of the human experience that we seek out and explore.

AN INFORMAL EXERCISE

There is no official exercise for this chapter. We will end, instead, with the following informal exercise. It is informal because of its inherently negative nature. We have consistently emphasized the positive throughout, but sometimes it is necessary to point out when things go wrong. But we do not have to make a big, formal deal about it.

The exercise is quite simple: Pick out several published qualitative research articles and inspect them for the presence of one or more of the deadly sins. Write down your findings and your justification for the identification of each of the deadly sins that you find. You may wish to share your results with classmates or the instructor, so long as you do not make a contest of it. Remember, each researcher did his or her work as an act of good faith, and so you must respect that as you perform this exercise. But I expect the results will be pretty eye-opening nonetheless.

CHAPTER 12

Once and Future Qualitative Research

CAPTURING QUALITATIVE RESEARCH

By now, it should be clear just how complex the qualitative perspective really is. How can we hope to capture a working understanding of this field? How can we be sure that our understanding is accurate, and how can we keep our understanding from becoming outmoded? In this final chapter, we will look at where we are by considering where the field has been, and where it might be headed in the future. As always, the present is wedged between "what was" and "what could be."

We will start by sketching out a brief account of some of the primary historical trends that eventually led to the "qualitative revolution" in the social sciences. We will then look at how qualitative research has affected practice in a number of fields. Finally, we will look at some promising trends for qualitative research, with an eye toward the future of our discipline.

THE BEGINNINGS OF THE QUALITATIVE TRADITION

The first step toward developing a working history of qualitative research is to look back on the beginnings of the tradition. This task is harder than it looks, as the qualitative perspective arose in many different ways in relation to many different issues. Following are three of the most crucial movements and influences in historical order. They are not so much defining moments, but rather important markers along the trail.

The March Toward Quantification

For much of recorded history in Western civilization, qualitative perspectives were prevalent if not dominant. Over the last 400 years, however, quantitative thinking has dominated Western culture. In order for us to appreciate the reemerging impact of qualitative ideas, we need to look at how quantitative ideas became so dominant in modern thought.

Crosby (1997) documents the rise of quantification in Western society and its profound impact upon the ways that we understand our world. He called this movement to quantify *pantometry*. Pantometry began to take shape around 1250, and settled into our routine and ordinary way of understanding reality by 1600. Ever since then, Western civilization has embraced pantometry in thought and deed.

What is pantometry? Crosby described it as:

> . . . visualizing the stuff of reality as aggregates of uniform units, as quanta: leagues, miles, degrees of angle, letters, guldens, hours, minutes, musical notes. The West was making up its mind (most of its mind, at least) to treat the universe in terms of quanta uniform in one or more characteristics, quanta that are often thought of as arranged in lines, squares, circles, and other symmetrical forms: music staffs, platoons, ledger columns, planetary orbits. Painters were thinking of scenes as geometrically precise visual cones or pyramids focusing on the observing eye. (pp. 10–11)

The drive to quantify literally exploded in Europe between

> . . . 1275 to 1325. Someone built Europe's first mechanical clock and cannon, devices that obliged Europeans to think in terms of quantified time and space. Portolano marine charts, perspective painting, and double-entry bookkeeping cannot be precisely dated because they were emerging techniques, not specific inventions, but we can say that the earliest surviving examples of all three date from that half century or immediately after. Roger Bacon measured the angle of the rainbow, Giotto painted with geometry in mind, and Western musicians, who had been writing a ponderous kind of polyphony called *ars antiqua* for several generations, took flight with *ars nova* and began to write what they called "precisely measured songs." There was nothing quite like this half century again until the turn of the twentieth century, when the radio, radioactivity, Einstein, Picasso, and Schoenberg swept Europe into a similar revolution. (Crosby, 1997, p. 19, italics his)

By the end of the 19th century, pantometry was at its height. Astronomers were trying to unravel the secrets of the universe by treating it as a huge clockwork sort of mechanism. Laplace boldly asserts that if we should ever be able to document all the actions and reactions that occur in the universe at one precise instant, that we could use that data to describe the entire past and to predict the entire future (Reese, 1996, p. 395). Quantum uniformity was seen to be everywhere.

But the advent of the 20th century saw the beginning of the end for the total dominance of pantometry in Western thought. Relativity and quantum mechanics rendered Laplace's clockwork universe unlikely, and Goedel proved that it was actually impossible (Reese, 1996, p. 265). For the first time since the 13th century, cracks began to show in the pantometric façade. The time was now ripe for new thinking. Part of that new thinking involved the way we look at science itself.

The Scientific Paradigm Shifts

One of the main documents in contemporary philosophy that helped ground the current qualitative culture was written by and for scientists. In 1962, Thomas Kuhn published his landmark work, *The Structure of Scientific Revolutions* (see Kuhn, 1970, for his revised and final version). This work has changed the way researchers in all fields look at the empirical world.

Kuhn's chief contribution was his introduction of the notions of *paradigm* and *paradigm shift* into the history of science. Prior to Kuhn, the prevailing view of science was evolutionary. That is, science started with a particular body of knowledge of the world. As a result of observation and experimentation, that view became more elaborated and more refined. Every now and then, a really powerful set of observations or experiments would occur. These powerful acts would propel the evolution of scientific understanding forward at an accelerated rate.

Kuhn replaced this monolithic evolutionary model with a paradigm model. Science, said Kuhn, is a social process. A paradigm is the complete set of beliefs and resultant practices that define a working group of scientists. For the most part, these paradigms are quite extensive and textured. For instance, Newtonian physics was a powerful scientific paradigm. Some of its basic principles were: (1) the universe can be understood from a mechanistic perspective; (2) these mechanistic forces are best modeled and understood mathematically; and (3) complex phenomena need to be trimmed back to see the simple and basic principles that actually define their actions.

Within the Newtonian paradigm, there was simply no place for many of the forms of empirical inquiry we have described in this book. They would not have counted as empirical inquiry and their questions were not raised in scientific circles. It was not so much the case that the scientific community was hostile to qualitative perspectives; it simply could not see them. And because they were a cohesive community, all the operant social forces worked against them taking such unusual perspectives. Science, like all forms of inquiry, gets pulled back to the center of the paradigm.

With a shift in paradigms, however, everything changes. Kuhn noted how wide-ranging these effects can be (Kuhn, in Anderson, 1995):

> Led by a new paradigm, scientists adopt new instruments and look in new places. Even more important, during revolutions scientists see new and different things when looking with familiar instruments in places they have looked before. It is rather as if the professional community had suddenly been transported to another planet where familiar objects are seen in a different light and are joined by unfamiliar ones as well. Of course, nothing of quite that sort does occur: there is no geographical transplantation; outside the laboratory everyday affairs generally continue as before. Nevertheless, paradigm changes cause scientists to see the worlds of their research-engagement differently. (pp. 189–190)

A number of qualitative theorists have embraced the notion that qualitative research represents a basic paradigm shift within the social sciences (e.g., Lincoln & Guba, 2000). By putting forth the notion that qualitative research is based upon a fundamental paradigm shift, these theorists and researchers paved the way for their claims that the "qualitative revolution" was at hand. But qualitative research still had to take a stance on the nature of reality and knowledge. Standard quantitative perspectives were just too restrictive. A new theoretical position was needed.

Social Science Tackles Social Reality

Building on the pioneering work of Alfred Schutz (1932/1967), Berger and Luckmann (1966) introduced yet another major concept within the emerging qualitative perspective. They sought to sort out the roles of objective and subjective characteristics in our understanding of (what we take as) our ordinary and everyday reality. How much of what we take as commonplace and ordinary is legitimized by the structure of our society? To what degree as individuals have we been socialized into accepting these dictates and doctrines as "natural" functions? And how do these dynamics shape what we accept as knowledge?

Berger and Luckmann (1967) called our attention yet again to the nature of knowledge as a sociological phenomenon. They took it a step further, by showing how various "knowledges" within social settings serve as the basis for a construction of a social reality—a reality that we both help build and which we unreflectively accept:

> Sociological interest in questions of "reality" and "knowledge" is thus initially justified by the fact of their social relativity. What is "real" to a Tibetan monk might not be "real" to an American businessman. The "knowledge" of the criminal differs from the "knowledge" of the criminologist. It follows that specific agglomerations of "reality" and "knowledge" pertain to specific social contexts, and that these relationships will have to be included in an adequate sociological analysis of these contexts. (p. 3)

With Berger and Luckmann's rejection of a monolithic and completely objective model of reality for social settings, a number of doors were opened. Their work served as justification for a wide range of notions. On the conservative end, their analysis was taken as an indication that we can no longer talk about one single understanding of reality for human experience as a whole. Our personal and social perspectives into our physical and cultural worlds help shape our activities in both worlds. At the other end of the conceptual spectrum, their work has been used to justify the notion that *all* reality is socially constructed, and that *all* knowledge is made instead of discovered or transmitted.

Wherever you see yourself along the continuum just described, Berger and Luckmann's (1967) treatise on the sociology of knowledge has had some impact. It also allowed social scientists to set aside the task of finding universal laws as the be-all and end-all of the social sciences. Exploring and understanding socially constructed realities became a legitimate endeavor in the social sciences, and thus helped support the growing qualitative revolution.

The Key Perspectives Fall into Place

By the end of the 1960s, it was becoming more and more clear that the social sciences were in a state of change. That change began to take form in both theory and practice.

We will look at theoretical changes within the context of individual fields, as most of these issues arose to address specific needs in specific areas. For instance, grounded theory was first formulated in sociology (Glaser & Strauss, 1967), and then was refined in such areas as the health sciences and education. Naturalistic inquiry arose within evaluation research (Lincoln & Guba, 1985), and ethnography has always been a standard part of cultural anthropology. Phenomenology was extended beyond its philosophical foundations and was developed as a research method within psychology (Moustakas, 1994). Though we find many fields sharing these and other methods, they are best understood within the cultures of their origin.

Change in practices followed from theoretical change. From a practice perspective, Creswell (1998) identifies five "traditions" of methods usage that came together in the social sciences during this period and which, from his vantage, define the more mature formulation of qualitative research we find in the social sciences today. His five "traditions" are biography, grounded theory, phenomenology, ethnography, and case study.

Crotty (1998), taking a far more theoretical and sophisticated perspective, points out that qualitative research came to be based on five theoretical oppositions to positivism. For Crotty, the five key movements of thought away from positivism are constructivism, interpretivism, critical inquiry, feminism, and postmodernism. Crotty's formulation is, in particular, quite useful for grounding our understanding of what we might call the initial qualitative "revolution," or the move against quantitative research.

Histories of Qualitative Research Within the Disciplines

There have been several accounts of the development and emergence of qualitative methods within various disciplines in the social sciences. Jacob (1987), Shulman (1988), and Lancy (1993) have looked at the development of qualitative ideas and methods in education. Bullough and Gitlin (1995) lay out "good practice" models for these educational ideas. Vidich and Lyman (2000) review historical issues in sociology and anthropology. And Morse (1994) wrote one of the first comprehensive sources for qualitative thinking and practices focused on the health sciences.

One thing is for sure—qualitative research will continue to change. Qualitative research has been in motion ever since it first started coming together as a cohesive movement, and there is no reason to suppose that it will not continue to grow and develop. That change will be most evident when we look at changes in the practice of qualitative research.

THE THREE DIRECTIONS OF QUALITATIVE PRACTICE

We can argue that qualitative research as a whole, throughout its brief history, has tried to position itself somehow in relation to prevailing quantitative models of empirical inquiry in the social sciences. We will try to make sense of the shifts of practices in qualitative research by considering three primary directions of orientation in relation to these prevailing quantitative practices.

In its early days, qualitative research gained momentum by developing a model of empirical inquiry that played *against* prevailing trends. Nowadays, the most powerful direction in the field has been a broad and comprehensive set of efforts to work *with* those same prevailing ideas. What will the future bring? Based on the past and the present, we can make some predictions. Before we do so, though, let us take a more careful look at practices during the past and the present.

Moving Against Quantitative Ideas

Qualitative research, as a comprehensive movement, first took shape as a revolutionary program against the quantitative status quo in empirical research in the social sciences. Its earliest champions took great care to show how this new movement operated as a sort of research counterculture. In essence, they saw themselves as leading a revolution against the older and more traditionally quantitative ways of looking at the social sciences. We can see this dimension by looking carefully at several of the early ideological pioneers of the field.

Revolutionary anthropological practices.
Cultural anthropology has always been an area that has valued process over system in its empirical approaches, so it is no wonder that other qualitative inquirers often drew guidance and inspiration from the long history of ethnography and fieldwork that characterized cultural anthropological work. But even within anthropology, there were revolutionary turns as well. Most notable was the advent of ethnography into ordinary and everyday settings, and the ongoing evolution of ethnography such that it became an important and useful tool in fields beyond anthropology (e.g., LeCompte & Preissle, 1993). For a comprehensive review of these historical issues, see Vidich and Lyman (2000).

Revolutionary sociological practices.

The first revolution within sociology was led by the Chicago school, which embraced the use of fieldwork over the creation of theoretical and mathematical sociological models (Bogdan & Biklen, 1998). After this initial assimilation of fieldwork methodology into sociology, there arose a need to use these new methods to do more than collect data. Glaser and Strauss (1967) led the way toward using qualitative methods to generate theory itself. We have discussed Glaser and Strauss in great detail already, so we will not go into any more detail here. It will suffice to note that their work had an impact far wider than sociology. To this day, grounded theory is arguably the method of choice for qualitative researchers in the health sciences, and for many in such fields as education and business. Again, Vidich, and Lyman (2000) touch upon many key sociological issues in the history of the development of qualitative research.

Revolutionary psychological practices.

While Glaser and Strauss were making strides within sociology and health sciences, Giorgi and Moustakas, among others, were making a similar assault on the bastions of psychology (Moustakas, 1994). Here, the battle was perhaps even more difficult. For 50 years, empirical psychology in the United States had been defined in behavioral terms. The emerging turn to cognitive psychology had opened certain conceptual inroads, but the experimental method was still entrenched as the only genuine way to approach the world of experience. The Duquesne school, which featured Giorgi, Moustakas, and others, brought the issue of phenomenology directly into the discussion and practice of research methods in psychology. While the Duquesne school never enjoyed great popularity within Western empirical psychology, it nonetheless served as an important starting point for the qualitative revolution within psychology.

Revolutionary educational practices.

In the field of education, no one did more to ground qualitative research as its own discipline than Egon Guba. Guba was just as combative as he was sincere, and so he and his intellectual successors triggered some of the most intense and severe qualitative versus quantitative debates on record.

Guba felt that qualitative research was fundamentally different from the positivistic models of research practiced by many within the area of educational research and evaluation (his own particular field). He sought to replace positivism with a model he called *naturalistic inquiry*. With Yvonna Lincoln, he crafted several treatises on the nature and implementation of naturalistic inquiry (see Lincoln & Guba, 1985 for the most comprehensive version of this model, and Guba & Lincoln, 1994 for one of his final statements on the topic).

It was not long before others began to apply these ideas to create systematic models of research (e.g., Erlandson, Harris, Skipper, & Allen, 1993). But there were others who sought to expand and extend these ideas. In particular, John Smith has been active in bringing and keeping the debate between qualitative and quantitative perspectives into the public forum (see Smith, 1983; Smith & Deemer, 2000; Smith & Heshusius, 1986). Elliot Eisner has also been active in this debate, both as a moderator (Eisner & Peshkin, 1990) and as a proponent of his own model of artistic connoisseurship in qualitative research (Eisner, 1991).

From the early 1960s to the beginning of the 1990s, the great debate between qualitative and quantitative methods in the social sciences continued. But gradually there emerged another consistent set of voices. These researchers were willing and eager to value the qualitative perspective, but not as an antagonist against quantitative methods. Instead, they called for cooperation between these two opposing views. This led to the next historical direction, which in many ways sums up the present state of the field.

Moving with Quantitative Ideas

Every revolution starts to wind down at some time and seek its place in the ordinary scheme of things. This was true of the qualitative revolution as well. By the advent of the 1990s, qualitative methods had gained a foothold of acceptance in many social science settings.

But the emergence of qualitative methods did not come without some tension. Miller, Nelson, and Moore (1998) documented the struggle for acceptance of a number of qualitative researchers. Cizek (1995) is fairly representative of the contempt that some social scientists felt for the emerging qualitative perspective. And Sokal and Bricmount (1998) extended the "fun" by concocting a famous prank against postmodern theory. They continued the assault by writing a follow-up book that sought to show that all contemporary nontraditional theory and research in the social sciences misunderstood the lessons of contemporary science and was therefore nothing more than "fashionable nonsense."

The call for a common vision.
On a more positive note, there was also a growing movement to incorporate qualitative and quantitative thought into one single coherent vision of social science research. Early pioneers began exploring the development of such notions as ethnostatistics (Gephart, 1988) and meta-ethnography (Noblit & Hare, 1988). The very titles of these methods suggest the blending of qualitative and quantitative ideas.

Conceptual and theoretical work designed to merge qualitative and quantitative theories and practices also began to appear. Firestone (1987) and Salomon (1991) were early and important attempts to go beyond the current "debate" and bring about methodological and theoretical union. Rossman and Wilson (1991) also supported this initiative, in their call for researchers to become "shamelessly eclectic."

The call for mixed methods.
The essence of the call for theoretical unity was quite simple. Here is the mantra: We need to choose our questions first and let the questions drive the methods we use. Sometimes, the questions lead us to use strictly quantitative methods. Other times, qualitative methods are necessary. But, according to most thinkers, more often than not the research question requires us to use *both* methods to some degree. This perspective came to be known as the mixed method approach. Greene, Caracelli, and Grabam (1989) were among the first to conceptualize this mixed method strategy.

Most mixed methods designs apply the following model:

- First, a research question is raised. Never mind how you might want to go about researching that question; just make sure it is well formulated and clearly stated.
- Now, it is time to think about how to go about answering that question. There are usually two components to any such answer.
- The first component deals with the issue of what it is we are trying to prove or verify. What are our hypotheses? How can we verify these hypotheses? How can we make sure our results are reliable, valid, and generalizable? These issues are addressed by the quantitative components of the mixed method design.

- The second component deals with the issue of making sure our research is as rich and vivid as possible. Here, we use qualitative methods to "add meat to the bones." We do not just settle for peoples' responses to questionnaires or surveys. We ask them to write their own thoughts to open-ended questions, usually attached at the end. We then do content analysis on those answers. Or we use structured interviews. With structured interviews, we can both collate data for hypothesis testing and also report the actual works to add a richer context.
- The final stage is to return to the research question. Have we answered our hypotheses? Have we qualified that answer with rich supporting data? If we have, then we have performed a successful mixed method project.

For better or worse, the blending of quantitative and qualitative methods into a common question-answering technique is the zeitgeist driving much contemporary qualitative work (Johnson & Onwuegbuzie, 2004; Morse & Chung, 2003). But there is one thing that is constant about research methodology in the social sciences: Things change.

Moving Away from Quantitative Ideas

What will the future bring? Will it bring an assimilation of qualitative and quantitative research methods into a single conceptual framework for doing empirical research in the social sciences? Or will qualitative research veer off once again, in pursuit of research questions and topics that can only make sense from a qualitative perspective? Candib, Stange, and Levinson (1999) and Gergen and Gergen (2000) are two recent and excellent explorations of these and other issues.

Also, and more importantly, how *should* qualitative research change?

I have tried to stay neutral throughout this book on a number of issues, but I wish to cast my vote on this matter and then defend my choice. I feel that qualitative research will be best served not by continuing its move to assimilate with quantitative research, but by moving instead *away* from quantitative research.

When I say that we need to move away from qualitative research theory and practice, I am not advocating a return to the "war" between qualitative and quantitative research. Far from it. As a matter of fact, I feel that this war was the main reason the two fields ended up moving together eventually.

Why would the qualitative versus quantitative struggle engender the eventual move toward each other? The answer is simple. When you are in conflict, you are in conflict over common ground. It was as if qualitative researchers wanted to wrest conceptual territory away from quantitative researchers, and claim it for their own. Because they were fighting over the same turf, it was inevitable that these two camps would start to move together. We can see this more clearly when we look at the moves that qualitative researchers used to "fight" the war.

One of the key strategies at the outset of the war between qualitative and quantitative methods was a replacement strategy. Traditional quantitative concepts were replaced by their qualitative counterparts. Objectivity was replaced by conformability, reliability was replaced by dependability, generalizability was replaced by transferability, internal validity was replaced by trustworthiness, external validity was replaced by triangulation, and so forth.

But in simple replacement we do not see a change in the underlying rules of research. Simply renaming concepts and setting up different criteria for their use is not enough to bring about genuine change. Sure, qualitative research talked about different sorts of epistemological and ontological stances, but when it came to research practices, the tools seemed to be based on old and familiar notions cast in new guises.

The replacement strategy ultimately led to a countermove by quantitative research to annex these qualitative terms under its own umbrella. Why wouldn't this be the case? For instance, generalizability has been around a lot longer, and has been studied and used far more often, than transferability. So it just makes sense to label transferability as a special case of generalizability, and move on. When you make this same move for each and every replacement concept, pretty soon you no longer have a unique set of ideas to ground your revolution upon.

The point that has not been addressed in all of this furor is as follows. The real problem with reducing all inquiry into one comprehensive and cohesive sets of rules and procedures is this: No one set of rules, no matter how good, can allow us to ask all the questions we need to ask. In particular, quantitative concepts are not very useful in dealing with questions of meaning unless we are looking at meaning as a means for getting to verification.

Qualitative research will finally be able to stand on its own feet when it feels comfortable asking questions that make no sense from any other perspective. All questions about meaning in the empirical world do not have to be separate from verification. Therefore, there will always be a place for mixed types of designs. But we must always remember that every sort of mixed designs will necessarily be quantitative at heart. The key concepts were forged from quantitative theory. Verification of hypotheses will always shape the interpretation of findings. At best, qualitative research can add contextual richness and sometimes explanatory richness. But those efforts will always be a subordinate part of the process. This is not a bad thing, but it does prevent us from asking questions about meaning on its own terms. To do that, we need to turn to the qualitative perspective alone.

What are some areas for research in which meaning is much more important than verification? Following are just a few examples. In my own research, I have been very interested in how people find sources of informal learning to enrich their lives. In this sort of research, meaning is front and center. Other researchers have been interested in tracking down that one unique person who can help us reconceptualize a field, and these researchers have brought their findings back to the world at large. Finally, qualitative research is very useful in dicovering heritage-in-use, or practices that convey a way of understanding the everyday world. Research efforts can simultaneously uncover and critique these "gold mines" of ordinary meaning that permeate our everyday worlds. The list of examples is endless, and they all have one thing in common. Most of their basic questions would not make sense, as stated and then researched, from a traditional quantitative perspective. To work in the quantitative research world, they would have to be operationalized, or theorized, or objectified. Being able to *not* have to do these things is one of the greatest strengths and promises of qualitative research.

QUESTIONS FROM THE FRONTIERS OF QUALITATIVE RESEARCH

We will end this book by looking at three areas at the frontiers of qualitative research. They will be presented as questions.

Is There a Spiritual Dimension to Qualitative Research?

Over the years, qualitative research methods have often been used to examine religious and other spiritual dimensions in various cultures and societies. Because spiritual issues often favor reflection and dialogue, it makes sense to use qualitative methods in their study.

In recent years, however, there has been a small but growing trend for some qualitative theorists and researchers to incorporate spiritual concepts into qualitative research itself. Ropers-Huilman (1999) uses the concept of witness as a metaphor to guide research practices. Witnessing commits researchers to six commitments—to meaning making, to bringing about change for others, to being open to change, to communicate our experiences and perspectives, to listen to others, and to explore issues of equity and care and to promote their greater understanding. These aspects of witnessing are very close to the way this concept is understood in a number of spiritual settings.

Others have sought to use spirituality to understand spirituality. Dillard, Abdur-Rashid, and Tyson (2000) used spiritual approaches to examine the role and use of spiritual concepts in the pedagogy of African American women teachers and researchers. Maher (2003) developed his Cognitive-Experiential Tri-Circle model to inform the use and search for spiritual concepts in field research.

Given that spirituality has been an important concept throughout human history, it makes sense that qualitative researchers should study it. The use of spiritual concepts within certain forms of qualitative research is more controversial. To many people, this suggests an infusion of religion into research.

Is it possible for research to be spiritual without being religious? The answer is yes. Consider the notion of the human spirit. Most forms of religions adhere in some fashion to the notion of the human spirit. However, the idea of the human spirit is much broader than the concept of religion. It simply holds that all human beings are at least potentially linked with one another in some fashion. That is, human beings are not just single, isolated individuals. When we form meaningful and productive units, like healthy and happy families and schools and businesses and even cultures, we build and sustain strong and enduring bonds among ourselves. If we can look at these larger units as having their own identities and histories and even personalities, then we are working within the domain of studying the human spirit. This form of spiritualism, at least, seems acceptable to most of us in the qualitative research community.

Is Qualitative Research Under Attack?

A few years ago, it was chic to declare that the qualitative-quantitative wars were finally over. Qualitative journals were proliferating in a number of fields. Important journals in many fields were publishing more and more qualitative articles. Studies that might have once been strictly quantitative were now using mixed methods. It seemed like a good time to be a qualitative researcher.

Now, in the minds of some, things have changed. Qualitative research has once again come under attack by those who champion a strictly quantitative approach to empirical research.

The focus of this perceived attack is the report by the National Research Council, or NRC (2002), an organization charged by the United States government to study proper modes of scientific research in education. The results of this report, coupled with funding guidelines for the No Child Left Behind educational act, has led to an insistence that randomized experimental design quantitative studies are to be considered the "gold standard" of educational research. Therefore, the chances for qualitative educational research being funded by the U.S. government have been diminished greatly, if not totally eliminated altogether.

A number of prominent members of the educational qualitative research community have responded vigorously to these circumstances. Howe (2004) raises serious questions about the wisdom of proposing experimentalism as the ideal research strategy in such a complex arena as education. Weinstein (2004) critiques the notion that randomized designs will allow for the sorts of certain knowledge that the NRC report seems to promise. Maxwell (2004) raises the specter of scientism and sees the NRC's actions as a reactionary and misguided attempt to reinstate older and outmoded models of science. Finally, Lincoln and Tierney (2004) illustrate how this apparent attack against qualitative research is manifested in such purportedly neutral areas as Institutional Review Board permissions for conducting research. Underlying all of these treatises and arguments is the sense that as qualitative research became more prominent and powerful within educational research, a counterattack was seen as necessary by certain advocates of a more quantitative approach. Whether these implicit charges prove to be true can only be determined over time. For now, it is certain that politics and research have become enmeshed in some areas of educational research in the United States.

The combination of research and politics is often a tricky matter. There has been an unstated assumption that most qualitative researchers lean toward such liberal political issues as cultural relativism and emancipatory politics. Hammersley (2001), however, argues that at least one early advocate of linking politics and research, namely Howard Becker, might have been misunderstood on that topic. It is certainly clear that some current qualitative researchers, such as Lather (2004) and St. Pierre (2004) are not afraid to raise political issues not only in the funding of qualitative research, but in its conduct as well.

How Should We Prepare the Next Generation of Qualitative Researchers?

Generations are usually defined in 25-year intervals. According to this metric, we are now in the early stages of the second generation of qualitative researchers. The members of the first generation were visionaries, explorers, adventurers, and the like. They have done their work well, and there now seems to be a stable and permanent place for at least some sort of qualitative research presence in empirical inquiry.

Our first important task is to maintain our vision and search for new ways to understand the field. Eisner (2001) reflects on his own struggles with doing qualitative research and integrating his own interest in the arts into his research practice. He expresses as well his series of things to hope for in the future—that qualitative research will continue to be practiced, that it will have an impact on not only theory but also policy, that graduate students will feel more and more free to look upon qualitative topics and methods in their own research programs, and that qualitative research will help lead the way for a more complex understanding of the phenomena of culture and society by all citizens.

The second key to the future is debate. Atkinson, Coffey, and Delamont (2001), in laying out their vision for the future of the field, emphasize the role and power of ongoing debate over methods, topics, findings, and strategies for research. In their view, friendly, constructive, and ongoing debate is one of the key ways to ensure both openness and freshness in the conduct and evolution of qualitative research.

The third and final key focuses on the formal educatoin of the next generation of qualitative researchers. Have we done a good job in educating qualitative researchers? Are we doing a good job now? Reisetter, Yexley, Bonds, Nikels, and McHenry (2003), for instance, offer us some valuable insights into these questions. However, we need to do more documentation of and research into our educational procedures and philosophies. And, needless to say, that research would be best approached qualitatively.

Six Quick Trips to the Far Frontiers

One final way to prepare the next generation is to challenge them with a set of new and revolutionary ideas. To that end, I would like to describe six new approaches to qualitative theorizing, data gathering, and analysis (Shank, in press), as follows:

- *Juxtaposing.* Juxtaposing allows us to contrast two areas of understanding to see how one might inform the other. The simplest form of juxtaposing involves the use of metaphors to expand and enhance our understanding of complex phenomena in natural settings. The key to juxtaposition is the notion that though the comparisons are arbitrary, there is nonetheless a powerful compulsion within the human mind to reconcile juxtaposed modes of understanding within some common framework. Why would we even want to pursue such a strategy in the first place? The answer is simple—if we are comparing two areas arbitrarily, then it is highly unlikely that they will be reconciled along any existing frameworks of understanding. Instead, we are more likely to be pursuing potential frameworks that are far from our current modes of understanding, and therefore our likelihood of finding transformative insights is greatly enhanced.

- *Appropriating.* Another method of transformation involves the new and creative use of other systems of examining and handling data. That is, researchers are free to appropriate existing analytical and explanatory techniques and strategies in ways that have not been used before. Just because, say, economic models or choreography charts were not designed for empirical inquiry does not mean that either their forms or their methods, or both, cannot be put into service to allow us to manipulate data in ways not available prior to such acts of appropriation.

- *Data prospecting.* When we do prospecting, the idea is to come up with data that need no further methodological justification to prove their worth. That is, prospecting involves sifting through data to find those one or two things that serve to open our eyes to things in a whole new way.

- *Data grading.* Data can be graded according to their value and contributions toward understanding. Data grading builds on the notion that not all data are as valuable as other data, and that it is a good research strategy is to take that fact into account. The best way to describe data grading is to talk about the system that serves as my model for the discovery and understanding of this process. I was thinking about sports cards. In the United States, we have cards for players in a variety of sports. These cards have been around, in one form or another, for over a century. As you might imagine, the value of any two sports cards might differ widely. These differences, however, exist within a systematic framework for determining value. Some key criteria include: How old is the card? What kind of condition is it in? How good was the player? How many copies of the card were made, or how many still exist? Similar criteria can be used to help us ground our data in qualitative research, such that we can make a clear, systematic, and open case for the inclusion and use of our data.

- *Ingredient theory.* Ingredient theory is a way to look at data not as components to systems, but as ingredients to holistic "recipes" of complex phenomena. It can be illustrated by examining some of the data in my emerging study where I am helping at-risk learners create little museums of their own. This study is an attempt to address a long-standing issue in museum research—why do some people feel excluded from museums even though museums often take great pains to try to attract these same people? After years of thinking about and exploring answers to this question, our team decided to concentrate on the notion of connection. People who like to go to museums feel "connected" to the experience, and the rest of us do not. Furthermore, that connection was not "built" by putting together the right components to get a "museum visitor." Connection has to be concocted. We need to find the right sorts of recipes so that we can bring the proper ingredients together for the proper people. Then we need to "cook" the pot so that we end up with an enduring and sustaining sense of connection.

- *Presence theory.* Presence theory is built around the simple but radical idea that things change not only over time, but also in the here and now. If things cannot change in the here and now, then we are forced to accept that these things are nothing more than the history of forces that have acted upon them. This view is no longer considered good science. From quantum theory to statistical models of the universe, we are confronted with the idea that the given thing, in the here and now, is indeterminate. But what is indeterminacy in the nature of something, other than the fact that it might possess freedom to be other than it is? When this freedom is integrated into the ongoing identity of something, we can say that we are looking at the "presence" of this thing. Presence is what makes things unique as themselves, but still allows us to talk about them in relation to other things as well. It is hard to talk about presence without lapsing into mystical-sounding language, but I can assure you that there is nothing mystical about this notion of presence. It is a real and tangible phenomenon, and it is a part of every process and entity that we experience. One of the goals of presence theory is to give us the language and set of concepts that allow us to explore these phenomena in a systematic, open, and empirical manner.

Exercise Ten—*Back to the Quiet Place*

Now that all of the chapters have been read, and at least some of the exercises have been performed, I have one last simple exercise to offer you. This exercise can either be written up and shared with the rest of the class, or else it can be something you do on your own for your own edification.

The rules of this exercise are simple: Go back to the site of your first exercise, and do it again. Do you see things the same way? Why or why not? What have you learned? How has it affected the way you see this setting?

As a capstone, you might want to write one last final reflective piece on the questions laid out earlier. Think of it, and this whole course, as a form of play. And thanks for playing!

References

Adler, P. A., & Adler, P. (1994). Observational techniques. In N. K. Denzin & Y. S. Lincoln (Eds.), *Handbook of qualitative research* (pp. 377–392). Thousand Oaks, CA: Sage.

Agee, J. (2002). "Winks upon winks": Multiple lenses on settings in qualitative educational research. *Qualitative Studies in Education, 15,* 157–173.

Aguinaldo, J. P. (2004). Rethinking validity in qualitative research from a social constructivist perspective: From "Is this valid research?" to "What is this research valid for?" *The Qualitative Report, 9,* 127–136.

Alexander, B. K. (2003). (Re)visioning the ethnographic site: Interpretive ethnography as a method of pedagogical reflexivity and scholarly production. *Qualitative Inquiry, 9,* 416–441.

Anderson, W. T. (Ed.). (1995). *The truth about truth: De-confusing and re-constructing the postmodern world.* New York: G. P. Putnam's Sons.

Angelides, P. (2001). The development of an efficient technique for collecting and analyzing qualitative data: The analysis of critical incidents. *Qualitative Studies in Education, 14,* 429–442.

Angrosino, M. V., & de Perez, K. A. M. (2002). Rethinking observation: From method to context. In N. K. Denzin & Y. S. Lincoln (Eds.), *Handbook of qualitative research* (2nd ed., pp. 673–702). Thousand Oaks, CA: Sage.

Arnett, R. C. (2002). Paulo Freire's revolutionary pedagogy: From a story-centered to a narrative-centered communication ethic. *Qualitative Inquiry, 8,* 489–510.

Atkinson, P., Coffey, A., & Delamont, S. (2001). A debate about our canon. *Qualitative Research, 1,* 5–21.

Attride-Stirling, J. (2001). Thematic networks: An analytic tool for qualitative research. *Qualitative Research, 1,* 385–405.

Aubusson, P. (2002). Using metaphor to make sense and build theory in qualitative research. *The Qualitative Report, 7*(4). Retrieved 16 August 2004 from http://www.nova,edu/ssss/ QR/QR7-4/aubusson.html

Baez, B. (2002). Confidentiality in qualitative research: Reflections on secrets, power, and agency. *Qualitative Research, 2,* 35–58.

Bal, M. (1997). *Narratology: Introduction to the theory of narrative* (2nd ed.). Toronto, Ontario, Canda: University of Toronto Press.

Bannerji, H. (2003). The tradition of sociology and the sociology of tradition. *Qualitative Studies in Education, 16,* 157–173.

Baptiste, I. (2001, September). Qualitative data analysis: Common phases, strategic differences [42 paragraphs]. *Forum Qualitative Sozialforschung/forum: Qualitative Social Research* [Online journal], *2*(3). Retrieved 4 November 2004 from http:// qualitative-research.net/ fqs-eng.htm

Barbour, R. S., & Kitsinger, J. (1999). *Developing focus group research: Politics, theory, and practice.* Thousand Oaks, CA: Sage.

Barnes, V., Clouder, D. L., Pritchard, J., Hughes, C., & Purkis, J. (2003). Deconstructing dissemination: Dissemination as qualitative research. *Qualitative Research, 3,* 147–164.

Barone, T. (2002). From genre blurring to audience blending: Reflections on the field emanating from an ethnodrama. *Anthropolgy and Education Quarterly, 33,* 255–267.

Barone, T. (2003). Challenging the educational imaginary: Issues of form, substance, and quality in film-based research. *Qualitative Inquiry, 9,* 202–227.

Barthes, R. (1957). *Mythologies.* NY: Hill and Wang.

Barthes, R. (1967). *Elements of semiology.* NY: Hill and Wang.

Beach, D. (2003). A problem of validity in education research. *Qualitative Inquiry, 9,* 859–873.

Belenky, M. F., Clinchy, B. M., Goldberger, J., & Tarule, J. M. (1986). *Women's ways of knowing.* NY: Basic books.

Berger, P. L., & Luckmann, T. (1966). *The social construction of reality: A treatise in the sociology of knowledge.* Garden City, NY: Doubleday.

Bettelheim, B. (1975). *The uses of enchantment.* NY: Vintage Books.

Bey, H. (1985). *T.A.Z: The temporary autonomous zone, ontological anarchy, poetic terrorism.* Brooklyn, NY: Autonomedia.

Bloom, C. M., & Erlandson, D. A. (2003). Three voices in portraiture: Actor, artist, and audience. *Qualitative Inquiry, 9*, 874–894.

Bloom, L. R. (1999). Interpreting interpretation: Gender, sexuality and the practice of *not reading straight*. *Qualitative Studies in Education, 12*, 331–345.

Bogdan, R. C., & Biklen, S. K. (1998). *Qualitative research for education: An introduction to theory and methods* (3rd ed.). Boston, MA: Allyn and Bacon.

Bogdevic, S. R. (1999). Participant observation. In B. F. Crabtree & W. L. Miller (Eds.), *Doing qualitative research* (2nd ed., pp. 47–70). Thousand Oaks, CA: Sage.

Bong, S. A. (2002, May). Debunking myths in qualitative data analysis [44 paragraphs]. *Forum Qualitative Sozialforschung/Forum: Qualitative Social Research* [Online journal], *3*(2). Retrieved 4 November 2004 from http://www.qualitative-research.net/fqs/fqs-eng.htm

Boufoy-Bastick, B. (2004, January). Auto-ethnography and critical incident methodology for eliciting a self-conceptualised worldview [36 paragraphs]. *Forum Qualitative Sozialforschung/Forum: Qualitative Social Research* [Online journal], *5*(1). Art. 37. Retrieved 4 November 2004 from http://www.qualitative-research.net/fqs-texte/1–04/1–04boufoy-e.htm

Bourdon, S. (2002, May). The integration of qualitative data analysis software into research strategies: Resistances and possibilities [30 paragraphs]. *Forum Qualitative Sozialforschung/Forum: Qualitative Social Research* [Online journal], *3*(2). Retrieved 4 November 2004 from http://qualitative-research.net/fqs/fqs-eng.htm

Boyatzis, R. E. (1998). *Transforming qualitative information: Thematic analysis and code development.* Thousand Oaks, CA: Sage

Brady, I. (2000). Authropological poetics. In N. K. Denzin & Y. S. Lincoln (Eds.), *Handbook of qualitative research* (2nd ed., pp. 949–980). Thousand Oaks, CA: Sage.

Breuer, F., & Reichertz, J. (2001, September). Standards of social research [40 paragraphs]. *Forum Qualitative Sozialforschung/Forum: Qualitative Social Research* [Online journal, *2*(3). Retrieved 4 November 2004 from http://qualitative-research.net/fqs/fqs-eng.htm

Bruner, J. S. (1996). *The culture of education.* Cambridge, MA: Harvard University Press.

Brunvand, J. H. (1981). *The vanishing hitchhiker: American urban legends and their meanings.* New York: W. W. Norton & Co.

Brunvand, J. H. (1984). *The choking doberman and other "new" urban legends.* New York: W. W. Norton & Co.

Brunvand, J. H. (1986). *The Mexican pet: More "new" urban legends and some old favorites.* New York: W. W. Norton & Co.

Brunvand, J. H. (1989). *Curses! Broiled again! The hottest urban legends going.* New York: W. W. Norton & Co.

Brunvand, J. H. (1993). *The baby train and other lusty urban legends.* New York: W. W. Norton & Co.

Bryant, A. (2003, January). A constructive/ist response to Glaser [25 paragraphs]. *Forum Qualitative Sozialforschung/Forum: Qualitative Social Research* [Online journal], *4*(1). Retrieved 4 November 2004 from http://qualitative-research.net/fqs-texte/1–03/1–03bryant-e.htm

Bullough, Jr., R. V., & Gitlin, A. (1995). *Becoming a student of teaching: Methodologies for exploring self and school context.* New York: Garland Publishing.

Butler, J. (1990). *Gender trouble.* NY: Routledge.

Buttrick, D. (1987). *Homiletic: Moves and structures.* Philadelphia, PA: Fortress Press.

Campbell, J. (1972). *Myths we live by.* New York: Penguin.

Candib, L. M., Stange, K. C., & Levinson, W. (1999). Qualitative research: Perspectives on the future. In B. F. Crabtree & W. L. Miller (Eds.), *Doing qualitative research* (2nd ed., pp. 347–362). Thousand Oaks, CA: Sage

Carey, L. J. (1999). Unexpected stories: Life history and the limits of interpretation. *Qualitative Inquiry, 5*, 411–427.

Chambers, E. (2000). Applied ethnography. In N. K. Denzin & Y. S. Lincoln (Eds.), *Handbook of qualitative research* (2nd ed., pp. 851–869). Thousand Oaks, CA: Sage.

Charmaz, K. (2000). Grounded theory: Objectivist and constructivist methods. In N. K. Denzin & Y. S. Lincoln (Eds.), *Handbook of qualitative research* (2nd ed., pp. 509–536). Thousand Oaks, CA: Sage.

Christians, C. G. (2000). Ethics and politics in qualitative research. In N. K. Denzin & Y. S. Lincoln (Eds.), *Handbook of qualitative research* (2nd ed., pp. 133–155). Thousand Oaks, CA: Sage.

Cizek, G. J. (1995). Crunchy granola and the hegemony of the narrative. *Educational Researcher, 24*(2), 26–30.

Clandenin, D. J., & Connelly, F. M. (1994). Personal experience methods. In N. K. Denzin & Y. S. Lincoln (Eds.), *Handbook of qualitative research* (pp. 413–427). Thousand Oaks, CA: Sage.

Clifford, J. (1986). On ethnographic allegory. In J. Clifford & G. F. Marcus (Eds.), *Writing culture: The poetics and politics of ethnography* (pp. 98–121). Berkeley, CA: University of California Press.

Clough, P. T. (2000). Comments on setting criteria for experimental writing. *Qualitative Inquiry, 6,* 278–291.

Coe, D. E. (1991). Levels of knowing in ethnographic inquiry. *International Journal of Qualitative Studies in Education, 4,* 313–331.

Cohen, M. Z., & Omery, A. (1994). Schools of phenomenology: Implications for research. In J. M. Morse (Ed.), *Critical issues in qualitative research methods* (pp. 136–156). Thousand Oaks, CA: Sage.

Corbin, J., & Morse, J. M. (2003). The unstructured interactive interview: Issues of reciprocity and risks when dealing with sensitive topics. *Qualitative Inquiry, 9,* 335–354.

Corden, R. (2001). Group discussion and the importance of a shared perspective: Learning from collaborative research. *Qualitative Research, 1,* 347–367.

Crawford, H. K., Leybourne, M. L., & Arnott, A. (2000, January). How we ensured rigour in a multi-site, multi-discourse, multi-researcher study [28 paragraphs]. *Forum Qualitative Sozialforschung/Forum: Qualitative Social Research* [Online journal], *1*(1). Retrieved 4 November 2004 from http://qualitative-research.net/fbs

Creswell, J. W. (1998). *Qualitative inquiry and research design: Choosing among five traditions.* Thousand Oaks, CA: Sage.

Crosby, A. W. (1997). *The measure of reality: Quantification and Western society, 1250–1600.* Cambridge, UK: University of Cambridge Press.

Crotty, M. (1998). *The foundations of social research: Meaning and perspective in the research process.* Thousand Oaks, CA: Sage.

Cunningham, D. J., & Shank, G. D. (1984). Semiotics: A new foundation for education? *Contemporary Education Review, 3,* 411–421.

Davies, B., Browne, J., Gannon, S., Honan, E., Laws, C., Mueller-Rockstroh, B., & Peteren, E. B. (2004). The ambivalent practices of reflexivity. *Qualitative Inquiry, 10,* 360–389.

Deely, J. (1990). *Basics of semiotics.* Bloomington: Indiana University Press.

Deleuze, G., & Guattardi, F. (1987). *A thousand plateaus: Capitalism and schizophrenia.* Minneapolis, MN: University of Minnesota Press.

deMarrais, K. (2004). Elegant communications: sharing qualitative research with communities, colleagues, and critics. *Qualitative Inquiry, 10,* 281–297.

Denzin, N. K. (1989). *Interpretive biography.* Thousand Oaks, CA: Sage.

Denzin, N. K. (1997). *Interpretive ethnography: Ethnographic practices for the 21st century.* Thousand Oaks, CA: Sage.

Denzin, N. K. (2001). The reflexive interview and a performative social science. *Qualitative Research, 1,* 23–46.

Denzin, N. K. (2003). Reading and writing performance. *Qualitative Research, 3,* 243–268.

Denzin, N. K., & Lincoln, Y. S. (1994). *Handbook of qualitative research.* Thousand Oaks, CA: Sage.

Derrida, J. (1981). *Positions.* Chicago, IL: University of Chicago Press.

Dillard, C. B., Abdur-Rashid, D., & Tyson, C. A. (2000). My soul is a witness: Affirming pedagogies of the spirit. *Qualitative Studies in Education, 13,* 447–462.

Doyle, L. H. (2003). Synthesis through meta-ethnography: Paradoxes, enhancements, and possibilities. *Qualitative Research, 3,* 312–344.

Duffy, T. M., & Cunningham, D. J. (1996). Constructivism: Implications for the design and delivery of instruction. In D. H. Jonassen (Ed.), *Handbook of research for educational communications and technology* (pp. 170–198). New York: Macmillan.

Eco, U. (1976). *A theory of semiotics.* Bloomington: Indiana University Press.

Eco, U. (1984). *Semiotics and the philosophy of language.* Bloomington: Indiana University Press.

Eco, U. (1990). *The limits of interpretation.* Bloomington: Indiana University Press.

Eichhorn, K. (2001). Sites unseen: Ethnographic research in a textual community. *Qualitative Studies in Education, 14,* 565–578.

Eisner, E. W. (1991). *The enlightened eye: Qualitative inquiry and the enhancement of educational practice.* Upper Saddle River, NJ: Prentice Hall.

Eisner, E. W. (2001). Concerns and aspirations for qualitative research in the new millenium. *Qualitative Research, 1,* 135–145.

Eisner, E. W., & Peshkin, A. (1990). Introduction. In E. W. Eisner & A. Peshkin (Eds.), *Qualitative inquiry in education: The continuing debate* (pp. 1–14). New York: Teachers College Press.

Elderkin-Thompson, V., & Waitzkin, H. (1999). Using videotape in qualitative research. In B. F. Crabtree & W. L. Miller (Eds.), *Doing qualitative research* (2nd ed., pp. 239–252). Thousand Oaks, CA: Sage.

Eliade, M. (1954/1959). *Cosmos and history: The myth of the eternal return.* New York: Harper & Row.

Ellis, C. (1995). The other side of the fence: Seeing black and white in a small Southern town. *Qualitative Inquiry, 1,* 147–167.

Ellis, C., & Bochner, A. P. (2000). Autoethnography, personal narrative, reflexivity: Researcher as subject. In N. K. Denzin & Y. S. Lincoln (Eds.), *Handbook of qualitative research* (2nd ed., pp. 733–768). Thousand Oaks, CA: Sage.

Ely, M. (1991). *Doing qualitative research: Circles within circles.* London: Falmer Press.

Ely, M., Vinz, R., Downing, M., & Anzul, M. (1997). *On writing qualitative research: Living by words.* London: Falmer Press.

Erickson, F., & Mohatt, G. (1982). Cultural organization of participation structures in two classrooms of Indian students. In G. Spindler (Ed.), *Doing the ethnography of schooling: Educational anthropology in action* (pp. 132–176). Prospect Heights, IL: Waveland Press.

Erlandson, D. A., Harris, E. L., Skipper, B. L., & Allen, S. D. (1993). *Doing naturalistic inquiry: A guide to methods.* Newbury Park, CA: Sage.

Espy, W. R. (1983). *The garden of eloquence: A rhetorical bestiary.* New York: Harper & Row.

Ezeh, P-Z. (2003). Integration and its challenges in participant observation. *Qualitative Research, 3,* 191–205.

Fadiman, A. (1997). *The spirit catches you and you fall down: A Hmong child, her American doctors, and the collision of two cultures.* New York: Farrar, Straus and Giroux.

Fairlie, H. (1979). *The seven deadly sins today.* Notre Dame, IN: University of Notre Dame Press.

Fanon, F. (1968). *The wretched of the earth.* New York: Grove Press.

Fetterman. D., Kaftarian, S., & Wandersman, A. (Eds.). (1996). *Empowerment evaluation: Knowledge and tools for self-assessment and accountability.* Thousand Oaks, CA: Sage Publications.

Fielding, N. G., & Lee, R. M. (1998). *Computer analysis and qualitative research.* London: Sage.

Fine, M., Weis, L., Centrie, C., & Roberts, R. (2000). Educating beyond the borders of shooling. *Anthropology and Education Quarterly, 31,* 131–151.

Finley, S. (2003). Arts-based inquiry in QI: Seven years from crisis to guereilla warfare. *Qualitative Inquiry, 9,* 281–296.

Firestone, W. (1987). Meaning in method: The rhetoric of quantitative and qualitative research. *Educational Researcher, 16*(7), 16–21.

Flick, U. (1998). *An introduction to qualitative research.* London: Sage.

Foley, D. E. (2002). Critical ethnography: The reflexive turn. *Qualitative Studies in Education, 15,* 469–490.

Fontana, A., & Frey, J. H. (2000). The interview: From structured questions to negotiated text. In N. K. Denzin & Y. S. Lincoln (Eds.), *Handbook of Qualitative Research* (2nd ed., pp. 645–672). Thousand Oaks, CA: Sage.

Foucault, M. (1984). *The Foucault reader.* New York: Pantheon Books.

Fraenkel, R. M. (1999). Standards of qualitative research. In B. F. Crabtree & W. L. Miller (Eds.), *Doing qualitative research* (2nd ed., pp. 333–346). Thousand Oaks, CA: Sage.

Franklin, K. K., & Lowry, C. (2001). Computer-mediated focus group sessions: Naturalistic inquiry in a networked enviornment. *Qualitative Research, 1,* 169–184.

Freire, P. (1968/1983). *Pedagogy of the oppressed.* New York: Continuum.

Gardner, G. (2001). Unreliable memories and other contingencies: Problems with biographical knowledge. *Qualitative Research, 1,* 185–204.

Garrick, J. (1999). Doubting the philosophical assumptions of interpretive research. *Qualitative Studies in Education, 12,* 147–156.

Garton, S. N., & Zweerink, A. (2002). Ethnography online: "Natives" practising and inscribing community. *Qualitative Research, 2,* 179–200.

Geertz, C. (1973). *The interpretation of cultures.* New York: Basic Books.

Gephart, R. P., Jr. (1988). *Ethnostatistics: Qualitative foundations for quantitative research.* Thousand Oaks, CA: Sage.

Gergen, K. (1994). *Toward transformation of social knowledge* (2nd ed.). Thousand Oaks, CA: Sage.

Gergen, M. M., & Gergen, K. J. (2000). Qualitative inquiry: Tensions and transformations. In N. K. Denzin & Y. S. Lincoln (Eds.), *Handbook of Qualitative Research* (2nd ed., pp. 1025–1046). Thousand Oaks, CA: Sage.

Geuss, R. (1981). *The idea of a critical theory: Habermas and the Frankfurt school.* Cambridge, UK: Cambridge University Press.

Gilchrist, V. J., & Williams, R. L. (1999). Key informant interviews. In B. F. Crabtree & W. L. Miller (Eds.), *Doing qualitative research* (2nd ed., pp. 71–88). Thousand Oaks, CA: Sage.

Gilgun, J. F. (1999). Fingernails painted red: A feminist, semiotic analysis of a "hot" text. *Qualitative Inquiry, 5,* 181–207.

Gilligan, C. (1982/1993). *In a different voice: Psychological theory and women's development.* Cambridge, MA: Harvard University Press.

Giroux, H. (1983). *Theory and resistance in education: A pedagogy for the opposition.* South Hadley, MA: Bergin & Garvey.

Giroux, H. (1992). *Border crossings: Cultural workers and the politics of education.* New York: Routledge.

Giroux, H. (1993). *Living dangerously: Multiculturalism and the politics of difference.* New York: Peter Lang.

Given, L. M. (2004). Mini-dise recorders: A new approach to qualiative interviewing. *International Journal of Qualitative Methods, 3*(2). Article 5. Retrieved 24 November 2004 from http://www.ulaberta.ca/~iiqm/backissues/3_2/html/pdf/given.pdf

Glaser, B. G. (1978). *Theoretical sensitivity.* Mill Valley, CA: The Sociology Press.

Glaser, B. (2002a). Conceptualization: On theory and theorizing using grounded theory. *International Journal of Qualitative Methods. 1*(2), Article 3. Retrieved 3 October 2004 from http://www.ualberta.ca/~ijqm/

Glaser, B. (2002b). Constructivist grounded theory? [47 paragraphs]. *Forum Qualitative sozialforschung/Forum: Qualitative Social Research* [Online journal], *1*(1). Retrieved 4 November 2004 from http://qualitative-research.net/fqs/fqs-eng.htm [4 November 2004].

Glaser, B. (2003, October). Naturalist inquiry and grounded theory [68 paragraphs]. *Forum Qualitative Sozialforschung/Forum: Qualitative Social Research* [Online journal], *5*(1), Art. 7. Retrieved 4 November 2004 from http://qualitative-research.net/fqs-texte/1–04/1–04glaser-e.htm

Glaser, B. (with J. Holton). (2004, May). Remodeling grounded theory [80 paragraphs]. *Forum Qualitative Sozialforschung/Forum: Qualitative Social Research* [Online journal], *5*(2), Art. 4. Retrieved 4 November 2004 from http://qualitative-research.net/fqs-texte/2–04/2–04glaser-e. htm

Glaser, B. G., & Strauss, A. L. (1967). *The discovery of grounded theory: Strategies for qualitative research.* Chicago: Aldine Publishing Company.

Gleick, J. (1987). *Chaos: Making a new science.* NY: Viking.

Glesne, C. (1999). *Becoming qualitative researchers: An Introduction* (2nd ed.). New York: Longman.

Goffman, E. (1959). *The presentation of self in everyday life.* Garden City, NY: Doubleday.

Golafshani, N. (2003). Understanding reliability and validity in qualitative research. *The Qualitative Report, 8.* 597–607.

Gold, R. L. (1958). Roles in sociological field observations. *Social Forces, 36,* 217–223.

Goldman-Segall, R. (1998). *Points of viewing, children's thinking: A digital ethnographer's journey.* Mahwah, NJ: Lawrence Erlbaum Associates.

Goldstein, L. S. (2000). Ethical dilemmas in designing collaborative research: Lessons learned the hard way. *Qualitative Studies in Education. 13,* 517–530.

Gonzalez, K. P. (2001). Inquiry as a process of learning about the other and the self. *Qualitative Studies in Education, 14,* 543–562.

Greenbaum, T. L. (1997). *The handbook for focus group research.* Thousand Oaks, CA: Sage.

Greenbaum, T. L. (2000). *Moderating focus groups: A practical guide for group participation.* Thousand Oaks, CA: Sage.

Greene, J. C. (1994). Qualitative program evaluation: Practice and promise. In N. K. Denzin & Y. S. Lincoln (Eds.), *Handbook of qualitative research* (pp. 530–544). Thousand Oaks, CA: Sage.

Greene, J. C. (2000). Understanding social programs through evaluation. In N. K. Denzin & Y. S. Lincoln (Eds.), *Handbook of qualitative research* (2nd ed., pp. 981–1000). Thousand Oaks, CA: Sage.

Greene, J. C., Caracelli, V. J., & Graham, W. F. (1989). Toward a conceptual framework for mixed-method evaluation designs. *Educational Evaluation and Policy Analysis, 11,* 255–274.

Grimm, J., & Grimm, W. (1815/1993). *Grimm's complete fairy tales.* New York: Barnes & Noble.

Groenewald, T. (2004). A phenomenological research design illustrated. *International Journal of Qualitative Methods, 3*(1). Article 4. Retrieved 2 November 2004 from http://www.ulaberta.ca/~iiqm/backissues/3_1/html/pdf/groenewald.pdf

Grondin, J. (1990/1994). *Introduction to philosophical hermeneutics.* Trans. by J. Weinsheimer. New Haven, CT: Yale University Press.

Guba, E. G., & Lincoln, Y. S. (1994). Competing paradigms in qualitative research. In N. K.

Denzin & Y. S. Lincoln (Eds.), *Handbook of qualitative research* (pp. 105–117). Thousand Oaks, CA: Sage.

Guillemin, M., & Gillam, L. (2004). Ethics, reflexivity, and "ethically important moments" in research. *Qualitative Inquiry, 10*, 261–280.

Habermas, J. (1971). *Knowledge and human interests*. Boston, MA: Beacon Press.

Hamer, L. (1999). A folkloristic approach to understanding teachers as storytellers. *Qualitative Studies in Education, 12*, 363–380.

Hammersley, M. (1990). *Reading ethnographic research: A critical guide*. New York: Longman.

Hammersely, M. (2001). Which side was Becker on? Questioning political and epistemological radicalism. *Qualitative Research, 1*, 91–110.

Hammersley, M., & Atkinson, P. (1983). *Ethnography: Principles in practice*. London: Routledge.

Hammond, L., & Spindler, G. (2001). Not talking past each other: Cultural roles in educational research. *Anthropology and Education Quarterly, 32*, 373–378.

Hanrahan, M., Cooper, T., & Burroughs-Lange, S. (1999). The place of personal writing in a PhD thesis: Epistemological and methodological considerations. *Qualitative Studies in Education, 12*, 401–416.

Harper, D. (2000). Reimagining visual methods: From Galileo to *Neuromancer*. In N. K. Denzin & Y. S. Lincoln (Eds.), *Handbook of qualitative research* (2nd ed., pp. 717–732). Thousand Oaks, CA: Sage.

Harre, R. (2004). Staking our claim for qualitative psychology as science. *Qualitative Research in Psychology, 1*, 3–14.

Harrington, W. (2003). What journalism can offer ethnography. *Qualitative Inquiry, 9*, 90–104.

Harrison, J., MacGibbon, L., & Morton, M. (2001). Regimes of trustworthiness in qualitative research: The rigors of reciprocity. *Qualitative Inquiry, 7*, 323–345.

Hawkes, T. (1977). *Structuralism and semiotics*. Berkeley, CA: University of California Press.

Heath, S. B. (1982). Questioning at home and at school: A comparative study. In G. Spindler (Ed.), *Doing the ethnography of schooling: Educational anthropology in action* (pp. 102–131). Prospect Heights, IL: Waveland Press.

Heath, S. B. (1983). *Ways with words*. Cambridge, UK: Cambridge University Press.

Heidegger, M. (1927). *Being and time*. New York: Harper & Row.

Hill, M. R. (1993). *Archival strategies and techniques*. Newbury Park, CA: Sage.

Hodder, I. (2000). The interpretation of documents and material culture. In N. K. Denzin & Y. S. Lincoln (Eds.), *Handbook of Qualitative Research* (2nd ed., pp. 703–716). Thousand Oaks, CA: Sage.

Hogan, K., & Gorey, C. (2001). Viewing classrooms as cultural contexts for fostering scientific literacy. *Anthropology and Education Quarterly, 32*, 214–243.

Holloway, I., & Todres, L. (2003). The status of method: Consistency and coherence. *Qualitative Research, 3*, 345–357.

hooks, b. (1984). *Feminist theory: From margin to center*. Boston: South End.

Horney, K. (1967). *Feminine psychology*. NY: W. W. Norton & Co.

Housely, W., & Fitzgerald, R. (2002). The reconsidered model of membership categorization analysis. *Qualitative Research, 2*, 59–83.

Howe, K. R. (2004). A critique of experimentalism. *Qualitative Inquiry, 10*, 42–61.

Hupcey, J. E. (2002). Issues of validity: The development of the concept of trust. *International Journal of Qualitative Methods, 1*(4). Article 5. Retrieved 3 October 2004 from http://www.ualberta.ca/~ijqm/

Husserl, E. (1960). *Cartesian meditations*. The Hague: Martinus Nijhoff.

Jackson, A. Y. (2003). Rhizovocality. *Qualitative Studies in Education, 16*, 693–710.

Jacob, E. (1987). Qualitative research traditions: A review. *Review of Educational Research, 57*, 1–50.

Jacob, E. (2001). The Council on Anthropology and Education as a crossroad community: Reflections on theory-oriented and practice-oriented research. *Anthropology and Education Quarterly, 32*, 256–275.

Jacobson, R. (1976). *Main trends in the science of language*. New York: Harper & Row.

Jagose, A. (1996). *Queer theory: An introduction*. New York: NYU Press.

Janesick, V. J. (1998). *"Stretching" exercises for qualitative researchers*. Thousand Oaks, CA: Sage.

Janesick, V. J. (1999). A journal about journal writing as qualitative research technique: History, issues, and reflections. *Qualitative Inquiry, 5*, 505–524.

Johnson, R. B., & Onwuegbuzie, A. J. (2004). Mixed method research: A research paradigm whose time has come. *Educational Researcher, 33*(7), 14–26.

Jones, K. (2004). Mission drift in qualitative research, or moving toward a systemaic review of qualitative studies, moving back to a more systematic narrative review. *The Qualitative Report, 9,* 95–112.

Kamberelis, G. (2003). Ingestion, elimination, sex, and song: Trickster as premodern avatar of postmodern research practice. *Qualitative Inquiry, 9,* 673–704.

Kemnis, S., & McTaggart, R. (2000). Participatory action research. In N. K. Denzin & Y. S. Lincoln (Eds.), *Handbook of Qualitative Research* (2nd ed., pp. 567–606). Thousand Oaks, CA: Sage.

Kincheloe, J. (1991). *Teachers as researchers: Qualitative paths to empowerment.* London: Falmer.

Kincheloe, J. (1993). *Toward a critical politics of teacher thinking: Mapping the postmodern.* Granby, MA: Bergin & Garvey.

Kincheloe, J. (2001). Describing the bricolage: Conceptualizing a new rigor in qualitative research. *Qualitative Inquiry, 7,* 679–692.

Kipnis, A. (2001). Articulating school countercultures. *Anthropology and Education Quarterly, 32,* 472–492.

Kluge, S. (2000, January). Empirically grounded construction of types and typologies in qualitative social research [20 paragraphs]. *Forum Qualitative Sozialforschung/Forum: Qualitative Social Research* [Online journal], *1*(1). Retrieved 4 November 2004 from http:// qualitative-research.net/fqs

Knight, M. G., Bentely, C. C., Norton, N. E. L., & Dixon, I. R. (2004). (De)constructing (in)visible parent/guardian consent forms: Negotiating power, reflexivity, and the collective within qualitative research. *Qualitative Inquiry, 10,* 390–411.

Korobov, N. (2001, September). Reconciling theory with method: From conversation analysis and critical discourse analysis to positioning analysis [36 paragraphs]. *Forum Qualitative Sozialforschung/Forum: Qualitative Social Research* [Online journal], *2*(3). Retrieved 4 November 2004 from http://qualitative-research.net/fqs/fqs-eng.htm

Koro-Ljungberg, M. (2001). Metaphors as a way to explore qualitative data. *Qualitative Studies in Education, 14,* 367–379.

Koro-Ljungberg, M. (2004). Impossibilities of reconciliation: Validity in mixed theory projects. *Qualitative Inquiry, 10,* 601–621.

Kosko, B. (1993). *Fuzzy thinking: The new science of fuzzy logic.* NY: Hyperion.

Kuhn, T. (1970). *The structure of scientific revolutions* (2nd ed.). Chicago: University of Chicago Press.

Kuzel, A. J. (1999). Sampling in qualitative inquiry. In B F. Crabtree & W. L. Miller (Eds.), *Doing qualitative research* (2nd ed., pp. 33–46). Thousand Oaks, CA: Sage.

Kvale, S. (1996). *Interviews: An introduction to qualitative research interviewing.* Thousand Oaks, CA: Sage.

Labuschagne, A. (2003). Qualitative research—Airy fairy or fundamental? *The Qualitative Report, 8,* 100–103.

Ladson-Billings, G. (2003). It's your world and I'm just trying to explain it: Understanding our expistemological and methodological challenges. *Qualitative Inquiry, 9,* 5–12.

Lakoff, G., & Johnson, M. (1980). *Metaphors we live by.* Chicago, IL: University of Chicago Press.

Lancy, D. F. (1993). *Qualitative research in education: An introduction to the major traditions.* New York: Longman.

Langer, C. L., & Furman, R. (2004, May). Exploring identity and assimilation: Research and interpretive poems [19 paragraphs]. *Forum Qualitative Sozialforschung/Forum: Qualitative Social Research* [Online journal], *5*(2). Retrieved 4 November from http://qualitative-research.net/fqs-texte/2-04/2-04 langerfurman-e.htm

Lapadat, J. C., & Lindsay, A. C. (1999). Transcriptions in research and practice: From standarization of technique to interpretive positionings. *Qualitative Inquiry, 5,* 64–86.

Lather, P. (1991). *Getting smart: Feminist research and pedagogy within the postmodern.* New York: Routledge and Kegan Paul.

Lather, P. (2004). This IS your father's paradigm: Government intrusion and the case of qualitative research in education. *Qualitative Inquiry, 10,* 15–34.

Latour, B. (1999). *Pandora's hope: Essays on the reality of science studies.* Cambridge, MA: Harvard University Press.

Laverty, S. M. (2003). Hermeneutic phenomenology and phenomenology: A comparison of historical and methodological considerations. *International Journal of Qualitative Methods, 2*(3). Article 3. Retrieved 2 November 2004 from http:// www.ulaberta.ca/~iiqm/backissues/2_3final html/pdf/laverty.pdf

Lawrence-Lightfoot, S., & Davis, J. H. (1997). *The art and science of portraiture.* San Francisco, CA: Jossey-Bass Publishers.

Lechte, J. (1994). *Fifty key contemporary thinkers: From structural-*

ism to postmodernity. London, UK: Routledge.

LeCompte, M. (2002). The transformation of ethnographic practice: Past and current challenges. Qualitative Research, 2, 283–299.

LeCompte, M. D., & Preissle, J. (1993). Ethnography and qualitative design in educational research (2nd ed.). San Diego, CA: Academic Press.

Lee, S., & Roth, W.-M. (2003, May). Becoming and belonging: Learning qualitative research through legitimate peripheral participation [64 paragraphs]. Forum Qualitative Sozialforschung/Forum: Qualitative Social Research [Online journal], 4(2). Retrieved 4 November 2004 from http:// qualitative-research.net/fqs-texte/2-03/2-03/leerpoth-e.htm

Levin-Rozalis, M. (2004). Searching for the unknowable: A process of detection—Abductive research generated by projective techniques. International Journal of Qualitative Methods, 3(2). Article 1. Retrieved 24 November 2004 from http://www.ulaberta.ca/~iiqm/backissues/3_2/html/pdf/rozalis.pdf

Levi-Strauss, C. (1966). The savage mind. Chicago, IL: University of Chicago Press.

Levi-Strauss, C. (1978). Myth and meaning. New York: Schocken Books.

Lieblich, A., Tuval-Mashiach, R., & Zilber, T. (1998). Narrative research: Reading, analysis, and interpretation. Thousand Oaks, CA: Sage.

Lincoln, Y. S. (1995). Emerging criteria for quality in qualitative and interpretive research. Qualitative Inquiry, 1, 275–289.

Lincoln, Y. S., & Guba, E. G. (1985). Naturalistic inquiry. Newbury Park, CA: Sage.

Lincoln, Y. S., & Guba, E. G. (2000). Paradigmatic controversies, contradictions, and emerging confluences. In N. K. Denzin & Y. S. Lincoln (Eds.), Handbook of Qualitative Research (2nd ed., pp. 163–188). Thousand Oaks, CA: Sage.

Lincoln, Y. S., & Tierney, W. G. (2004). Qualitative research and Institutional Review Boards. Qualitative Inquiry, 10, 219–234.

Lyotard, J. F. (1979). The postmodern condition. Minneapolis, MN: University of Minnesota Press.

Madriz, E. (2000). Focus groups in feminist research. In N. K. Denzin & Y. S. Lincoln (Eds.), Handbook of Qualitative Research (2nd ed., pp. 835–850). Thousand Oaks, CA: Sage.

Maher, F. A., & Tetreault, M. K. T. (1993). Doing feminist ethnography: Lessons from feminist classrooms. International Journal of Qualitative Studies in Education, 6, 19–32.

Maher, M. (2003). The potential role of spirituality in conducting field research: Examination of a model and a process. The Qualitative Report, 8, 13–31.

Malone, S. (2003). Ethics at home: Informed consent in your own backyard. Qualitative Studies in Education, 16, 797–815.

Mandelbrot, B. B. (1983). The fractal geometry of nature. NY: W. H. Freeman and Co.

Manning, P. K. (1995). The challenges of postmodernism. In J. van Maanen (Ed.), Representation in ethnography (pp. 245–272). Thousand Oaks, CA: Sage.

Marcus, G. E. (1986). Afterword: Ethnographic writing and anthropological careers. In J. Clifford & G. F. Marcus (Eds.), Writing culture: The poetics and politics of ethnography (pp. 262–266). Berkeley, CA: University of California Press.

Marshall, C., & Rossman, G. B. (1995). Designing qualitative research (2nd ed.) Thousand Oaks, CA: Sage.

Maxwell, J. A. (2004). Reemergent scientism, postmodernism, and dialogue across differences. Qualitative Inquiry, 10, 35–41.

Maykut, P., & Morehouse, R. (1994). Beginning qualitative research: A philosophic and practical guide. London: Falmer Press.

McAuliffe, D. (2003). Challenging methodological traditions: Research by email. The Qualitative Report, 8, 57–69.

McCaslin, M. L., & Scott, K. W. (2003). The five-question method of framing a qualitative research study. The Qualitative Report, 8, 447–461.

McCracken, G. (1988). The long interview. Newbury Park, CA: Sage.

McLaren, P. (1986). Schooling as ritual performance: Toward a political economy of educational symbols and gestures. London: Routledge & Kegan Paul.

McTaggart, R. (1991). Action research: A short modern history. Geelong, Victoria, Australia: Deakin University Press.

Mead, M. (1949). Male and female. NY: William Morrow & Co.

Meadmore, D., Hatcher, C., & McWilliam, E. (2000). Getting tense about genealogy. Qualitative Studies in Education, 13, 463–476.

Meiners, E. R. (1999). Writing (on) fragments. Qualitative Studies in Education, 12, 347–362.

Mello, R. A. (2002). Collocation analysis: A method for conceptualizing and understanding narrative data. Qualitative Research, 2, 231–243.

Merriam, S. B. (1998). *Qualitative research and case study applications in education*. San Francisco, CA: Jossey-Bass.

Metcalfe, M. (2003, January). The literature review as expert witness [45 paragraphs]. *Forum Qualitative Sozialforschung/ Forum: Qualitative Social Research* [Online journal], *4*(1). Retrieved 4 November 2004 from http://qualitative-research.net/ fqs-texte/1–03/1–03metcalfe-e.htm

Miles, M. B., & Huberman, A. M. (1994). *Qualitative data analysis* (2nd ed.). Thousand Oaks, CA: Sage.

Miller, S., & Fredericks, M. (2003). The nature of "evidence" in qualitative research methods. *International Journal of Qualitative Methods, 2*(1). Article 4. Retrieved 2 November 2004 from http://www.ulaberta.ca/~iiqm/backissues/2_1/html/miller.html

Miller, S. M., Nelson, M. W., & Moore, M. T. (1998). Caught in the paradigm gap: Qualitative researchers' lived experience and the politics of epistemology. *American Educational Research Journal, 35*, 377–416.

Miller, W. L., & Crabtree, B. F. (1999). Depth interviewing. In B. F. Crabtree & W. L. Miller (Eds.), *Doing qualitative research* (2nd ed., pp. 89–108). Thousand Oaks, CA: Sage.

Moore, T. (1996). Developing a mythic sensibility. In J. Young (Ed.), *Saga: Best new writings on mythology* (pp. 20–27). Ashland, OR: White Cloud Press.

Morgan, A. K., & Drury, V. B. (2003). Legitimising the subjectivity of human reality through qualitative research method. *The Qualitative Report, 8*, 70–80.

Morgan, D. L. (1988). *Focus groups as qualitative research*. Newbury Park, C.A: Sage.

Morgan, D. L. (1998). *The focus groups guidebook*. Thousand Oaks, CA: Sage.

Morgan, D. L. & Krueger, R. A. (1997). *The focus group kit*. Thousand Oaks, CA: Sage.

Morse, J. M. (1994). "Emerging from the data": The cognitive processes of analysis in qualitative inquiry. In J. M. Morse (Ed.), *Critical issues in qualitative research methods* (pp. 23–43). Thousand Oaks, CA: Sage.

Morse, J. M., & Chung, S. E. (2003). Toward holism: The significance of methodological pluralism. *International Journal of Qualitative Methods, 2*(3). Article 2. Retrieved 2 November 2004 from http://www.ulaberta.ca/~ijqm/backissues/2_3final/html/pdf/morsechung.pdf

Morse, J. M., Barrett, M., Mayan, M., Olson, K., & Spiers, J. (2002). Verification strategies for establishing reliability and validity in qualitative research. *International Journal of Qualitative Method, 1*(2), Article 2. Retrieved 3 October 2004 from http://www.ualberta.ca/~ijqm/

Morse, J. M., & Mitcham, C. (2002). Exploring qualitatively-derived concepts: Inductive-deductive pitfalls. *International Journal of Qualitative Methods, 1*(4), Article 3. Retrieved 3 October 2004 from http://www.ualberta.ca/~ijqm/

Morse, J. M, & Pooler, C. (2002). Analysis of videotaped data: Methodological considerations. *International Journal of Qualitative Methods, 1*(4), Article 7. Retrieved 3 October 2004 from http://www.ualberta.ca/~ijqm/

Moss, G. (2004). Provisions of trustworthiness in critical narrative research: Bridging intersubjectivity and fidelity. *The Qualitative Report, 9*, 359–374.

Moustakas, C. (1990). *Heuristic research: Design, methodology, and applications*. Newbury Park, CA: Sage.

Moustakas, C. (1994). *Phemomenological research methods*. Thousand Oaks, CA: Sage.

Murray, S. B. (2003). A spy, a shill, a go-between, or a sociologist: Unveiling the "observer" in participant observer. *Qualitative Research, 3*, 243–268.

National Research Council (2002). *Scientific research in education* (R. J. Shavelson & L. Towne, Eds., Committe on Scientific Principles for Educational Research). Washington, DC: National Academy Press.

Noblit, G. W., & Hare, R. D. (1988). *Meta-ethnography: Synthesizing qualitative studies*. Thousand Oaks, CA: Sage.

Nygren, L., & Blom, B. (2001). Analysis of short reflective narratives: A method for the study of knowledge in social workers' actions. *Qualitative Research, 1*, 369–384.

Oliva, M. (2000). Shifting landscapes/shifting langue: Qualitative research from the in-between. *Qualitative Inquiry, 6*, 33–57.

Onyx, J., & Small, J. (2001). Memory-work: The method. *Qualitative Inquiry, 7*, 773–786.

Oringderff, J. (2004). "My way": Piloting an online focus group. *International Journal of Qualitative Methods, 3*(3). Article 5. Retrieved 24 November 2004 from http://www.ulaberta.ca/~iiqm/backissues/3_1/html/pdf/oringderff.pdf

Parker, L., & Lynn, M. (2002). What's race got to do with it? Critical race theory's conflicts with and connections to qualitative research methodology and epistemology. *Qualitative Inquiry, 8*, 7–22.

Paterson, B., Bottorff, J., & Hewatt, R. (2003). Blending observational methods: Possibilities, strategies, and challenges. *International Journal of Qualitative Methods, 2*(1). Article 3. Retrieved 2 November 2004 from http://www.ulaberta.ca/~iiqm/backissues/2_1/html/patersonetal.html

Patton, M. Q. (2002). *Qualitative research and evaluation methods* (3rd ed.). Thousand Oaks, CA: Sage.

Patton, M. Q. (1999). Myths as normative frames for qualitative interpretation of life stories. *Qualitative Inquiry, 5*, 338–352.

Paulos, J. A. (1998). *Once upon a number: The hidden mathematical logic of stories.* New York: Basic Books.

Pedelty, M. (2001). Teaching anthropology through performance. *Anthropology and Education Quarterly, 32*, 244–253.

Peirce, C. S. (1898/1992). *Reasoning and the logic of things.* Cambridge, MA: Harvard University Press.

Peirce, C. S. (1903/1992). *Pragmatism as a principle and method of right thinking: The 1903 Harvard lectures on Pragmatism.* Albany, NY: State University of New York Press.

Peirce, C. S. (1992). *The essential Peirce: Volume 1(1867–1893).* N. Houser & C. Kloesel (Eds.). Bloomington, IN: Indiana University Press.

Peirce, C. S. (1998). *The essential Peirce: Volume 2(1893–1913).*

The Peirce Edition Project (Eds.). Bloomington, IN: Indiana University Press.

Penn-Edwards, S. (2004). Visual evidence in qualitative research: The role of videorecording. *The Qualitative Report, 9*, 266–277.

Penrod, J. (2002). Advancing uncertainty: Untangling and discerning related concepts. *International Journal of Qualitative Methods, 1*(4), Article 6. Retrieved 3 October 2004 from http://www.ualberta.ca/~ijqm/

Peshkin, A. (1982). The researcher and subjectivity: Reflections of an ethnography of school and community. In G. Spindler (Ed.), *Doing the ethnography of schooling: Educational anthropology in action* (pp. 47–67). Prospect Heights, IL: Waveland Press.

Peshkin, A. (2001). Angles of vision: Enhancing perception in qualitative research. *Qualitative Inquiry, 7*, 238–253.

Phillips, D. C., & Burbules, N. C. (2000). Postpositivism and educational research. Lanham, MD: Rowman & Littlefield.

Pichert, J. W., & Anderson, R. C. (1977). Taking different perspectives on a story. *Journal of Educational Psychology, 69*, 309–315.

Piirto, J. (2002). The question of quality and qualifications: Writing inferior poems as qualitative research. *Qualitative Studies in Education, 15*, 431–445.

Pillow, W. (2002). When a man does feminism should he dress in drag? *Qualitative Studies in Education, 15*, 545–554.

Pipher, M. (1994). *Reviving Ophelia: Saving the selves of adolescent girls.* New York: Ballantine Books.

Pinar, W. F. (1998). *Queer theory in education.* Mahweh, NJ: Erlbaum.

Polkinghorne, D. E. (1988). *Narrative knowing and the human sciences.* Albany, NY: State University of New York Press.

Pratt, M. L. (1986). Fieldwork in common places. In J. Clifford & G. F. Marcus (Eds.), *Writing culture: The poetics and politics of ethnography* (pp. 27–50). Berkeley, CA: University of California Press.

Precourt, W. (1982). Ethnohistorical analysis of an Appalachian settlement school. In G. Spindler (Ed.), *Doing the ethnography of schooling: Educational anthropology in action* (pp. 440–453). Prospect Heights, IL: Waveland Press.

Psathas, G. (1995). *Conversation analysis: The study of talk-in-interaction.* Thousand Oaks, CA: Sage.

Queneau, R. (1947/1958). *Exercises in style.* New York: New Directions.

Rapley, T. J. (2001). The art(fulness) of open-ended interviewing: Some considerations on analysing interviews. *Qualitative Research, 1*, 303–323.

Ratner, C. (2002, September). Subjectivity and objectivity in qualitative methodology [29 paragraphs]. *Forum Qualitative Sozialforschung/Forum: Qualitative Social Research* [Online journal], *3*(3). Retrieved 4 November 2004 from http://qualitative-research.net/fqs/fqs-eng.htm

Ray, M. A. (1994). The richness of phenomenology: Philosphic, theoretic, and methodologic concerns. In J. M. Morse (Ed.), *Critical issues in qualitative research methods* (pp. 117–133). Thousand Oaks, CA: Sage.

Reese, W. L. (1996). *Dictionary of philosophy and religion: Eastern and Western thought* (Expanded Ed.). Atlantic Highlands, NJ: Humanities Press.

Reisetter, M., Yexley, M., Bonds, D., Nikels, H., & McHenry, W. (2003). Shifting paradigms and mapping the process: Graduate students respond to qualitative research. *The Qualitative Report, 8,* 462–480.

Richardson, L. (1995). Narrative and sociology. In J. van Maanen (Ed.), *Representation in ethnography* (pp. 198–221). Thousand Oaks, CA: Sage.

Richardson, L. (2000). Writing: A method of inquiry. In N. K. Denzin & Y. S. Lincoln (Eds.), *Handbook of Qualitative Research* (2rd ed., pp. 923–948). Thousand Oaks, CA: Sage.

Riessman, C. K. (1993). *Narrative analysis.* Newbury Park, CA: Sage.

Ritchie, S. M., & Rigano, D. L. (2001). Researcher-participant positioning in classroom research. *Qualitative Studies in Education, 14,* 741–756.

Rockwell, E. (2000). Teaching genres: A Bahktinian approach. *Anthropology and Education Quarterly, 31,* 260–282.

Rolling, Jr., J. H. (2004). Messing around with identity constructs: Pursuing a poststructural and poetic aesthetic. *Qualitative Inquiry, 10,* 548–557.

Ropers-Huilman, B. (1999). Witnessing: Critical inquiry in a poststructural world. *Qualitative Studies in Education, 12,* 21–35.

Rorty, R. (1979). *Philosophy and the mirror of nature.* Princeton, NJ: Universtity of Princeton Press.

Rorty, R. (1983/1997). Postmodern bourgeois liberalism. In L. Menand (Ed.) *Pragmatism: A reader* (pp. 329–336). NY: Random House.

Rossman, G. B., & Wilson, B. L. (1991). Numbers and words revisited: Being "shamelessly eclectic." *Evaluation Review, 9,* 627–643.

Roth, W. M. (2004, February). Qualitative research and ethics [15 paragraphs]. *Forum Oualitative Sozialforschung/Forum: Oualitative Social Research* [Online journal], *5*(2). Art. 7. Retrieved 4 November 2004 from http://qualitative-research.net/fqs-texte/2–04/2–04roth2-e.htm

Roulston, K. (2001). Data analysis and "theorizing as ideology." *Qualitative Research, 1,* 279–302.

Roulston, K., deMarrais, K., & Lewis, J. B. (2003). Learning to interview in the social sciences. *Qualitative Inquiry, 9,* 643–668.

Rubin, H., & Rubin, I. (1995). *Qualitative interviewing: The art of hearing data.* Thousand Oaks, CA: Sage.

Ryan, G. W., & Bernard, H. R. (2000). Data management and analysis methods. In N. K. Denzin & Y. S. Lincoln (Eds.), *Handbook of qualitative research* (2nd ed., pp. 769–802). Thousand Oaks, CA: Sage.

Sacks, O. (1985/1990). *The man who mistook his wife for a hat, and other clinical tales.* New York: Quality Paperback Book Club.

Salomon, G. (1991). Transcending the qualitative-quantitative debate: The analytic and systemic approaches to educational research. *Educational Researcher, 20*(6), 10–18.

Salus, P. H. (1995). *Casting the net: From ARPANET to INTERNET and beyond.* Reading, MA: Addison-Wesley.

Sandelowski, M., & Barroso, J. (2002). Reading qualitative studies. *International Journal of Qualitative Methods, 1*(1), Article 5. Retrieved 3 October 2004 from http://www.ualberta.ca/~ijqm/

Saussure, F. (1959). *Course in general linguistics.* New York: Philosophical Library.

Schatzman, L., & Strauss, A. L. (1973). *Field research: Strategies for a natural sociology.* Englewood Cliffs, NJ: Prentice-Hall.

Schmitt. R. (2000, January). Notes toward the analysis of metaphor [16 paragraphs]. *Forum Qualitative Sozialforschung/Forum: Qualitative Social Research* [Online journal], *1*(1). Retrieved 4 November 2004 from http://qualitative-research.net/fqs

Schofield, J. W. (1990). Increasing the generalizability of qualitative research. In E. W. Eisner & A. Peshkin (Eds.), *Qualitative inquiry in education: The continuing debate* (pp. 201–232). New York: Teachers College Press.

Schutz, A. (1932/1967). *The phenomenology of the social world.* Evanston, IL: Northwestern University Press.

Schwandt, T. A. (1999). On understanding understanding. *Qualitative Inquiry, 5,* 451–464.

Scott, B. B. (1989). *Hear then the parable.* Minneapolis, MN: Fortress Press.

Scott, K. W. (2004). Relating categories in Grounded Theory analysis: Using a conditional relationship guide and reflective coding matrix. *The Qualitative Report, 9,* 113–126.

Seale, C. (1999). Quality in qualitative research. *Qualitative Inquiry, 5,* 465–478.

Segall, A. (2001). Critical ethnography and the invocation of voice: From the field/in the field—single exposure, double standard? *Qualitative Studies in Education, 14,* 579–592.

Seidman, I. E. (1991). *Interviewing as qualitative research.* New York: Teacher's College Press.

Seymour, W. S. (2001). In the flesh or online? Exploring qualitative research methodologies. *Qualitative Research, 1,* 147–168.

Shank, G. (1987). Abductive strategies in educational research. *American Journal of Semiotics, 5*(2), 275–290.

Shank, G. (1993). Abductive multiloguing: The semiotic dynamics of navigating the Net. *The Electronic Journal of Virtual Culture, 1*(1). [online journal]. Available at ftp://ftp.lib.ncsu.edu/pub/stack/aejvc/aejvc-v1n01-shank-abductive

Shank, G. (1994). Shaping qualitative research in educational psychology. *Contemporary Educational Psychology, 19,* 340–359.

Shank, G. (1996). If O-ring booster seals were alive. *Mind, Culture, and Activity, 3*(3), 203–212.

Shank, G. (1998). The extraordinary ordinary powers of abductive reasoning. *Theory and Psychology, 8,* 841–860.

Shank, G. (in press). Six alternatives to mixed methods in qualitative research design. To appear in *Qualitative Research in Psychology.*

Shank, G., & Cunningham, D. J. (1996a). Mediated phosphor dots: toward a Post-Cartesian model of computer mediated communication via the semiotic superhighway. In C. Ess (Ed.), *Philosophical Issues in Computer-Mediated Communication.* Albany, NY: SUNY Press, 27–41.

Shank, G., & Cunningham, D. J. (1996b). Modeling the six modes of Pericean abduction for educational purposes. In *MAICS 1996 Proceedings.* Available online at http://www.cs.indiana.edu/event/maics96/Proceedings/shank.html

Shank, G. & Cunningham, D. (1992). The virtues of an educational semiotic. *Midwest Educational Researcher.* 5(2) 2–8.

Shields, C. M. (2003). "Giving voice" to students: Using the Internet for data collection. *Qualitative Research, 3,* 397–414.

Shulman, L. S. (1988). Disciplines of inquiry in education: An overview. In R. M. Jaeger (Ed.), *Complementary methods for research in education* (pp. 3–17). Washington, DC: AERA.

Silverman, D. (2000). Analyzing talk and text. In N. K. Denzin & Y. S. Lincoln (Eds.), *Handbook of Qualitative Research* (2nd ed., pp. 821–834). Thousand Oaks, CA: Sage.

Sinding, C., & Aronson, J. (2003). Exposing failures, unsettling accomodations: Tensions in interview practice. *Qualitative Research, 3,* 95–117.

Smaling, A. (2002). The argumentative quality of the qualitative research report. *International Journal of Qualitative Methods. 1*(3), Article 4. Retrieved 3 October 2004 from http://www.ualberta.ca/~ijqm/

Smaling, A. (2003). Inductive, analogical, and communicative generalization. *International Journal of Qualitative Methods, 2*(1), Article 5. Retrieved 2 November 2004 from http://www.ulaberta.ca/~iiqm/backissues/2_1/html/smaling.html

Smeyers, P., & Verhersschen, P. (2001). Narrative analysis as philosophical research: Bridging the gap between the empirical and the conceptual. *Qualitative Studies in Education, 14,* 71–84.

Smith, J. A. (2004). Reflecting on the development of interpretative phenomenological analysis and its contribution to qualitative research in psychology. *Qualitative Research in Psychology, 1,* 39–54.

Smith, J. K. (1983). Quantitative vs. qualitative research: An attempt to clarify the issue. *Educational Researcher, 12*(3), 6–13.

Smith, J. K., & Deemer, D. K. (2000). The problem of criteria in the Age of Relativism. In N. K. Denzin & Y. S. Lincoin (Eds.), *Handbook of Qualitative Research* (2nd ed., pp. 877–896). Thousand Oaks, CA: Sage.

Smith, J. K., & Heshusius, L. (1986). Closing down the conversation: The end of the quantitative-qualitative debate among educational researchers. *Educational Researcher, 15*(1), 4–12.

Sokal, A., & Bricmount, J. (1998). *Fashionable nonsense: Postmodern intellectuals' abuse of science.* New York: Picador USA.

Soltis, J. F. (1990). The ethics of qualitative research. In E. W. Eisner & A. Peshkin (Eds.), *Qualitative inquiry in education: The continuing debate* (pp. 247–257). New York: Teachers College Press.

Sondergaard, D. M. (2002). Poststructural approaches to empirical analysis. *Qualitative Studies in Education, 15,* 187–204.

Spence, D. P. (1982). *Narrative truth and historical truth: Meaning and interpretation in psychoanalysis.* New York: W. W. Norton & Company.

Spiers, J. A. (2002). The pink elephant paradox (or, avoiding the misattribution of data). *International Journal of Qualitative Methods, 1*(4), Article 4. Retrieved 3 October 2004 from http://www.ualberta.ca/~ijqm/

Spiers, J. A. (2004). Tech tips: Using video management/analysis technology in qualitative research.

International Journal of Qualitative Methods, 3(1). Article 5. Retrieved 2 November 2004 from http://www.ulaberta.ca/~liqm/backissues/3_1/html/pdf/spiersvideo.pdf

Spivak, G. (1988). *In other worlds: Essays in cultural politics*. London: Routledge.

Spradley, J. P. (1979). *The ethnographic interview*. New York: Holt, Rinehart and Winston.

Spradley, J. P. (1980). *Participant observation*. New York: Holt, Rinehart and Winston.

Spry, T. (2001). Performing authethnography: An embodied methodological practice. *Qualitative Inquiry, 7*, 706–732.

Stake, R. E. (1995). *The art of case study research*. Thousand Oaks, CA: Sage.

Stanley, L., & Wise, S. (1993). *Breaking out again: Feminist ontology and enistemology*. New York: Routledge.

St. Pierre, E. A. (2000). Poststructural feminism in education: An overview. *Qualitative Studies in Education, 13*, 477–515.

St. Pierre. E. A. (2004). Refusing alternatives: A science of contestation. *Qualitative Inquiry, 10*, 130–139.

Strauss, A. (1988). Teaching qualitative research methods courses: An interview with Anselm Strauss. *International Journal of Qualitative Studies in Education, 1*, 91–99.

Strauss, A. (1995). Notes on the nature and development of general theories. *Qualitative Inquiry, 1*, 7–18.

Strauss, A., & Corbin, J. (1998). *Basics of qualitative research: Techniques and procedures for developing grounded theory*. Thousand Oaks, CA: Sage.

Stringer, E. T. (1996). *Action research: A handbook for practitioners*. Thousand Oaks, CA: Sage.

Sturges, J. E., & Hanrahan, K. J. (2002). Comparing telephone and face-to-face qualitative interviewing: A research note. *Qualitative Research, 2*, 107–118.

Tedlock, B. (2000). Ethnography and ethnographic representation. In N. K. Denzin & Y. S. Lincoln (Eds.), *Handbook of Qualitative Research* (2nd ed., pp. 455–486). Thousand Oaks, CA: Sage.

Temple, B., & Young, A. (2002). Qualitative research and translation dilemmas. *Qualitative Research, 2*, 161–178.

Tenni, C., Smyth, A., & Boucher, C. (2003). The researcher as autobiographer: Analyzing data written about oneself. *The Qualitative Report, 8*, 1–12.

Terkel, S. (1975). *Working*. New York: Viking.

Thompson, S. (1946). *The folktale*. Berkeley, CA: University of California Press.

Thome, S., Kirkham, S., & O'Flynn-Magee, K. (2004). The analytical challenge in interpretive description. *International Journal of Qualitative Methods, 3*(1). Article 1. Retrieved 2 November 2004 from http://www.ulaberta.ca/~iiqm/backissues/3_1/html/pdf/theorneetal.pdf

Tierney, W. G. (2002). Get real: Representing reality. *Qualitative Studies in Education, 15*, 385–398.

Tilley, S. A. (2003a). Transcription work: Learning through coparticipation in research practices. *Qualitative Studies in Education, 16*, 835–581.

Tilley, S. A. (2003b). "Challenging" research practices: Turning a critical lens on the work of transcription. *Qualitative Inquity, 9*, 750–773.

Torronen, J. (2002). Semiotic theory on qualitative interviewing using stimulus texts. *Qualitative Research, 2*, 343–362.

van Maanen, J. (1988). *Tales of the field: On writing ethnography*. Chicago, IL: University of Chicago Press.

van Maanen, J. (1995). An end to innocence: The ethnography of ethnography. In J. van Maanen (Ed.), *Representation in ethnography* (pp. 1–35). Thousand Oaks, CA: Sage.

Vidich, A. J. & Lyman, S. M. (2000). Qualitative methods: Their history in sociology and anthropology. In N. K. Denzin & Y. S. Lincoln (Eds.) *Handbook of Qualitative Research* 2e (pp. 37–84). Thousand Oaks, CA: Sage.

von Glasersfled, E. (1984). An introduction to radical constructivism. In P. Watzlawick (Ed.), *The invented reality* (pp. 17–40). New York: Norton.

Vygotsky, L. (1962). *Thought and language*. Cambridge, MA: MIT Press.

Vygotsky, L. (1978). *Mind in society*. Combridge, MA: Harvard University Press.

Walsh, M. (2003). Teaching qualitative research using QSR NVivo. *The Qualitative Report, 8*, 251–256.

Wax, M. L. (2002). The school classroom as frontier. *Anthropology and Education Quarterly, 33*, 118–130.

Webb, E. J., Campbell, D. C., Schwartz, R. D., & Sechrest, L. (2000). *Unobstrusive measures* (Revised Edition). Thousand Oaks, CA: Sage.

Weinstein, M. (with narrative by T. Dulce). (2004). Randomized design and the myth of certain knowledge. Guinea pig narratives and cultural critique. *Qualitative Inquiry, 10*, 246–260.

Weitzman, E. A. (2000). Software and qualitative research. In N. K.

Denzin & Y. S. Lincoln (Eds.), *Handbook of qualitative research* (2nd ed., pp. 803–820). Thousand Oaks, CA: Sage.

Wells, G. (1999). *Dialogic inquiry: Towards a sociocultural practice and theory of education.* New York: Cambridge University Press.

Whyte, W. F. (1955). *Street corner society: The social structure of an Italian slum.* Chicago, IL: University of Chicago Press.

Witzel, A. (2000, January). The problem-centered interview [27 paragraphs]. *Forum Qualitative Sozialforschung/Forum: Qualitative Social Research* [Online journal], *1*(1). Retrieved 4 November 2004 from http://qualitative-research.net/fqs

Wolcott, H. F. (1990). *Writing up qualitative research.* Thousand Oaks, CA: Sage.

Wolcott, H. F. (1995a). *The art of fieldwork.* Walnut Creek, CA: Altamira Press.

Wolcott, H. F. (1995b). Making a study "more ethnographic." In J. van Maanen (Ed.), *Representation in ethnography* (pp. 79–111). Thousand Oaks, CA: Sage.

Wolcott, H. F. (2003). A "natural" writer. *Anthropology and Education Quarterly, 34,* 324–338.

Wolfinger, N. H. (2002). On writing fieldnotes: Collection strategies and background expectancies. *Qualitative Research, 2,* 85–95.

Woods, P. (1999). *Successful writing for qualitative researchers.* London: Routledge.

Woods, P., Boyle, M., Jeffrey, B., & Troman, G. (2000). A research team in ethnography. *Qualitative Studies in Education, 13,* 85–98.

Yin, R. (1994). *Case study research: Designs and methods* (2nd ed.). Newbury Park, CA: Sage.

Zeller, N., & Farmer, F. M. (1999). "Catchy, clever titles are not acceptable": Style, APA, and qualitative reporting. *Qualitative Studies in Education. 12,* 3–19.

Index